MW01004439

Characters on the Couch

T 730656

Characters on the Couch

Exploring Psychology through Literature and Film

DEAN A. HAYCOCK, PhD
Foreword by Tara Deliberto, PhD

An Imprint of ABC-CLIO, LLC
Santa Barbara, California • Denver, Colorado

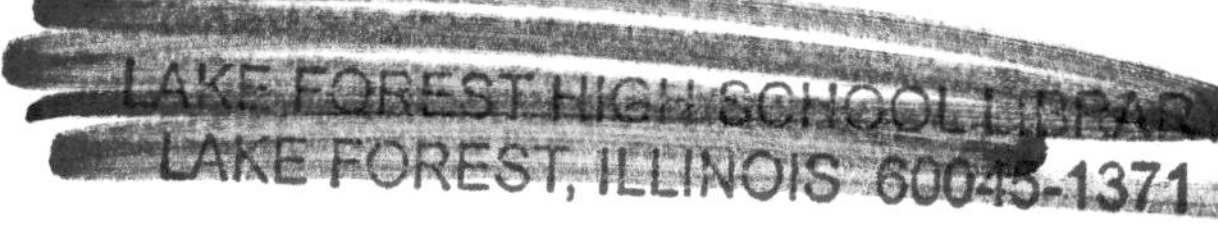

Copyright © 2016 by ABC-CLIO, LLC

All rights reserved. No part of this publication may be reproduced, stored in a retrieval system, or transmitted, in any form or by any means, electronic, mechanical, photocopying, recording, or otherwise, except for the inclusion of brief quotations in a review, without prior permission in writing from the publisher.

Library of Congress Cataloging-in-Publication Data

Names: Haycock, Dean A., author. | Deliberto, Tara, writer of foreword.
Title: Characters on the couch : exploring psychology through literature and film / Dean A. Haycock ; foreword by Tara Deliberto.
Description: Santa Barbara, California : Greenwood, [2016] | Includes bibliographical references and index.
Identifiers: LCCN 2016016059 (print) | LCCN 2016031566 (ebook) | ISBN 9781440836985 (hardcopy : acid-free paper) | ISBN 9781440836992 (ebook)
Subjects: LCSH: Psychology and literature. | Characters and characteristics in literature. | Characters and characteristics in motion pictures. | Psychology in literature. | Psychoanalysis and literature. | Psychologists in literature. | Identity (Psychology) in motion pictures.
Classification: LCC PN56.P93 H39 2016 (print) | LCC PN56.P93 (ebook) | DDC 801/.92—dc23
LC record available at https://lccn.loc.gov/2016016059

ISBN: 978-1-4408-3698-5
EISBN: 978-1-4408-3699-2

20 19 18 17 16 1 2 3 4 5

This book is also available as an eBook.

Greenwood
An Imprint of ABC-CLIO, LLC

ABC-CLIO, LLC
130 Cremona Drive, P.O. Box 1911
Santa Barbara, California 93116-1911
www.abc-clio.com

This book is printed on acid-free paper ∞

Manufactured in the United States of America

For Marie E. Culver

Contents

Foreword

Fiction allows us to explore the character of a person far beyond the limits of what is afforded to us in reality.

In reality, when endeavoring to understand a person's psychological makeup, the information we have is limited to experiences such as observing and listening as the person interacts with others, personally witnessing a given reaction to a situation in your presence, and hearing what a person tells you directly.

In fiction, a character can be on display at all times, when at ease and under duress, with others but also when alone. We can even be privy to the character's innermost thoughts and private internal experiences. If bestowed this type of data, as a plot progresses, we can draw connections between a character's inner experience and its subsequent actions and reactions. Of course, this kind of informational luxury is something that reality simply cannot afford.

Further, when consuming fiction, we have the ability to make observations in a completely objective fashion, without ever having a single interpersonal exchange with a character. Fictional characters do not address us personally when they speak; they do not produce facial expressions in reaction to something we have said or done, nor do they ever make active attempts to manipulate our thoughts, emotions, and behavior. As such, when assessing the character of a fictional person, we run much less of a risk of being clouded by our own biases and defenses.

Taken together, the psychological assessment of fictional characters—rather than real people—can be a wonderfully didactic tool for early students of clinical psychology: if done well. And Dean Haycock, PhD, has done this *very* well. In this book, *Characters on the Couch*, Dr. Haycock offers us a thoughtful psychological assessment a variety of captivating fictional characters that embody very real diagnoses. And it is imperative to the student of psychology that real diagnoses be well understood because they affect real people.

The essence of a person's struggle is *never* captured by the diagnostic criteria for his or her mental illness. Knowing that a diagnosis, for instance anorexia, involves fear of fatness and low weight does not tell you that a person with anorexia nervosa may be tearing her family apart with grief as they helplessly watch her disappear. Contextually understanding a person's life in this latter way is absolutely critical to being an empathetic and effective psychologist.

In fact, because contextualizing the lives of people with a given diagnosis is so important to the training of psychologists, an official book exists that does this: the *DSM Casebook*. But while the *Casebook* chapters provide short case presentations of fabricated patients presenting to treatment, *Characters on the Couch* provides a psychological assessment of well-written, masterfully portrayed, very interesting, and memorable fictional characters as observed through storytelling. As such, *Characters on the Couch* is a wonderful educational complement to the *Casebook* (having coauthored a section of the *DSM-IV* and *DSM-5 Casebooks* myself, I can tell you).

In *Characters on the Couch,* the author's psychological assessments contextualize the lives of fascinating and unforgettable fictional people with mental illness by explaining:

- adversity a character has encountered because of a given illness;
- how others may respond to the person because of their illness;
- the impact of a given illness on the life of a person with it;
- the impact of a given illness on loved ones of a person with it;
- ways in which a given illness can be limiting;
- a person's internal experience, secondary to a given illness.

In short, although all students of abnormal or clinical psychology can easily look up the criteria for any given diagnosis, not everyone takes the time to understand the impact of mental illness on the lives of people it affects. Because this latter effort can greatly improve the skill level of a psychologist, I believe you are quite fortunate to have discovered this book.

—Tara Deliberto, PhD
Assistant Professor of Psychology
in Clinical Psychiatry,
Weill Cornell Medicine,
New York-Presbyterian Hospital

Preface

Popular fictional characters display an impressive and wide range of psychological attributes, both positive and negative. We admire some because they display knowledge, resilience, courage, humanity, justice, and temperance. We sometimes sympathize with, or are intrigued by, characters that show signs of personality disorders and mental illness: psychopathy, narcissism, antisocial personality, paranoia, depression, bipolar disorder, and schizophrenia, among many other conditions.

This book explores the psychological attributes and motivations of 101 characters with these and other conditions and personality traits. The selections include examples of both accurate and misleading depictions of psychological traits and conditions, and so enable readers to distinguish realistic from inaccurate representations of human behavior. This will help readers recognize misconceptions about psychological illnesses and hopefully will help dispel stigma and prejudice associated with these conditions.

Stories simulate our social world, says cognitive psychologist Keith Oatley, the author of *Such Stuff as Dreams: The Psychology of Fiction*. Oatley, who is himself a novelist, notes that literature in all forms—short stories, novels, plays, and poetry—increases our understanding of the wide variety of people we deal with and also helps us in our interactions with them.

And finally, of course, literature and films are about much more than psychology. While psychological insights are often essential elements of a story, good storytelling requires well-developed characters, appropriate settings, engaging plots, realistic conflicts, and relevant, meaningful themes.

SPOILER ALERT

This book contains many "spoilers," references to events or plot lines that a reader might not want to know before reading a story or viewing a film for the first time. While there is no intention to reveal important plot developments unnecessarily, it is often necessary to do this to point out important psychological traits and features of many characters chosen for discussion. Read the stories or watch the films before reading about them in secondary sources such as this one. This will allow you to form your own impressions of the characters and, of course, avoid spoilers.

DISCLAIMER

The discussions and observations in this book apply only to the *fictional* characters they address. Only mental health professionals can diagnose mental illnesses in real people. Some periods of sadness or a few sessions of grief should not be confused with clinical depression. A psychotic episode does not mean a person has schizophrenia any more than one fist fight means someone has an antisocial personality. Nor does performing a few good deeds mean a person has an overall positive personality.

Such diagnoses require firsthand evaluations involving interviewing, taking histories, making observations, evaluating test results, and even talking to acquaintances, friends, and family. In nearly all cases, it is unethical and irresponsible for anyone to diagnose a living person without examining that person personally.

SCOPE AND ORGANIZATION OF THE BOOK

The main section of this book consists of 101 profiles of fictional characters found in novels, novellas, short stories, plays, poems, graphic novels, comic books, and films. Many are well-known and often cited in references to popular culture. Others are more obscure and are more likely to be found on rarely visited library shelves than on tablets.

For most entries, each character description begins with an emblematic quote or short passage from the story in which the character appears. This is followed by a brief summary of the plot. The character's profile and psychological traits are then briefly reviewed to set up a discussion of the psychological concept(s) embodied by the character. Throughout, background information about the psychological problem or strength displayed by the character is included where appropriate. Specific examples using quotations from the book or film suggest, and often demonstrate, the character's key psychological trait(s) or disorder(s).

In a few entries, the format is modified to reflect the nature of the topic or the focus of the selection. This is the case, for example, with subjects in the psychologists in films section, in descriptions of poems and dreams, and in a few other selections.

The selections are divided into seven subdivisions:

1. **Mental and Personality Disorders.** Characters whose behaviors suggest personality or mental disorders are presented roughly in the order found in the *Diagnostic and Statistical Manual of Mental Disorders, 5th Edition* (*DSM-5*). Other indications of pathological psychology also appear in this section.
2. **Positive Psychological Traits.** In 2004, Peterson and Seligman identified six character strengths and virtues, which they described as universal and stable personality traits associated with positive psychological health. This led to the VIA Classification of Character Strengths & Virtues (CSV). (VIA was originally an acronym of "Values in Action" but that phrase was dropped in 2007 so that the more important concept of core character would not be overlooked.) In a sense, the CSV is like the *DSM-5* because it provides a framework and criteria for describing behavior. It differs because it describes features related to wellness rather than illness. It uses well-defined criteria to identify core psychological characteristics or personality traits and features that promote strengths. Insights into these positive features of human psychology can complement insights into the painfully negative aspects of personality and mental disorders. See Appendix B for a complete description.
3. **Negative Psychological Traits and Features.** This section includes examples of characters that do not have mental disorders but whose psychological outlook is dominated by hate.
4. **Emotional Instability/Neuroticism.** Unhappy personalities liable to seek therapy are included in this section.
5. **Freudian Themes.** Some authors created characters that are more easily understood by referring to an older theoretical psychological model of the working of the mind than they are by more recent theories of personality and mental illnesses.
6. **Psychologists in Films.** Two famous experiments frequently included in psychology textbooks have been depicted on the big screen.
7. **Psychological Growth, Development, Maturity, Loss, and Aging.** Aging is accompanied by psychological development and new challenges. A range of examples is included in this section, which illustrate different stages of psychological development and growth.

In addition to the psychological profiles, this reference work includes a detailed glossary of psychological and literary terms, and a list of sources and recommended readings. Author/director spotlight sidebars have also been included alongside some of the main entries.

Acknowledgments

Marie E. Culver supported this work as she has done all of my writing. Her comments helped to clarify many of the chapters. Anna Millhauser provided essential research material concerning *The Picture of Dorian Gray*, *The Marriage Plot*, and *The Assistant*. She also improved the early manuscript with her excellent editing, observations, and suggestions. I appreciate the efforts of N. Magendra Varman and the copy editor for making the manuscript suitable for publication. My editor at ABC-CLIO, Maxine Taylor, was supportive and helpful all during the writing of this book. Trevor J. Oakley, Teen Services Librarian at the Saratoga Springs Public Library in Saratoga Springs, New York, helpfully suggested several relevant young adult titles. I'm grateful to clinical psychologist Dr. Tara Deliberto of Weill Cornell Medicine for taking the time to read the book, offer suggestions, and write the foreword. I also appreciate the generosity of the VIA Institute on Character for allowing me to reproduce the list and descriptions of "Character strengths and virtues."

Introduction

> Words mean more than what is set down on paper. It takes the human voice to infuse them with shades of deeper meaning.
>
> —Maya Angelou,
> *I Know Why the Caged Bird Sings*

Storytellers have been incorporating hidden and not-so-hidden psychological issues and insights into their stories long before psychology became a science. The protagonist of *The Epic of Gilgamesh*, one of the oldest known works of literature, struggled with bereavement, despair, and the fear of death more than 4,000 years ago—just like people today. The same psychological concerns—and scores of other positive and negative, normal and abnormal traits and motivations—have provided material for writers ever since. It is the purpose of writers to portray, explore, and illuminate the thoughts and actions of their characters. It is the purpose of psychologists to understand and explain human behavior. There is no way good literature and psychology can be separated.

Well-written stories—in print, on the stage, or on the screen—can be useful supplements to psychology textbooks and lectures, but they must be evaluated in their context as fiction. And because good fiction reflects the positive and the negative aspects of human struggles, triumphs, and daily experience, select titles can provide useful examples of psychological principles only if the reading is combined with basic knowledge of psychology and mental health.

Psychological traits featured in works of literature and film, of course, need not be exact copies or even close approximations of real human experiences. "It's partly true, too, but it isn't all true," Holden Caulfield observes in *Catcher in the Rye*. "People always think something's all true."

Psychological profiles of literary characters can offer readers more than clinical accuracy; characters like Mr. Kurtz in *Heart of Darkness* and Luke Jackson in

Cool Hand Luke are more useful and powerful as symbols of conflict in society than as examples of accurate pathological or positive psychological forces in an individual. Through well-constructed drama, we can see and capture key, defining features of human behavior, often better than we can see them in what we perceive as mundane, day-to-day interactions. Fiction from the pen (or keyboard) of a talented writer can spotlight human behavior in a way that lets us see and understand others and ourselves better. And it can show us the greater forces that influence history.

LEARNING FROM FICTIONAL CHARACTERS

Fictional characters provide a useful and rich source of psychological and psychiatric material for readers and for mental health workers in training. They are even used in medical schools' training programs to help train future psychiatrists.

Wall Street Journal columnist Melinda Beck reported in 2010 that a semester-long class called "Therapy Bites" was so successful at the University of South Carolina School of Medicine that a session was devoted to the class at the American Psychiatric Association's annual conference that year. The session, "Therapy Bites: Promoting Competency in Psychotherapy through an Exploration of Popular Fiction," described the class as an effective way to teach psychiatrists about neurotic behavior as illustrated by characters in the popular books of the *Twilight* series. It's true that the fictional characters Edward and Bella belong to a subgroup of humanity that does not exist, vampires, but some of their traits, including arrested psychological development, poor self-image, and frequent negative thoughts, are very real and common. Readers can recognize, sympathize, and identify with them.

Psychiatrist Glen Gabbard, MD, told the *Wall Street Journal* that "Students in the mental-health disciplines can sometimes learn as much about what it means to be human from studying popular films and novels as they can from sitting with a patient." Gabbard, the author of *The Psychology of the Sopranos*, is a clinical professor of psychiatry at Baylor College of Medicine in Houston, Texas, and a professor of psychiatry at the State University of New York Upstate Medical University in Syracuse, New York.

When Gabbard refers to "studying popular films and novels," he is referring, of course, to their characters. Characters are the individuals through which readers experience and relate to a work of fiction; they drive, or are sometimes driven by, the plot. The thoughts and actions of well-developed characters affect us, sometimes by giving us insights and other times by evoking moods or emotions. Fictional characters, like real persons, have personality traits, strengths, and flaws. Some, like Ophelia in *Hamlet* and Bruce Banner/"The Incredible Hulk" have mental disorders. Others, like Atticus Finch in *To Kill a Mockingbird* and Marge Gunderson in *Fargo*, are mentally healthy and, indeed, have traits readers and moviegoers might envy.

In 2015, psychiatrist Susan Friedman, MD, of the University of Auckland in New Zealand and her colleagues published three articles in psychiatric journals pointing out the benefits of using *Star Wars* characters to illustrate a variety of mental health conditions. The long list of problems they identify in a galaxy far, far away include "borderline and narcissistic personality traits, psychopathy, PTSD, partner violence risk, developmental stages, and of course Oedipal conflicts" as well as "histrionic, obsessive-compulsive, and dependent personality traits, perinatal psychiatric disorders, prodromal schizophrenia, pseudodementia, frontal lobe lesions, pathological gambling, and even malingering." They conclude that "Star Wars has tremendous potential to teach psychiatric trainees about mental health issues."

PSYCHOLOGY AND PSYCHIATRY

"Psychology is the study of the mind and behavior," according to the American Psychological Association. It "embraces all aspects of the human experience—from the functions of the brain to the actions of nations, from child development to care for the aged. In every conceivable setting from scientific research centers to mental healthcare services, 'the understanding of behavior' is the enterprise of psychologists."

Psychology includes the study of both mental health and mental disorders and is therefore less specialized than psychiatry, a branch of medicine. Psychiatrists, for the most part, focus their attention on diagnosing, treating, and preventing emotional and mental health problems. The emphasis in modern biological psychiatry is to treat mental disorders with medications when appropriate. More and more psychiatrists leave psychotherapy or "talk-therapy" to therapists and psychologists.

Traditionally, psychologists, like psychiatrists, concentrated on the study of mental problems because the suffering associated with mental illness demanded more immediate attention than psychological traits regarded as healthy and positive.

PSYCHOLOGICAL ILLNESS AND MENTAL DISORDERS

Today, both APAs, the American Psychological Association and the American Psychiatric Association, rely heavily on the fifth edition of the *Diagnostic and Statistical Manual of Mental Disorders* or *DSM-5* to describe hundreds of disorders divided into 22 categories. Often referred to as "The Bible" of psychiatry, *DSM-5* is a 947-page description of the mental disorders that psychologists and psychiatrists encounter when treating patients.

The American Psychiatric Association publishes the manual, which is much like a dictionary or catalog. The manual enables mental health workers to compare people's symptoms, behaviors, and medical histories with those listed under different categories. It also provides them with a common vocabulary to describe the illnesses they encounter. This makes it possible for mental health workers and insurance companies to categorize and diagnose personality and mental disorders in a uniform way. The detailed descriptions of the disorders greatly increase the likelihood that clinicians are talking about the same thing when they refer to a particular mental health problem or to the same patient. Even with the guidance of the exhaustive manual, physicians and psychologists may not always agree on a diagnosis for a particular person.

Criticism of the Diagnostic and Statistical Manual of Mental Disorders

A desperate and highly agitated man rushes into his doctor's office and pleads for help. "Doctor, please help me. I am tortured by a nameless fear!"

"Don't worry," says the psychiatrist in a reassuring tone, "We have a name for everything."

This old joke captures the frustration of some mental health care providers and, at the same time, alludes to one of the main criticisms of modern mental health care: we know the names of every mental illness but the causes of very few. Neuroscience is just beginning the long and expensive process of uncovering the causes of mental disorders.

Recently, scientists have determined that the development of some of the most serious disorders affecting mental health appears to share common biological pathways and similar genetic risk factors. Some of the disorders that may turn out to be more alike than we suspected just a few years ago include major depression, such as that experienced by Sylvia Plath's character Esther Greenwood in *The Bell Jar*; bipolar disorder, as accurately depicted by Jeffrey Eugenides's character Leonard Bankhead in *The Marriage Plot*; and schizophrenia, illustrated by Aksenty Ivanovich Poprishchin in Nikolai Gogol's short story "Diary of a Madman." On a level that is still poorly understood, autism spectrum disorders might have some biological commonalities with these disorders. Dustin Hoffman provides a skillfully portrayed, if slightly misleading, depiction of a person on the autism spectrum with exceptional abilities in the film *Rain Man*. (No one person with autism spectrum disorder and savant abilities has all the skills attributed to Hoffman's character, although many have one or a few of the skills he demonstrated.)

Unfortunately, for the most part we lack a detailed understanding of why people develop psychological and psychiatric problems. The best explanation we have is that some people have predispositions, often genetic, that make them susceptible to mental illness. Sometimes this vulnerability combined with stresses results in the development of mental disorders. Without a deep understanding of why mental disorders develop, it is not possible to treat the root causes of these illnesses. As a result, mental health workers have had to limit themselves to listing, categorizing, and describing the disorders to diagnose them and provide the drugs and other treatments that experience has shown are most effective at relieving symptoms. Many of the drugs first used to treat mental disorders, now called psychotropic medications, were discovered serendipitously—that is, by accident. The hope is that someday increased understanding of the biological basis of mental illness will allow researchers to develop more effective treatments that target root causes of the disorders.

One consequence of this situation is that the authors of the *DSM-5*, and indeed the fields of psychology and psychiatry in general, are criticized for the choices they make in defining disorders and choosing what to include in the descriptive manual. This has been going on for over 60 years, since the first edition of the manual appeared.

A frequently voiced criticism of the *DSM* is that it is not scientifically valid because the biological bases of the disorders in the dictionary-like manual are unknown. But until neuroscientists can figure out the biological causes of mental disorders and treat them based on that knowledge, mental health workers have no choice but to rely on the current classifications. Every day they face people who suffer from psychological torment; they don't have the luxury of waiting until neuroscientists figure out what is going wrong in the brains of these people. Psychologists and other mental health professionals must relieve the suffering as best as they can using whatever tools they have. Despite the criticism, we now know more about many disorders—including schizophrenia, autism spectrum disorder, borderline personality disorder, major depression, and bipolar disorder—than we did just 10 years ago.

POSITIVE PSYCHOLOGY

Of course, not all psychology is about mental disorders. For more than a century, some psychologists have expressed interest in developing, nurturing, promoting, and maintaining positive psychological traits. Pioneering psychologist William James, for instance, discussed positive mental health at the turn of the last century. "Believe that life is worth living, and your very belief will help create the fact," he advised in *Pragmatism and Other Writings*. Recently, psychologists Martin Seligman, Christopher Peterson, and others have encouraged fellow psychologists to study positive traits. This has resulted in the establishment of a subdiscipline of psychology called positive psychology.

Positive psychology brings together different aspects of research related to the investigation of traits that contribute to the well-being, happiness and satisfaction of people, and other benefits and advantages of mental health.

Research indicates that enhancing positive emotions is associated with an increase in people's perceptions of possibilities and interests. People with negative emotions are more likely to have narrowed interests and are less likely to see the many possibilities when faced with challenges. In other words, negative emotions aren't as good as positive emotions in allowing people to see the broad picture when seeing multiple options could be very helpful.

Neuroscientists report that brain activity in people expressing positive emotions is consistent with these findings. Brain imaging studies indicate that the brains of people with positive emotions may show greater information-processing activity than the brains of people with negative emotions.

Positive psychology cannot eliminate the normal disappointments, sadness, and unpleasantness that all humans experience from time to time. In fact, it's not unusual for positive emotions to appear and disappear quickly. Positive psychology's purpose is to increase knowledge that will help people deal with these negative experiences and improve the quality of their lives, increasing their chances of flourishing.

The key core character strengths and virtues identified by the nonprofit VIA Institute on Character are listed below:

1. **Wisdom and knowledge,** including traits that reflect a love of learning and a desire to use knowledge for good purposes. Examples are creativity, curiosity, judgment, love of learning, and perspective. Atticus Finch in Harper Lee's popular novel *To Kill a Mockingbird* exemplifies these and other positive traits.
2. **Courage** reflects the will and emotional strength required to overcome opposition from within and without to accomplish worthwhile goals—for example, bravery, perseverance, honesty, and zest. Will Kane, played by Gary Cooper, in the movie *High Noon* has many of these features.
3. **Humanity** reflects strong interpersonal relationships and effectively helping others. Love, kindness, and social intelligence are included in this category. Santiago's friendship with Manolin in the novella *The Old Man and the Sea* includes love, loyalty, respect, and kindness.
4. **Justice** refers to ideals that promote a healthy society on a large and small scale. This is made possible by teamwork, fairness, and leadership. A good example of these traits appears in Henry Fonda's portrayal of Juror #8, in the film *12 Angry Men*.
5. **Temperance** is the ability to avoid excess and negative outlooks. This is made easier with forgiveness, humility, prudence, and self-regulation. Will Kane, in the film *High Noon*, has this trait along with courage.
6. **Transcendence** helps many people by providing meaning for their lives. This can take the form of spirituality, gratitude, hope, humor, or the basic appreciation of beauty and excellence. Peter Parker (Spider-Man) demonstrates this virtue with his humor and optimism.

Although violent, antisocial characters often seem to dominate films and even fiction today, in fact, it is not difficult to find characters, both in film and in literature, that embody aspects of positive mental health.

PERSONALITY

Psychologists have been trying to describe the relationship between aspects of people's personalities and their behavior for decades. These attempts have resulted in theories suggesting that personality is determined by a finite number of personality traits. The type and number of these traits vary with different theories. The most complex theory includes 4,000 personality traits. The least complex theory postulates only three.

The most popular current theory is supported by half a century of research. It includes five core personality traits, which are determined in part by genetics. These universal personality traits are often referred to as "The Big Five Dimensions of Personality." They can be described as follows:

- **Extroversion–Introversion** incorporates a range of characteristics that describe a person's tendency to talk and be sociable, to express emotions, to be assertive, and to be excitable. Extremely extroverted people are at one end of the spectrum while people who lack these traits—extreme introverts—are at the opposite end. The majority of people are somewhere in the middle of the spectrum.
- **Agreeableness–Antagonism** covers positive social attitudes and behaviors such as affection, trust, kindness, and altruism.
- **Conscientiousness–Undirectedness** is characterized by traits that are associated with good planning and organization. This involves setting goals, controlling impulses, and generally being thoughtful.
- **Emotional Stability**–Emotional Instability (formerly Neuroticism) reflects the degree of negative emotionality in a person's life. Moodiness, irritability, anxiety, dissatisfaction, sadness, and generalized worry are examples of negative emotionality.
- **Openness–Incuriousness** reflects the positive traits of intellectual curiosity as indicated by wide-ranging interests, insightfulness, and imagination.

These core personality traits influence a person's behavior and reactions to different situations. The categories are too broad to capture all aspects of an individual, although many personalities are well described by the profile that results from measuring these traits. An extremely extroverted person, for example, might have most or all of the traits consistent with extroversion. But psychologists recognize that some people have diverse personalities. It's possible that one person might have one or two traits in a dimension like extroversion while another might have them all. Personality is a highly complex part of human nature, and this complexity is reflected in well-developed fictional characters just as it is apparent in living human beings.

For most people, the traits and characteristics described by "The Big Five" help define characteristics of generally mentally healthy lives. If none of the dimensions of personality are associated with troubling unhappiness or threats to a person's mental health, then there is no need for psychological or psychiatric intervention or care. But according to the National Institute of Mental Health, this is not the case for approximately 4 percent of the adult population in the United States. They suffer from serious mental illnesses that have significant negative effects on their ability to work, to take care of themselves, and to live a fulfilling life. Remarkably, nearly 19 percent of the adult population has some mental illness ranging from mild impairments to serious mental illnesses. The full range of all these serious mental disorders is described in the *DSM-5*.

Dimensional versus Categorical Features

Like the core values described in the VIA Classification in Character Strengths & Virtues, personality traits exist on a scale or spectrum. People express these traits to varying degrees. The *DSM-5*, in contrast, uses a categorical classification system that implies that a person either has a particular mental disorder or does not have it.

In fact, it is likely that there are different degrees of mental illness. This is suggested in the *DSM-5* by the descriptions: mild, moderate, or severe. And the various illnesses listed in the *DSM-5* category "Schizophrenia Spectrum and Other Psychotic Disorders" likely reflect the dimensional aspect of mental disorders.

PSYCHOANALYSIS VERSUS BIOLOGICAL PSYCHIATRY/PSYCHOLOGY

When many people think of psychology or psychiatry, they still think of a patient lying on the couch talking to a therapist seated out of sight. This persistent image can be traced to the founder of psychoanalysis, the Austrian neurologist Sigmund Freud. In the late 19th and early 20th centuries, Freud pioneered the exploration of factors he thought influenced behavior and explained mental distress.

He developed a once-influential theory about psychological development and how events, particularly during childhood, contributed to psychological problems. He theorized that unconscious drives play a major role in people's behavior. The clichéd image of the patient lying on a couch is derived from psychoanalysis, the "talk therapy," Freud developed to help patients deal with their hidden conflicts. Alexander Portnoy in the satirical novel *Portnoy's Complaint* delivers his book-length monologue while lying on a psychoanalyst's couch.

Freudian theory and psychoanalysis have been out of favor among many mental health care providers for decades, although some adherents continue to defend his theory and claim that new evidence may support it. But psychoanalysis has largely been replaced by therapies like cognitive-behavioral therapy, which addresses present issues rather than repressed past issues troubling a patient.

Scientifically obtained evidence that a treatment works or that an explanation is valid is much more useful than a simple assertion by an "expert" that a patient's behavior is due to an untested theory he or she has constructed based on his experience with his own patients. Thus, when Sigmund Freud insists that young male children go through a developmental stage during which they come to hate their fathers and want their mothers all to themselves, we have to ask, based on what study? How many children were examined and showed these preferences? Were the children's preferences in the study influenced by factors that might not apply to a larger population? Were they specific to culture, socioeconomic status, or ethnicity?

Freud's greatest contribution was not to science but to literature. Although he himself was a trained medical doctor, so far his work has had negligible influence on modern science. His theory of the subconscious has provided tremendously useful insights for psychologists and psychiatrists, and it has strongly influenced many people's impressions of how past experiences have shaped their lives. Unfortunately, modern neuroscience has not advanced enough to satisfactorily relate brain structure and function to many important aspects of mental health, which is something Freud hoped would one day happen. Freud's concept of the subconscious, however, continues to play a big role in the plots of many psychological novels and films and in our lives.

PROBLEMS EXPLORING PSYCHOLOGY THROUGH LITERATURE AND FILM

Fictional characters cannot be expected to, and do not always, fit into specific diagnostic categories. Authors don't write books to provide clinical descriptions of mental health and mental illness. Psychologists and psychiatrists do that. Writers give their characters particular traits they need in order to come alive for the reader, to drive the plot, to provide insights into our lives, and to tell a good story. It's important, as author Erica Jong believes, that we do not "take literature literally." We read fiction, Jong suggests, "to show us what we are afraid to show ourselves."

Mental health problems experienced by real people don't always fit into neat, specific diagnostic categories either. As the misanthropic physician Dr. Gregory House, played by Hugh Laurie on the television show *House*, insists: "everybody lies." Patients sometimes lie by making false or misleading statements to their mental health care providers and sometimes they lie by omitting important facts about their condition. In this regard, evaluating the psychological characteristics of fictional characters is not much different from the problems faced by doctors working with real patients.

Some well-known fictional characters that have attained a prominent place in popular culture have been seriously misdiagnosed by the reading and viewing public. Norman Bates in Alfred Hitchcock's movie *Psycho* is a good example. Norman is not psychopathic, a common assumption; he suffers from an inaccurate version of dissociative identity disorder (with Hitchcockian homicidal features of course). Well-known characters like Norman provide an opportunity to correct the misconceptions about their psychological profiles.

It is essential that other causes of troubling behaviors be eliminated before an accurate diagnosis can be made. For example, the side effects of several medications and illegal drugs can produce symptoms identical to mental disorders. Physical disease can as well. A good example is symptoms displayed by the main character in the film *The Madness of King George*. The film portrays the psychotic behavior of King George III, who is now suspected of having suffered from porphyria. People with this genetic disorder have abnormally elevated levels of natural chemicals in their body. These chemicals accumulate because patients have a defective gene that cannot efficiently produce an essential component of red blood cells. The built-up chemicals have wide-ranging effects that can result in disorientation, confusion, hallucinations, or paranoia.

The classic depiction of schizophrenia in Gogol's short story "Diary of a Madman" still requires that those doing the diagnosing eliminate a list of other possible causes for the main character's behavior. These include any medical condition, drug (including alcohol) abuse, mania, a lasting developmental disorder, major depression, and temporal lobe epilepsy.

Exploring the diverse aspects of personality and mental health by studying fictional characters can be both entertaining and educational. A worthwhile goal of studying the behavior of fictional characters is to increase the understanding of these human strengths and frailties. It should also increase our empathy for those who suffer from mental disorders, inspire us to promote positive mental health in ourselves, and decrease the persistent stigma that surrounds mental illness.

"THE GOLDWATER RULE"

The examples and explorations of psychology in this book should never be applied to living persons. It is unethical for mental health care providers to diagnose living persons without examining them in person. The American Psychiatric Association first warned its members against engaging in this unprofessional behavior in response to an embarrassing episode in 1964.

Magazine publisher Ralph Ginsberg asked 12,356 psychiatrists to pass judgment on the mental health of Republican presidential candidate Senator Barry Goldwater of Arizona, who at the time was running against Lyndon Johnson. Ginsberg published the impressions and "diagnoses" provided by more than one thousand doctors who responded to his unscientific poll in *Fact* magazine. The cover of the issue that featured the article, "The Unconscious of a Conservative: A Special Issue on the Mind of Barry Goldwater," read simply "Fact: 1,189 Psychiatrists Say Goldwater Is Psychologically Unfit to Be President!" Approximately one-quarter of the psychiatrists implied that Goldwater was mentally ill and so should not serve as president of the United States. To their credit, a little less than one-quarter of the psychiatrists acknowledged that they did not have enough information to pass judgment. Those who thought they could pass judgment described the politician as being megalomaniacal and psychotic. Some said he had had a paranoid personality. Some speculated that he suffered from narcissistic personality disorder and even paranoid schizophrenia.

Goldwater sued Ginsberg for libel. He won. The Supreme Court awarded him $1.00 in compensation for the libel and punished Ginsberg and *Fact* magazine by ordering them to pay Goldwater an additional $75,000. The irresponsible journalistic exercise was condemned by the American Medical Association and the American Psychiatric Association. Nine years after the article appeared, the latter group issued the following guideline for psychiatrists, known as the "Goldwater Rule," which in reality is a more of a directive or guideline than a rule, although one that has significant influence today.

> On occasion psychiatrists are asked for an opinion about an individual who is in the light of public attention or who has disclosed information about himself/herself through public media. In such circumstances, a psychiatrist may share with the public his or her expertise about psychiatric issues in general. However, it is unethical for a psychiatrist to offer a professional opinion unless he or she has conducted an examination and has been granted proper authorization for such a statement.

Likewise, the American Psychological Association's code of ethics stipulates that psychologists provide expert opinions "only for individuals they have directly examined."

Psychologists and psychiatrists working for intelligence agencies are generally held exempt from this rule. Developing confidential psychological profiles of foreign leaders might provide an advantage when dealing with them. In extreme circumstances, such profiles, if accurate, could help predict behavior of a hostile foreign leader who might pose a real threat. Psychological profiles have been prepared for Adolf Hitler, Saddam Hussein, Osama bin Laden, and many other personalities by psychologists and psychiatrists working for the U.S. government. In fact, any head of government or key player in foreign relations with whom the U.S. government has to deal may be subjected to psychological profiling. Criminal and forensic psychologists and psychiatrists are also exempted from the guidelines to aid in the apprehension of dangerous criminals.

Fortunately, as previously mentioned, the Goldwater Rule applies only to living persons, not to fictional ones. This leaves teachers and students of psychology and psychiatry, and readers in general, the opportunity to practice recognizing both positive and negative psychological traits in the large and diverse population of the world's fictional characters.

REALITY, FICTION, AND DRAMATIC LICENSE

It is not unusual for authors to use significant mental or personality disorders as hurdles for their protagonists to overcome and so inspire readers or viewers. These plot twists or turning points are often clearly "out of character." To satisfy the writer's or director's desire for a happy or satisfying ending, the true challenges of mental disorders are sometimes ignored, downplayed, or overlooked.

The highly manipulative and narcissistic mother, Ingrid Magnussen, in the book and film *White Oleander* [Spoiler Alert!], eventually—out of character—sacrifices her freedom for her daughter. This key plot development near the end of the story provides a heartwarming conclusion. In reality, it would not be unusual if Ingrid, without therapy, continued with her self-serving and controlling behavior no matter how much it hurt her daughter. Such "downer" endings are hardly popular with audiences, and so we will continue to see less-than-typical happy endings, especially in films. Fortunately, this isn't always the case.

Writers also adapt and borrow aspects of psychological traits and psychological insights to color and improve their stories. As previously mentioned, they are not required or expected to provide clinically accurate portrayals of psychological conditions. The "psychopathic," cannibalistic, serial killer, and brilliant psychiatrist Hannibal Lecter exists only in the books in which he appears: *Red Dragon*, *The Silence of the Lambs*, *Hannibal*, and *Hannibal Rising*, all by Thomas Harris. A more clinically accurate depiction of the very rare homicidal, psychopathic individual is the character Anton Chigurh in Cormac McCarthy's novel *No Country for Old Men* and in the film version with the same title.

Hannibal Lecter's creator wasn't trying to provide a clinical picture of psychopathy. He was creating an intriguing character, one that proved to be immensely popular in his books and their film adaptations. McCarthy, by contrast, successfully depicted the very dark aspects of a changing, modern world, using a more clinically accurate portrayal of a very rare and extreme psychopathic personality.

Few individuals have personality disorders as extreme as Anton Chigurh. Instead of falling neatly into discrete categories, most people can have an array of traits that define their personalities and behaviors. But when someone is on the extreme end of a spectrum of behavior covering degrees of paranoid thinking, for example, the person may be diagnosed with an illness such as paranoid personality disorder. Another example is empathy, a positive trait in most cases. But on the extreme ends of the empathy spectrum, there can be serious problems. Extreme sensitivity to all the suffering in the world can debilitate a person and render him or her anxious and depressed. High levels of empathy are one feature of an innate trait sometimes referred to as sensory processing sensitivity seen in "highly sensitive people," according to research psychologists such as Elaine and Arthur Aron. Complete lack of empathy, on the opposite side of the spectrum, is common in psychopathy and narcissism.

Many popular and/or critically acclaimed creative works describe characters' psychological health issues accurately and convincingly. Often these characters have diagnosable mental or personality disorders. Examples are Malcolm Lowry's doomed character Geoffrey Firmin in *Under the Volcano*. Both Geoffrey and his creator Malcolm Lowry suffered from alcohol use disorder, formally known as alcoholism.

Laurie Halse Anderson's character in *Wintergirls*, Lia, is another example of a character whose psychological traits are clearly and intentionally described thoroughly enough for them to be diagnosed, in this case with anorexia nervosa.

Sylvia Plath herself and her character Esther Greenwood in *The Bell Jar* clearly experienced severe depressive episodes. However, a diagnosis of bipolar disorder can't be ruled out for Plath and for her character since a complete history would be needed to distinguish major depressive disorder from bipolar disorder. There are some indications Plath may have suffered from bipolar disorder.

And of course Plath was not alone among writers. William Blake, Alfred Lord Tennyson, Lord Byron, Ernest Hemingway, Charles Dickens, Virginia Woolf, John Berryman, Robert Lowell, Delmore Schwartz, Anne Sexton, and many other writers and artists appear to have been affected by mood disorders or alcohol use disorder. In fact, there is some evidence to suggest an association between bipolar disorder, depression, and creativity. Firsthand experience with mental health problems obviously can greatly influence an author's depiction of the fictional lives of his or her characters.

Both accurate and not-so-accurate depictions of psychological behaviors in fiction can provide opportunities to learn about and explore psychology, as long as the distinctions between the accurate and the not-so-accurate portrayals are clearly pointed out.

Sometimes writers rely on a limited number of select personality traits to define their characters. These profiles may work well in terms of a writer's literary goals, but they do not always—and they are not meant to—provide enough information for a reader, or even a clinical psychologist or psychiatrist, to make a definitive diagnosis. The fictional characters discussed in this book provide more than enough material to illustrate important and specific psychological traits and behaviors without the need to diagnose or apply a label to each one of them. As mentioned, in some notable instances authors have diagnosed their characters and that is reflected in the discussions in this book. In other cases, characters are described as having features of a mental disorder rather than having been diagnosed with a mental disorder.

READING'S EFFECTS ON READERS' PSYCHOLOGY

Finally, consider the effect reading has on the psychology of the reader. A reader can observe and evaluate a character. A reader can identify with, and live vicariously through, a character. Or a reader can both analyze and identify with an intriguing character.

Evaluating a character has the potential to develop observation and analytical skills in a reader, particularly when the reader's background knowledge is brought into the analysis. Identifying with a character—seeing the character's fictional world through the character's eyes—has the potential to change the way the reader sees the world. If the reader is open to different perspectives, reading can change a reader's opinions and attitudes, which in turn can change the reader's behavior.

Experimental psychologists like Dan R. Johnson of Washington and Lee University are gathering evidence that suggests reading does indeed affect behavior.

Johnson, for example, reported that reading increased displays of empathy in readers, after taking into account the amount of empathy the readers had before the experiment. It also increased prosocial behavior and perception of emotions. Reading then may change readers just as characters are changed by their fictional experiences.

CHARACTER PROFILES

Part 1

Mental and Personality Disorders

Neurodevelopmental Disorders

Profile #1: Charlie Gordon in the Novel *Flowers for Algernon* by Daniel Keyes

Even a feeble-minded man wants to be like other men.

PLOT SUMMARY

Thirty-two-year-old Charlie Gordon works at Donner's Bakery in New York City. He sweeps the floor and performs other simple tasks. He thinks his fellow employees are his friends, but in fact, they ridicule him and have fun at his expense. Charlie doesn't recognize their cruelty. He is treated much better by Alice, who teaches a night class for intellectually impaired adults.

With Alice's help, Charlie is chosen to undergo an experimental procedure designed to increase his intelligence. This operation was first performed, with apparent great success, on a mouse named Algernon. The scientists who lead the research project ask Charlie to record his impressions in a personal journal to provide a record of his progress before and after surgery. The novel consists of these journal entries.

Following the operation, Charlie slowly begins to make progress with Alice's help. Incrementally, his writing and grammar improve. Then his reading comprehension increases. He reads more and more challenging books as his intelligence expands more than anyone expected.

Unfortunately, Charlie's intellectual progress comes with serious psychological complications. He realizes that his coworkers at the bakery were not true friends and that they now resent his intellectual superiority. He begins to recall unpleasant childhood memories involving his mother, who could not accept his impairment and often punished him for it. He also begins to realize that he is romantically attracted to Alice but finds it impossible to make love to her. His feelings for Alice bring back memories of the beatings he received from his mother before his operation whenever he expressed curiosity about sex.

As Charlie's intelligence grows, it begins to surpass that of everyone around him, including the scientists who operated on him. He leaves the study and succeeds in having an affair with a woman he meets. He returns to the study only when the scientists offer him a chance to direct his own research.

Meanwhile, Algernon, the laboratory mouse that underwent the intelligence-enhancing procedure before Charlie, worsens and dies prematurely. Charlie discovers that, due to a flaw in the design of the procedure he underwent, he is doomed to return to his former mental state of intellectual impairment. During this return journey, he attempts to reconcile his relationship with his mother and family. He also advises the scientists who viewed him as an experimental subject to humanize their outlook and to lose their pretensions. Charlie's final entry in his journal is a request for the scientists to put flowers on Algernon's grave.

CHARLIE'S PSYCHOLOGICAL TRAITS

Charlie is gentle, innocent, and easygoing, but socially isolated and lonely. He has trouble learning even mildly challenging tasks and understanding concepts that others quickly grasp. This makes it difficult for him to be accepted as an equal by his peers. Despite his challenges, he wants to learn, to improve himself, and to better comprehend what he struggles to understand.

MODERATE INTELLECTUAL DISABILITY

Charlie (before his operation) had an intellectual disability, a condition once known as mental retardation. It is possible that his brain did not develop normally before he was born. His difficulty understanding and learning as well as others his age was apparent early during his childhood development. In fact, an alternative label for intellectual disability is intellectual development disorder.

There are four levels of severity of intellectual disability: mild, moderate, severe, and profound. Charlie's moderately severe disability is consistent with his ability to care for his personal needs like eating, dressing, and hygiene—although it probably took him longer to learn these skills than children with average ability. He may also need to be reminded from time to time to maintain these skills. He has a job that requires little or no problem-solving or communication skills. He can form friendships, might develop romantic relationships, and could maintain relationships with family members but he sometimes has trouble "reading people"—that is, interpreting how others feel and deciphering what they mean. This is illustrated by his inability to appreciate that his coworkers ridicule him.

A diagnosis of intellectual disability may be made if three criteria are met, criteria that appear to apply to Charlie.

(Note: The misspellings and grammar and punctuation errors in these quotes are present in the original text since they reflect Charlie's writing ability at different times during his intellectual "round trip" journey.)

Charlie's intellectual deficits made it difficult for him to solve problems, learn from past experiences, perform successfully in school, use good judgment, and develop other mental skills necessary to care for himself independently.

" . . . all my life I wantid to be smart and not dumb and my mom always tolld me to try and lern just like Miss Kinnian tells me but its very hard to be smart and even when I lern something in Miss Kinnians class at the school I ferget alot."

Charlie's intellectual deficits appeared early, during childhood development.

"You're fooling yourself, Rose It's not fair to us or to him Pretending he's normal Driving him as if he were an animal that could learn to do tricks." As Charlie's mental abilities improve after his operation, he recalls this childhood memory of his father challenging his mother's refusal to accept the fact that her child was intellectually challenged and could not learn as well as other children.

He was unable to function effectively and adapt to the demands of everyday life in such a way that he could function effectively in a variety of situations including school, family life, at work, and in social situations.

"Dr. Strauss feels that emotionally I'm still in that adolescent state where being close to a woman, or thinking of sex, sets off anxiety, panic, and hallucinations." Also, "I never knew before that Joe and Frank and the others liked to have me around just to make fun of me. Now I know what they mean wen they say 'to pull a Charlie Gordon.' I'm ashamed." And finally: "If your smart you can have lots of friends to talk to and you never get lonely by yourself all the time."

By taking readers along with Charlie on his heart-wrenching journey from intellectual disability to intellectual superiority and back again, the author gives readers a chance to identify with individuals who struggle with challenges presented by mental health issues.

Profile #2: Benjy Compson in the Novel *The Sound and the Fury* by William Faulkner

" 'Did you come to meet Caddy,' she said, rubbing my hands. 'What is it. What are you trying to tell Caddy' Caddy smelled like trees and like when she says we were asleep." (Note: Punctuated as it appears in the text.)

PLOT SUMMARY

The Sound and the Fury begins with Benjy Compson, one of four children in a once aristocratic Mississippi family. Benjy's father, Jason III, suffers from alcohol use disorder and his mother, Caroline, suffers from severe anxiety about her health. Thirty-three-year-old Benjy can't speak, and he has difficulty making sense of events he has witnessed or experienced. Like his brothers Quentin and Jason IV, he has an obsession with their sister Caddy. She was the only member of his family who showed concern for him.

From Benjy's stream-of-consciousness narration, we learn that he and his caretaker Luster are out for a walk. We readers can read Benjy's thoughts, impressions, and misimpressions about the past and present but his intellectual disability allows him to verbally express himself only with moans and cries. At one point during their walk, the pair stop on the sidelines of a golf course. The course is built on land once owned by the Compsons. Benjy can't comprehend that it is no longer his family's land where he once spent time with his beloved sister Caddy.

Benjy's memories are not sequential, although it becomes clear as the novel progresses that they are all relevant to the dynamics of the siblings' relationships to each other and especially to Caddy. Benjy's memories flit from the death of his grandmother to his siblings playing in a stream on the land. He recalls the time he approached a young school girl, an encounter after which he was accused of attacking her. This incident eventually led to his castration to prevent similar "scandals" and prevent him from ever having children. And he remembers Caddy's first kiss and her wedding. And how, in time, he lost her. After he returns home from his walk with Luster, the family servant Dilsey is nice to him while his own brother Jason is dismissive and scornful.

Quentin is the narrator of the second section of the book. We hear his thoughts on the day he takes his own life, 18 years before Benjy's account. Caddy's emerging sexuality disturbs him, and plays a central role in Quentin's story.

The third section belongs to Jason IV. It features Jason's thoughts on the day before Benjy and Luster visited the golf course. As his behavior toward Benjy suggests, Jason is unpleasant, manipulative, and cruel. It also becomes clear in this section that Caddy's illegitimate daughter lives with the Compsons. Caddy herself has been banished from the Compson home. Now divorced, she lives in a neighboring county and sends money home for her daughter, money that Jason steals. Jason ultimately exemplifies the depths to which the Compsons have fallen over the course of several generations since the Civil War.

The fourth section of the novel describes in the third person events that takes place on Easter Sunday, the day after Benjy's narration. Jason tries to retrieve $7,000, which Caddy's illegitimate daughter took from him. Jason had confiscated the money from the checks Caddy had sent for her daughter. In this section, we also see Dilsey at church. She realizes that the structure of the Compson family has decayed to a point beyond recovery. Benjy, of course, is incapable of understanding this.

Benjy becomes terribly upset and bellows when Luster takes him for a carriage ride along a route that is not part of Benjy's routine. After Jason accosts Luster and Benjy, striking them, Luster returns to the route familiar to Benjy. Benjy is relieved and calms down as he passes the landmarks he recognizes. Order returns and he gives no thought to his brother Jason or to his recent encounter with terrifying change.

We learn in an appendix that Jason commits Benjy to an institution after their mother dies and he sells the family home. Caddy has long since moved away, never to return. The once aristocratic Southern family crumbles.

BENJY'S PSYCHOLOGICAL TRAITS

In contrast to Charlie Gordon in *Flowers for Algernon*, 33-year-old Benjy has an intellectual disability that leaves him unable to speak (although we hear his thoughts in the first section of the book). He remembers significant events in his life but the sequence and timing of his memories are jumbled. And he doesn't understand the greater significance of any of them; they have meaning only in terms of his needs and wants. Benjy needs and wants Caddy—her love, kindness, and understanding—back in his life. Now he has a caretaker, a teenager named Luster, who accompanies him everywhere. In the company of his caretaker, Benjy is able to enjoy going for walks and carriage rides, but he becomes upset if the routine changes. The severity of his disability, therefore, is significantly greater than Charlie Gordon's. Benjy has a profound intellectual disability.

William Faulkner

Born in 1897—only two years before Ernest Hemingway—William Faulkner wrote in a style so different from Hemingway's terse, simple, declarative style that perhaps it isn't surprising that these two giants of American literature competed with each other. Faulkner: "He has never been known to use a word that might cause the reader to check with a dictionary to see if it is properly used." Hemingway: "Poor Faulkner. Does he really think big emotions come from big words?"

Faulkner's novels and short stories about the death of an old Southern lifestyle are complex and challenging for most readers. His sentences are sometimes astoundingly long. His plots are not straightforward. He often takes you into the minds of his characters by letting you hear their internal monologues, their private thoughts. This stream-of-consciousness presentation is often made more challenging when Faulkner shifts the point of view to a new character. And yet even Hemingway acknowledged that the Mississippi-born Faulkner was "the best of us all."

For much of his career, Faulkner paid a price for freeing himself to write what he wanted to write and not what publishers wanted him to write.

He was often short of money. For a time he took a job writing Hollywood scripts but loathed the work. His struggles were not made easier by the fact that he, like Hemingway, had a severe problem with alcohol. Although he was not a steady drinker, his binges were uncontrolled and led to injuries and time recovering in a sanitarium.

Faulkner finally received widespread recognition and respect at the age of 52 in 1949 when he won (again, like Hemingway) the Nobel Prize in literature "for his powerful and artistically unique contribution to the modern American novel." He also received two Pulitzer Prizes and two National Book Awards.

Throughout his career he wrote more than 100 short stories and close to 20 novels including *The Sound and the Fury*, *Absalom, Absalom!*, *As I Lay Dying*, and *Light in August*.

Faulkner died from a heart attack in 1962, weeks after suffering an excruciatingly painful back injury falling from a horse.

PROFOUND INTELLECTUAL DISABILITY

In addition to satisfying the common criteria for intellectual disability described in the entry about *Flowers for Algernon*, Benjy's more severe disability is indicated by the following observations:

Benjy communicates nonverbally.

" 'Shut up that moaning.' Luster said." Faulkner has to use a great deal of literary license when he gives Benjy a significant vocabulary. The words Faulkner attributes—or perhaps even "loans"—to Benjy allow readers to appreciate what Benjy feels but cannot articulate even to himself. They provide insight into Benjy's feelings and his limited understanding but they do not reflect his ability to speak. Those around Benjy hear only his thoughts and emotions expressed as moans.

But he is capable of maintaining relationships with family members or individuals he knows well.

"Caddy smells like trees." Benjy is devoted to his sister Caddy or, more accurately, to her memory, since she has left the family home. She is the only family member who showed him affection and love. He remembers all the times they played outside when they were children. He associates her with the trees and flowers they played among. Long after she left, he still moans with grief when anyone mentions her name. Understanding so little, Benjy even moans when he hears golfers on the nearby golf course refer to golf caddies. For Benjy, there is only one Caddy.

His well-being requires his caretaker's constant presence.

"LUSTER. A man, aged 14. Who was not only capable of the complete care and security of an idiot twice his age and three times his size, but could keep him entertained." The author describes Benjy's caretaker in an appendix. Before Luster, a servant named Hirsch watched over Benjy. "Idiot" is a long-outdated term, now considered inaccurate and insulting.

He can enjoy recreational activities such as walking and carriage rides (but must be accompanied by a caretaker).

"Ben's voice roared and roared. Queenie moved again, her feet began to clop-clop steadily again, and at once Ben hushed."

Once Luster returns to the carriage route Benjy expects to travel along, Benjy's distress instantly subsides and he again placidly watches the familiar landmarks pass by.

Benjy's conception of the world is limited to what he can see and touch and remember. He is not capable of understanding symbols or symbolic processes.

" 'It's froze.' Caddy said. 'Look.' She broke the top of the water and held a piece of it against my face. 'Ice. That means how cold it is.' "

Benjy's section of the book reveals that he largely lives in the past with his memories of Caddy and the outdoor adventures they shared along with its sights and smells.

Profile #3: Raymond Babbitt in the Film *Rain Man*; Screenplay by Ronald Bass

---

Dr. Bruner: "He's an autistic savant. People like him used to be called idiot savants. There's certain deficiencies, certain abilities that impair him."
Charlie: "So he's retarded."
Dr. Bruner: "Autistic. There's certain routines, rituals that he follows."

PLOT SUMMARY

Charlie Babbitt (played by Tom Cruise) is a shallow, materialistic young adult who is unhappy with the terms of his late father's will. He learns that his father has left a significant portion of his assets to Raymond, a brother Charlie did not know he had. Charlie travels to Cincinnati, Ohio, to meet Raymond and finds him living at Wallbrook, a live-in health care facility that provides security and routine for his brother who has autism spectrum disorder. Charlie wants to bring Raymond to a lawyer in Los Angeles in the hope of receiving a greater portion of his father's estate.

Since Raymond is afraid to fly, an irritated Charlie agrees to make the long trip by automobile. During the road trip, Charlie discovers Raymond's considerable handicaps as well as his remarkable talents. Charlie exploits Raymond's impressive memory skills by teaching him to count cards before stopping off in Las Vegas to beat the casinos at the blackjack table. This and other adventures shared by the brothers during their road trip have a positive effect on the narcissistic Charlie. He begins to see his talented brother who has a significant disability as more than simply an irritating obstacle preventing him from getting what he thinks is his due inheritance. In the end, despite his own emotional growth and a new appreciation and fondness for his brother, Charlie can't be sure if Raymond has changed or developed any affection for him.

RAYMOND'S PSYCHOLOGICAL TRAITS

Raymond is a 38-year-old man with autism spectrum disorder. (Among the 3 million plus persons in the United States with this disorder, males account for up to six times as many cases as females, according to psychiatrist Darold A. Treffert, MD.) He is unusual because he has savant syndrome, a rare condition in which people with developmental disorders, including autism spectrum disorder, have exceptional abilities or skills in a specialized field. Raymond has an extraordinary memory as well as remarkable but specialized mathematical skills. The term "autistic savant" has been used routinely in the past to describe a person like Raymond who is on the autism spectrum with savant syndrome.

AUTISM SPECTRUM DISORDER

Most people on the autism spectrum—an estimated 9 out of 10—do not have any savant abilities. Among people who are not on the spectrum, fewer than 1 out of 100 have such special abilities. As the word "spectrum" indicates, autism spectrum disorder covers a wide range of abilities and behaviors. The diagnostic criteria are complex because they cover a group of disabilities all related to problems of brain development. These problems can significantly affect a person's ability to behave, communicate, and interact successfully in social situations. The severity of symptoms varies but the symptoms typically include difficulty with both verbal and nonverbal communication. In some cases, individuals engage in repetitive behaviors such as rocking, spinning, and flapping arms or hands. At one end of the spectrum, these symptoms can be debilitating. At the opposite end, people function quite well.

Until the publication of the *Diagnostic and Statistical Manual of Mental Disorders, 5th edition* (*DSM-5*) in 2015, the label "Asperger's syndrome" was used to describe a condition marked by normal intelligence and normal language abilities but impaired interpersonal or social skills. This diagnosis was dropped from the *DSM-5* because high-functioning autism turned out to be the same as Asperger's syndrome. In other words, people with Asperger's syndrome were on the spectrum, albeit at a much higher level of functioning than those whose disabilities placed them further toward the opposite end of the spectrum. Critics argue that the replacement label—high-functioning autism—isn't always an accurate fit for people previously diagnosed with Asperger's syndrome. Many of these high-functioning individuals don't feel they are disadvantaged. Some say they appreciate their unique way of looking at the world and their unique abilities.

SAVANT SYNDROME

Rain Man introduced moviegoers to the struggles of people on the autism spectrum and to the remarkable abilities of people with savant syndrome. It also may have given many people unfamiliar with autism the mistaken impression that everyone on the spectrum has savant abilities. Viewers might also conclude, incorrectly, that people on the autism spectrum who have savant skills routinely have multiple abilities. Raymond, for example, can effortlessly memorize listings in telephone books, baseball statistics, and cards dealt in a Las Vegas casino. He also can instantly count the number of toothpicks that spill from a box onto the floor and correctly answer difficult arithmetic problems instantly. Most people with savant syndrome do not have this many special abilities.

Raymond's character was inspired by a man named Kim Peek, who was not on the autism spectrum. Kim had an extraordinary memory but had considerable difficulty mastering the skills necessary to live an independent life. Kim, who died in 2011 at the age of 58, had been called a mega-savant. He read and memorized thousands of books. He had the remarkable ability to read and memorize both pages of an open book at the same time. This extraordinary skill was undoubtedly related to the fact that he was born without the major communication pathway, the corpus callosum, linking the two hemispheres of his brain. It is possible that both hemispheres of his brain could process information independently without cross-referencing or interfering with the other hemisphere.

Unlike most of us, Kim appeared to have well-developed language processing abilities in both sides of his brain. While both Raymond and Kim were savants and had neurodevelopmental conditions, only Raymond was on the autism spectrum. Kim was diagnosed with a neurodevelopmental abnormality that left him without major communication pathways linking the two sides of his brain. Neuroscientists are not yet able to explain the mechanism that underlies savant abilities in either group.

The National Institute of Mental Health lists the following characteristic features of autism spectrum disorder (unrelated to savant syndrome):

Persistent deficits in social communication and social interaction across multiple contexts

Vern: "He likes you, that's just his way of showing it."
Susanna: "When I touched him, he pulled away."
Vern: "Don't take it personal. He never touched me and I'm closer to him than anyone in the world. Known him for nine years. It's not in him. If I left tomorrow without saying goodbye, he probably wouldn't notice."
Susanna: "He wouldn't notice if you left?"
Vern: "I'm not sure but I don't think people are his first priority."

Raymond's caretaker, Vern, explains Raymond's social deficits to Charlie's girlfriend, Susanna.

Restricted, repetitive patterns of behavior, interests, or activities

Dr. Bruner: "The way he eats, sleeps, walks, talks, uses the bathroom. It's all he has to protect himself. Any break from this routine leaves him terrified."
Charlie learns how accurate Dr. Bruner's explanation is when Charlie travels with Raymond.
Raymond: "Gotta get my boxer shorts at K-Mart."
Charlie: "What difference does it make where you buy underwear? What difference does it make? Underwear is underwear! It's underwear wherever you buy it! In Cincinnati or wherever!"
Raymond: "K-Mart."

Symptoms must be present in the early developmental period (typically recognized in the first two years of life)

Charlie: "When I was a kid and I was scared, the Rain Man would come and sing to me."
Susanna: "What happened to him?"
Charlie: "Nothing. I grew up."

After his father's death, Charlie learns about his older brother Raymond who has been institutionalized for several decades. Raymond has been on the autism spectrum his entire life. In time, Charlie realizes that what he thought was an imaginary friend he called Rain Man was, in fact, his brother Raymond. Charlie was so young when Raymond was sent to Wallbrook, he confused his earliest memories of his real brother with an imaginary friend.

Symptoms cause clinically significant impairment in social, occupational, or other important areas of current functioning

Doctor: "Ray, do you know how much a candy bar costs?"
Raymond: " 'Bout a hundred dollars."

Doctor: "Do you know how much one of those new compact cars costs?"
Raymond: " 'Bout a hundred dollars."

Raymond is not capable of understanding enough to live independently.

Raymond is a savant because he is both intellectually impaired and has extraordinary specialized skills.

Doctor: "Ray, how much is 4343 × 1234?"
Raymond: "5-3-5-9-2-6-2."
. . .
Doctor: "Ray, do you know how much a square root of 2130 is?"
Raymond: "4-6 point 1-5-1-9-2-3-0-4."
Charlie: "That's amazing! He is amazing! He should work for NASA or something like that."
Doctor: "If you had a dollar and you spent 50 cents, how much money would you have left?"
Raymond: "About 70."
Doctor: "70 cents?"
Raymond: "70 cents."
Charlie: "So much for the NASA idea."

Another example:

Waitress: "Good Morning! Coffee?"
Raymond [sees her name tag]: "Sally Dibbs, Dibbs Sally. 461-0192."
Sally Dibbs: "How did you know my phone number?"
Charlie: "How did you know that?"
Raymond: "You said read the telephone book last night. Dibbs Sally. 461-0192."
Charlie: "He, uh, remembers things. Little things sometimes."

Profile #4: Dylan Mint in the Young Adult Novel, *When Mr. Dog Bites* by Brian Conaghan

"I want to shout out.
"I want to scream.
"I want to bellow, holler, and yell soooooo badly it hurts like hell."

PLOT SUMMARY

When Dylan Mint, a student at Drumhill Special School, is stressed, he shouts and swears uncontrollably. And he twitches—uncontrollably. These are enormously distressing behaviors for anyone; for a 16-year-old they seem disastrous. He fights to suppress the shouting and swearing and tics—involuntary movements and vocalizations—but that is a challenge in a school filled with many unsympathetic peers. One exception is his good friend Amir. Amir has a high-functioning form of autism spectrum disorder, previously referred to as Asperger's syndrome. Dylan is loyal to and protective of his friend.

Things get worse when Dylan overhears a conversation between his mother and a doctor that leads him to conclude that he doesn't have long to live. Determined to experience as much as he can before the end, he composes a short but ambitious Bucket List. This includes the goal of seducing a fellow student, the object of his affection, Michelle Malloy. As Dylan goes to work checking off the three items on his list, which he labels "Cool Things to Do before I Cack It," he learns unexpected lessons not only about swearing but also about life, as well as death, sex, and love.

DYLAN'S PSYCHOLOGICAL TRAITS

Dylan is positive, resilient, determined, loyal, and family-oriented. His life, however, is dominated by a tic disorder, specifically Tourette's disorder with coprolalia.

TOURETTE'S DISORDER

Tourette's disorder is characterized by sudden, involuntary jerking movements (motor movements), and shouting or other vocalizations called tics. It is estimated to affect between 3 and 8 out of every 1,000 school-aged children, according to the American Psychiatric Association. Two to four times as many males as females have the disorder. Dylan is in the minority of people with Tourette's disorder, perhaps 10 to 15 percent, because his disorder includes coprolalia. This means his complex tics can take the form of cursing or insults like socially unacceptable slurs. The doctors who diagnosed Dylan would have drawn their conclusion after they had observed or seen the following in his medical history:

His symptoms appeared before he was 18 years of age.

"Even though I was a sixteen-year-old man."

He displayed more than one instance of motor tics plus one or more instances of vocal tics at some time since his illness appeared. Dylan's sudden, nonrhythmic movements could affect his limbs, head, or neck and would not have occurred necessarily at the same time as the shouting, swearing, or other vocal tics.

"SMALL VOLCANO ALERT!

It starts with Mr. Right Eye and quickly moves to Mr. Jaw, then the red hot-lava flows and Mr. Head shakes at super rapid speed.
Whoosh!
Whoosh!
Whoosh!
Mr. Head is dizzy Miss Lizzie. That's the worst bit.
Mr. Sweaty arrives with Mr. Pong and Mr. Panic.
Mr. and Mrs. Eyes start to pee themselves.
Mr. Throat doesn't miss the boat.
Here he comes: Mr. and Mrs. Bloody Twitch.
That is how life's a bitch for Dylan Mint.
Not far behind is Mr. Tic. Can't stand that prick.
It's the docs who like to call them 'tics.'
I prefer 'volcanoes' myself, because they are like mega eruptions in my head."

Dylan's tics have occurred over at least a 12-month period but they may have increased or decreased in frequency during this time. Also, his symptoms are not caused by any neurological or other medical condition nor were they side effects of medications or drugs of abuse, such as cocaine or methamphetamine.

"I don't suppress it—the docs with the big brains told me not to. 'Always allow it to escape, Dylan, always allow it to escape,' one bright-spark doc said." These comments show that Dylan is under the care of physicians who have diagnosed his Tourette's disorder. During their evaluation, they would have eliminated other possible conditions, including medications and medical conditions, that might be responsible for his symptoms.

Psychotic Disorders

Profile #5: Travis Bickle in the Film *Taxi Driver*; Screenplay by Paul Schrader

Travis's diary: "The headaches got worse. I think I got stomach cancer. I shouldn't complain though. You are only as healthy as you feel."

PLOT SUMMARY

Travis Bickle (played by Robert De Niro) can't sleep. He starts driving a cab at night in New York City to fill up this time. As he drives night after night, he slowly but steadily becomes more and more disgusted with the people of the city, the hustlers, the drug users, the "creeps and the prostitutes." Although he is often anxious and always lonely, he nevertheless manages to persuade Betsy (played by Cybill Shepherd) to go out with him, first to a diner and then to a movie.

Betsy rejects him after he takes her to a pornographic movie on their first date. The experience increases Travis's sense of isolation, suspiciousness, and hatred of the city.

Soon he fixates on Iris, a 12-year-old prostitute (played by Jodie Foster), whom he wants to rescue. When he becomes suicidal and depressed, Travis makes plans to assassinate Betsy's boss, a presidential candidate. Travis's odd appearance, which includes a Mohawk haircut and a long-sleeved military jacket worn in the summer, attracts the attention of the candidate's secret service agents who chase Travis. Travis escapes and drives to the apartment where Iris works. There, in a bloody, violent ending, Travis ironically becomes a hero who lives to drive his cab again.

TRAVIS'S PSYCHOLOGICAL TRAITS

Travis's thoughts and speech are not in tune with other people's. He lacks interpersonal skills and the ability to read social cues. Consequently, he cannot establish relationships with others. He is lonely, friendless, and socially isolated. It is likely that people would describe him as odd or eccentric. He lives with a high level of anxiety that never subsides. His profile strongly resembles a man with schizotypal personality disorder.

Travis becomes suicidal and depressed, leading to a violent and bloody shoot-out in the film's climax. After Travis survives, the depression subsides enough for his schizotypal personality to again become his most prominent feature.

SCHIZOTYPAL PERSONALITY DISORDER

Schizotypal personality disorder (SPD) is characterized by disturbed or odd thought patterns and speech, as well as significant problems forming relationships. Unusual behavior and appearance often create the impression of eccentricity. SPD is often accompanied by depression and anxiety. It is distinct from schizophrenia because it does not involve persistent delusions and hallucinations. Travis would need to satisfy at least five criteria to receive a diagnosis of SPD.

Travis's speech and thinking are odd.

Travis: "I had black coffee and apple pie with a slice of melted yellow cheese. I think that was a good selection."

After meeting Betsy at a diner, Travis reviews the experience. He places a great deal of importance on small details about the meeting rather than on impressions of their conversation or personal chemistry. Most people would think food orders were a trivial matter when meeting a new person. But Travis does not think like most people. Also, his diary entries are often elaborate but stereotyped, and his speech is often vague, as when he answers a prospective employer's question about his education: "Some. Here, there. You know."

Travis's behavior or appearance is odd.

When he attends a campaign rally with the intention of shooting the candidate, he is the only one in the crowd with a Mohawk haircut, which in the mid-1970s stood out more than it might today.

Travis reports having unusual perceptual experiences.

"Sometimes I go out and I smell it. I get headaches, it's so bad, ya know. It's like, they never go away."

"It" refers to those Travis calls the "scum" and the "animals" who come out at night as he rides the streets in his cab.

Travis is frequently suspicious of people or has paranoid feelings.

"You talkin' to me? You talkin' to me? You talkin' to me? Then who the hell else are you talking—You talkin' to me? Well, I'm the only one here."

Talking to himself in the mirror, Travis imagines dealing with potential threats. Throughout the film, he repeatedly conveys his suspicious nature bordering on paranoia through his sideways glances with and without the aid of his rearview mirror.

Travis has no close friends or relationships.

Travis: "Loneliness has followed me my whole life, everywhere. In bars and cars, sidewalks, stores, everywhere. There's no escape. I'm God's lonely man."

Travis could have close relationships with relatives and still satisfy this criterion, but he hasn't seen his parents for years. He also tells them and others that he is working for the government on secret business and can't tell them where he lives or how they can contact him.

Travis's emotional expressions are constrained.

He hardly smiles and never laughs. He does show frustration and frequently appears anxious.

Travis has odd beliefs that influence how he acts.

When he decides to assassinate a politician, Travis declares to himself: "The idea had been growing in my brain for some time. True force. All the king's men cannot put it back together again." And: "Now I see it clearly. My whole life is pointed in one direction. I see that now. There never has been any choice for me."

Other criteria for SPD are believing that ordinary events have a special relevance or meaning and having weird beliefs or magical thinking that influences a person's actions.

It is important to point out that none these or any of the criteria listed indicate that the type of violence portrayed in *Taxi Driver* is common in people with SPD or any other mental disorder. The public's perception that mental illness is closely associated with violence is fed by news stories that heavily publicize events involving mentally ill suspects. In fact, a mentally ill person is statistically more likely to become a victim of a crime than to commit a crime.

Profile #6: Alan Strang in the Play *Equus* by Peter Shaffer

Psychiatrist: "What did he [Equus] say to you?"
Alan: "I see you. I will save you."

PLOT SUMMARY

At the age of 12, Alan Strang experiences a life-changing horseback ride. It gives him a powerful feeling of control, meaning, and freedom. As a youth predisposed to mental illness, the stresses of his upbringing—including significant conflict between his hyper-religious mother and his ardently atheistic father—lead him to create a personal religion. This bizarre belief system prominently features his obsession with horses. It merges his religious conflicts and his sexual fascination with horses. He worships the animals as gods ruled by Equus, the horse spirit.

At age 17, Alan has an unsuccessful sexual experience with a girl in the stable where he works part-time. He is guilt-ridden and tormented by his behavior, since his mother taught him that sex without love is a sin. Because his god Equus—a substitute for his mother's god Jesus Christ—is omnipotent, Alan is convinced that Equus has seen his "sin." Equus has witnessed that sin through the eyes of the six horses in the temple of Alan's religion, the stable. This delusion leads Alan to pick up a spike and blind the half-dozen horses. Following the mutilation, Alan's mother insists that Alan is personally responsible for his behavior, while his father blames religion.

Psychiatrist Dr. Martin Dysart is assigned to treat Alan at Rokesby Psychiatric Hospital in the United Kingdom. He believes he can help Alan overcome his delusions, but the disaffected and disillusioned psychiatrist has serious doubts about the ethics of treating the young man. Dysart comes to envy the boy's passion, never having experienced passion in his own life. He worries that "curing" Alan will take away Alan's zest for life and leave the young man empty.

Dysart's existential crisis is a dramatic affectation that can only be seriously entertained on stage, at cocktail parties, or in literature courses. Doubting the usefulness of removing Alan's pain is naïve at best and cruel and unethical at worst. It grossly underestimates the suffering that untreated mentally ill individuals like Alan struggle against on a daily basis. It is often fashionable to discount psychological and psychiatric treatments as misguided efforts that take away individuality and creativity. But such arguments never address the severe suffering that accompanies mental illness. Such a debate cannot be approached responsibly and seriously solely from a literary standpoint. The discussion must involve medical and psychological insights and knowledge gathered through years of studying and treating mental illnesses.

Eccentricity is not mental illness. Behavior patterns are not considered mental disorders unless they cause significant distress or they threaten the health or well-being of a patient or other individuals. Alan is not eccentric; he is mentally ill. He is tormented and dangerous. He needs help, not pity from a psychiatrist questioning his own career choice who is worried about the implications of taking away his patient's delusional "passion" when he is successfully treated.

Dr. Dysart's own passionless life, of course, explains his doubts about the value of relieving the symptoms of Alan's mental illness. It explains his literary affectation but it betrays an insensitivity and a lack of understanding of the seriousness of mental illness. Any competent doctor would realize that there is nothing artistic or enviable about a passion that emanates from the delusions of a human being in pain.

ALAN'S PSYCHOLOGICAL TRAITS

Alan is a lonely 17-year-old who has a poor relationship with his parents. Because of his upbringing, he is sexually repressed and tormented by religious conflict. On multiple occasions he has experienced sexual pleasure from riding horses. Alan believes he has a special relationship with a god of his own invention. This grandiose delusion is centered on a horse spirit named Equus, which resides in every horse.

DELUSIONAL DISORDER—GRANDIOSE TYPE

The key feature of delusional disorder is a patient's firm conviction, lasting at least one month, that at least one false belief is real. This belief is not supported by facts or evidence, or is contrary to the beliefs common to a patient's culture. It also must impair the person's ability to function day to day. Alan's disorder appears to be of the grandiose type. This form of the disorder involves the delusion that a person is extraordinarily talented or is privy to some special insight or discovery. Alan's belief that he has a unique insight into the existence of Equus, the omnipotent horse god, is consistent with this diagnosis. Belief in other deities such as those worshiped by Christians, Jews, Muslims, and members of other religions are not considered delusions because they are common in the world's cultures and do not impair people's ability to function.

Alan's psychiatrist believes he can cure him. He would have to base a diagnosis of delusional disorder based on the following five observations:

Clear evidence of at least one delusion lasting 30 days or longer exists.

Alan: "No one knows him but him and me."
Psychiatrist: "You can tell me, Alan. Name him."
Alan: "Equus."
Psychiatrist: "Thank you. Does he live in all horses or just some?"
Alan: "All."

Alan has believed in an omnipotent horse god named Equus for years, long before he was forced into treatment.

Alan's symptoms do not support a diagnosis of schizophrenia. Hallucinations may be present in delusional disorder but they are not a key feature of the illness and are clearly related to the subject or theme of the delusion.

Alan: "He [Equus] was there. Through the door. The door was shut, but he was there! . . . He'd seen everything. I could hear him. He was laughing."

Alan reports hearing the voice of Equus on several occasions, but these auditory hallucinations are consequences of his delusional beliefs; they are not like the voices people with schizophrenia often hear in their heads. And while Alan does have a delusion, he shows no signs of disorganized speech, severely disorganized behavior, or diminished emotional expressions (negative symptoms). Because his auditory hallucination is intimately associated with his delusion, he does not meet the criteria for schizophrenia.

Aside from the delusion and its influence, other behaviors are generally normal and do not draw attention to him. His ability to care for himself and function day to day was not affected up until he blinded the horses.

No one knew about Alan's delusion until the violent episode in the stable. Before then, he had the confidence of his employer and people did not pay much attention to him. He behaved normally enough to attract the interest of at least one woman his own age.

There is no indication that Alan suffers from major depression or mania.

Until his psychiatrist gains his confidence, Alan sings when questioned in the hospital just as he did during his trial. This behavior appears to be a dismissal of authority rather than a symptom of mental illness because he immediately resumes speaking when he begins to trust his doctor.

And, as is true with most diagnoses, the symptoms cannot be explained by use of medications or other drugs or by the presence of physical or other mental illness.

Profile #7: Alonso Quixano in the Novel *Don Quixote* by Miguel de Cervantes

> His fantasy filled with everything he had read in his books, enchantments as well as combats, battles, challenges, wounds, courtings, loves, torments, and other impossible foolishness, and he became so convinced in his imagination of the truth of all the countless grandiloquent and false inventions he read that for him no history in the world was truer.

PLOT SUMMARY

Alonso Quixano is a middle-aged, moderately well-off, stick-thin bachelor living in the Spanish countryside. He is obsessed with the myth of noble knights and their selfless quests to defend honor and vanquish evil. Alonso is such a devoted reader of chivalric romances that he neglects running his estate and begins to sell off parcels of his land to buy more books on his favorite topic.

Alonso eventually becomes so absorbed by the tales of chivalry, and so devoted to the ideals they promote, that he convinces himself that he is a valiant knight: Don Quixote of La Mancha. He takes a boney, worn-out horse as his noble steed, which he christens Rocinante, and declares that an unrefined, rough-looking country girl named Aldonza Lorenzo is the beautiful Dulcinea del Toboso, his ideal lady and inspiration for all of his noble quests.

Completely deluded, and obsessed with chivalric codes of honor and behavior, Don Quixote improvises a helmet, a suit of armor, and a makeshift lance.

After his first solo adventure—during which he receives a beating—he acquires a squire, a peasant named Sancho Panza. Sancho is in touch with reality but naïve enough to believe that Don Quixote can keep his promise of rewarding him for loyal service with a small kingdom of his own.

Together, the knight and his squire embark on a long series of misadventures during which they challenge many imaginary evil sorcerers, enemies, and scoundrels. They are sometimes humored but often ridiculed and abused by the people they encounter. The knight's quest continues until a sense of sad reality returns.

Don Quixote starts out as a ludicrous, silly, deluded adventurer. Yet, the knight seems to have captured the heart of his creator, Cervantes, at some point during the writing of the book. The character that started as a parody of romantic escapism is transformed into an endearing reminder of idealism versus the petty, baser features of human nature: disloyalty, selfishness, greed, and surrender in the face of hardship and cruelty.

ALONSO'S PSYCHOLOGICAL TRAITS

Alonso lives an unremarkable life as a well-to-do landowner in the Spanish countryside well into his middle age. He appears undernourished and not well rested. He is solitary and particularly fond of reading. He showed no signs of mental illness before developing serious delusions. Although lack of sleep troubled Alonso around the time he became delusional, there is no indication that sleep deprivation is a permanent part of his life during the months he suffers his grandiose delusion.

DELUSIONAL DISORDER—GRANDIOSE TYPE

The defining feature of Alonso's mental condition is his unshakable belief, which he has held for at least one month, that he is in reality a knight. It only takes one such false belief to qualify as delusional disorder. Alonso's disorder is of the grandiose type because he sees himself as an exceptional, brave, honest, virtuous, and heroic figure in a world that does not exist, one that recognizes and values codes of chivalry, and one in which evil sorcerers threaten, and brave knights protect, the innocent.

Other types of delusions are erotomanic (the inaccurate belief someone is in love with the person), jealous (belief a partner is unfaithful), persecutory (belief a person is the object of conspiracy or is being targeted in a potentially harmful way), somatic (beliefs involving some aspect of bodily sensations or functions), and mixed (in which no one theme stands out).

If belief in knight errantry was common in Alonso's culture, he might not be considered delusional. But since he is convinced he is a character found only in books, he suffers from a delusion. (Compare with Alan Strang in *Equus*.)

Alonso misinterprets people and events as players in his delusional world populated by noble knights, virtuous ladies, and grand quests. He has no symptoms of schizophrenia or other mental illness. He takes no medication. Any

hallucinations he has are clearly related to his delusion and so do not change his diagnosis.

Alonso as Don Quixote:	"Good fortune is guiding our affairs better than we could have desired, for there you see, friend Sancho Panza, thirty or more enormous giants with whom I intend to do battle and whose lives I intend to take, and with the spoils we shall begin to grow rich, for this is righteous warfare, and it is a great service to God to remove so evil a breed from the face of the earth."
Sancho:	"What giants?"
Don Quixote:	"Those you see over there, with the long arm; sometimes they are almost two leagues long."
Sancho:	"Look, your grace, those things that appear over there are not giants but windmills, and what looks like their arms are the sails that are turned by the wind and make the grindstone move."

Sancho can never convince his master that his delusions are not real.

In the past, critics suggested that Alonso suffered from paranoia or folie à deux. It is true that he often explains his failures during his adventures by blaming "enchanters" who persecute him, but these excuses are part of the medieval chivalric romantic tradition that defines his delusion. It is part of his delusion, not a separate illness.

Folie à deux is a delusion or psychosis shared by two people. Alonso has a delusion. Sancho frequently tries to convince his master that he is misinterpreting sights and events. He often goes along with Alonso in order to get his reward. Although Sancho is unsophisticated and has less-than-average intelligence, he contrasts Alonso's delusion with reality. Sancho does not share Alonso's delusion and so does not suffer from folie à deux.

Profile #8: Jerry Fletcher in the Film *Conspiracy Theory*; Screenplay by Brian Helgeland

---

> A good conspiracy is unprovable. I mean, if you can prove it, it means they screwed up somewhere along the line.

PLOT SUMMARY

Cabdriver Jerry Fletcher (played by Mel Gibson) sees conspiracies everywhere: fluoridation of the water supply is a plot to enslave the population, Nobel

Prize winners are forced to become sperm donors to create an elite class of offspring, and even some of his innocent cab customers are threats. Conspiracies dominate Jerry's life. He lectures his passengers about the plots he is convinced underlie the power structure of the world. When not driving his cab, Jerry searches newspapers and cross-references the "leads" and "evidence" he finds to support his conspiracy theories. He writes up the conclusions of his extensive research in a newsletter which he mails to each of his dozen subscribers, moving about the city, dropping each newsletter into a different mailbox. Convinced he is the subject of an investigation, he equips his apartment with scores of locks and safety features. He even puts locks on his refrigerator, on the mental canisters of pudding in it, and on his kitchen and file cabinets. He goes so far as to booby-trap his apartment in case it is ever invaded by the conspirators he sees everywhere.

Jerry frequently visits Alice Sutton (played by Julia Roberts) in her Department of Justice office to alert her to the conspiracies he thinks he has uncovered. Alice is kind to Jerry despite the annoyance he has become. Although he is not a threat to her, he nevertheless stalks her by sitting in his cab outside her apartment and watching her through her window as she exercises.

In entertaining Hollywood fashion, Jerry stumbles across a real government conspiracy, one which had even involved him years ago. Everything he has obsessed and worried about comes true. He becomes the target of rogue intelligence agents and manages to drag Alice into his plight and flight.

JERRY'S PSYCHOLOGICAL TRAITS

Jerry shows signs of stalking behavior, delusions of persecution, and paranoia. The stalking behavior in this film is limited to his parking outside Alice's apartment building and watching her exercise. Although he does not pose a threat to Alice, it is inappropriate behavior, as is his keeping a "shrine" of her photos in his apartment. Understandably Alice is alarmed when she discovers this aspect of Jerry's behavior. (Jerry tells her the shrine was there when he moved into the apartment.) In reality, stalking behavior can be a much more serious threat to the person stalked. Contrast Jerry's Hollywood type "romantic crush" stalking with a more serious depiction of pathological stalking behavior in the cases of Claude Frollo in *The Hunchback of Notre Dame* or Martin Burney in *Sleeping with the Enemy.*

Jerry's delusions (before he is entangled in a real conspiracy) are more central to the plot than his stalking behavior. The majority of people with paranoid delusions like Jerry's are extremely serious and quite humorless. Mel Gibson, however, makes his character more likable by giving it a sense of humor. This is an effective moviemaking tweak that you probably won't often find in the real world should you encounter someone who shares Jerry's view of the world. Delusions are very real—and very serious—to people who suffer from them.

DELUSIONAL DISORDER—PERSECUTORY TYPE

Jerry has had conspiratorial delusions for more than a month and he is certain that his false beliefs are real. Some people with delusional disorder have only one false belief; Jerry seems to have dozens of them. None of them is supported by convincing evidence. Jerry's delusions appear to be of the persecutory type. This subtype of the disorder involves the delusion that some entity is conspiring against the person or trying to prevent the person from pursuing his or her goals. This describes the nature of Jerry's delusions. Other people with persecutory delusions may feel they are being spied on, drugged, harassed, or targeted maliciously in other ways.

Clear evidence exists of at least one delusion lasting 30 days or longer.

Jerry Fletcher: "July eighth, 1979, all the fathers of Nobel Prize winners were rounded up by United Nations military units, all right, and actually forced at gunpoint to give semen samples in little plastic jars, which are now stored below Rockefeller Center underneath the ice skating rink."

Jerry is quite serious when he asserts this. He is just as serious when he announces that "The Vietnam War was fought over a bet that Howard Hughes lost to Aristotle Onassis."

Aside from the delusion and its influence, other behaviors are generally normal and do not draw attention. His ability to care for himself and function day-to-day is not affected.

Jerry earns a living as a cabdriver, is physically healthy and, although he looks over his shoulder, suspecting innocent people of being part of government conspiracies, does not stand out in a crowd.

Jerry's symptoms do not support a diagnosis of schizophrenia. Hallucinations may be present in delusional disorder but they are not a key feature of the illness and are clearly related to the subject of the delusion or to the theme of the delusion.

Jerry's symptoms do not match the criteria for schizophrenia and hallucinations are not among his symptoms.

And, as is true with most diagnoses, the symptoms cannot be explained by use of medications, other drugs, or by the presence of physical or other mental illness.

Not everyone who believes in conspiracy theories is mentally ill. Mental illness only exists when it creates situations or problems that threaten the psychological or physical well-being of an individual and/or people the individual interacts with. Just because you believe that a vast, unwieldy and unlikely conspiracy involving Lyndon Johnson, the CIA, Fidel Castro, and the Mafia in the assassination of President John F. Kennedy—despite the lack of evidence supporting this view and strong evidence against it—does not mean you need therapy. Jerry Fletcher, however, despite his sense of humor, was tormented by his belief in conspiracy theories and so was a good candidate for therapy that might relieve his torment.

Some research suggests that people like Jerry Fletcher often have a system of beliefs that includes a strong distrust of authorities such as politicians, government officials, the military, and large corporations. Conspiracy theorists are uncomfortable with the fact that they have little or no influence with these powerful agencies. This perceived weakness makes them feel helpless and threatened. "Uncovering" and "exposing" the imagined misdeeds of these powerful, controlling forces gives such individuals a sense of control which they are desperate to have.

The belief that governmental authorities have covered up the fact that Earth has been visited by aliens arriving in UFOs is another common conspiracy theory. The psychological and spiritual significance of this belief for conspiracy theorists is similar to the psychological and spiritual significance Jerry's beliefs have for him.

Clinical and forensic psychologist Stephen Diamond, PhD, summarized in his *Psychology Today* blog, "Evil Deeds," a likely answer to the question: What is the psychospiritual significance of the UFO phenomenon? Diamond recalls psychiatrist Viktor Frankl's views that "we all possess an innate, instinctual 'will to meaning': an inherent need to make sense of life, to find some purpose."

If, for some reason, a person does not find satisfying explanations for the significance or purpose of their lives, he or she may become more than a little uncomfortable. The discomfort may even reach levels of "despair, rage, depression and embitterment." To fill this "existential vacuum," as Frankl called it, people seek meaning. "Meaning makes suffering more bearable," Diamond explains. "So naturally, we tend to seek meaning in life as much as possible. We want to make sense of the seemingly senseless. Attribute meaning to the apparently absurd. Assign significance to the imaginary."

Perhaps it is because of this intense need to make sense out of what seems like a scary, uncontrollable world that accounts for a characteristic commonly seen in conspiracy buffs. This is an inability or refusal to consider evidence that conflicts with their conclusions. Instead of weighing counterarguments and evidence that does not agree with their conclusions, they commonly dismiss these arguments and evidence out of hand or quickly come up with new evidence to support their views and conclusions. They may even go so far as to assert that any counterarguments are, in fact, part of the conspiracy they believe exists. As Jerry Fletcher said: "A good conspiracy is unprovable."

This inclination to believe that any contrary information is part of a large conspiracy, and the adoption of a conspiratorial worldview, was once called "sick think," a phrase once applied to a paranoid CIA official named James Jesus Angleton by the head of his organization. As the agency's counterintelligence chief, Angleton seriously harmed the morale of his organization when he searched for a Soviet mole he was convinced was hiding in the ranks of his spy agency. He was so obsessed and taken in by his conviction that there was a traitor in the CIA that he dismissed any arguments or facts that countered his belief as being part of the conspiracy to hide the identity of the Soviet double agent. Because Angleton could not distinguish between real and suspected traitors, and because he would not consider arguments or facts that countered his views, he caused serious damage among the ranks of his fellow intelligence operatives and even destroyed some of their careers.

Sometimes, of course, there are double agents in the CIA. And the National Security Agency's practice of vacuuming up phone, email, and other electronic communications of U.S. citizens not suspected of terrorist activities are examples of troubling policies that are indeed evocative of conspiracies. The difference between these examples and those typically believed by conspiracy theorists is the degree and quality of supporting evidence. It's necessary to consider all the facts, both for and against the existence of a conspiracy, if it is to be considered valid.

Conspiracy theorists often cannot distinguish between events and facts that are related to conspiracy and those that are not. Dismissing counterarguments without considering their merits or judging them as being part of a conspiracy is a sign of "sick think." This type of response may be seen in people suffering from schizotypal paranoia and in those who have an overwhelming distrust of authorities against whom they feel weak and threatened. Healthy people consider the possibility they may be wrong but rely heavily on evidence or lack of evidence in distinguishing what they believe is true and real, and what are simply possibilities.

Profile #9: Ophelia in the Play *Hamlet* by William Shakespeare

Claudius: " . . . poor Ophelia/Divided from herself and her fair judgment/Without the which we are pictures, or mere beasts."

PLOT SUMMARY

Hamlet, the Prince of Denmark, suspects that his uncle Claudius killed his father, the King, to steal his Crown. Claudius further outrages Hamlet by marrying Hamlet's mother, Gertrude. After his father's ghost commands Hamlet to avenge him, Hamlet spends much of the play struggling to overcome his doubts about his mission and himself. Others pay the ultimate price as Hamlet worries, procrastinates, and then ultimately acts.

Among the many victims in the drama is Ophelia, the teenage daughter of the Lord Chamberlain, Polonius. She loves Hamlet but she must obey her father's orders not to associate with the troubled prince. Hamlet's cruel words produce yet more distress.

After Hamlet mistakes Ophelia's father for Claudius and kills him, Ophelia is psychologically broken and eventually drowns herself. Her death begins a cascade that ends with the deaths of Claudius, Gertrude, Ophelia's brother Laertes, and Hamlet himself.

OPHELIA'S PSYCHOLOGICAL TRAITS

Hamlet's on and off love interest is a sensitive, passive teenager who, like most women in Elizabethan England, is forced by societal standards to obey and not challenge the decisions of the men in her life. After her father first forbids her from speaking to Hamlet and then forces her to spy on him, she becomes very troubled. Following the death of her father, her speech shows signs of disorganized thinking, which she often delivers in song. Her family asserts that she is "mad" although the contents of her seemingly incomprehensible speech hint at the events that trigger her affliction.

PSYCHOSIS

It seems certain that Ophelia experienced psychosis. Based on the sudden onset of her disorganized speech and lack of previous symptoms, it is possible she suffered from brief psychotic disorder with marked stressors.

A diagnosis of brief psychotic disorder requires the presence of at least one of the following: disorganized speech, hallucinations, or delusions. (In addition to one or more of these symptoms, a patient could also have symptoms of gross disorganization or catatonic behavior.) Ophelia has disorganized speech that has lasted for at least 1 but not more than 30 days. Her suicide, however, prevents us from knowing how long Ophelia's symptoms would have lasted. Consequently, we don't know if she would meet the criteria for any of several possible diagnoses. For example, had she lived, it would be necessary to rule out other psychotic disorders including schizophrenia, as well as bipolar disorder and major depressive disorder with psychotic features.

It is clear from the plot of *Hamlet* that Ophelia's disorganized speech is closely linked to two highly stressful events. One is Hamlet's rejection of her love and the other is the murder of her father. Ophelia's behavior in response to these troubling events may well be due to a brief reactive psychosis.

William Shakespeare, of course, rarely if ever wasted lines in his plays. Ophelia's disjointed, incoherent speech contains plenty of hints about what troubles the disturbed teenager.

Disorganized speech

Ophelia sings: "You must sing A-down a-down—And you, Call him a-down-a—Oh, how the wheel becomes it! It is the false steward that stole his master's daughter . . . There's rosemary, that's for remembrance. Pray you, love, remember. And there is pansies, that's for thoughts."

Laertes: "A document in madness, thoughts and remembrance fitted."

Ophelia: "There's fennel for you, and columbines There's rue for you, and here's some for me; we may call it herb of gracea Sundays. Oh, you must wear your rue with a difference. There's a daisy. I would give you some violets, but they withered all when my father died. They say he made a good end (sings) For bonny sweet Robin is all my joy . . . "

Ophelia's speech seems incoherent to Gertrude, Laertes, and Claudius. She appears to be a severely troubled person who does not make sense. Her listeners hear only nonsense (although, as discussed in the next section, there is literary meaning in the nonsense).

MARKED STRESSORS

Ophelia's symptom appears to be in response to extremely stressful events.

Hamlet: " . . . I loved you not."

Ophelia: "I was the more deceived."

Hamlet rejects her love.

Claudius: "Oh, this is the poison of deep grief. It springs / All from her father's death . . . "

Claudius attributes Ophelia's symptoms to the loss of her father.

Although Ophelia has indeed lost her "wits," as Laertes refers to her mental health, Shakespeare has hidden meaning in Ophelia's symptom. The individual flowers she hands out, for example, had individual associations that Shakespeare's audience might have recognized: faithfulness, adultery, and wilted happiness, for instance. All are references to what has happened to her or to what has happened around her. She also alludes to her father's death. Shakespeare thus manages to convey both mental illness and symbolic meaning in the symptom he uses to illustrate Ophelia's psychological disintegration.

Profile #10: Nina Sayers in the Film *Black Swan*; Screenplay by Mark Heyman, Andrés Heinz, and John McLaughlin

Nina's mother: "What happened to my sweet girl?"
Nina: "She's gone!"

PLOT SUMMARY

Ballerina Nina Sayers (played by Natalie Portman) is chosen to play the Swan Queen in a production of Swan Lake. Her ballet director, Thomas (played by Vincent Cassel), tells her that the role requires an innocent, sweet, and tender portrayal on one hand, and a more worldly, adult, and sexual portrayal on the other hand.

Nina was raised by, and still lives with, a controlling, smothering mother who hinders her development as an independent adult. She is overwhelmed by her own efforts to incorporate the opposing sides of the Swan Queen into both her ballet performance and her personal life. The conflict results in a magnificent performance on opening night but at a price that makes a celebratory curtain call impossible.

NINA'S PSYCHOLOGICAL TRAITS

Nina displays a range of problems. She is undernourished with unhealthy eating habits and appears to have an eating disorder. There are obsessive-compulsive aspects in her excessive preoccupation with her athletic performance and physical "perfection." Her anxiety about her performance is excessive and debilitating.

Already emotionally fragile with a weak self-image, Nina also suffers from extreme anxiety, which is a driving force behind her self-destructive behavior. She is stressed by performance anxiety, Thomas's sexual harassment, her terror at transitioning from a child to an adult, and competition from a fellow dancer. The stress associated with her anxiety, likely in association with a genetic predisposition, contributes to her hallucinations.

Her age is consistent with schizophrenia (symptoms in women appear on average at age 25 and in men at age 18), but she lacks some important features of that disorder, for example, negative symptoms. Patients with negative symptoms have reduced emotional expressions. They also aren't self-motivating and they are socially withdrawn. If anything, Nina is too motivated in her doomed and misguided goal "to be perfect."

PSYCHOSIS

Psychosis is not a mental disorder; it is a symptom that can appear in several mental disorders including schizophrenia, bipolar disorder, and major depressive disorder. Other medical conditions and drugs can also produce psychosis. People with psychosis are not in touch with reality. They experience hallucinations (sensing things that are not real) and/or delusions (being convinced that beliefs are accurate despite good evidence that they are not).

Visual hallucinations

Commuting to and from the ballet studio, Nina, dressed in pink and white, sees herself dressed in black leaving her subway car. She experiences this hallucination several times in other locations.

In a literary sense, this figure represents her looming, threatening dark side. It also portends her emerging psychosis. Later she sees her mother's drawings come to life and mock her. At one point, she hallucinates a sexual encounter with Lily, a fellow dancer (played by Mila Kunis). Her hallucinations become more vivid with time. They culminate in a lethal encounter with Lily and finally Nina's physical transformation into the Swan Queen, complete with webbed feet and feathers.

Auditory hallucinations

Her mother's self-portraits move and cry "It's my turn. It's my turn!"

In both her apartment and the ballet studio, Nina hears faint laughter when no one is there. Auditory hallucinations are more common than visual ones but filmmakers strongly rely on images to tell their stories.

In typical Hollywood fashion, Nina is weighed down with other select symptoms of mental disorders, which rarely appear together in one person.

OBSESSIVE-COMPULSIVE TRAITS

Thomas: "In four years, every time you dance I see you obsess getting each and every move perfectly right but I never see you lose yourself. Ever. All that discipline, for what?"

Also, after a day of practice with the ballet company, Nina returns to the apartment she shares with her mother and immediately resumes practicing in the living room.

EATING DISORDER

Nina: "Oh, Mom, not too big. That's way, way too much."

When her mother buys a cake to celebrate Nina's getting the part of the Swan Queen, Nina is alarmed about the calories. By itself, this comment would not suggest an eating disorder but in combination with her other behaviors, including vomiting, meager meals, and weight loss, it illustrates her obsession with diet and weight control. A dresser in the ballet company tells her: "You've lost weight."

SELF-HARM

Mom: "You've been scratching yourself again."
Nina: "No, I haven't. Mom."
Mom: "I thought you'd outgrown this disgusting habit."

Using her fingernails, Nina scratches her back as if to free hidden swan wings. Self-harm like this may be done to distract or release extreme anxiety when a person is unable to express their intense feelings.

PARANOID THINKING

Nina: "Lily. You made her my alternate?"
Thomas: "Well, there's always an alternate. Lily's the best choice."
Nina: "No, but she wants my role."
Thomas: "Every dancer in the world wants your role."
Nina: "No, this is different. She's after me. She is trying to replace me."
Thomas: "Nobody's after you."

Nina's paranoia about Lily worsens after this exchange. She later hallucinates a life-or-death struggle with Lily. This struggle, like all her struggles, is with her own mental illness. Her self-harming behavior, together with her stress and hallucinations, leads to a dramatic end of both the ballet and Nina's struggles.

Profile #11: The Narrator in the Short Story "The Tell-Tale Heart" by Edgar Allan Poe

---

> And now have I not told you that what you mistake for madness is but over acuteness of the senses?

PLOT SUMMARY

The troubled narrator of Poe's story works as a caretaker for an elderly gentleman. The narrator admits to being "dreadfully nervous" and equipped with an extraordinarily acute sense of hearing. It is, however, his strong insistence that he is not mentally ill that raises questions about his sanity. The question becomes a certainty when the narrator reveals his obsession with the appearance of the old man's diseased eye. The eye, perhaps one with a cataract, reminds the narrator of a vulture's eye. He sees it as an Evil Eye. And he concludes that he must kill the old man to escape its gaze.

After carefully planning the murder for days, the narrator attacks his unsuspecting elderly victim as he sleeps, killing him. He notices that it takes a while for the man's heart to stop beating. When it finally does, the narrator dismembers the man's body, hides the body parts under the floorboards, and removes all evidence of his crime. But someone heard the old man scream and called the police. Three officers arrive before sunrise to question the narrator about the reported disturbance.

Convinced he has committed a perfect crime, the narrator is composed and confident as he invites the officers into the house. He entertains them for a while and shows no sign of the anxiety that typically torments him. After a short while, however, his composure begins to break because he detects a soft, steady ticking sound. The sound grows louder and becomes a thumping sound, a sound like a beating heart. When the tormenting sound grows unbearably loud, the narrator cracks. His "devastating" nervousness returns and he yells to the police officers, "I admit the deed!—tear up the planks!—here, here!—it is the beating of his hideous heart!"

Edgar Allan Poe

Short-story writer, poet, critic, and magazine editor Edgar Allan Poe became a leading figure in American literature despite the financial hardships, mental health problems, and personal tragedies he endured during his 40-year-long life. He pioneered the genres of horror and detective fiction and has been called the architect of the American short story. He also stressed the importance of structure and style in his and others' writings.

Poe was born in 1809 in Boston, Massachusetts, and orphaned at age three when he was adopted by a wealthy Virginia couple. They provided a good home for Poe until his stepfather objected to Poe's intention to become a writer. At age 16, he was largely on his own. He joined the army and self-published a pamphlet of poems that attracted little or no notice. Two years later he published a second collection of poetry. He transferred from the army's enlisted ranks to West Point but was dismissed at his own request for disobedience and "gross neglect of duty."

By age 20, Poe's writing career began to progress with more published poems and short stories, and he got a job with a literary magazine. In his mid-20s, he married his 13-year-old cousin, Virginia. The following year he lost his job as a result of his drinking. The stress of losing his job created a sense of anxiety, which seemed to affect him the rest of his life. He obtained work at other magazines, succeeded in boosting their sales, and wrote prolifically. Unfortunately, his drinking, restlessness, and inability to get along with coworkers and writers prevented him from holding a job longer than two years.

Based on accounts of Poe's persistent nervous anxiety, irritable nature, and melancholy, psychologist Erica Giammarco concludes that Poe would score high on the neuroticism (negative emotionality) scale in the five-factor model of personality. Historical evidence also suggests that other well-documented behaviors and traits, including distrustfulness, argumentativeness, and lack of self-control, would place him low in conscientiousness and agreeableness.

Despite his difficult nature, by his early 30s, Poe's reputation as a writer continued to grow but his beloved wife was dying from tuberculosis. Poe drank more, suffered ill health, and had trouble earning a living. Virginia died in January 1847. Although Poe's alcoholism and depression worsened, he continued to write. Two years later he became engaged, but on October 3, 1849, he was found unconscious in a bar in Baltimore, Maryland. He died four days later.

Poe's difficult life is reflected in his finely crafted writing, which often featured troubled characters that lived tormented dreams and experienced terrifying horrors.

THE NARRATOR'S PSYCHOLOGICAL TRAITS

The psychotic narrator's paranoia and auditory hallucinations immediately raise the possibility that he may suffer from schizophrenia. His anxiety is also consistent with schizophrenia. His "dreadful" nervousness may be linked to his psychosis or could be a sign of anxiety disorder. Both of these conditions are discussed elsewhere in this volume. More than most fictional characters, however, the narrator displays a trait that is common among many people suffering from serious mental illnesses like schizophrenia and bipolar disorder: anosognosia.

ANOSOGNOSIA

When the narrator insists that he does not suffer from "madness," he provides a clear example of anosognosia, or lack of awareness of his illness. The inability to appreciate the seriousness of one's illness complicates the treatment of about half of everyone with schizophrenia and about 40 percent of people with bipolar disorder. It is a major problem. Obviously, it would be a challenge to persuade the narrator of Poe's horror story to seek or submit to treatment since he adamantly refuses to concede that he is ill. The narrator is convinced that the heart of his murdered victim, which he has hidden under the floorboards of the house, is beating louder and louder. For him, it is a fact. Why should he doubt it?

Anosognosia has been linked to impaired brain function or damage to parts of the right side of the brain, notably the right frontal lobe and a portion of the adjacent parietal lobe. It is not the same thing as denial. Unlike denial, which is a psychological mechanism used to avoid dealing with unwanted information, anosognosia is a consequence of impaired brain function. If the narrator sensed he was ill but insisted he wasn't, it would be denial. The narrator, however, is unable to comprehend that he is ill.

The narrator lacks insight or awareness of his true mental condition.

"True!—Nervous—very, very dreadfully nervous I had been—and am; but why will you say that I am mad? The disease has sharpened my senses—not destroyed—not dulled them. Above all was the sense of hearing acute. I heard all things in the heaven and in the earth. I heard many things in hell. How, then, am I mad? Hearken! and observe how healthfully—how calmly I can tell you the whole story."

Profile #12: Aksenty Ivanovich Poprishchin in the Short Story "Diary of a Madman" by Nikolai Gogol

> I confess, lately I had begun sometimes to hear and see things no one had ever seen or heard before.

PLOT SUMMARY

Aksenty Ivanovich Poprishchin is a 40-something, low-level civil servant who begins to develop signs of schizophrenia. He documents his thoughts in a journal. Later, during a phase when his symptoms subside, he refers to his writing as the "Diary of a Madman."

He is convinced dogs speak and write letters to each other. He sees a message no one else sees between the lines of books: "Eat people!" He becomes convinced that his family, and perhaps even he, practiced cannibalism. His erratic behavior leads to trouble at work, as does his interest in the boss's daughter.

Eventually his symptoms worsen as he comes to believe he is the new king of Spain. He dates his entries more than 150 years in the future. Finally, he believes he is being taken to Spain by Spanish officials when he is actually being taken to an insane asylum.

AKSENTY'S PSYCHOLOGICAL TRAITS

Aksenty is a middle-aged civil servant whose main job is sharpening writing implements for his boss. He is, needless to say, not respected at work and even demeaned. Aksenty's coworkers are not yet aware that he sees odd things and has strange thoughts, but his diary entries reveal his delusions, hallucinations, and disordered thought patterns, all classic symptoms of schizophrenia. He suffers paranoia and obsessions, and exhibits bizarre behavior.

SCHIZOPHRENIA

Schizophrenia is a brain disease that causes people to lose touch with reality. In Greek, "schizo" means split and "phren" means mind. The "split" in schizophrenia refers to a break between reality and delusion. It has nothing to do a "split personality." (The closest thing to a "split personality" would be dissociative identity disorder, once known as multiple personality disorder. See Eve White in *The Three Faces of Eve*.)

Schizophrenia may be diagnosed when at least two of the following five symptoms are present. These are: (1) hallucinations, (2) delusions, (3) incoherent or disorganized speech, (4) highly disorganized behavior, and (5) negative symptoms, which include low emotional expressiveness or lack of motivation. At least one of the symptoms must be one of the first three on the list. People with schizophrenia display a variety of symptom combinations and features. It is not uncommon for people to believe they are receiving special instructions or are privy to secret information meant just for them, referred to as ideas of reference. Psychiatrists call the disorder a "heterogeneous clinical syndrome." Like autism, it exists on a spectrum. Compare Aksenty's schizophrenia symptoms to those of John Nash in *A Beautiful Mind*.

Disorganized behavior

"I was nearly going to the office, but various considerations kept me from doing so. I keep on thinking about these Spanish affairs. . . . These events, to tell the truth, have so shaken and shattered me, that I could really do nothing all day. Mawra told me that I was very absent-minded at table. In fact, in my absent-mindedness I threw two plates on the ground so that they broke in pieces."

As Aksenty's illness worsens, he begins missing work and acting strangely. One of the many signs and symptoms of the disease are impaired ability to function at work and in social settings.

Ideas of reference

"The year 2000: April 43rd.—Today is a day of splendid triumph. Spain has a king; he has been found, and I am he. I discovered it today; all of a sudden it came upon me like a flash of lightning."

Reading in the newspaper about problems the Spanish are experiencing with the succession of a new king, Aksenty, who is not Spanish and has no connection with the country, assumes he is the king of Spain. Eric Lewin Altschuler, MD, PhD, points out in his article about the short story in the *British Medical Journal* that Aksenty takes the problem personally and so exhibits "the sign of 'ideas of reference,' " which is commonly seen in people with schizophrenia. A modern example is seen in patients convinced that they are receiving personal messages from television broadcasts directed only at them.

Thought disorder

"The moon is generally repaired in Hamburg, and very imperfectly. It is done by a lame cooper, an obvious blockhead who has no idea how to do it. He took waxed thread and olive-oil—hence that pungent smell over all the earth which compels people to hold their noses. And this makes the moon so fragile that no men can live on it, but only noses. Therefore, we cannot see our noses, because they are on the moon."

A common feature of schizophrenia, thought disorder is evidence of an inability to generate ideas in a rational, logical and orderly manner. (See Ophelia in *Hamlet*. Ophelia's relatives conclude that her thoughts are seriously disordered shortly before she takes her life.)

Hallucinations

" 'No, Fidel, you are wrong,' I heard Meggy say quite distinctly. 'I was—bow—wow!—I was—bow! wow! wow!—very ill.' What an extraordinary dog! I was, to tell the truth, quite amazed to hear it talk human language."

An early indication of Aksenty's illness is his belief that dogs can speak and he can understand them.

Delusions

"No date. The day had no date.—I went for a walk incognito on the Nevski Prospect. I avoided every appearance of being the king of Spain. I felt it below my dignity to let myself be recognized by the whole world, since I must first present myself at court."

Aksenty has the grandiose delusion that he is royalty.

Gogol's short story contains, as Altschuler wrote in the *British Medical Journal* in 2001, "one of the oldest and most complete descriptions of schizophrenia."

Profile #13: John Nash in the Film *A Beautiful Mind*; Screenplay by Akiva Goldsman, Inspired by Sylvia Nasar's Biography

Alicia (John Nash's wife): "What's wrong with him?"
Psychiatrist: "John has schizophrenia. People with this disorder are often paranoid."

PLOT SUMMARY

Shortly after the end of World War II, John Forbes Nash, Jr. (played by Russell Crowe), enters Princeton University to study for a doctoral degree in mathematics. He struggles to identify and solve a truly original mathematical problem to secure his reputation. After many false starts, he succeeds in producing brilliant, Nobel Prize–quality work in the field of game theory.

Five years after graduation, however, he becomes convinced he is engaged in top secret code-breaking work for the U.S. government, work that puts him in life-threatening danger from Communist agents. He struggles painfully with his delusions and psychotic episodes as he strives to advance in his academic career and succeed as a father and husband. After years of turmoil and suffering—and with the support of his wife Alicia (played by Jennifer Connelly)—John succeeds in discarding his delusions and learns to recognize and live with his hallucinations. John manages to reach the highest level of scientific accomplishment despite suffering from a severe mental disorder that incapacitates him for years.

JOHN'S PSYCHOLOGICAL TRAITS

In graduate school, John is brilliant but socially awkward. He is ambitious and driven to excel to live up to his image of himself and to impress his fellow students. At the same time, he is experiencing the first psychotic symptoms that, after graduation, will lead to a diagnosis of schizophrenia.

SCHIZOPHRENIA

John suffered from delusions and hallucinations, two key symptoms of schizophrenia, for years. For other defining features of the disease, see Aksenty Ivanovich Poprishchin in "Diary of a Madman."

Hallucinations

Alicia: "What are you talking about? What hallucinations?"

Psychiatrist: "One so far that I am aware of: an imaginary roommate named Charles Herman. I phoned Princeton. According to their housing records John lived alone."

The movie character John Nash (although not the man on whom the character was based) saw, spoke with, and depended for emotional support upon a man who became his best friend after graduate school. The man, like several other characters John speaks to and interacts with, is a hallucination.

Delusions

Psychiatrist: "Which is more likely? That your husband, a mathematician with no military training, is a government spy fleeing the Russians or that he has lost his grip on reality?"

John is convinced that he is engaged in top secret code-breaking work for the U.S. government. He spends hour after hour scanning newspapers and magazine articles looking for "patterns" and "clues" that do not exist. He delivers his reports to a secret dead drop, which, in reality, is an abandoned mailbox. He hallucinates his "control," an American intelligence agent (played by Ed Harris).

Evidence of significantly impaired functioning in important activities, such as employment, taking care of oneself, or interacting with others

John: "The truth is that I don't like people much. And they don't much like me."

The poignancy of John's statement becomes clear when it is revealed that he is talking to his roommate who will become his best friend: a hallucination. Poor socializing skills and problems at work are common in this disorder. John spends all of his time at work looking for hidden messages.

Some signs of illness have been continuously present for at least half a year.

Psychiatrist: "Possibly since graduate school. At least that's when his hallucinations seem to have begun."

Years after graduate school, John's hallucinations and delusions are not only still troubling him, but also have forced his hospitalization.

This film was inspired by a biography of the same name. It was not meant to be a documentary and so the filmmaker took some liberties with John's story and, like most biographical films, changed key facts. For example, in the film, John remains married. In reality, his wife divorced him, although she eventually remarried him and cared for him. In the film, John gives a moving Nobel Prize acceptance speech. In reality, Nobel Prize winners don't give speeches; they give seminars. The real John Nash was not asked to give a seminar because the Nobel Prize committee was concerned his behavior might embarrass them. In the film, John's delusion involves spying. In reality, the real John Nash suffered a variety of different delusions, which included believing he was a biblical figure, a slave, and a messiah. Often he stated that he did not regard himself as ill, a condition called anosognosia. (See the narrator in *A Tell-Tale Heart.*)

In sum, the movie did a good job of presenting a sympathetic portrait of a person affected by a very serious mental illness, which affects approximately 1 percent of the world's population. Unlike more than 90 percent of people with schizophrenia, both the movie character and the real John Nash were able to regain much of their ability to think rationally without the aid of psychotherapeutic medications. The real John Nash worked hard to reject his delusional thinking and he succeeded remarkably well.

Profile #14: The Boy in the Short Story "Signs and Symbols" by Vladimir Nabokov

> For the fourth time in as many years, they were confronted with the problem of what birthday present to take to a young man who was incurably deranged in his mind.

PLOT SUMMARY

Two aged, unnamed Russian immigrants living a bleak life in New York City sometime after World War II wonder "what birthday present to take to a young man who was incurably deranged in his mind." The young man is their son who has been in the sanitarium for four years. The son's doctors say he is afflicted with "referential mania." They even publish a description of the case.

The parents' long trip to deliver the gift basket they choose as a present requires time on the subway, on a bus, and on foot. Upon their arrival they learn from a nurse, whom they don't like, that their son cannot see them this day; he has tried to take his own life once again.

The old couple make the long trip home. They spend a quiet, unhappy evening together. The wife looks through a photo album, recalling deceased family members and the odd behavior their son showed even as a six-year-old boy.

The husband, unable to sleep, suggests that they consider taking their son out of the sanitarium and caring for him at home. They discuss plans to watch him around the clock and hide anything he might use to harm himself. Twice their conversation is interrupted by phone calls. Each time it is a wrong number.

After a bit more discussion, they resolve to do it: they will bring their son home. Then, the phone rings again.

THE BOY'S PSYCHOLOGICAL TRAITS

The couple's child is described throughout the short story as a boy, although he is now 20 years old. He suffers from severe delusions, negative symptoms, and paranoia. In 1947 when the story is set, the boy's appearance (shuffling gait, sullen face, confused, ill-shaven) would not be unusual in patients with schizophrenia. This was before the introduction of psychotropic medications in the early 1950s.

The "referential mania" his doctors diagnosed would today be called schizophrenia. For the boy "everything is a cipher and of everything he is the theme. All around him, there are spies . . . He must be always on his guard and devote every minute and module of life to the decoding of the undulation of things."

Unlike most patients with schizophrenia, the boy began to show signs of mental disturbance while still a child.

CHILDHOOD SCHIZOPHRENIA

Symptoms of schizophrenia in men typically begin in the late teens to mid-20s. In women, symptoms usually develop in the late 20s. They include delusion, hallucinations, disorganized thinking and speech, and other negative symptoms (lack of interest and motivation together with diminished emotional expression).

Rarely, symptoms appear in children. When they do, the disease eventually produces the same symptoms as it does in adults, but they often take longer to appear. The different nature of early symptoms and the gradual buildup to typical adult symptoms can make it challenging to diagnose the disease in children.

The child, for instance, may develop language and motor skills like crawling and walking later than usual. The child may also show abnormal movements like rocking back and forth. Of course, other disorders, like autism spectrum disorder, must be ruled out before a diagnosis of childhood schizophrenia is possible.

During the teen years, adult-like schizophrenia symptoms may become more obvious, including hallucinations, but not necessarily delusions. Some other symptoms may be confused with behaviors common in teens: low level of motivation, pulling away from social contacts, low grades, irritability, moodiness, difficulty sleeping, and odd behavior. In time, however, the symptoms of schizophrenia become clear.

Hints of childhood schizophrenia are discussed in following sections.

Problems at school

"She remembered the shame, the pity, the humiliating difficulties of the journey, and the ugly, vicious, backward children he was with in the special school where he had been placed after they arrived in America."

After his 10th birthday, the boy had difficulty in school and showed signs of unusual behaviors. This led to his enrollment in a school for children with emotional and behavioral problems.

Sleep disturbance

"The boy, aged six—that was when he drew wonderful birds with human hands and feet, and suffered from insomnia like a grown-up man."

The drawing could have been expressions of creativity or expressions of an unusual view of the world. Sleep disturbance may be seen in cases of childhood schizophrenia.

Indications of thought and speech disorder

"The boy again, aged about eight, already hard to understand . . . "

As the mother looks through her photos, she recalls that her son's disturbed thought and speech developed early.

Emerging paranoia

At age eight, " . . . afraid of the wallpaper in the passage, afraid of a certain picture in a book, which merely showed an idyllic landscape with rocks on a hillside and an old cart wheel hanging from the one branch of a leafless tree . . . "

Development of delusions with age

"And then came a time in his life, coinciding with a long convalescence after pneumonia, when those little phobias of his, which his parents had stubbornly regarded as the eccentricities of a prodigiously gifted child, hardened, as it were, into a dense tangle of logically interacting illusions, making them totally inaccessible to normal minds."

Although symptoms in childhood appear gradually, in time patients develop the full range of schizophrenia symptoms. Delusions, for example, are less common at first but often develop in time.

Prominent negative symptoms

"Desires he had none." And he appeared with a " . . . poor face sullen, confused . . . "

Negative symptoms refer to the lack of certain traits we normally associate with a mentally healthy person. Without these traits, a person lacks the ability to function effectively. Motivation, enthusiasm, sense of joy, expressive speech, and normal expression of emotions may all be missing in someone with negative symptoms. Even as a child, the boy showed signs of negative symptoms.

High risk of poor outcome

"... a nurse they knew and did not care for appeared at last and brightly explained that he had again attempted to take his life."

Without treatment, children with schizophrenia often completely lose touch with reality as their thoughts become more disorganized. Like the boy, they would be hospitalized and face a bleak future. Even today, 5 or 6 percent of people with schizophrenia take their own lives and 20 percent attempt to do so.

Had the boy been born in the second half of the 20th century, his chances of receiving effective treatment would have been significantly improved. Identifying people like the boy very early and beginning treatment right away can significantly improve their lives.

Profile #15: Ebenezer Scrooge in the Novella *A Christmas Carol* by Charles Dickens

---

> Marley's Ghost bothered him exceedingly. Every time he resolved within himself, after mature inquiry, that it was all a dream, his mind flew back again, like a strong spring released, to its first position, and presented the same problem to be worked all through, "Was it a dream or not?"

PLOT SUMMARY

Seven years after the death of his business partner and last close human contact, Jacob Marley, Ebenezer Scrooge is visited first by Marley's pitiful, eternally roaming spirit and, shortly after, by three ghosts who represent Christmas Past, Present, and Future.

The visions Ebenezer sees during the night reveal to him both the suffering and the joy in the world. They also reveal to him the damage he does by not using his time and money to relieve the suffering and experience the joy.

When he wakes on Christmas morning, he has undergone a radical change. He raises his underpaid clerk's salary and promises to help his sole employee's struggling family. He reestablishes contact with his nephew and reaches out to his community, and "it was always said of him, that he knew how to keep Christmas well, if any man alive possessed the knowledge."

EBENEZER'S PSYCHOLOGICAL TRAITS

Businessman Ebenezer Scrooge is successful and wealthy but he has deliberately neglected interpersonal relationships. As a child, his only close family relationship was his sister, now deceased. He spent most of his time in a boarding school. As a young adult, his desire to be rich led to his breakup with his fiancée.

Now, he is humorless and rejects all opportunities to interact with his nephew Fred and Fred's circle of friends. He overworks and underpays his clerk, Bob Cratchit. He takes no interest in Cratchit's personal problems, which include poverty (due in large part to Ebenezer's exploitation of his labor) and a sickly, handicapped son called Tiny Tim. Ebenezer gives nothing to charity and has no interest in anyone with whom he does not do business.

However isolated and grumpy he was prior to his ghostly visions, it is not clear that Ebenezer had a psychological illness. His social isolation and unpleasant personality did not distress him enough to cause him to seek help. Among the ranks of billionaires profiled in *Forbes* magazine, it is not difficult to find people just as devoted to material wealth or obsessed with their achievements as is Ebenezer. Like many of them, Ebenezer is a workaholic. He is excessively devoted to his business and to increasing its profitability.

His complete dedication to his work and his rigid schedule might cause some to see Ebenezer as an example of a person with obsessive-compulsive traits. After all, he has more than enough money to ease off a bit and enjoy life. Since, however, his lifestyle does not cause him distress or harm, a diagnosis of obsessive-compulsive personality disorder does not apply.

BRIEF PSYCHOTIC DISORDER WITHOUT MARKED STRESSORS

When a psychotic symptom like hallucination, delusion, disorganized speech, or disorganized behavior appears suddenly and lasts at least one day but less than one month, brief psychotic disorder should be considered, providing the person returns to his normal state of health after the episode. Since there were no apparent stressful events before his psychotic symptoms appeared, the description "without marked stressors" applies to this diagnosis, which fits Ebenezer's experience on Christmas Eve. (See Ophelia in *Hamlet* for a possible case of psychosis *with* marked stressors.)

Hallucinations

"The curtains of his bed were drawn aside; and Ebenezer, starting up into a half-recumbent attitude, found himself face to face with the unearthly visitor who drew them: as close to it as I am now to you, and I am standing in the spirit at your elbow."

During the one night his psychotic symptoms last, Ebenezer experiences both visual and auditory hallucinations involving four "ghosts" and scores of people these visions reveal to him.

Delusions

" 'Good Spirit,' he pursued, as down upon the ground he fell before it: 'Your nature intercedes for me, and pities me. Assure me that I yet may change these shadows you have shown me, by an altered life!' "

At first, Ebenezer doubts that he has actually seen a ghost after his visit from his late friend and business partner Jacob Marley. He doubts his senses because, he explains to his visitor, "a little thing affects them. A slight disorder of the stomach makes them cheats. You may be an undigested bit of beef, a blot of mustard, a crumb of cheese, a fragment of an underdone potato. There's more of gravy than of grave about you, whatever you are!"

With the successive hallucinations of three more ghosts during the evening, however, Ebenezer comes to believe that he is actually being visited by spirits and that he is interacting with them. For Ebenezer, the ghosts are real on Christmas Eve. Those who don't believe in ghosts might say that Ebenezer's brief psychotic episode lasted less than a day and changed him considerably.

Profile #16: King George III in the Film *The Madness of King George*; Screenplay by Alan Bennett, Based on His Stage Play

King George III: "I am the King of England."
Doctor: "No, sir. You are the patient!"

PLOT SUMMARY

In 1788, England's King George III (played by Nigel Hawthorne) suffers a painful episode of abdominal pain. This is soon followed by symptoms of confusion, uncensored thoughts, and inappropriate behavior, mania, hallucinations, and violent displays of temper. The monarch's 18th-century physicians are clueless and helpless in the face his mysterious illness. The king's political enemies—including his eldest son (played by Rupert Everett) who wants to assume the throne—scheme to undermine him using his mental illness as an excuse. They are opposed by the queen (played by Helen Mirren) and his Prime Minister William Pitt (played by Julian Wadham).

THE KING'S PSYCHOLOGICAL TRAITS

The film version of King George III depicts a thoughtful and conscientious—if self-centered—man. He has a good knowledge of the people and the land he rules (in conjunction with Parliament) and has a sincere interest in both.

His reign is marked by an illness that produces a range of symptoms including physical pain, confusion, disorientation, mania, psychosis, hallucinations, and paranoia. Many physicians today attribute the king's symptoms to a hereditary disease called porphyria.

PSYCHOTIC DISORDER DUE TO ACUTE PORPHYRIA

Porphyria is the result of the body's inability to effectively produce heme. Heme is a key component of hemoglobin, the molecule that carries oxygen in red blood cells from the lungs to all organs in the body. There are many steps in its production. Porphyria is a genetic disorder in which one of many enzymes required for the production of heme is defective. This results in the buildup of chemicals called porphyrins. Excess amounts of porphyrins are harmful. Different forms of the disease are caused by mutations affecting different enzymes involved in the production of porphyrins.

Acute porphyrias affect the nervous system. In addition to physical pain, they can produce multiple symptoms of mental illness. These symptoms may subside after a week or two. The patient may then slowly recover until there is another attack.

As many as 9 out of 10 people who carry a gene for the disease, including descendants of King George III, show no symptoms. But some things, like alcohol, stress, and certain medications, can trigger symptoms. Some researchers believe that toxic levels of arsenic (which were detected in the king's hair centuries after his death) may have triggered his severe symptoms. A major source of the arsenic was medicines prescribed by his doctors.

Abdominal pain

King: "I had a very smart bilious attack. Very smart, indeed."

The king's ill health begins with severe abdominal pain, a characteristic symptom of acute porphyria.

Confusion

King George to his servant: "Yours?"
Servant: "You know my name, Sir."
King: "Don't tell me what I know and don't know! What is it?"

The king becomes confused about the identity of three of his servants, whose names he knew well before he became ill.

Urine may appear dark.

Servant: "It's the King's water, Sir. It's blue."
Officer: "So?"
Servant: "Well, it's been this color since this business [the king's mental symptoms] began."

The Greek word "porphyrus" means purple. The urine of some patients experiencing attacks of acute porphyria has a red or purple color, which becomes darker when exposed to light.

Hallucinations

King: "The children! The children!"
Queen: "The children are asleep, Sir."
King: "You must wake them up!"
Queen: "Why?!"
King: "London is flooded! We must take the children and flee for higher ground!"

During his illness, the king suffers from a visual hallucination involving a nonexistent flood.

Delusions

King: "I make the weather by means of mental powers."

At times the king believed he had grandiose powers. Reasoning with him could not convince him otherwise.

Mania

King: "I follow my words. I run after them . . . I have to talk to keep up with my thoughts . . . "
Queen: "Do you think that you are mad?"
King: "I don't know. I don't know. Madness isn't such a torment. Madness isn't half blind. Madmen can stand. They skip. They dance. I talk. Talk and talk and talk. I can hear the words, so I have to speak them. I have to empty my head of the words. Something has happened. Something is not right."

The king, in life and in the film, experienced exhausting manic attacks during which, one member of his court wrote, "He often spoke till he was exhausted, and, the moment he could recover his breath, began again, while the foam ran out of his mouth."

The king also experienced periods of rationality and good health between attacks. He knew he was ill and once confided to one of his sons that he wished "to God that I may die, for I am going to be mad."

Bipolar Disorder

Profile #17: Leonard Bankhead in the Novel *The Marriage Plot* by Jeffrey Eugenides

> You took ridiculous physical risks, jumping out of a third-floor dorm room into a snowbank, for instance. It made you spend your year's fellowship money in five days. It was like having a wild party in your head, a party at which you were the drunken host who refused to let anyone leave.

PLOT SUMMARY

Three friends, English major Madeleine Hanna, Mitchell Grammaticus, and Leonard Bankhead, graduate from Brown University in 1982. Leonard is a charismatic, moody, and intellectually brilliant loner. Madeleine is intrigued by his brilliant and brooding personality. Mitchell, meanwhile, is convinced that he and Madeleine belong together. Mitchell yearns for Madeleine but devotes his time to seeking spiritual meaning. Madeleine and Leonard move in together.

In the year following graduation, neither Leonard nor Mitchell succeeds in making a smooth transition into "the adult world." It becomes clear to Madeleine that Leonard's charisma and energy are temporary features of a mental illness. Leonard experiences extreme mood shifts, ranging from severe depression to mania with its characteristic racing thoughts, hyperactivity, and irresponsible and self-destructive behavior. Madeleine, who had always avoided unstable people, finds herself married to one.

LEONARD'S PSYCHOLOGICAL TRAITS

Leonard has the advantages of being tall (6′3″), attractive, intellectually brilliant (a biology and philosophy major), and intriguing to women. Unfortunately, part of his initial appeal to Madeleine can be traced to hypomania, an abnormal mood characterized by high levels of optimism and hyperactivity. Tragically, Leonard's hypomania is replaced by mania; his vitality and energy become uncontrolled and extreme. His extreme highs alternate with extreme lows as Leonard becomes clinically depressed.

BIPOLAR DISORDER

Leonard's serious mental disorder was called manic depression in the past. He has a form of the disease now called bipolar I disorder. It produces very severe changes in mood. These range from the extreme euphoric highs of mania to the depths of severe depression or to hypomanic episodes. If his manic episodes were less severe and less debilitating, but he still suffered from episodes of severe depression, he would be diagnosed with bipolar II disorder.

Bipolar disorder has been cited by a few people as an example of a false mental disorder, particularly by people who claim the "highs" associated with it are positive experiences, which can increase creativity. This argument ignores the devastating effect serious bipolar and other mental disorders can have on individuals and their families. A condition becomes a mental illness only when it produces significant distress in a person or poses a threat to that person or others. Bipolar disorder is not a positive experience for Leonard, for Madeleine, or for anyone who suffers with it.

Mood change—mania

"The qualities he was displaying—extroversion, vitality, boldness—were the qualities that had attracted Madeleine to him in the first place. Only now they were amplified, like a stereo with the volume turned up so loud that the sound distorted."

It's misleading to describe hypomania simply as a less severe form of mania. It can be a forerunner of mania. Madeleine learned this as she became more involved with Leonard.

"No one understood what he was talking about. He became angry, irritable."

The irritability Leonard displays is not uncommon during manic episodes.

Behavioral changes—racing thoughts, talkativeness

"He called everybody. He talked for fifteen minutes, or a half hour, or an hour, or two hours . . . From them, he moved on to other people, people he knew well or had barely met, students, departmental secretaries, his dermatologist, his advisor." And, "Words became other words inside his head, like patterns in a kaleidoscope." Finally, "He started finishing Madeleine's sentences. As if her mind was too slow. As if he couldn't wait for her to gather her thoughts. He riffed on the things she said, going off on strange tangents, making puns."

Thoughts pass so quickly through Leonard's mind during his manic episodes that both he and his listeners cannot keep up with them. He tries to process these racing thoughts by speaking rapidly and shifting from one topic to another (see *The Madness of King George*).

Behavioral changes—easily distracted, no need for sleep

"He kept stopping along the Champs-Élysées to admire things he'd never shown interest in before—suits, shirts, cuff links, Hermès neckties." And, "It had started with Leonard not being able to sleep . . . He felt too wired to go to bed, he said, and so began staying up until three or four in the morning. When he forced himself to turn off the lights and get into bed, his heart raced, and he broke into a sweat."

Other symptoms of Leonard's mania include his belief he had exceptional abilities ("he was more sensitive, deeper"), his high-risk behavior, and his impulsivity (he "could leave one girl's bed at five a.m., cross campus, and slide into bed with somebody else" and spend his "year's fellowship money in five days").

When Leonard's abnormal mood swings produce severe depression, he displays symptoms like those described in the next entry: Sylvia Plath's *The Bell Jar*.

Depressive Disorders

Profile #18: Esther Greenwood in the Novel *The Bell Jar* by Sylvia Plath

> How did I know that someday—at college, in Europe, somewhere, anywhere—the bell jar, with its stifling distortions, wouldn't descend again?

PLOT SUMMARY

In the 1950s, college student Esther Greenwood's writing talents help her secure a month-long appointment as a guest editor for a prestigious New York magazine. She and the other awardees stay at the same women-only hotel and celebrate their good fortune together in Manhattan. Esther, however, does not feel the joy she believes she should feel, given her enviable situation. Instead, her emotions are deadened. She worries about her future and endures several scary experiences in New York, including food poisoning, unrewarding relationships, and even an attempted date rape on her last night in the city.

Disappointed by her unfaithful college boyfriend and would-be fiancé, Esther embarks on a mission to lose her virginity. Back home in Massachusetts, she is also disappointed when she is not accepted into a special program for young writers. The depression, which she first experienced in New York, returns. It drains her of nearly all her interests and desires. She can't read or write or sleep. She even stops bathing.

Her mother intervenes and takes her to a psychiatrist. Unfortunately, the electroconvulsive therapy (then called "electroshock therapy") that she receives is improperly administered. It terrifies her and fails to relieve her suffering. This leads her to attempt suicide and to commitment to a city hospital psychiatric ward.

The novelist who sponsored Esther's college scholarship comes to her aid by arranging for her to move to a better, private psychiatric hospital. There, Esther finally meets a psychiatrist she can relate to and trust. A combination of therapies improves her mental health enough so that she is allowed outside visits. During one of these trips, she succeeds in losing her virginity with a college professor. In time, Esther's health improves enough so that she can return to school. Nevertheless, she is convinced that "the bell jar," a metaphor for the depression that descended and isolated her from the rest of the world, remains a threat that will not disappear.

Sylvia Plath

Sylvia Plath's parents were teachers who encouraged her academic achievement and learning as she grew up. Sylvia's intelligence and talent were apparent from an early age. Unfortunately, they were accompanied by anxiety and significant self-consciousness. Her father, Otto, taught at Boston University, and her mother taught in a high school. Her father died of diabetes mellitus less than two weeks after Plath's eighth birthday, an event that had a profound effect on her and left her with anger and resentment, which she expressed in some of her poems.

Before she entered Smith College in 1950 at age 18, Plath had already written scores of short stories, won magazine writing prizes, and published poetry in newspapers. Her talent and ambition helped her get a scholarship to Smith College where she continued to excel. But this is where serious signs of psychological problems, perhaps related to the depressive symptoms that had plagued her father's family, became apparent. She received outpatient therapy, including electroconvulsive therapy, which was then called "shock treatment."

During her junior year—when perhaps overwork was a contributing factor—she took an overdose of sleeping pills. After spending six months in the hospital, she was able to return to school. She continued to excel in her academic studies, but her psychological problems troubled her off and on until her death. Her mother was very supportive, but for much of her life, Plath harbored resentment at her dependence on her mother. She also continued to feel the pain of having lost her father at such a young age.

Plath's success in college led to a Fulbright fellowship to study at Cambridge University in 1955. Without neglecting her studies, she found time to pursue outside interests. She explored her sexuality and objected to the then-rampant double standard of behavior that allowed men but not women to have sexual experiences outside of marriage.

While in England, she met Cambridge poet Ted Hughes and married him in 1956. Both continued to write poetry despite many rejections from publishers. The pair supported and encouraged each other for five or six years. And by 1961, Plath had nearly completed her first and only novel *The Bell Jar*.

Her marriage, sadly, then became troubled. Hughes was unfaithful and Plath once again suffered depression. Still, she was able to find satisfaction for a time as the mother of two children and enjoyed the friendships she was able to establish with other women. Then in December 1962, she moved with her children, two-year-old Frieda and infant Nicholas, to an apartment in London. Unfortunately, the winter of 1962–63 was the worst the city had experienced in 100 years. This did nothing to help the struggling single mother deal with her severe depression. *The Bell Jar* was published in January 1963 (under the pseudonym Victoria Lucas because Plath feared the book was not literary or serious enough). A few weeks later, Plath died from an overdose of sleeping pills and gas inhalation.

The novel that she feared was not good enough to be considered literature, together with her poetry published before and after her death, assured her a place as one of the finest writers from North America.

ESTHER'S PSYCHOLOGICAL TRAITS

It is clear that Esther suffered from major depressive disorder.

MAJOR DEPRESSIVE DISORDER

This diagnosis is made when a person shows five or more of the symptoms listed below—all within a two-week time frame. At least one of the first two symptoms on the list—depressed mood or loss of interest or pleasure—must be present. And all of the observed or reported symptoms must reflect a noticeable change from the person's previous behavior. Of course, the symptoms can't be related to medication or drug side effects or to another medical condition. One such medical condition that can at first look like major depression is bipolar disorder. Often patients receive treatment for major depression without any signs of mania. Only later, when the patient's depression gives way to an abnormally energetic mood does the presence of bipolar disorder become clear.

Long-lasting depressed mood

"I didn't know why I was going to cry, but I knew that if anybody spoke to me or looked at me too closely the tears would fly out of my eyes and the sobs would fly out of my throat and I'd cry for a week. I could feel the tears brimming and sloshing in me like water in a glass that is unsteady and too full." Clinical major depression such as Esther's is far more severe and debilitating than the "down" or "blue" moods everyone experiences occasionally and which are a normal part of life.

Loss of interest or pleasure

"I guess I should have been excited the way most of the other girls were, but I couldn't get myself to react. I felt very still and very empty, the way the eye of a tornado must feel, moving dully along in the middle of the surrounding hullabaloo." And: "To the person in the bell jar, blank and stopped as a dead baby, the world itself is the bad dream."

Significant weight loss or gain when not dieting, or change in appetite nearly every day

"In a dull, flat voice—to show I was not beguiled by his good looks or his family photograph—I told Doctor Gordon about not sleeping and not eating and not reading."

Sleeping too little or too much

"My mother told me I must have slept, it was impossible not to sleep all the time, but if I slept it was with my eyes wide open, for I had followed the green, luminous course of the second hand and the minute hand and the hour hand of the bedside clock through their circles and semicircles, every night for seven nights, without missing a second, or a minute, or an hour."

Nearly daily indications of physical agitation or lack of activity tied to mood

"I was still wearing Betsy's white blouse and dirndl skirt. They drooped a bit now, as I hadn't washed them in my three weeks at home. The sweaty cotton gave off a sour but friendly smell."

Nearly daily fatigue or lack of energy

"I wondered why I couldn't go the whole way doing what I should any more. This made me sad and tired. Then I wondered why I couldn't go the whole way doing what I shouldn't, the way Doreen did, and this made me even sadder and more tired."

Nearly daily feelings of inappropriate or excessive guilt or a feeling of worthlessness which goes merely beyond blaming oneself for being depressed

"Wherever I sat—on the deck of a ship or at a street café in Paris or Bangkok—I would be sitting under the same glass bell jar, stewing in my own sour air." Esther's depression, the "bell jar" that encases her, keeps her enclosed in feelings of her own worthlessness.

Nearly daily indications that the ability to think or concentrate has been significantly diminished, or an inability to make decisions

" 'I can't sleep. I can't read.' I tried to speak in a cool, calm way, but the zombie rose up in my throat and choked me off. I turned my hands palm up."

Recurrent, persistent thoughts about death including suicide plans or attempts

"It would take two motions. One wrist, then the other wrist. Three motions, if you count changing the razor from hand to hand. Then I would step into the tub and lie down."

Esther first begins reading tabloid newspaper stories about people taking their lives and attempting to take their lives. She speculates about the details involved in seppuku, ritual Japanese suicide. Then she begins to think about taking her own life.

Later she thinks:

"Death must be so beautiful. To lie in the soft brown earth, with the grasses waving above one's head, and listen to silence. To have no yesterday, and no tomorrow. To forget time, to forgive life, to be at peace."

The Bell Jar is a semi-autobiographic novel written by a talented novelist and poet. It describes depression from a first-person viewpoint and is still as relevant today as it was when it was published in 1963.

Profile #19: The Narrator in the Poem "I Felt a Funeral in My Brain" by Emily Dickinson

My mind was going numb.

Emily Dickinson's untitled poem beginning with the line "I felt a funeral in my brain" has been subjected to many analyses over the years. It uses imagery of death and is frequently interpreted as a work depicting the torment associated with a descent into major depressive or another mental disorder. Some writers suggest that it reflects Dickinson's experience with migraine headaches, although there is no evidence the poet, who rarely left her home, suffered from migraines.

An alternative reading might support the suggestion that it depicts the loss of one consciousness and the emergence of another, more spiritual one, although in a rather morose way. Whatever meaning or meanings Dickinson intended, the imagery of the poem undeniably evokes depressive symptoms, however you interpret the outcome of the "funeral" in her brain.

I felt a funeral in my brain,
And mourners, to and fro,
Kept treading, treading, till it seemed
That sense was breaking through.

And when they all were seated,
A service like a drum
Kept beating, beating, till I thought
My mind was going numb.

And then I heard them lift a box,
And creak across my soul
With those same boots of lead,
Then space began to toll

As all the heavens were a bell,
And Being but an ear,
And I and silence some strange race,
Wrecked, solitary, here.

And then a plank in reason, broke,
And I dropped down and down—
And hit a world at every plunge,
And finished knowing—then—

IMAGERY OF DEPRESSION AND MENTAL ILLNESS

Major depressive disorder or clinical depression is a mood disorder that produces long-lasting feelings of extreme sadness and despair. It also prevents people from experiencing pleasure. It is a true illness with both psychological and physical symptoms. It is not, as some people assume, the result of "not trying." A person with clinical depression cannot "just snap out of it" at will. Fortunately, lifestyle changes including diet and exercise, psychotherapy, and psychotropic medication are able to help the majority of people who have to face the challenges of serious depression.

Recurrent, persistent thoughts about death

"I felt a funeral in my brain . . . And then I heard them lift a box,/And creak across my soul"

The powerful image of a person feeling a funeral in her brain indicates the she has suffered a loss and is witnessing one at the same time. Being present at the service suggests unpleasant developments to come.

Diminished ability to think or concentrate or make decisions

" . . . till I thought/My mind was going numb."

Depressed mood, loss of interest or pleasure

"And I and silence some strange race, / Wrecked, solitary, here."

Dickinson's poems, as well as her lifestyle, have raised questions about her mental health. She rarely left her home, leading some to wonder if she had agoraphobia. Others wonder if she had some bipolar traits affected by the seasons since she appears to have been more productive in the summer than in the winter. Although "I Felt a Funeral in My Brain" may have been written in the summer of 1862, many of her poems written in the summer are joyous and exuberant. Her winter poems are often bleak and despondent.

Georgetown University psychiatrist Norman Rosenthal told the *L.A. Times*, "If there was ever a poet that I would diagnose in all likelihood suffered from SAD [seasonal affective disorder], Emily would be our lady." SAD is bipolar disorder with a seasonal pattern. It is characterized by the regular onset of certain moods—mania, hypomania, or depression—during the same season year after year.

Profile #20: Leonard Peacock in the Young Adult Novel *Forgive Me, Leonard Peacock* by Matthew Quick

> "I'm going to kill you later today," I say to that guy in the mirror, and he just smiles back at me like he can't wait.

PLOT SUMMARY

It is Leonard Peacock's 18th birthday. His mother forgot about it, but that isn't the most important thing troubling Leonard today. Today is the day he is planning to kill his former best friend and then himself.

He packs his grandfather's old P-38 World War II pistol into his backpack along with four presents. The presents are goodbye gifts for the people he likes best. Walt is his retired neighbor who is killing himself with cigarettes and spends much of his time watching Humphrey Bogart movies, often with Leonard. Baback is a fellow student and violin virtuoso. Lauren is a religious homeschooled girl he likes but will never date. And Herr Silverman is his history teacher. Leonard is enrolled in his class about the Holocaust.

Leonard visits each of them as the day progresses and struggles with what he intends to be his final act.

LEONARD'S PSYCHOLOGICAL TRAITS

Leonard is angry, lonely, and socially isolated. His burnt-out rock star father abandoned Leonard and his mother years ago. His mother is preoccupied with herself and gives him little attention. He has been sexually abused, bullied, and abandoned.

No one sees how hurt and damaged Leonard is. On this special day, his birthday, he resolves to do something desperate so people will know how great his pain is. Leonard is in the middle of a psychiatric crisis.

PSYCHIATRIC EMERGENCY

Despite the extensive coverage they receive in the media, behavioral emergencies involving violence are rare. Millions of people in the United States experience stress and millions more have mental disorders, yet the vast majority pose no threat to others.

When multiple factors push an individual like Leonard to a point where he plans to harm himself and/or others, early identification of risk factors could help prevent a tragedy if people pay attention and make an effort to help.

George E. Tesar, MD, of the Cleveland Clinic compiled a list of more than 40 risk factors for aggression, which covers both suicide and homicide. As Leonard follows his plans for what he expects to be his last day, his actions, intentions, and statements on this one day alone show that he has at least 10 of these risk factors.

Risk Factors for Suicidal or Homicidal Aggression

Risk factors for aggression are divided into 11 categories: current or past suicidal or homicidal thoughts and behavior, psychiatric diagnoses, physical illnesses, psychosocial issues, childhood traumas, genetic and familial factors, psychological symptoms, behavioral features, cognitive features, demographic features, and additional features such as substance abuse, poor relationship to a psychotherapist, and access to firearms.

Leonard's 10 identified risk factors fall into 6 of these categories.

Homicidal or suicidal thoughts and behavior

Suicidal or homicidal ideas or plans

Leonard: "In addition to the P-38, there are four gifts, one for each of my friends. I want to say good-bye to them properly. I want to give them each something to remember me by. To let them know I really cared about them and I'm sorry I couldn't be more than I was—that I couldn't stick around—and that what's going to happen today isn't their fault."

Leonard has made detailed plans to kill his former best friend, Asher Bell, and then himself after saying good-bye to the four people he feels closest to.

Childhood traumas

Sexual or physical abuse

"Herr Silverman finally says, 'you know that men can be raped, right?'

I don't say anything, but I wonder if that's what happened to me because I didn't put up a fight at first, and then when I did, it seemed like I was just trying to stop something that had been going on for a long time and it was not likely to end soon—like jumping off a moving train because it was making you sick but the conductor couldn't stop for some reason."

Late in the day, Leonard becomes convinced that Herr Silverman sincerely cares about him, Leonard tells him about the abuse he suffered: "and all the words came out in a rush—like I'm trying to purge. I tell him everything."

Other psychological symptoms

Shame or humiliation

Leonard: "I'm sorry I couldn't be more than I was."

The abandonment and abuse Leonard has suffered has undermined his sense of worth. He feels responsible for and humiliated by the ill-treatment he has received.

Psychic pain

Leonard: "I feel like I'm broken—like I don't fit together anymore. Like there's no more room for me in the world or something. Like I've overstayed my welcome here on Earth, and everyone's trying to give me hints about that constantly. Like I should just check out."

The pain Leonard feels is so great that the only solution he can think of is to use violence against himself and his friend who betrayed him. This will not only get him the attention he wants from people who ignore him, but also end his psychological suffering.

Psychological turmoil

"And I know that your childhood wasn't all that great—that you felt a lot of pain, and that you are in a lot of pain right now. But maybe you have to go through all that so you'll learn just how important having a happy childhood can be, so you will provide one for our daughter."

On the advice of his teacher, Leonard has written a series of letters to himself as if they were coming from the future. For this exercise he imagines he is married with a child and manning a lighthouse in a postapocalyptic world. No ships ever pass by the lighthouse, but he faithfully maintains it nonetheless. This "future Leonard" reassures the 18-year-old Leonard that life is worth living and will improve.

Psychosocial issues

Poor family relationships

Leonard: "These people we call Mom and Dad, they bring us into the world and then they don't follow through with what we need, or provide any answers at all really—it's a fend-for-yourself free-for-all in the end, and I'm just not cut out for that sort of living."

Leonard has been physically abandoned by his father and psychologically abandoned by his mother. He wants close relationships but has no one to develop them with. He spends time with his neighbor Walt but their interactions are limited to quoting lines from Humphrey Bogart movies to one another. Later in the day, he will share intimate secrets with Herr Silverman and make a life-saving connection.

Demographic features

Leonard falls into the categories of being *male*, an *adolescent or young adult*, and *white*. All three are risk factors for aggression, which include suicidal and/or homicidal thoughts or intentions. Other risk factors are being single, widowed, or divorced (especially for males); being elderly; and being bisexual or homosexual.

Additional features

Finally, Leonard has access to a firearm, his grandfather's World War II Nazi "trophy" pistol. Access to firearms is another risk factor for aggression.

The risk factors that Leonard demonstrates on his birthday are the same for both suicide and homicide. Acts like those Leonard planned "are often triggered by frustration, anger, fear, or hopelessness; the circumstances—real or perceived—that fostered those feelings; and any type of intoxicant that intensifies distressing feelings or perceptions and increases impulsivity," according to Dr. Tesar's report on psychiatric emergencies for the Cleveland Clinic. Leonard did not need to use an intoxicant to intensify his distress; his past experiences provided enough distress to motivate him to plan and prepare for lethal aggression.

Profile #21: Miss Havisham in the Novel *Great Expectations* by Charles Dickens

> In an armchair, with an elbow resting on the table and her head leaning on that hand, sat the strangest lady I have ever seen, or shall ever see.

PLOT SUMMARY

A young boy named Pip sits by himself in a graveyard looking at his parents' tombstones. But Pip is not alone; an escaped convict hiding behind another tombstone grabs him before he can react. The fugitive demands that Pip bring him food and a file he can use to file through his leg irons. Pip runs off but returns with food and a file. The convict is recaptured shortly afterward but takes the blame for stealing the items Pip brought to him. Pip returns to the home he shares with his sister and her husband.

Pip's encounter with the convict is one of two that will radically change his life. The second occurs when Pip's uncle Pumblechook takes him to the home of the very reclusive, eccentric dowager, Miss Havisham. Pip is to be a playmate for Miss Havisham's niece Estella, a haughty, snobbish, beautiful young girl. Pip immediately sees that Miss Havisham's house has become a filthy tomb, uncleaned in decades with all the clocks stopped at 40 minutes after 8. This is the time in the morning of her wedding day when Miss Havisham learned that her fiancé decided he would not to go through with the wedding.

In time, Pip falls in love with the coldhearted Estella and hopes Miss Havisham will make him a gentleman worthy of her niece. Instead, Miss Havisham arranges a blacksmith apprenticeship for the disappointed boy.

As a young adult, while living in London, Pip is visited by the convict he had encountered in the graveyard when he was a boy. After serving his sentence in Australia, the convict had acquired legitimately a great deal of money. With his help, Pip gains a fortune and so becomes a gentleman by English 19th-century standards. And after many years apart, he and Estella, now a widow and more sad than haughty, meet once again in the ruins of Miss Havisham's estate.

MISS HAVISHAM'S PSYCHOLOGICAL TRAITS

Miss Havisham wears the wedding dress she wore on the day her marriage was scheduled to take place. She wears only one shoe because that is what she had on when she learned her fiancé had rejected her. The clocks are all stopped at that moment and her wedding cake sits mummified on a table covered in cobwebs, a mansion for mice.

Miss Havisham's extreme reaction to being jilted can be traced not only to the shock and disappointment she felt, but also to the social stigma she knew she would suffer in Victorian society. Pip's uncle tells Pip that she experienced "a bad illness" after getting the news and upon recovery she "laid the whole place waste" and never repaired or cleaned it. We are not told the nature of the illness she suffered but it is likely it was related to the shock she received that day.

Miss Havisham is not psychotic. She is not under the delusion that her fiancé will return and marry her. She does not hallucinate. Her thoughts are not bizarre or disturbed, except in her preoccupation with being rejected. She doesn't have stressful flashbacks or, to our knowledge, other symptoms during which she relives the traumatic event. Instead, she has resolved to remember it and memorialize the event so others will remember it too. Miss Havisham's behavior does, however, suggest complicated grief.

COMPLICATED GRIEF

The vast majority of people who experience a shock like the one Miss Havisham experienced eventually recover. They are changed by it but they resume a normal life. If their grief lasts longer than six months—Miss Havisham's has lasted for decades—they suffer from what is called complicated grief. It is a serious condition and requires psychotherapy and perhaps medications that were not available in Victorian England. Had Miss Havisham consulted her contemporary doctors, she likely would have been diagnosed with "hysteria," a catchall diagnosis which in her era was often used to describe troublesome behavior in women.

Daily, acute pain of loss

" 'Do you know what I touch here?' she said, laying her hands, one upon the other, on her left side . . . 'What do I touch?'

'Your heart.'

'Broken!'

She uttered the word with an eager look, and with strong emphasis, and with a weird smile that had a kind of boast in it. Afterwards, she kept her hands there for a little while, and slowly took them away as if they were heavy."

Miss Havisham's heart was broken decades ago upon receiving the worst news a young bride could receive. She has never recovered from the grief she felt that morning. It coexists with a bitterness and an overwhelming desire for vengeance.

These traits are consistent with other features of complicated grief including the following:

Long-lasting anger

Miss Havisham: "I stole her heart away and put ice in its place."

Miss Havisham's anger is so great that she raises Estella to break men's hearts. Near the end of her life, she regrets what she has done.

Preoccupation with the insult or injury

" 'What do you think that is?' she asked me, again pointing with her stick; 'that, where those cobwebs are?'
'I can't guess what it is, ma'am.'
'It's a great cake. A bride cake. Mine!' "

Miss Havisham lives every minute with reminders of the worst day of her life. She wears the once white, now yellowing, wedding dress she wore that day, the single shoe she had on when she received the bad news, and frequently refers to her self-imposed, pitiful situation.

Depressed mood

Pip: "In seclusion, she had secluded herself from a thousand natural and healing influences."

Miss Havisham's one and only source of "pleasure" is the anticipation of using Estella to hurt boys like Pip and the men she'll meet when she is older. Otherwise, she is joyless.

Lack of resilience

" 'At the hour and minute,' said Herbert, nodding, 'at which she afterwards stopped all the clocks.' "

Miss Havisham is one of the least resilient characters in literature. When she received shockingly bad news, she literally stopped time for herself in order to never forget what happened to her. "Look at me," she says to Pip at their first meeting. "You're not afraid of a woman who has never seen the sun since you were born?"

Miss Havisham is wealthy and so is able to maintain her unhealthy, eccentric lifestyle. If she had not been wealthy and responded in the same way, she would likely have been placed in what was called, in Victorian England, a lunatic asylum. (Sadly, the deplorable state of psychiatric incarceration in Miss Havisham's time very likely would not have offered a more wholesome environment than her trashed and unkempt home.)

Miss Havisham's initial shock and extended grief, combined with an extraordinary lack of resilience at not being able to recover from the pain of rejection and her misguided desire for revenge, help explain how she became an unforgettable Dickensian creation.

Anxiety Disorders

Profile #22: John "Scottie" Ferguson in the Film *Vertigo*; Screenplay by Samuel A. Taylor et al.

It's because of this fear of heights I have, this acrophobia. I wake up at night seeing that man fall from the roof and I try to reach out to him.

PLOT SUMMARY

San Francisco police detective John "Scottie" Ferguson (played by James Stewart) has to retire after discovering he has an abnormal, incapacitating fear of heights. His fear is accompanied by vertigo, which causes dizziness and the feeling that his surroundings are spinning. Scottie learns he has a phobia while chasing a criminal across high rooftops. He slips and stops himself from falling by clinging to a rain gutter on the tall building. A fellow police officer falls to his death while trying to rescue Scottie. Scottie now feels responsible for his colleague's death.

Scottie lives alone in retirement and without a focus in his life. He accepts a freelance job offer from a former classmate named Gavin Elster (played by Tom Helmore). Elster wants Scottie to follow his wife Madeleine. The reason, Elster explains, is that Madeleine is disturbed and may be suicidal; she believes she is possessed by the spirit of a dead woman.

During his investigation, Scottie falls in love with Madeleine. He saves her from one apparent suicide attempt, but, due to his fear of heights, he is later unable to stop her from seemingly jumping to her death from a church's bell tower. He finds himself alone and guilt ridden over a second death.

Scottie's life changes radically several months later when he sees a woman who looks remarkably like Madeleine. After some hesitation, but in response to his persistent efforts, she agrees to date him. He becomes obsessed with her and tries to make her dress and look like Madeleine. Despite his obsession, it doesn't take him long to realize that he has been set up and used as part of a plot by Elster to kill his wife. His reaction to this realization leads to a new tragedy for Scottie and for the woman who haunts him.

Hitchcock's film is considered a masterpiece because it is about much more than acrophobia, vertigo, and obsessive romantic love, although these are crucial elements of the story. In fact, the plot is more than a little farfetched. In the hands of a less-skillful director, it might easily have been a forgettable movie. It is a film classic because the main characters are all troubled psychologically. They are unable to overcome their isolation and loneliness. Of all his great films, *Vertigo* was particularly important for Hitchcock.

SCOTTIE'S PSYCHOLOGICAL TRAITS

Scottie feels guilty because a fellow police officer dies trying to save him. He feels guilty after he thinks he has contributed to the death of a woman he loves, again involving a fall from a great height. These traumas seem to

Alfred Hitchcock

One of the most famous directors in film history was born in London's East End in 1899. He began directing in 1923 when he filled in for an ailing director on the film *Always Tell Your Wife*. He directed his first movie, *The Pleasure Garden*, in 1925.

Over the next half century, Hitchcock became the premier director of suspense and thriller films. He pioneered and perfected the genre to such a degree that the adjective "Hitchcockian" is defined as "very exciting and full of suspense (= the feeling that something bad is about to happen but you do not know what or when)" in the *Macmillan Dictionary*. His films include *The Birds*, *Psycho*, *North by Northwest*, *Vertigo*, *Dial M for Murder*, *Rear Window*, *Strangers on a Train*, *Notorious*, and nearly 50 others.

To build and maintain the suspense that these and his other films are known for, Hitchcock frequently relied on scripts that stressed the troubled psychological traits of their characters. He achieved this by very careful preparation and planning of his films. He did not improvise during filming or change the scripts once he had approved them. Every scene was thought out in detail and filmed as he had planned.

According to his biographer, Donald Spoto, and accounts offered by several actors and crew members who worked with him, Hitchcock's own troubled psychology may have influenced his films. Spoto claims that Hitchcock's psychological profile includes sadistic tendencies evidenced by cruel practical jokes, obsession with several of the (blonde) female stars of his films, misogyny, fetishes, anxiety, and guilt.

A year before his death in 1980, Hitchcock was knighted by Queen Elizabeth.

contribute to his specific phobia: a fear of heights, or acrophobia, which he evidently had developed even before the officer died trying to save him.

SPECIFIC PHOBIA—ACROPHOBIA AND VERTIGO

A specific phobia is a long-lasting, irrational fear that is far out of proportion to the risk posed by the situation or object that produces the fear. Scottie fears heights. Other specific phobias center on the categories of animals like snakes or dogs, blood/injection/surgery-related procedures and items like needles, and situations like enclosed spaces.

Acrophobia is characterized by strenuous efforts to avoid heights that evoke the fear. Like other phobias, acrophobia is not a temporary condition such as, for example, nervousness commonly associated with speaking in public. Phobias cause debilitating physical and psychological problems that can seriously interfere with a person's ability to function and to maintain a relatively good quality of life.

Besides intense anxiety, a person with acrophobia is often affected by vertigo when looking down from a height. Vertigo is a feeling of dizziness and lack of balance. When it is not associated with disease of the inner ear or other parts of the body's vestibular system that maintains a sense of balance, it may be linked to distress caused by anxiety and depression.

Several studies indicate that anxiety, a psychological disorder, may be a factor in approximately half of the patients who seek help for dizziness. The results of other studies indicate that dizziness is frequently linked to reactive anxiety and depression. This suggests that the problem is not the result of a primary psychiatric or psychological disorder, but that it is a response to something that has happened to the patient.

Avoiding the source of the fear becomes a top priority.

Judy, Scottie's love interest: "He knew of your illness. He knew you'd never get up the stairs to the tower."

Gavin Elster manipulated Scottie to unknowingly help him commit a murder. His plan was completed in a bell tower. Elster fooled Scottie into delivering the victim to the tower but the plan required that Scottie not make it to the top of the tower. Scottie's fear of heights assured this.

Anxiety interferes with normal day-to-day functioning.

Scottie: "I know. I know. I have acrophobia which gives me vertigo and I get dizzy."

Scottie shows symptoms whenever he looks down from a high place.

The phobia produces physical reactions like increased heart rate, sweating and trouble breathing, as well as psychological reactions, like severe anxiety and panic.

Scottie: "Watch this. Here we go. There. (He steps onto the first step of a step ladder.) There. Now. I look up, I look down. I look up. I look down. There's nothin' to it."

Scottie attempts to control the symptoms of his acrophobia and vertigo by gradually exposing himself to increasing heights. This approach is called desensitization. He pushes himself too far, however, and faints when he steps onto the top step before he has desensitized himself sufficiently.

Recognition that the fear is exaggerated and out of proportion to the real threat without having control of the fear

Elster: "Is it a permanent, physical disability?"
Scottie: "No, no. It just means that I can't climb stairs that are too steep or go to high places like the bar at the Top of the Mark. But there are plenty of street-level bars in this town."

Scottie downplays the seriousness of his phobia because he knows it appears unreasonable to others. But in fact, Scottie's condition is so serious that he will faint if he stands on a short step ladder and looks out the window of a multistory building.

Thinking about the fear can sometimes result in anxiety.

Scottie: "It's because of this fear of heights I have, this acrophobia. I wake up at night seeing that man fall from the roof and I try to reach out to him, it's just . . . "

Scottie wakes from several dreams involving heights that result in severe anxiety.

Facing the fear results in terror or uncontrollable panic.

Scottie: "I made it. I made it."

The film's climax is set in the same bell tower Scottie had not been able to climb earlier. This time, inexplicably, he manages to reach the top without experiencing symptoms of his phobia or vertigo. This is unlikely since phobias that last into adulthood don't disappear by themselves for the majority of sufferers.

Profile #23: Dr. Helen Hudson in the Film *Copycat*; Screenplay by Ann Biderman and David Madsen

Dr. Helen Hudson: "This is the only space that I have in the world."

PLOT SUMMARY

Forensic psychologist Dr. Helen Hudson (played by Sigourney Weaver) is traumatized after being attacked by Daryll Lee Cullum (played by Harry Connick Jr.), a murderer she testified against in court. Now afraid to leave her apartment, she is drawn into a new case involving a serial killer who deliberately changes his modus operandi to copy the murderous methods of infamous killers of the past.

Behind the latest crimes is Cullum, inspiring followers from his prison cell. A pair of police officers convince a reluctant Helen to help them solve the crimes. Helen's involvement in the case threatens her personal and psychological safety.

HELEN'S PSYCHOLOGICAL TRAITS

This highly educated professional was able to use her above-average intelligence to establish a successful career and to the gain the respect of her colleagues. She suffered a serious setback professionally and personally when she was traumatized in a violent attack. Helen's character seems to have been written to display the key traits of panic disorder with agoraphobia. The attack that sparked this disorder and her phobia may also have produced posttraumatic stress. Her use of alcohol goes beyond typical social drinking and raises the possibility of substance abuse.

ANXIETY DISORDER—AGORAPHOBIA

The most important feature of this type of anxiety disorder is the extreme anxiety associated with being in situations or places from which it would be difficult or embarrassing to leave, or in which there would be no one to help if the patient had a panic attack. Often the fear is centered on the outdoors, on large open spaces, or anywhere groups of people or crowds are present. This can include buses, planes, or trains. People with this disorder commonly avoid any place that could result in them feeling helpless, embarrassed, and unable to escape if they developed panic-like symptoms. Agoraphobia usually develops after people have had one or more panic attacks and fear being in a similar situation. In some cases, individuals are able to move about if accompanied by a companion. In other cases, like Helen Hudson's, people dealing with this disorder will not venture out of their homes or apartments.

Dr. Helen Hudson's behavior is consistent with a diagnosis of agoraphobia because she experiences great fear or anxiety when she finds herself in at least two of the following situations.

She finds herself alone outside her familiar house or apartment.

To retrieve a newspaper dropped out of reach outside her apartment door, Helen tries to pull it closer using a broom handle. When that doesn't work, she ventures just a few steps beyond her front door to retrieve the paper and experiences serious anxiety as a result. In fact, she could not tolerate any of the following situations: finding herself in a parking lot, on a bridge, in a mall, or in other open space.

Other situations that can produce fear or anxiety are being on any type of public transportation including planes, trains, ships, buses, or automobiles; being in a crowd or standing in a line; or being in a theater, shop, or other enclosed space.

Among other requirements for a diagnosis of agoraphobia, the symptoms must be persistent and have typically been present for six months or longer.

We see in the following scene that Dr. Helen Hudson meets this criterion: Waking up in panic, Dr. Helen Hudson goes to her computer and enters an online forum called "The Stressline." Using the alias "She Doc," she types:

She Doc: "Anyone awake? Need to talk. She Doc."
Kate Minn: "Hello She Doc. Panic attack?"
She Doc: "Big time. Bad memories. You housebound?"
Kate Minn: "Six months. You?"
She Doc [mutters under her breath with a relieved and slightly amused smile "I got you beat"]: "Thirteen and counting."

It is possible to have agoraphobia without panic disorder but Helen appears to have both.

Helen's assistant: "It's just a good old-fashioned panic attack. She hyperventilates until she passes out then her breathing returns to normal and she's fine."

Panic attack is not a mental disorder but when someone experiences panic attacks repeatedly and unexpectedly, the pattern can lead to a diagnosis of panic disorder. Helen experiences periodic rapid surges of intense fear involving shortness of breath, trembling, heart pounding, and fainting. It is clear that the physical assault Helen Hudson experienced resulted in extreme trauma and the development of multiple disorders.

Profile #24: Arthur Dimmesdale in the Novel *The Scarlet Letter* by Nathaniel Hawthorne

> Notwithstanding his high native gifts and scholar-like attainments, there was an air about this young minister,—an apprehensive, a startled, a half-frightened look.

PLOT SUMMARY

Following an adulterous affair, Hester Prynne gives birth to a girl. She is shamed by her Puritan community for having a child out of wedlock and forced by the authorities to wear a scarlet letter "A" after she completes a three-year jail term. Hester is remarkably strong and resilient despite the rejection she faces from her fellow Puritans. Her child, Pearl, grows up to be healthy and lively, a reflection of her mother's strength.

Both mother and child are in stark contrast to Pearl's secret father, Rev. Arthur Dimmesdale. At first only Hester and Arthur know their secret. Later, Hester's husband Chillingworth, who was away for years, suspects the couple's secret after he begins treating Arthur's for his physical ailments. One day, Chillingworth discovers that the Reverend's guilt had driven him to carve a letter "A" over his damaged heart.

When Chillingworth sees the scar, he is convinced Arthur is the father of his estranged wife's child. He begins to undermine Arthur's health instead of improving it. Arthur suffers emotionally and physically for both committing and hiding what he and his community view as an unforgivable sin.

Years later, Hester Prynne's daughter Pearl marries a wealthy man and lives in Europe. And Hester and Arthur are buried under the same tombstone marked with the letter "A."

ARTHUR'S PSYCHOLOGICAL TRAITS

The Rev. Arthur Dimmesdale is tormented by what he views as a mortal sin. The worry and anxiety he feels contribute to his failing health. He is frequently agitated and cannot limit or control his worry.

GENERALIZED ANXIETY DISORDER

Excessive worry and anxiety

"Who is that man, Hester?" gasped Mr. Dimmesdale, overcome with terror. "I shiver at him! Dost thou know the man? I hate him, Hester! . . . I tell thee, my soul shivers at him! This muttered the minister again. Who is he? Who is he? Canst thou do nothing for me? I have a nameless horror of the man!"

Arthur's agitation and worry are obvious when he sees Roger Chillingworth. He and the rest of Boston do not know it, but Chillingworth is Hester Prynne's husband who has returned after years away.

Difficulty limiting worry

" 'Hester,' said he, 'hast thou found peace?'
She smiled drearily, looking down upon her bosom.
'Hast thou?' she asked.

'None!—nothing but despair!' he answered.' " And later: "I have laughed, in bitterness and agony of heart, at the contrast between what I seem and what I am!"

At least three of the following symptoms: reduced stamina, restlessness, difficulty concentrating, irritability, disturbed sleep, tense muscles, or episodes when the mind goes blank

"It seemed hardly the face of a man alive, with such a death-like hue: it was hardly a man with life in him"; "there was an air about this young minister,—an apprehensive, a startled, a half-frightened look"; and "He kept vigils, likewise, night after night, sometimes in utter darkness."

Arthur has symptoms of reduced stamina, restlessness, and insomnia.

Another mental disorder that might apply to Arthur is major depressive disorder with anxious distress. In addition to meeting the criteria for major depression (see Esther Greenwood in *The Bell Jar*), Arthur would have to have at least two additional symptoms such as tenseness, restlessness, difficulty concentrating, anticipating disaster, or fearing loss of control. Worry and anxiety, however, seem to dominate Arthur's illness more than classic features of major depression such as depressed mood, lack of interest, and inappropriate guilt. Arthur's worry can be traced to the birth of his daughter who is seen as illegitimate by his Puritan congregation. That stressful event in his life, combined with an apparent predisposition to anxiety, accounts for much of the reverend's psychological distress.

Profile #25: Francis Morton in the Short Story "The End of the Party" by Graham Greene

"What's the matter?" Peter asked.
"Oh, nothing. I don't think I'm well. I've got a cold. I oughtn't to go to the party."

Peter was puzzled. "But, Francis, is it a bad cold?"

"It will be a bad cold if I go to the party. Perhaps I shall die."

PLOT SUMMARY

Nine-year-old Peter Morton is very protective of his identical twin Francis. He comforts him, reassures him, and provides much needed companionship. When the boys' parents and nanny tell them they will attend a children's party at a neighbor's house, Francis protests. The last time he attended the party he had to play hide-and-seek in the dark and the experience terrified him.

The adults dismiss Francis's fears as childish and insist he and his brother attend the party. Peter tries to protect his brother but becomes separated from him in the darkness during the game Francis dreads. When Peter finds his brother, it is too late.

FRANCIS'S PSYCHOLOGICAL TRAITS

Francis is sensitive, introverted, and anxious. His fear of the dark goes beyond a typical childhood fear. The experience of being in the dark, and even the anticipation of it, produces anxiety and extreme distress in the young boy.

Specific Situational Phobia—Fear of the Dark

Like John "Scottie" Ferguson in the film *Vertigo*, Francis suffers severely from a situational specific phobia. Francis has an extreme and debilitating phobia called nyctophobia.

Fear of the dark is common in childhood. Since this and other fears are typical features of childhood, it is important that the severity and duration of the associated anxiety are closely considered before diagnosing a phobia. Only when fear produces symptoms like those listed below, does it become a phobia. Most cases of specific phobia develop in children around Francis's age; the median age is 7 to 11.

Francis has an excessive or irrational fear of the dark.

"I'm afraid of going. I won't go. I daren't go. They'll make me hide in the dark, and I'm afraid of the dark. I'll scream and scream and scream."

The last time Francis played hide-and-seek in the dark, he was panicky and let out a terrified scream when someone touched his arm.

Francis experiences great stress when he is in the dark and avoids being in it.

"But Francis crouched with fingers on his ears, eyes uselessly closed, mind numbed against impressions, and only a sense of strain could cross the gap of dark."

Forced to attend the party, Francis crouches on the floor and covers his head with his arms when the lights go out for a game of hide-and-seek.

Francis has physical symptoms typical of anxiety or a panic attack. These may include an accelerated heart rate, sweating, trembling, shortness of breath, lightheadedness, or nausea or diarrhea.

"It was true he felt ill, a sick empty sensation in his stomach and a rapidly beating heart, but he knew the cause was only fear, fear of the party, fear of being made to hide by himself in the dark, uncompanioned by Peter and with no nightlight to make a blessed breach."

Francis's response to the dark or thinking about it causes his heart to pound and produces a feeling of nausea.

Francis experiences anxiety when he anticipates being in the dark.

"Panic nearly overcame him when, all unready, he found himself standing on the doorstep, with coat collar turned up against the cold wind, and the nurse's electric touch making a short trail through the darkness . . . He was nearly overcome by the desire to run back into the house and call out to his mother that he would not go to the party, that he dared not go."

After Francis is forced to attend the party and play in the dark, his phobia produces an unusual outcome: death. Author Graham Greene uses this unrealistic plot development to highlight the insensitivity of the twins' parents and nanny when they ignore the obvious distress Francis experiences just thinking about the party. A study by Kate Waters of University College London and her colleagues found that new onset panic disorder or panic attacks in people younger than 50 may be associated with an increased risk of heart disease and heart attacks later in life. But Francis's death is more of an effective plot device than it is an accurate reflection of the danger associated with a phobia like fear of the dark.

Obsessive-Compulsive Disorder

Profile #26: Melvin Udall in the Film *As Good as It Gets*; Screenplay by Mark Andrus and James L. Brooks

> I've got this, what—ailment? My doctor, a shrink that I used to go to all the time, he says that in fifty or sixty percent of the cases, a pill really helps.

PLOT SUMMARY

Melvin Udall (played by Jack Nicholson) writes romance novels for a living. It's a curious occupation for a man who dislikes people and has no interest in being liked. He is prejudiced, homophobic, and rude to everyone. He is so unpleasant that only one waitress, Carol (played by Helen Hunt), will serve him at his favorite local diner where he eats every day sitting at the same table.

After his neighbor, Simon (played by Greg Kinnear), is attacked and beaten, Melvin reluctantly agrees to care for his dog. Melvin's discovery that he feels affection for the dog leads to a small opening in the isolating and self-protective defenses he uses to avoid human contact. In time, enough of his defenses fall away that he is able to have a chance at winning the affection of his favorite waitress.

MELVIN'S PSYCHOLOGICAL TRAITS

Melvin doesn't like people. He is self-centered and uses rudeness to keep others away. Underneath his misanthropic exterior, Melvin suppresses a romantic outlook, which is only expressed in the romance novels he writes quite successfully. He has consulted a psychiatrist about his diagnosed condition of obsessive-compulsive disorder, a condition that makes his life very difficult.

OBSESSIVE-COMPULSIVE DISORDER

The defining features of this disorder are obsessions and compulsions. Obsessions are unreasonable thoughts, urges, or even images that are unwanted. They occur over and over and often lead to anxiety or distress. People try to escape them by ignoring them or by distracting themselves by performing a compulsive act. This act could be another thought or it could be a physical action.

Compulsions are repetitive mental or physical behaviors such as counting objects or washing one's hands repeatedly. Not performing these acts results in distress or anxiety. The compulsive activities are performed to prevent such distress. People with obsessive-compulsive disorder have the following characteristics:

Troubled by compulsions, obsessions, or both

To relieve anxiety associated with this condition, Melvin refuses to step on cracks on the sidewalk. He also washes his hands in a ritualistic manner and locks and unlocks the door to his apartment repeatedly. He will only eat with plastic cutlery that he carries with him, will only eat at one table in his local restaurant, and will only be served by his favorite waitress, Carol.

Melvin feels driven to engage in these repetitive behaviors in order to prevent or reduce the distress he would feel if he did not engage in these activities.

Stepping on a crack in the sidewalk poses no realistic threat to Melvin but he avoids stepping on these cracks to avoid the unpleasant feelings he would experience if he did so. The same applies to his other compulsive behaviors.

Melvin's compulsive behavior is easy to see. He doesn't show signs of having obsessive thoughts, which is another symptom of this disorder in some people. If Melvin had obsessions, he would have repeated and persistent unwanted thoughts that distressed him. He would attempt to counter these thoughts by trying to think of something else or by performing a compulsive act.

Spends one hour or more time per day engaging in obsessive or compulsive acts, or the acts cause distress or interfere with normal day-to-day functioning.

Melvin: "I mean, wouldn't your life be easier if you weren't . . . "
Simon: "You consider your life easy?"
Melvin: "All right, I give you that one."

Melvin acknowledges that his disorder impairs the quality of his life. He feels great distress, for example, when he finds people sitting at his usual table at his favorite diner. His favorite waitress, Carol, tells him "It's not your table, behave! This once, you can sit at someone else's station." Of course, Melvin's compulsion—his desire to avoid the anxiety or distress he feels if he cannot sit at that table—prevents him from changing his behavior. He refuses to take medication, which could relieve his symptoms.

Melvin's unpleasant, rude behavior is not a symptom of his obsessive-compulsive disorder. The screenwriter gave Melvin these traits to make his character funnier. Melvin's character would be amusing (particularly if portrayed by Jack Nicholson) if he did not have obsessive-compulsive disorder. But by giving Melvin a mental disorder, the writers provided him with an obstacle to overcome in order to win Carol's affection, or at least her tolerance. In reality, of course, the symptoms of obsessive-compulsive disorder are not funny. When left untreated, they can and do make people's lives miserable.

Trauma and Stress-Related Disorders

Profile #27: Dr. Martin Ellingham in the Television Series *Doc Martin*, created by Dominic Minghella, Mark Crowdy, and Craig Ferguson

Doc Martin to his therapist: "You will diagnose attachment disorder."
Therapist: "I see you've done some homework."

PLOT SUMMARY

Martin Ellingham is a successful London surgeon until he develops a fear of blood. This phobia makes it impossible for him to continue in his chosen specialty, so he moves to Portwenn, a small fishing village in Cornwall, to practice general medicine. His abrasive attitude, off-putting demeanor, and complete lack of bedside manner define his relationship with his patients and fellow villagers. They soon begin to overlook his unpleasant personality, in part because he is the only physician in the region.

Although Martin marries and has a child, his coldness has left him estranged from his wife Louisa with whom he would like to be closer emotionally. In the seventh season of the series, he consults a therapist about his self-diagnosed attachment disorder and asks her "How long will this take to fix?" To which she replies "This isn't surgery, Martin. This is a process."

DOC MARTIN'S PSYCHOLOGICAL TRAITS

Martin is an intelligent, efficient professional. He is completely dedicated to the practice of medicine and to the health and well-being of the people of Portwenn. He just doesn't connect with them, or with anyone, on an emotional level. He tries to suppress and deny his emotions. He has diagnosed himself with a dismissive style of avoidant attachment, what he calls attachment disorder.

He has also correctly diagnosed himself with hemophobia, the fear of blood.

DISMISSIVE STYLE OF AVOIDANT ATTACHMENT

Although Martin indicates that he has attachment disorder, a more accurate term for his personality problem is "dismissive style of avoidant attachment." The word "attachment" refers to how a person relates to others. Attachment patterns form during infancy and early childhood. They play a major role in determining adult attachment patterns.

The *DSM-5* describes reactive attachment disorder as a condition seen in infants or very young children who do not form attachments with the adults who have the responsibility of caring for them. These children have the ability to form attachments but never have the opportunity to connect with their caregivers. Cold, emotionally unavailable parents can cause children to stop seeking an emotional attachment to them. As a result, the children may become self-contained and form an avoidant attachment.

When these children become adults, their childhood experiences may produce a dismissive personality. Martin has many of the dismissive attachment patterns common to this type of personality.

Martin suffered from reactive attachment disorder as a young child.

Martin: "I was an unwanted child. I failed to develop a normal attachment to my parents, resulting in an inability to form adult relationships."

Martin is a loner and seeks emotional distance from others.

Paramedic: "You're joking, right?"
Martin: "No, I don't make jokes."

Martin suppresses his feelings.

Martin: "I exhibit poor communications skills."

Martin concentrates on cerebral interests.

Martin: "I think happiness is overrated."

Martin is completely dedicated to his medical practice with few or no outside interests. He is beginning, however, to wish his wife were happy. He seeks therapy in the hope that he will be able to make her so.

Martin regards friendships and relationships as unimportant.

Receptionist: "Doc, you okay there?"
Martin: "Be quiet!"
Receptionist's friend: "You've got plenty to live for! Probably."
Martin: "Oh, will you shut up?!"
Constable: "Steady on, Doc. Don't snap at her. It's not our fault."
Martin: "Oh, no, of course it isn't. It's never anybody's fault, is it? Not in the Village of the Idiots."

He has no friends and his emotional distance and dismissive attitude toward others have alienated his wife. The writers of Doc Martin make Martin more sympathetic by having him develop a sincere desire to change. In this case, the character wants to establish an emotional connection with his wife. Unfortunately, some unhappy, troubled individuals never try to change their behavior or seek therapy. In fiction, characters that show no signs of change or desire to change are often too one-sided to capture the sustained or invested interest of viewers or readers.

Profile #28: Septimus Warren Smith in the Novel *Mrs. Dalloway* by Virginia Woolf

It was a case of complete breakdown—complete physical and nervous breakdown, with every symptom in an advanced stage.

PLOT SUMMARY

Over the course of a summer day in 1923, five years after the end of World War I, Clarissa Dalloway is running errands in preparation for a party she is going to have in her home this evening. Her actions are routine and mundane, but her thoughts show her to be sensitive and more complex than her activities would suggest. During the day, she hears about the tragedy of a World War I veteran called Septimus Warren Smith. She never knew Septimus but feels a connection with him.

Septimus Smith's thoughts and actions reveal the psychological damage he has suffered as a result of his war experiences. He often thinks of his friend Evans, a war casualty, and he is terribly troubled by his worsening symptoms. His wife, Lucretia, drags him to consult with doctors but they can do nothing to help him. One physician damages him further by treating him like a faker. Feeling no hope and fearful for his future, Septimus takes his own life by throwing himself out a window. It is his way of retaining control, control he feels he is losing to his illness and to the doctors and society that would control him but not help him.

Clarissa empathizes with Septimus and comes to terms with the idea of his death. She also comes to understand that it is important for her to live her life as best as she can.

SEPTIMUS'S PSYCHOLOGICAL TRAITS

Like many young Englishmen in the beginning of the 20th century, Septimus began life full of optimism, promise, and faith in the British Empire. He loved Shakespeare's plays and sonnets and—typical of his generation—he believed there was glory in war. His experiences in the trenches in World War I destroyed these illusions. Such disillusion is also forcefully depicted by the characters in the classic German novel *All Quiet on the Western Front* by Erich Maria Remarque, set during World War I.

Unlike the characters in Remarque's novel, and the estimated 10 million soldiers lost on both sides of the conflict during World War I, Septimus survives the war. But he returns to England suffering from a condition known in his time as "shell shock." Today this condition is called posttraumatic stress disorder (PTSD).

Virginia Woolf was one of the first authors to depict the signs and symptoms of this debilitating disorder caused, in this case, by exposure to the horrors of war. Septimus is a walking casualty who has flashbacks of the death of a friend. His traumatic experiences have also affected his emotions, sometimes causing him to feel numb and at other times causing him to feel agitated. In his flashbacks, he is surrounded by fire. He often speaks of suicide.

POSTTRAUMATIC STRESS DISORDER

Symptoms of PTSD can begin as early as three months or as long as several years after a traumatic event. Most cases develop sooner rather than later. Some people recover in less than six months, but Septimus has a chronic case of the disorder. Today, he would be diagnosed with PTSD if he had the following symptoms for at least a month: (a) at least one avoidance and (b) one reexperiencing symptom; and (c) at least two arousal and reactivity symptoms and (d) two cognition and mood symptoms.

Virginia Woolf

During the 59 years of her life between 1882 and 1941, the English novelist, essayist, and critic Virginia Woolf dealt with a nightmarish childhood and severe mental disorder. Yet she is recognized as one of Great Britain's leading modernist authors in the first half of the 20th century. One of her most impressive accomplishments was writing fiction in a style that lets readers share experiences with her characters and build impressions of them, rather than providing readers with explicit, photo-like descriptions of her characters' interests, motivations, and personalities.

Woolf had a head start becoming a great novelist because she was born into a literary family. This advantage, however, was tragically counterbalanced by the sexual abuse she suffered starting at age 6 at the hands of her two half-brothers. The abuse lasted until she was in her early 20s. This trauma had profound effects on her.

When she was 30, Virginia married Leonard Woolf from Cambridge, England. The couple shared an interest in literature and criticism. Together they founded Hogarth Press and published stories by "L. and V. Woolf." The stories were well received and Hogarth Press went on to publish important works by promising unknown writers including a poet named T. S. Eliot.

In addition to promoting the works of new talent, Virginia Woolf hosted an intellectual circle of Cambridge University–educated friends at her home in Bloomsbury. This group included scholar of Chinese and Japanese literature Arthur Waley, critic and writer Lytton Strachey, economist John Maynard Keynes, poet Victoria Sackville-West, and painter Roger Fry. This artistic and literary social circle became known as the Bloomsbury Group.

Woolf's achievements were interspersed with incapacitating mood swings that, at times, included hallucinations. The stress associated with her childhood sexual abuse was undoubtedly a major factor in her struggle with bipolar disorder and perhaps posttraumatic stress disorder. "My own brain is to me the most unaccountable of machinery—always buzzing, humming, soaring, diving and then buried in mud," she wrote in a letter when she was 50. "And why? What's this passion for?"

Among the more than 20 important works by Woolf are *Mrs. Dalloway, To the Lighthouse*, *Jacob's Room*, and *Orlando*. Woolf is also recognized as an early feminist; her famous 1929 essay *A Room of One's Own* promoted women's rights.

In 1941, as World War II raged, Woolf realized she was facing the onset of another devastating depressive episode. She took her own life by drowning herself in Sussex, England. Shortly before her death, she wrote to her husband: "I feel certain that I am going mad again. I feel we can't go through another of those terrible times. And I shan't recover this time. I don't think two people could have been happier 'til this terrible disease came."

Woolf's illness frequently interfered with her productivity, yet she produced notable and often more original works of literature and literary essays than many of her better known contemporaries. Virginia Woolf's accomplishments in the face of severe mental illness and traumatic experience will remain a remarkable testament to her abilities and to the potential for creative accomplishment despite tremendous disadvantages.

Avoidance Symptoms

Feeling emotionally numb

"When Evans was killed, just before the Armistice, in Italy, Septimus, far from showing any emotion or recognising that here was the end of a friendship, congratulated himself upon feeling very little and very reasonably. The War had taught him."

Septimus saw his friend Evans killed and felt nothing. Before he was shipped home after the war "he became engaged one evening when the panic was on him—that he could not feel." He continues to experience emotional numbness five years after the end of the war.

Feeling strong guilt, depression, or worry

Septimus's depressed mood is reflected in his frequent talk of suicide.

Staying away from places, events, or objects that are reminders of the traumatic experience

Septimus lives with his wife in London, so revisiting the battlefields in France where he was traumatized is not an issue.

Losing interest in activities that were enjoyable in the past

On this day, Septimus's wife is dragging him to see doctors, leaving little time for recreational activities. When they stop to rest, Septimus just stares straight ahead and, in this way, even prevents his wife from enjoying the moment.

Having trouble remembering the dangerous event

Septimus experienced the full horror of war in the trenches. He especially remembers the death of his friend and officer Evans. This criterion, therefore, does not apply to Septimus. He remembers it too often.

Reexperiencing Symptoms

Flashbacks

"And he would lie listening until suddenly he would cry that he was falling down, down into the flames!"

It's possible the flames Septimus fears are flashbacks or related to them. He also has become sensitized to excess stimulation from the bustle of city life.

Frightening thoughts

"He said people were talking behind the bedroom walls. Mrs Filmer thought it odd."

This frightening thought may have crossed the line to become an auditory hallucination.

Bad dreams

We do not have a chance to find out what kind of dreams Septimus may be having because the novel is set during a day he does not survive.

Arousal and Reactivity Symptoms

Being easily startled

"In the street, vans roared past him; brutality blared out on placards; men were trapped in mines; women burnt alive . . . "

Septimus is startled by traffic and upset by the news.

Feeling tense or "on edge"

"Septimus Warren Smith, aged about thirty, pale-faced, beak-nosed, wearing brown shoes and a shabby overcoat, with hazel eyes which had that look of apprehension in them which makes complete strangers apprehensive too. The world has raised its whip; where will it descend?"

Septimus has constant arousal symptoms, which is common with PTSD. They produce stress and affect his concentration and his ability to function normally. Two other arousal and reactivity symptoms are *difficulty sleeping* and *angry outbursts*.

Cognition and Mood Symptoms

Trouble remembering key features of the traumatic event

This does not apply to Septimus because he remembers the death of his friend often.

Negative thoughts about oneself or the world

"So he was deserted. The whole world was clamouring: Kill yourself, kill yourself, for our sakes."

Septimus's negative thoughts will contribute to his suicide.

Distorted feelings like guilt or blame

"I have—I have," he began, "committed a crime—"

"He has done nothing wrong, whatever," Rezia assured the doctor.

Septimus may feel guilty for surviving the war while his friend did not.

Loss of interest in enjoyable activities

"She could not sit beside him when he stared so and did not see her and made everything terrible; sky and tree, children playing, dragging carts, blowing whistles, falling down; all were terrible."

Septimus's inability to enjoy himself prevents his wife from enjoying herself as well. Septimus's cognition and mood symptoms make him feel alienated from everyone, including his wife.

The exact cause of PTSD is unknown. Researchers believe it is probably the result of a combination of factors. People genetically predisposed to anxiety and depression, for example, may be at greater risk for developing PTSD. Personality type or temperament, past exposure to traumatic events, and individual differences in the way a person's brain chemistry responds to stress all may contribute to the development of this serious mental health problem.

AN UNDETERMINED DISORDER WITH PSYCHOTIC FEATURES

Hallucinations

"No crime; love; he repeated, fumbling for his card and pencil, when a Skye terrier snuffed his trousers and he started in an agony of fear. It was turning into a man! He could not watch it happen! It was horrible, terrible to see a dog become a man! At once the dog trotted away."

Septimus experiences many hallucinations including one in which he thinks birds are communicating with him in Greek. Like her fictional character, Virginia Woolf experienced the same hallucination in which birds seemed to be talking to her in Greek during one of her mental health crises due to bipolar disorder.

Delusions

"Septimus, was alone, called forth in advance of the mass of men to hear the truth, to learn the meaning, which now at last, after all the toils of civilization—Greeks, Romans, Shakespeare, Darwin, and now himself—was to be given whole to . . . 'To whom?' he asked aloud. 'To the Prime Minister,' the voices which rustled above his head replied."

There is, however, a complication in Septimus's case. He has hallucinations that are not related to his flashbacks—that is, he hears things and see things that are not there. And he has delusions—that is, firmly held beliefs that are clearly false. These symptoms are more like the symptoms Virginia Woolf experienced herself when she suffered from bipolar disorder with psychotic symptoms. Since PTSD is associated with an 80 percent increased risk of being diagnosed with another mental disorder such as bipolar disorder, depression, or anxiety, it is possible that Septimus suffered PTSD and bipolar disorder with psychotic symptoms or depression with psychotic features.

Dissociative Disorders

Profile #29: Eve White in the Film *The Three Faces of Eve*; Screenplay by Nunnally Johnson, Based on Corbett Thigpen and H. Cleckley's Book

> Alistair Cooke, narrator: "Well, in a literal and terrifying sense, inside this demure young woman two very vivid and different personalities were battling for the mastery of her character. She was, in fact, a case of what is called multiple personality, something that all psychiatrists have read about and very few have ever seen."

PLOT SUMMARY

Psychiatrist Curtis Luther is surprised when his patient Eve White, a repressed, shy housewife suffering from headaches and periods of lost memory, is transformed suddenly into Eve Black, an extroverted, flirtatious personality who is very different from Eve White. Eve Black refers to Eve White as "she," not as "I," and denies being married. Dr. Luther believes Eve suffers from multiple personality disorder (which is now called dissociative identity disorder [DID], according to the *DSM-5*). He consults Dr. Day, a more experienced psychiatrist, and together they attempt to understand and help Eve.

In the course of Eve's therapy, Jane, a third personality, emerges. Before the psychiatrists discover the traumatic events of Eve's childhood that contributed to the development of her multiple personalities, she struggles with a strained marriage, domestic violence, promiscuity, and divorce. Eventually therapy yields results. Eve White and Eve Black fade away leaving Jane. As Jane, the patient is able to maintain a single, positive personality. She even manages to start a new family with a new spouse.

EVE'S PSYCHOLOGICAL TRAITS

Each of Eve's identities has different traits. Eve White is shy, introspective, insecure, and inhibited. Eve Black is assertive, extroverted, flirtatious, and uninhibited. Jane is stable, secure, focused, and calm. The presence of three identities in Eve indicates she has DID.

DISSOCIATIVE IDENTITY DISORDER

DID is one of the most controversial topics in the mental health field. It is said to occur when a patient has two or more separate and distinct personalities or identities. The individual identities take control of a person completely, with distinct handwriting, body language, and even brain wave patterns, according to some reports. The appearance of one identity typically leaves the other identity or identities with no recollection of the occurrence. Hence, blackouts are a key feature of the disorder. Patients also complain of headaches.

Some skeptics believe DID doesn't exist, that it is a belief and a behavior planted into the minds of troubled, highly suggestible patients by their well-meaning but naïve therapists, a symptom of a schizophrenia-like disorder, borderline personality disorder, or other condition. They cite the case of "Sybil." As told in a book and a film of the same name, "Sybil" was a patient who presented 16 distinct personalities during therapy. Her therapist believed Sybil suffered from multiple personality disorder (as it was then known), a result of severe sexual and physical abuse by Sybil's mother. Several years after the book and film were released, however, a respected psychiatrist named Herbert Spiegel, MD, expressed his opinion that Shirley Mason, (Sybil's real name) did not in fact have multiple personalities. Instead, Spiegel believed Mason's therapist had misinterpreted various emotional states as separate personalities and gave Mason the idea that she had multiple personalities.

Nevertheless, based on a variety of other cases, the American Psychiatric Association concludes that there is enough evidence to suggest that DID is a real phenomenon and it is included in the *DSM-5.*

Eve's identity is disrupted by at least two distinct personalities. These disruptions markedly interrupt her sense of self. They produce changes in her behavior, emotional responses, thought processes, and memories.

Dr. Luther: "Now, when you say 'spell,' do you mean you faint or anything like that?"

Eve White: "No, sir, it's not like faintin'. It's more like . . . Well, it's like the other day I was playing out in the back yard with Bonnie [her daughter] and all of a sudden I got this splitting headache and then the next thing I knew, I mean, the next thing I was conscious of, it was the next morning."

Another example:

Dr. Day: "Are we to understand that you're no longer Mrs. White?"

Jane: "No, I'm not."

Dr. Day: "Nor Eve Black?"
Jane: "No."
Dr. Day: "Then may I ask, what is your name?"
Jane: "I don't know." Shortly after her appearance, the third identity chooses the name Jane.

Eve repeatedly is unable to remember major or minor events or important information about herself. These memory gaps are more serious than simple forgetfulness.

Dr. Luther: "Well, amnesia means 'loss of memory.' Is that what happens to you?"
Eve White: "Yes, I guess that's it."

Another example:

Eve Black: "Now I'm having blackout spells too."
Dr. Luther: "You mean, lapses of time when you don't remember what's happened?"
Eve Black: "Uh-huh. Let me tell you, it scares me too."

Eve's symptoms are distressing enough to interfere with her daily functioning. They are also very distressing for her husband.

The Hollywood ending in which Jane emerges as the final, stable third personality may have sent audiences home from movie theaters feeling good, but in reality, the patient Eve was based upon was not cured soon after the identity called "Jane" appeared. Chris Costner Sizemore, the real-life inspiration for Eve, struggled with DID for 18 more years. During this time, she says she dealt with a total of not 3 but 22 different identities. She sought treatment from eight different doctors. Finally, in 1974, a stable identity emerged.

Profile #30: Jason Bourne in the Film *The Bourne Identity*; Screenplay by Tony Gilroy and William Blake Herron, Based on the Novel by Robert Ludlum

---

Bourne: "I can't remember anything that happened before two weeks ago."
Marie: "Lucky you."
Bourne: "No, I'm serious. I don't know who I am. I don't know where I'm going. None of it."
Marie: "What, like, amnesia?"
Bourne: "Yes."

PLOT SUMMARY

An unconscious man is pulled from the Mediterranean Sea by the crew of an Italian fishing boat. A medic on board named Giancarlo removes two bullets from the unconscious man's back. He then cuts out a small capsule embedded under the skin of the man's hip. The capsule provides a Swiss bank account number. It is clear when the man regains consciousness that he is panicky and has no memory of his identity.

The unidentified man spends weeks on the ship as a crew member. All the while he tries unsuccessfully to figure out who he is and where he has been. When the fishing vessel returns to port, Giancarlo gives him enough money to reach Switzerland. The bank account leads to a safety deposit box filled with cash, a pistol, and multiple international passports. Each passport has a different name but the same photograph: his. The name on the American passport is Jason Bourne.

Bourne never completely recovers his memories of what he has done or who he is, but he realizes he speaks multiple languages, including English, French, Spanish, Italian, German, and Russian. He also has retained his exceptional skills in self-defense, use of weapons, and intelligence tradecraft.

He meets a German woman named Marie who accompanies him on his search for his identity. Almost immediately, Bourne becomes the target of multiple assassination attempts and the subject of an intense hunt by the Central Intelligence Agency and local police. Eventually he learns that he too was an assassin.

He is not, however, quite as ruthless and cold-blooded as his handlers—who "reprogrammed" him during his training—expected him to be. When faced with the prospect of killing a man in the presence of the man's children, Bourne could not complete the task. The conflict between what he has been trained and programmed to become—an efficient and remorseless assassin—and his concern for the innocent bystanders led to a psychological crisis.

JASON BOURNE'S PSYCHOLOGICAL TRAITS

Jason Bourne initially suffers panic when he regains consciousness and does not know who or where he is. His inability to remember his past life and identity often leave him frustrated and anxious. These are reactions to his main psychological feature: dissociative amnesia. Bourne has a particularly rare type of amnesia called *generalized amnesia*, which involves completely forgetting one's identity and life history. *Localized amnesia*, characterized by an inability to remember events that occurred during specific periods of time, is more common than generalized amnesia.

DISSOCIATIVE AMNESIA

Dissociative amnesia may be diagnosed when a person cannot remember basic, key facts such as his or her name, background, or personal history.

University of California, Los Angeles, psychiatrist Dr. Reef Karim was asked by the producers of the film to comment on Bourne's diagnosis. "Amnesia," he explained, "is a legitimate problem. It's not something that is just conjured in this movie. It involves mostly neurologic or metabolic processes in the body."

Karim went on to describe how a psychoanalyst would explain Bourne's condition. "Bourne has the drive to do his job: to kill somebody. But there is an unconscious conflict of: 'Maybe I shouldn't be doing this. Maybe this is wrong.' When that happens and you alter your behavior, you might not remember because it was so traumatic. And if it's dissociative amnesia, it means you don't remember *you*. And the dissociative amnesia was almost a defense mechanism for him to need to separate himself in order to try to maybe make things better in his way of dealing with himself."

Karim added that the film's screenwriters gave Bourne *selective* dissociate amnesia: "They had him forget who he was but they gave him kinesthetic memory. They allowed him to continue to remember all the training and the things that he learned over time."

The memory loss that accompanies dissociative amnesia cannot be attributed to any medical conditions or be a result of medications or drugs. The diagnosis also assumes that the memory loss is not caused by other mental disorders such as PTSD, acute stress disorder, or DID, among others. Bourne's case satisfies the criteria for dissociative amnesia.

Bourne cannot remember his name, where he is from, or any people from his past due to a traumatic or highly stressful event.

Giancarlo: "My name is Giancarlo. Who are you? What's your name? What's your name?"
Bourne: "I don't know."

Another example:

Marie: "So do you think there's, like, a family waiting for you?"
Bourne: "I don't know."

Bourne's amnesia troubles him deeply or impairs his ability to function normally at work or socially.

Giancarlo: "Yes, yes. It will come back."
Bourne: "No, it's not coming back, goddamn it! That's the point! I'm down here looking through all this s**t. For two weeks I'm down here. It's not working. I don't even know what to look for."
Giancarlo: "You need to rest. It will come back."
Bourne: "What if it doesn't come back? . . . We get in there tomorrow; I—I don't even have a name."

Profile #31: Marcel in the Novel *Swann's Way* by Marcel Proust

> I had only the most rudimentary sense of existence, such as may lurk and flicker in the depths of an animal's consciousness; I was more destitute of human qualities than the cave dweller.

PLOT SUMMARY

Marcel dips a small French cake called Madeleine into a cup of hot tea. This simple, everyday experience evokes "gusts of memory" about his life in the small French town of Combray. Marcel's memories fill not just *Swann's Way* but six additional volumes in Proust's fictional autobiographical novel, *Remembrance of Things Past* (also known as *In Search of Lost Time*).

One of Marcel's early memories is of his fear of going to sleep in the evening. He dreads waking up late at night and experiencing the disquieting sensation that he has lost his sense of self. He yearns each evening for his mother to kiss him goodnight and at the same time anticipates it with worry because it means he will then face the long bedtime hours alone.

MARCEL'S PSYCHOLOGICAL TRAITS

An introverted aspiring writer, Marcel enjoys reading about the arts and pondering the past. His high level of anxiety helps explain why he enjoys his solitude. One source of Marcel's childhood anxiety is his fear of waking up at night and not knowing where or who he is.

DEPERSONALIZATION/DEREALIZATION

Marcel describes childhood episodes during which he is distressed by a sense of being detached from himself, a phenomenon called depersonalization. It can produce feelings of observing yourself or your thoughts as if you are outside yourself. Some people report feeling like they have no control over their movements or speech. Senses may seem numbed, and thoughts and memories lack emotional content.

Derealization produces symptoms of feeling cut off, emotionally disconnected, or alienated from familiar people and things.

Many people report having had rare or occasional episodes of depersonalization. If these episodes cause distress, are repeated and frequent, and are not caused by medications, drugs, or another mental disorder, then depersonalization/

derealization disorder may be diagnosed. Key features of this disorder include the following:

A person experiences repeated or persistent episodes of depersonalization and/or derealization.

"And when I awoke at midnight, not knowing where I was, I could not be sure at first who I was . . . And then my thoughts, too, formed a similar sort of recess, in the depths of which I felt that I could bury myself and remain invisible even while I looked at what went on outside."

The ability to distinguish between reality and fantasy, to tell the difference between external reality and one's imagination, is not affected during the experiences.

". . . but then the memory, not yet of the place in which I was, but a various other places where I had lived, and might now very possibly be, would come like a rope let down from heaven to draw me up out of the abyss of not being . . . "

Somatic Symptoms

Profile #32: Roderick Usher in the Short Story "The Fall of the House of Usher" by Edgar Allan Poe

---

> A letter, however, had lately reached me in a distant part of the country—a letter from him—which, in its wildly importunate nature, had admitted of no other than a personal reply. The MS. gave evidence of nervous agitation. The writer spoke of acute bodily illness—of a mental disorder which oppressed him—and of an earnest desire to see me, as his best, and indeed his only personal friend, with a view of attempting, by the cheerfulness of my society, some alleviation of his malady.

PLOT SUMMARY

An unnamed narrator receives a letter from an old school friend, Roderick Usher, pleading with him to visit. Although he wasn't particularly close to Roderick, the narrator travels to the isolated country House of Usher and finds

Roderick suffering from worry and fear. The narrator learns that Roderick has a twin sister, Madeline, who is dying from an unknown illness. At times, she enters a death-like trance. Roderick, anxious and agitated, is convinced a terrible fate awaits him and his sister.

The narrator tries to comfort Roderick but when Madeline is declared dead and her body placed in a tomb in the house, Roderick's fears are realized. Madeline has been buried alive. Bloodied from clawing her way out of her tomb, she rushes at Roderick who is overcome with fear and dies.

RODERICK'S PSYCHOLOGICAL TRAITS

Roderick is intellectual, physically weak, and emotionally sensitive. He and his twin sister are the last two members of the Usher family, living and dying in their decaying family home. He worries constantly about his health and his sister's imminent death. He is convinced they are doomed.

HYPERESTHESIA

"He suffered much from a morbid acuteness of the senses; the most insipid food was alone endurable; he could wear only garments of certain texture; the odours of all flowers were oppressive; his eyes were tortured by even a faint light; and there were but peculiar sounds, and these from stringed instruments, which did not inspire him with horror."

Some of Roderick's symptoms might be related to somatic symptom disorder. He complains of a painfully increased sense of smell, taste, sight, and touch. In medical terms, this is an unusually intense example of a condition called hyperesthesia. In most cases, this condition is associated with an increased sensitivity to touch and often involves a burning sensation caused by damage to nerves in the skin, peripheral neuropathy. In Roderick's case, all of his senses are hypersensitive. Poe appears to be using this hypersensitivity as an indication of Roderick's mental condition.

SOMATIC SYMPTOM DISORDER

"It was, however, the only book immediately at hand; and I indulged a vague hope that the excitement which now agitated the hypochondriac, might find relief (for the history of mental disorder is full of similar anomalies) even in the extremeness of the folly which I should read."

Roderick appears to meet many of the criteria for somatic symptom disorder, the current name for what used to be called hypochondria: (1) his physical complaints cause him great distress. In Roderick's case, they are one reason he has become a recluse; (2) he thinks about and talks about his symptoms frequently and his symptoms produce a high level of anxiety; and (3) his symptoms are long-lasting, six months or more.

ANXIETY

"In the manner of my friend I was at once struck with an incoherence—an inconsistency; and I soon found this to arise from a series of feeble and futile struggles to overcome an habitual trepidancy—an excessive nervous agitation. For something of this nature I had indeed been prepared, no less by his letter, than by reminiscences of certain boyish traits, and by conclusions deduced from his peculiar physical conformation and temperament."

Trepidancy refers to shaking or trembling linked to nervous agitation. Roderick appeared to have a nervous or anxious disposition even when he was a student. This nervous agitation worsened after he retreated as an adult into his crumbling family estate and shared the house with his dying twin sister.

Roderick's anxiety also reflects an important part of Poe's symbolism in the story. The twins seem to represent two crucial aspects of one being. The narrator recalls a conversation with Roderick: "He entered, at some length, into what he conceived to be the nature of his malady. It was, he said, a constitutional and a family evil, and one for which he despaired to find a remedy."

The constitutional and family evil hints at a history of incest. The Usher twins thus may be closer than twins born in less troubled families. Madeline's body is failing while Roderick's mind is failing. The twins' fate suggests that mind and body cannot be safely separated. In his typically gruesome fashion, Poe may be rejecting the idea that the mind and the body are distinct entities, a philosophical view called dualism.

Profile #33: Beatrice Trueblood in the Short Story "Beatrice Trueblood's Story" by Jean Stafford

> When Beatrice Trueblood was in her mid-30s and on the very eve of her second marriage, to a rich and reliable man—when, that is—she was in the prime of life and on the threshold of a rosier phase of it than she had ever known before—she overnight was stricken with total deafness.

PLOT SUMMARY

Beatrice Trueblood is engaged to Marten ten Brink. Unfortunately, she is convinced that she and Marten are incompatible. She cannot tolerate the possibility of a quarrelsome marriage but she is convinced that she will quarrel with the man she has promised to wed.

The last time she and her fiancé argued, he said: "You mustn't think you can shut your mind to these things. You can't shut your ears to them." She replied softly: "I am exhausted with talk, Marten. I will not hear another word."

As Beatrice's friend Mrs. Onslager tells her guests, "And two months before the wedding *this* thunderbolt comes out of nowhere." "*This*" is the sudden, unexplained onset of Beatrice's deafness.

BEATRICE'S PSYCHOLOGICAL TRAITS

Beatrice is introverted, gentle, and soft-spoken. She was raised in a home filled with shouting and arguing. Her mother, who struggled with alcohol use disorder, and her nagging father fought viciously. Consequently, she loathes the thought of conflict, argument, and domestic strife.

CONVERSION DISORDER

Author Jean Stafford's account makes it clear that Beatrice did not lose her hearing because she had a neurological or other medical condition. The implication is that Beatrice's deafness is caused by what used to be called "hysteria." In Victorian times, physicians used the term "hysteria" to describe all sorts of complaints made by women: emotional outbursts, unhappiness, anxiety, nervousness, and even discontent. This diagnosis was tainted with sexism and was wisely removed from psychiatric and psychological texts in the later part of the last century.

Today Beatrice's condition would be classified as conversion disorder (or functional neurological symptom disorder). There is nothing wrong with the components of Beatrice's inner ear or with the auditory nerves that carry sound to the centers in her brain that enable her to hear. Her deafness is a result of her psychological state. "You are being fanciful," her friend writes, "although he did not think she was at all fanciful. 'You can't wish yourself deaf.' But Beatrice insists that she *has* done just that." Later she laments: "My God, the mind is diabolical! . . . Even in someone as simple as I."

Beatrice's symptoms involve the impairment of at least one sense. In her case, it is hearing. In others, the sense of sight or use of limb muscles could be affected.

" . . . in a far, soft, modest voice, she said, 'I am deaf. That explains it.' "

Her symptom is not caused by another medical or neurological condition.

"So, from Johns Hopkins, New York hospital, the Presbyterian, the Leahy Clinic, and God knows where, the same account comes back: there's nothing physical to explain it, no disease, no lesion, there's been no shock, there were no hints of any kind beforehand."

Her symptoms are seriously interfering with her ability to function normally in her day-to-day life.

"What had begun to harry was that her wish to be deaf had been granted. This is exactly how she put it, and Onslager received her secret uneasily. She had not bargained for banishment, she said; she had only wanted a holiday. Now, though, she felt that the Devil lived with her, eternally wearing a self-congratulatory smile." And: "And now I'm sorry because I'm so lonely here, inside my skull. Not hearing makes one helplessly egocentric."

Eating Disorders

Profile #34: Lia Overbrook in the Young Adult Novel *Wintergirls* by Laurie Halse Anderson

> I had to eat at Thanksgiving (vultures all around the table), but since then it's been mostly water and rice cakes. ~~I am so hungry that I could gnaw off my right hand.~~ I stick three pieces of gum in my mouth, throw out Emma's potato chips, and fill the tank. I am disgusting. (Note: Words are crossed out in the quotes in this entry as they are in the novel.)

PLOT SUMMARY

Eighteen-year-old Lia Overbrook learns that her best friend Cassie called her 33 times before she died alone in a hotel room after binging and purging for hours. Lia took none of her calls. She imagines Cassie is haunting her and urging her to follow her in death. Her guilt for neglecting her friend adds to the many other problems Lia struggles with, including her dissatisfaction with her parents, her appearance, herself, and life in general. The only person she feels affection for is her eight-year-old stepsister Emma, the daughter of her father's new wife.

Obsessed with her body image and desperate to exert control over her life, Lia starves herself. Her psychological and physical problems increase, putting her life in danger. Her survival after a suicide attempt will depend on her willingness to get help in coming to terms with her emotional problems.

LIA'S PSYCHOLOGICAL TRAITS

Lia suffers from anorexia nervosa. To distract herself from her psychological suffering, she cuts herself. She also has visual and auditory hallucinations of her dead friend Cassie. She shows no other signs of psychosis. It is possible that on some level she is aware that Cassie's ghost is a manifestation of her intense guilt for not being available when Cassie needed her.

ANOREXIA NERVOSA

People affected by this eating disorder have a pathological fear of gaining weight, or they persist in engaging in behaviors that prevent weight gain. They are also unable to accurately perceive and experience their true body weight and shape.

As a result, this mental illness causes patients to eat so little that they lose excessive amounts of body weight and consequently disturb their metabolism, threatening their health and their lives. Some people, like Lia's friend Cassie, have a type of eating disorder that involves binge eating and purging. Purging can involve self-induced vomiting or use of diuretics, laxatives, or enemas. Those who do not binge eat or purge are said to have the "restricting type" of anorexia nervosa.

Anorexia nervosa ranks number three among common chronic illnesses in adolescents. Approximately 10 times as many females as males are treated for this condition, but like other eating disorders, people of all genders, ages, socioeconomic classes, and races can develop anorexia nervosa.

People may be diagnosed with anorexia nervosa if they have following characteristics:

They persistently restrict energy intake enough to develop a dangerously low body weight.

Stepmother: "Why don't you have one of the muffins? I bought oranges yesterday, or you could have toast or frozen waffles."

Lia: "~~Because I can't let myself want them~~ because I don't need a muffin (410), I don't want an orange (75) or toast (87), and waffles (180) make me gag."

The observations and thoughts Lia either doesn't want people to hear or knows she can't say without betraying her obsession with losing weight are crossed out in her dialogue. The numbers in parentheses are calorie counts that she has memorized.

They have an intense and unreasonable fear of gaining weight or persistently behave in ways that interfere with weight gain, despite already being underweight.

Stepmother: "That's too small to be a full serving."
Lia: "~~I could eat the entire box~~ I probably won't even fill the bowl. 'My stomach's upset.' "

Lia fights hunger all the time but her desire for control is so great she resists her hunger and rewards herself for limiting her calories.

They experience disturbances in the way they perceive their body weight and shape, allow body weight and shape to unduly influence their self-evaluation, or fail to recognize the threat their low body weight poses to their health.

Lia: "I am the space between my thighs, daylight shining through."

And,

Lia: "I grab my books and stand up. *Too fast.* The floor tries to pull me down face-first, but my night-scummy teacher is watching so I make myself strong enough to float away, stars swimming in my eyes."

In the first quote, Lia interprets her dangerously underweight physical condition in a positive way. In the second, her malnutrition results in physical weakness caused by low blood sugar and/or low blood pressure. She can hardly stand without fainting. Still, she does not acknowledge the danger her eating habits pose to her health.

Lia's eating disorder puts her at great risk. In fact, psychiatrist Dr. Jon Arcelus of the Loughborough University Centre for Research into Eating Disorders and his colleagues report that anorexia nervosa appears to be the deadliest of all psychiatric disorders. Anorexia nervosa increases the risk of death 5.86 times. The increased risks of death from schizophrenia, major depression, and bipolar disorder are 2.8, 1.5, and 1.9, respectively.

It is a mystery why Lia and other people with anorexia nervosa starve themselves and see their bodies as being larger than they actually are. Self-imposed and social pressure, as well as atypical and unrealistic role models in the popular media, may play a role, but these factors don't explain why some individuals develop eating disorders and others do not. The factors that make susceptible individuals obsess about food and body weight are still unidentified, but many psychiatrists today regard the disorder as a brain disease. Researchers are beginning to identify specific brain circuits that may function abnormally in persons with eating disorders. Some of these brain differences could be consequences of having an eating disorder and some could be present in susceptible individuals before symptoms appear. Identification of the later could lead to effective treatments.

Profile #35: Janie Ryman in the Young Adult Novel *Purge* by Sarah Darer Littman

> Was there ever a period of time when I was able to love food unreservedly, without thinking of it as "the enemy" the minute it was in my stomach?

PLOT SUMMARY

The great humiliation happens at her sister's wedding. Of all places, that is where her embarrassing secret is revealed to family, friends, and strangers. After binging at the wedding, she is found covered in vomit in the bathroom. Later, feeling shame and despair, 16-year-old Janie tries to take her life, an action that leads to her stay at the Golden Slopes rehabilitation center for teens with eating disorders.

Her stay is also the beginning of her reluctant exploration—through her journal, therapy sessions, and interactions with other teens—of the reasons behind her binging and purging. It requires her to understand her unhealthy need for control and her intense dissatisfaction with her body and with herself.

JANIE'S PSYCHOLOGICAL TRAITS

Janie experiences several highly stressful events that contribute to her need to maintain control in her life. She has a painful and traumatic fight with her best friend Kelsey, and she is treated poorly by the boy with whom she has her first sexual experience. Social pressures at school, a comment by her father that she looks "a little chunky in the butt," and her mother's overemphasis on what she eats add to her insecurity. Achieving "control" over herself becomes a key aspect of Janie's troubled psychology.

BULIMIA NERVOSA

Janie demonstrates three features that lead psychiatrists to diagnose her with bulimia nervosa: (1) she repeatedly engages in binge eating. This means that on repeated occasions, and in a relatively short amount of time (for example, a few hours), she consumes more food than most people would ever consider eating in that space of time. And during this time, she feels a lack of control; (2) she then tries to compensate for her binging and forces herself to vomit; and (3) Janie's opinion of herself, her sense of her self-worth, is overly dependent on her weight and body shape.

A strongly negative self-image that overemphasizes the importance of body shape and weight

"As soon as I finish eating, it's like this tape starts playing in my head: 'You are SO FAT! What the hell did you eat that for?' "

Janie is not "so fat" but she has an inaccurate impression of her body that is a hallmark of people suffering from such eating disorders. Her negative self-image is reflected in 9 of the 10 words she uses to describe herself: "Fat, Sad, Bulimic, Screwed up, Defective, Smart, Ugly, Empty, Confused, Scared."

Unhealthy behaviors used to compensate for eating

" 'The main emotion I have is that I want to purge,' I say. 'And frustration that I have to sit here and tell you about it and can't go off and do it.' "

Self-induced vomiting is the most common way of purging. Other purging behaviors include excessive exercise, fasting, or use of laxatives.

Binging and purging occurs approximately once a week for at least three months.

"Bulimia has become so much a part of me that I can't remember what it felt like not to purge."

Janie responds positively to psychotherapy and returns home. If she shows no symptoms for more than a year, she has a good chance of recovery. In some people, symptoms may decrease over time without treatment, but the disorder increases the risk of death by all causes, not just suicide. Close to 2 percent of people with bulimia nervosa die per decade. Treatment like that which Janie received is effective. It can restore physical and psychological health and it can save lives.

Sleep–Wake Disorder

Profile #36: Mike Waters in the Film *My Own Private Idaho*; Screenplay by Gus Van Sant

Scott Favor: "He's not dead. He's just passed out. It's a condition. It's called narcolepsy."

PLOT SUMMARY

Mike Waters (played by River Phoenix) stands on an empty highway in Idaho. Suddenly he drops to the pavement, asleep.

Mike and his best and only friend Scott Favor (played by Keanu Reeves) are male prostitutes. Mike comes from a broken family; Scott comes from a wealthy, successful family. Scott's father is a mayor. Scott has ambitions to eventually enter politics himself after he gives up hustling, which for him is voluntary. It is an act of defiance directed against his father. In contrast, Mike has no one to defy; he is poor and desperate.

The two friends meet in a seedy section of Portland, Oregon, and in time decide to search for Mike's mother. The search takes Mike from Portland to Italy to Idaho. Along the way, they prostitute themselves for money and for drugs.

This slowly paced, independently produced film ignores Hollywood standards and clichés. It is loosely based on Shakespeare's *Henry IV*, told as a road movie. It depicts Mike's search for a safe place in the world. From time to time, Scott imagines an idyllic image of Idaho, hence the title of the film, *My Own Private Idaho*.

The story captures the tragedy of someone who is lost, aimless, and seeking to connect with others during an unsuccessful journey. Mike fails to find his mother and he even loses Scott when his best friend leaves with a woman. The film ends with Mike suffering yet another sleep attack in the middle of the same road where his journey began.

MIKE'S PSYCHOLOGICAL TRAITS

Mike is lonely and, with the exception of Scott, without strong social ties. His untreated narcolepsy heightens his separation from everyone except his one friend.

NARCOLEPSY

Narcolepsy is a chronic sleep disorder that causes a person to become very drowsy during the day and to suddenly fall asleep. No matter what people with narcolepsy are doing, they have trouble staying awake for long periods. Narcolepsy is incurable but it can be managed with medications and lifestyle adjustments. Sadly, Mike's narcolepsy is untreated.

To receive a formal diagnosis of narcolepsy, Mike would have to have frequent episodes of spontaneously falling asleep.

Mike has involuntarily fallen asleep at least three times a week over a period of at least 90 days. (Napping or feeling an overwhelming urge to sleep would also qualify.)

Scott: "He always does this."

Dialog and events in the film suggest that Mike has frequent episodes and easily satisfies this criterion. Mike says: "I've been tasting roads my whole life." His statement refers to the episodes when he literally collapses while standing on a road, as shown in the film. More poignantly, it refers as well to his homeless, difficult, drifting life on the road. Since he is a drifter, many of these episodes occur when he is on the road.

Mike would also have to meet at least one of three additional criteria. One is the occurrence of cataplexy at least twice a month. Cataplexy is a medical condition often associated with narcolepsy. People with this condition collapse due to loss of muscle tone when they experience strong emotions or laughter. They do not, however, lose consciousness. Mike's symptoms do not look like cataplexy.

The other two criteria involve testing in a clinical setting, something we know Mike has not received. One would measure how quickly he enters the rapid eye movement phase of sleep. Mike would most likely enter this phase more rapidly than someone who did not have narcolepsy.

The other test would look for the presence of a molecule called hypocretin in Mike's spinal fluid. This brain chemical plays a role in regulating wakefulness and rapid eye movements. It is often present in low levels in cases of narcolepsy.

Scott: "Narcolepsy doctors are saying it's brought on by certain chemical reactions in the brain."

Gender Dysphoria

Profile #37: Roy Applewood in the Television Film *Normal*; Teleplay by Jane Anderson

I don't know how to express this to you other than in a letter. I'm going to have a surgery next year to correct a condition I have that is known as gender dysphoria. In other words, I'm a woman born in a man's body and I'll be getting a sex change. I hope you'll understand that I would like to find some peace and happiness in my life.

PLOT SUMMARY

Roy and Irma Applewood (played by Tom Wilkinson and Jessica Lange, respectively) appear to have been happily married for a quarter century. They are well-respected in their rural hometown and live a comfortable life.

Their lives change radically after celebrating their wedding anniversary. Roy can no longer handle the distress caused by the fact that he has always felt like a woman trapped in a man's body. He tells Irma and their pastor that he has decided to have a sex change operation. The announcement threatens Roy's relationship with his family, friends, and coworkers.

Many members of his community are ignorant of gender dysphoria and are intolerant of Roy's decision. Eventually, Roy receives the support of his wife, teenage daughter, and his friend and boss, Frank. This helps him as he transitions from Roy to his true self, Ruth.

ROY'S PSYCHOLOGICAL TRAITS

Roy is a well-respected member of his community. For decades, he's been known as a good husband and father. But all of his adult life, he has hid from everyone the secret of who he is, the source of his unhappiness. Although he was born with a male body, his true identity and self-image is female.

GENDER DYSPHORIA

Because Roy can no longer handle the distress caused by the lack of fit between his female identity and his biologically assigned gender, he appears to have gender dysphoria. The diagnostic criteria for this condition for children differ from those for adolescents and adults. Roy is in his 50s and so a doctor would look for the following indications during a psychological or psychiatric examination to make a diagnosis. Such an evaluation should be done to decide if providing hormone therapy and elective surgery, if desired, would be the best way to relieve Roy's psychological distress. If Roy had experienced the following for at least six months (and in his case he has endured them for years), then the diagnosis would be clear.

One criterion for gender dysphoria is that it causes significant distress for the person.

Roy: "It's not out of nowhere. I've been hiding it for years. It has been an agony. I can't go on living my life like this. I'd rather die."

In addition, Roy would only need to satisfy two of these additional criteria to receive the diagnosis.

A strong desire not to have the primary and/or secondary sex characteristics one was born with because they do not agree with the gender the person identifies with

Roy: "I've been struggling with something for a long time. I've prayed for years for it to go away, but it won't . . . I was born in the wrong body. I'm a woman. I've known it all my life."

A strong desire in a biological male to have the primary and secondary sex characteristics of a biological female, and vice versa

Roy: "I'd like to have the operation to change my sex."

A significant lack of fit between the gender a person identifies with and the primary and secondary sex characteristics he or she was born with. (Primary sex characteristics are physical features directly involved in reproduction, for example, male testes and female ovaries. Secondary sex characteristics are physical features specific to males or females that do not directly play a role in reproduction. Examples include broad shoulders, Adam's apple, deep voices, and beards in males, and breasts, wider hips, less body hair, and a higher voice in females.)

Roy: "I'm a woman born in a man's body."

Other criteria often met by people with gender dysphoria are as follows:

Being convinced that one has the personality, feelings, and reactions normally associated with the other gender

A strong desire to be treated as someone who belongs to an alternative gender

A strong conviction that a person feels and reacts in a way typical of the other gender

Gender dysphoria has attracted controversy. Like most topics that generate heated debate, the vacuum created by the lack of scientifically confirmed facts is quickly filled with often emotional arguments driven by personal beliefs and opinions. Psychological and psychiatric diagnoses, and the disciplines themselves, are often the targets of a vocal minority which doesn't recognize their usefulness. These critics feel someone's gender should not be changed. Until we can pinpoint the biological basis of gender identity beyond doubt, this topic will be open to ideological and religious debate, as opposed to factual debate.

As an adult, Roy Applewood's case is clear. Roy spent decades living uncomfortably in a male body, all the time feeling as if he was a female. Roy lived a false life for decades and the years were marked by intense feelings of unhappiness that he kept from everyone, even those closest to him. It is Roy's choice if he wants to have a physical body that matches the gender he identifies with.

Disruptive, Impulse Control, and Conduct Disorders

Profile #38: Bruce Banner/The Hulk in the Film *The Avengers*; Screenplay by Joss Whedon

Security guard: "Are you an alien?"
Bruce Banner: "No."
Security guard: "Well, then, son, you've got a condition."

PLOT SUMMARY

Dr. Bruce Banner (played by Mark Ruffalo) has moved to Calcutta where he provides medical care for the poor. There he hopes to lessen the chance that he will lose his self-control and temper. When Bruce does lose it, he turns into the Hulk, a giant, inhumanly muscled, bullet-proof, seemingly indestructible, perpetually enraged green monster. This aspect of his personality is attributed to his accidental exposure to intense gamma radiation during a nuclear weapon test.

Despite the threat Bruce's poor anger control issues pose to others, he is recruited by Natasha (played by Scarlett Johansson) to join a group of superheroes to stop a threat posed yet again by a super villain. This time the villain is Loki, an extraterrestrial being inspired by the Norse god of mischief. During the time he is teamed up with his superhero companions, Bruce struggles to control his temper and unleash it only upon Loki and his agents.

BRUCE'S PSYCHOLOGICAL TRAITS

Bruce Banner had a stressful, unhappy childhood. His father, Brian, showed signs of paranoia and was jealous of his infant son. Brian frequently abused Bruce's mother. Brian eventually killed his wife during one of his angry outbursts and was committed to a psychiatric hospital. Bruce was raised by his aunt who recognized his superior intelligence. She sent them to a private school for gifted children. Bruce suppressed his emotions, fearful of becoming like his father.

As an adult, Bruce appears subdued, soft-spoken, and mild-mannered—until he becomes angry. When he loses control, he rages, roars, and strikes out at people and things in an uncontrolled manner. This anger is accompanied by his transformation into the Hulk.

The Hulk's character has evolved since he was introduced in 1962. Several of his incarnations show symptoms of dissociative identity disorder. Tom DeFalco, author of *Hulk: The Incredible Guide*, explains: "Banner's MPD [multiple personality disorder, an out-of-date term for dissociative identity disorder] can be traced to his traumatic childhood. Exposure to gamma rays allowed him to manifest his darker personalities as the Hulk. Each Hulk incarnation has distinctive characteristics, expressing key aspects of Banner's psyche, and they all battle for supremacy within his subconscious."

Although this evolving comic book hero represented alternate Bruce personalities in the past, the version of the character in the film *The Avengers* does not stress this aspect of his psychology. He appears to have one personality subject to terrible outbursts of anger represented by the Hulk. Bruce Banner in *The Avengers* appears to suffer from intermittent explosive behavior.

INTERMITTENT EXPLOSIVE DISORDER

Impulsive aggression is not limited to comic book characters like Bruce Banner's violent, short-tempered Hulk. In fact, psychiatrist Emil F. Coccaro, MD, notes that intermittent explosive disorder (IED) is just as common as a number of other psychiatric disorders.

When people have frequent angry outbursts that result in verbal or physical harm or injury to property, self, or others, they should be evaluated for IED. This disorder causes people to impulsively become aggressive and angry when frustrated or faced with a social threat. Many instances of domestic abuse and road rage may be related to IED. These people's impulsive aggression is "over-the-top"; it is out of proportion to the situation they face. The spontaneous, uncontrolled aggression can take the form of physical assaults against people, animals, or things. It can also take the form of temper tantrums or screaming arguments.

Found mostly in people below the age of 40, IED is more common in people with a high school education or less. The disorder seems to be more common in the United States than in Asia or the Middle East. This might be an effect of culture, or it might be due to differences in how people respond to questions about their aggressive behaviors.

A key factor in the diagnosis of IED is not whether someone or something was injured or damaged, but that the outburst is explosive, the result of impulsive, as opposed to planned, aggression. A diagnosis of IED, of course, would not apply to anyone whose outbursts are due to another disorder, or who is chronologically or developmentally under the age of six.

Bruce has had at least three unplanned explosive outbursts of anger during which he has destroyed property and assaulted others over the course of a single year. He would also meet this criterion if he had only verbal outbursts on average a couple of times a week over a three-month period.

Natasha: "You've been more than a year without an incident. I don't think you want to break that streak."
Bruce: "Well I don't every time get what I want."

Bruce's escape to Calcutta has temporarily relieved his symptoms. In the past, he easily met this criterion with frequent episodes of unplanned, explosive, and angry outbursts. Furthermore, he is about to be placed in a position where his anger, although manipulated by his fellow superheroes, will repeatedly result in explosive episodes.

The ferocity of the outbursts far exceeds the events that elicit them.

Natasha: "You know, for a man who is supposed to be avoiding stress you've picked a hell of a place to settle."
Bruce: "Avoiding stress isn't the secret."
Natasha: "What is? Yoga?"

Only in the comic book world do the provocations that bring forth Bruce Banner's uncontrolled anger match his destructive responses. This is because the Hulk violence at times is directed at villains trying to destroy or conquer the world. Although Natasha mistakenly believes that stress elicits Bruce's uncontrolled outbursts, she knows that, whatever causes the Hulk to appear, his outbursts are always way out of proportion to whatever elicits them. When Bruce deliberately unnerves Natasha by pretending to get angry, he raises his voice and slaps a tabletop. Natasha jumps back and points a pistol at him, expecting the extreme ferocity that marks his real outbursts.

The outbursts are impulsive, uncontrolled, and unplanned.

Bruce: "That's my secret, Captain. I'm always angry."

Although Natasha believes stress brings on Bruce's terrible angry outbursts, Bruce knows that they are based on anger, a destructive feeling he is forever trying to control.

During one episode of IED, the Hulk attacks his allies, his putative superheroes-in-arms. The impulsiveness and pointlessness of the explosive outburst are apparent as Thor (played by Chris Hemsworth) struggles to resist the Hulk: "We are not your enemies, Banner. *Try to think*."

Bruce Banner is a comic book and movie character but the trait that so burdens his life, IED, is a real disorder. Although it is represented by Bruce's transformation into the Hulk, it is important to realize that, in the real world, IED causes real and serious problems both for those afflicted by the disorder and for the targets of their verbal and/or physical rages.

Profile #39: Ronald Bartel in the Film *Backdraft*; Screenplay by Gregory Widen

After it took your dad . . . the fire . . . did it look at you Brian? Did it talk to you?

PLOT SUMMARY

Brothers Stephen and Brian McCaffrey (played by Kurt Russell and William Baldwin, respectively) lost their heroic firefighter father when they were children. They have been competing with each other ever since. Their rivalry continues as Chicago firefighters. Senior firefighter Stephen supervises Brian but doubts that his younger brother is capable of being a good firefighter.

Brian transfers to the arson investigation unit and begins training under veteran arson inspector Donald "Shadow" Rimgale (played by Robert De Niro). Together, Brian and Shadow investigate a series of intense fires involving backdrafts, which occur when oxygen rapidly flows into an oxygen-depleted burning environment. The resulting burst of intense flame can be catastrophic.

Ronald Bartel (played by Donald Sutherland), who is in prison as a result of his fire-setting crimes, plays an important role in this case. The investigation eventually leads to a conspiracy involving a highly unlikely conspirator.

RONALD'S PSYCHOLOGICAL TRAITS

Ronald is fascinated by fire. He calls it "the animal" because for him it is a living creature; it breaths, eats, moves, and hunts. He cannot resist its allure. His speech pattern and sometimes behavior hint at a mild intellectual deficit, unless he is discussing fire. And unlike people with pyromania, Ronald is also an arsonist. His repeated crimes and clear lack of remorse for the victims of the fires he has set indicate significant antisocial personality traits.

Ronald is not an accurate representation of most people who have pyromania. Like Hannibal Lecter in *The Silence of the Lambs*, he is a character in whom the screenwriter has combined multiple features of criminal and psychological problems to create a memorable, but probably unrealistic, villain.

PYROMANIA AND POSSIBLE PSYCHOPATHIC TRAITS

Defining features of pyromania are multiple instances of setting fires and experiencing arousal or tension before the acts. Ronald would seem to meet the criteria for a positive diagnosis, but other, antisocial, traits would make a diagnosis complicated. There are six diagnostic criteria for pyromania, several of which would exclude Ronald. Thus, he is not representative of a person with pyromania although he has many key traits that define the disorder.

Has set fires deliberately and purposefully on multiple occasions

Rimgale: "Ronald here likes telephones. Used to tape wooden matches to the bell striker and wrap it in cotton. Came up with a whole little thing there, didn't you Ronald? When you got bored, what did you do? You just started making calls . . . mostly day care centers and retirement homes, wasn't it?"

Ronald has been convicted of setting multiple fires. One way he set them was by repeatedly rigging phones in day care centers and retirement homes so they would catch fire when they rang. He made sure they rang by calling them.

Feels tense or aroused before setting fires

Since we meet Ronald in prison, we can't get a sense of his feelings before he set fires in the past. But when Ronald questions Brian, it strongly suggests that he might have: "After it took your dad . . . the fire . . . did it look at you Brian? Did it talk to you?" Ronald's lurid, desperate demeanor as he questions Brian reveals excitement and arousal, feelings that would presumably have been present when he started fires.

Attracted to, interested in, curious about, or fascinated with fire and fire-related topics

Ronald: "So you've come pick Ronald's brains because nobody knows 'the animal' like Ronald."

Experiences relief, pleasure, or gratification upon setting fires or seeing the results of fires

Rimgale: "What did you do to that little girl, Ronald?"
Ronald: "I burned her."
Rimgale: "You burned her. What do you do to old ladies, Ronald?"
Ronald: "Burn them."
Rimgale: "What about the world, Ronald? What would you like to do to the whole world?"
Ronald: "Burn it all."

Here, Ronald's undeniable pleasure, and presumed relief of tension, upon setting fires and seeing the results crosses from pyromania to, perhaps, psychopathic behavior. These features, strictly speaking, would make a simple diagnosis of pyromania inaccurate.

Fire-setting is not the result of having another mental disorder such as mania, antisocial personality disorder, or conduct disorder.

Ronald's history strongly suggests he has more mental health issues than simple pyromania. As written, the character probably has antisocial personality disorder or psychopathy.

Sets fires to relieve tension or for pleasure but* not *to make money or gain personal benefits, to make a political statement, to hide a crime, to exact revenge, or to express anger. Also fire-setting behavior cannot be a result of a neurological condition, intellectual disability, or drug (including alcohol) abuse.

Ronald has set fires for both pleasure and for money. He therefore exploited his interest in fire-setting to make a criminal living. Again, strictly speaking, this fact would make a simple diagnosis of pyromania inaccurate.

The arsonist does not start fires because he cannot control his impulse to start fires. He starts fires because he has a motivation to gain something. A person with pyromania starts fires to relieve an intense psychological tension to start fires. Ronald is a very unrepresentative, although interesting, fictional combination of an arsonist who can't resist his impulse to set fires.

Profile #40: Alex DeLarge in the Novel *A Clockwork Orange* by Anthony Burgess

But what I do I do because I like to do.

PLOT SUMMARY

At age 15, Alex is the leader of a violent gang of three other teenage criminals: Georgie, Pete, and Dim. He and his "droogs," as he calls them, rampage through a futuristic totalitarian country full of passive victims. He narrates his experiences, which include robbery, mugging, breaking and entering, theft, rape, and ultimately, murder. He tells his story using a rich slang called "nadsat," a mixture of standard and Cockney English, Russian, and a few other languages.

After Alex alienates his fellow droogs, Dim hits him with a chain while they are robbing an elderly woman's home. Alex is knocked down and arrested when the police arrive. He is sentenced to 14 years in prison. He manages to manipulate his way into an experimental program called "Reclamation Treatment" in the hopes of being released early. Alex doesn't know that the treatment consists of injections of nausea-producing drugs coupled with watching movies depicting the "ultraviolence" he loves. The nausea soon becomes linked to violence (and inadvertently to his cherished Beethoven symphony). Alex is declared "cured" of his criminality because he now becomes incapacitated with nausea at the thought of violence.

Once freed, Alex's treatment is reversed after he injures himself in a suicide attempt. Although he can once again tolerate violence, he eventually decides to abandon it by choice.

ALEX'S PSYCHOLOGICAL TRAITS

Alex is an intelligent, quick-witted, and articulate teenager with a deep appreciation for classical music, particularly Beethoven. He is also violent and manipulative. His personality is dominated by his conduct disorder.

CONDUCT DISORDER

If Alex were 18 years of age or older, he would undoubtedly be described as an example of an extreme sadistic, criminal psychopathic personality. But that description should never be applied to minors because it condemns them prematurely to a diagnosis that could change, as it does in Alex's case.

Psychiatrists instead use a diagnosis of conduct disorder for minors who show disturbing antisocial behavior. Children with conduct disorder persistently and repeatedly commit acts that violate the rights of others or violate standards of behavior that society considers normal for their age. The diagnosis is made when a child demonstrates at least 3 of 15 specific behaviors over the course of a year. The criteria are divided into categories of aggression, property destruction, thievery or deceitfulness, and serious rule violation.

Assault, bullying, threats, intimidation, using a weapon to injure a victim, or other forms of cruelty or aggression directed against persons or animals

Alex: "Our pockets were full of deng, so there was no real need from the point of view of crasting any more pretty polly to tolchock some old veck in an alley and viddy him swim in his blood while we counted the takings and divided by four, nor to do the ultra-violent on some shivering starry grey-haired ptitsa in a shop and go smecking off with the till's guts. But, as they say, money isn't everything."

Alex admits to beating victims and robbing them not out of a need for "polly" or money but because he and his gang of "droogs" enjoy the violence.

(Nadsat translations: deng = money; cresting = stealing; polly is rhyming slang for lolly, a Romany word for money; tolchock = to strike; veck = man; viddy = to see; ptitsa = woman; smecking = laughing.)

Causing the destruction of property with or without the use of fire

Alex: "Then there was like quiet and we were full of like hate, so smashed what was left to be smashed—typewriter, lamp, chairs . . . "

During a home invasion, Alex and his gang beat a writer, rape his wife, and wreck their house. The woman does not survive, but her husband does. After Alex is released from prison, he finds refuge with the writer, who does not recognize Alex at first. When he realizes who Alex is, he gets revenge by forcing him to listen to Beethoven, once Alex's favorite composer but now one whose music is linked to the extreme nausea he feels when he sees or thinks of violence.

Stealing or deceitfulness including conning behavior

Alex: " 'I've been doing nothing I shouldn't, sir,' I said. 'The millicents [police] have nothing on me, brother, sir I mean.' "

Alex repeatedly lies when he tells his "post-corrective advisor" or parole officer that he has done nothing illegal.

Breaking commonly accepted rules of society

Alex: "The next morning I woke up at oh eight oh oh hours, my brothers, and as I still felt shagged and fagged and fashed and bashed and my glazzies were stuck together real horrorshow with sleepglue, I thought I would not go to school."

Parents, schools, and the courts expect children to obey basic rules put in place for their protection and benefit. Attending school, not running away from home, and not staying out all night are examples. We can imagine what Alex was like when he was 13 years old but we don't know for sure; the story describes his life after his 15th birthday. If he had started skipping school or started staying out all night before he was 13, he might add two more criteria to the long list he meets for conduct disorder.

Callousness—lack of empathy

Alex: "I see what is right and approve, but I do what is wrong."

The *DSM-5* recognizes the rare existence of youth like Alex who clearly display an alarming disregard for the feelings of others and a chilling, uncaring attitude regarding the consequences of their behavior. These young people are described as having conduct disorder with "callous—lack of empathy."

Substance-Related and Addictive Disorders

Profile #41: Bobby in the Film *Panic in Needle Park*; Screenplay by Joan Didion and John Gregory Dunne, Based on the Book by James Mills

---

I'm not hooked. Just chippin'.

PLOT SUMMARY

Bobby (played by Al Pacino) spends much of his time in "Needle Park," a gathering place for heroin addicts and other drug users on Manhattan's Upper West Side. He meets and falls in love with Helen (played by Kitty Winn), a sad, homeless girl. Soon Helen samples heroin in Bobby's hotel room. Now both addicted, Bobby and Helen cling to each other as they desperately hustle any way they can for money to buy heroin. The stress of feeding their drug habits, however, leads to betrayal when Helen is arrested for selling illegal pills. After much resistance and hesitation, Helen cooperates with the police to help them arrest Bobby. Despite the betrayal, Helen meets Bobby when he is released from prison and together they walk back into their lives in Needle Park, bound by their need for one another.

BOBBY'S PSYCHOLOGICAL TRAITS

Bobby is funny and personable enough to win Helen's affection. He demonstrates a sincere concern for her, but their relationship is soon dominated by their need to obtain heroin. The drug becomes a third, and often selfish, partner in their relationship.

OPIOID USE DISORDER

The original definition of "opioid" referred to any synthetic narcotic that produced physiological effects similar to those produced by opium. More recently, the term "opioid" frequently refers to synthetic narcotics as well as opium and its derivatives. Examples of opioids under this wider definition include painkillers such as morphine, heroin, methadone, oxycodone, and hydrocodone.

Bobby and Helen are addicted to heroin but they will take other illegal drugs if they cannot obtain their opiate of choice. Heroin produces an immediate stimulation or "rush" followed by an intense state of relaxation. It obliterates pain. Bobby and Helen demonstrate more than 2 of the 11 criteria that, over the course of one year, would qualify them for diagnosis of opioid use disorder.

They increase the amount of opioids they use over time or use them longer than they planned.

Bobby tells his brother and girlfriend: "I'm not hooked. Just chippin'." Bobby may have started out "chipping"—that is, using heroin only occasionally—but now he is obviously addicted. He injects himself with heroin intravenously regularly throughout the film.

Bobby repeatedly attempts or announces his intention to cut back or stop using opioids.

Bobby: "I'm quittin'." "Never again." And "Never again. I swear to God." He never quits or even seriously tries.

Bobby and Helen spend a lot of time trying to buy heroin, using it, or recovering from using it.

"This really sucks!" Bobby says as he searches desperately in several neighborhoods for heroin he has paid for. On another occasion Bobby tests Helen's devotion to him: "I want you to do me a favor. I want you to go up to 119th street for me. I want you to score for me."

They demonstrate a craving for opiate drugs.

Bobby: "Where are you going?"
Helen: "Baby, we don't have any money."
Bobby: "What are you talking about? We're gonna have thousands and thousands of dollars."
Helen: "Not in time to get either one of us straight today."

When Bobby discovers Helen preparing to inject herself with the heroin he had been saving for himself, he confronts her. "That's my wake up. You stole my wake up." Helen: "I needed it." Bobby: "I take you back and you steal my wake up?"

Their opioid use makes them unable to function successfully at home and at work (or at school, if they had jobs or were students).

"What do you mean? I want my key!" Bobby yells at the clerk of the cheap hotel. The clerk replies: "Not until you pay your rent."

They have given up regular jobs, recreations, and nearly all social life not connected to their heroin addictions.

"Say, uh, you still selling grass in the Village?" Bobby's older brother asks him. "When I get a chance," Bobby replies before adding: "I copped a television yesterday." When Helen works as a prostitute to pay for drugs, Bobby tells her "I don't want you to do that." But when he needs heroin, he uses the money she makes from prostitution.

They repeatedly use opioids despite the danger of physical threats.

"All your friends are here. You're here," Helen observes. Bobby answers "Some friends. You know I've been beat by half the people out there. Half of 'em."

Bobby continues to use opioids even though he knows that his addiction is causing him physical or psychological harm.

"I'm a germ," Bobby tells Helen, "You should split." When Bobby fails to show up as promised, another addict tells Helen: "I just heard Bobby's O.D.'d." The two rush to Bobby's aid and prevent him from dying from the overdose. Heroin overdoses usually kill by shutting down a person's breathing. They can also seriously lower blood pressure and cause heart failure.

Bobby and Helen develop tolerance to opioids.

Drug tolerance causes a person to use increasing amounts of a drug to achieve a sought-after effect or "high." If the person continues to use the same amount of drug over time, the drug's effect will diminish. Bobby says to Helen: "You're taking too much; you know that? We got plenty. You don't have to take it all at once."

Withdrawal occurs when opioids are unavailable or use is stopped.

The panic in *Panic in Needle Park* results from a drug shortage in the city, preventing people addicted to opiates from obtaining their supplies. A male heroin user recalls seeing "guys kicking their habit in the streets. Puking in the alleyway." Withdrawal symptoms include dysphoric mood (which may include depression, anxiety, and a general feeling of dissatisfaction or discomfort), muscle aches, nausea, vomiting, sweating, diarrhea, insomnia, fever, and other unpleasant effects. Helen clearly displays her withdrawal-related dysphoric mood when she tries to fool a doctor into giving her an opiate prescription. "Please," she pleads, "I need something."

Bobby knows "someone who shot paregoric and shoe polish." Desperate to avoid the effects of withdrawal, this user resorted to injecting substances he hoped would offset withdrawal symptoms. (Paregoric is a medicine used to treat intestinal pain and diarrhea. It contains anise oil, benzoic acid, camphor, glycerin, diluted alcohol, and some opium powder. Its use reveals the desperate steps addicted individuals will take to avoid withdrawal.)

Bobby continues to use heroin despite its negative effects on his personal life.

When Helen begins to kiss him in bed, Bobby, who has recently taken heroin, manages to mumble: "I can't. I can't. I can't. When I'm doing junk. When I'm straight, okay?" Also, Bobby tells Helen: "Another thing. I been in jail eight times." Later in the film, Helen says to Bobby: "It's been a long time . . . since we laughed about anything."

Profile #42: Geoffrey Firmin in the Novel *Under the Volcano* by Malcolm Lowry

---

> And what right had Yvonne to assume it, assume either that he was not sober now, or that, far worse, in a day or two he would be sober?

PLOT SUMMARY

Former British consulate Geoffrey Firmin, known as "The Consul," has moved through his adult life under the very heavy influence of alcohol. He spends November 2nd, 1938, the last, tragically eventful day of his life, in Quauhnahuac, Mexico, during All Souls' Day. It is the final day of Mexico's Day of the Dead celebration.

Looking for reconciliation and perhaps a life together in some other country, his ex-wife Yvonne joins him. She hopes to revive their failed relationship and to save Geoffrey from himself. Geoffrey drinks his way through the day, visiting one cantina after another, unable to act on his desire to reconnect with his wife or to consider a life without alcohol. The presence of Geoffrey's half-brother, Hugh, and his childhood friend, Jacques, doesn't help Geoffrey or Yvonne as their stay in Mexico heads toward tragedy. The novel, rich in powerful symbolism and finely crafted, vivid prose, captures the alienation and struggles of a man battling threats from within and from without—but mostly from within.

Malcolm Lowry

Beginning in 1936, Englishman Malcolm Lowry began writing a novel. With significant editing help from his second wife Margerie Bonner, he produced his most acclaimed book, *Under the Volcano*, 10 years later. He was 27 years old when he started, and, after its publication, he would live only 10 more years, dying at age 48. His death was closely related to the same illness that contributed to the death of his masterwork's main character, Geoffrey Firmin: alcohol use disorder. The disorder appeared early in Lowry's life; he began drinking before his 15th birthday. He never stopped and although he was popular in bar rooms, he was deeply insecure and unhappy.

When he was 18, Lowry signed on as a deckhand on a freighter headed to Japan. He used the experience to write his first novel, *Blue Voyage*. When he was 20, he enrolled at Cambridge University. Although he did not distinguish himself as a student, his writing skill was recognized by those who knew him. His time at the university was severely marred, however, by the suicide of his roommate. This death troubled him deeply for the rest of his life.

After the publication of *Under the Volcano* in 1947, Lowry's heavy drinking continued. He never published again. He consulted a psychiatrist in 1955 but did not appear to benefit from whatever advice or treatment he received. In 1957, while living in England, he argued with his wife, who fled their home. He died shortly later after taking an overdose of sleeping pills.

While some critics appreciated the depth and complexity of *Under the Volcano*'s narrative, it did not attract many readers until after Lowry's death. The structure of the book shows the influence of techniques used in the films of his time. (Lowry wrote one screenplay in his lifetime. It was a treatment of *Tender Is the Night* by F. Scott Fitzgerald. It was never made into a movie.) *Under the Volcano* contains flashbacks and provides comparisons of images, recollections, and thoughts representing different impressions of events. Much like Lowry himself, the main character of his masterpiece is a tragic and lonely figure who suffered from a devastating disorder.

GEOFFREY'S PSYCHOLOGICAL TRAITS

"The Consul," as he is known, despite his resignation from the British diplomatic service, is burned out, nearly completely disillusioned, and rarely sober. He hears voices and experiences severe blackouts.

ALCOHOL USE DISORDER

Alcohol use disorder is one of eight substance use disorders. The others are cannabis (e.g., marijuana); hallucinogens (e.g., LSD); inhalants (e.g., glues); opioid (e.g., heroin); sedatives, hypnotics, or anxiolytics (e.g., valium);

stimulants (e.g., methamphetamine, cocaine); and tobacco (e.g., cigarettes). A person with alcohol or other substance use disorder will continue to use the substance even though its use causes serious problems in his or her life, problems that cause distress or that impair the ability to function in a healthy manner day-to-day. Geoffrey displays most or all of the indications that he suffers from alcohol use disorder.

Geoffrey has increased the amount of alcohol he uses over time or uses it longer than he had once planned to use it.

"Far above him a few white clouds were racing windily after a pale gibbous moon. Drink all morning, they said to him, drink all day. This is life!"

If Geoffrey repeatedly attempted or announced his intention to cut back or stop drinking alcohol, it would be consistent with this type of disorder.

"The Consul," however, is in an alcoholic depression and seems intent on drinking himself into oblivion to escape an existence he sees as worthless.

Geoffrey spends a great deal of time drinking, assuring he finds the next bar, or recovering from alcohol's effects.

" . . . what beauty can compare to that of a cantina in the early morning?" And "Closing his eyes again, standing there, glass in hand, he thought for a minute with a freezing detached almost amused calm of the dreadful night inevitably awaiting him whether he drank much more or not . . . he returned to the bar."

Geoffrey demonstrates a craving for alcohol.

Early in the morning, before breakfast, Yvonne turns down his offer of a drink. " 'She might have said yes for once,' a voice said in the Consul's ear at this moment with incredible rapidity, 'for now of course poor old chap you want horribly to get drunk all over again don't you.' "

Alcohol use leaves Geoffrey unable to function successfully at home or at work.

"Unless of course it seemed utterly impossible, one dreaded the hour of anyone's arrival unless they were bringing liquor."

Geoffrey continues to use alcohol despite its negative effects on his personal life.

"And this is how I sometimes think of myself, as a great explorer who has discovered some extraordinary land from which he can never return to give his knowledge to the world: but the name of this land is hell." And "How indeed could he hope to find himself, to begin again when, somewhere, perhaps, in one of those lost or broken bottles, in one of those glasses, lay, forever, the solitary clue to his identity? How could he go back and look now, scrabble among the broken glass, under the eternal bars, under the oceans?"

Geoffrey has no regular job, no recreation, and no social life that is not connected to his use of alcohol.

"Why am I here, says the silence, what have I done, echoes the emptiness, why have I ruined myself in this willful manner, chuckles the money in the till, why have I been brought so low, wheedles the thoroughfare, to which the only answer was—The square gave him no answer."

Geoffrey continues to drink alcohol even though he knows that his addiction is causing him physical or psychological harm.

"You fool, you stupid fool . . . You've even been insulated from the responsibility of genuine suffering. . . . Even the suffering you do endure is largely unnecessary. Actually spurious. It lacks the very basis you require of it for its tragic nature. You deceive yourself."

Geoffrey develops tolerance to alcohol.

Tolerance causes a person to use increasing amounts of alcohol to achieve a sought-after effect. If a person continues to drink the same amount of alcohol over time, its psychological (but not its harmful physical) effects can decrease. "But my lord, Yvonne, surely you know by this time I can't get drunk however much I drink."

Withdrawal occurs when alcohol is unavailable or someone with alcohol use disorder stops drinking.

It takes a short time without alcohol for Geoffrey to experience withdrawal symptoms. For instance, his hands shake too much for him to shave himself after only a few hours without a drink.

Geoffrey repeatedly abuses alcohol despite the danger of physical threats.

Drunk, unable to defend himself, Geoffrey argues with corrupt local policemen who forcibly remove him from a bar, shoot him, and throw him into a ravine. "Christ," he remarked, puzzled, "this is a dingy way to die." Following his murder, "Somebody threw a dead dog after him down the ravine."

Profile #43: Ray and Jewel Kaiser in the Novel *Bob the Gambler* by Frederick Barthelme

So far, what I figure is you're kind of obsessed with gambling.

O.K, so we're obsessed. You know how much we've lost?

PLOT SUMMARY

Ray Kaiser isn't getting much work as an architect in Biloxi, Mississippi, as his interest in gambling grows. His interest began when his wife, Jewel, won a thousand dollars at Paradise, an offshore gambling casino. Bored with their domestic life, the couple begin spending more time and more money at the casino. First they play slot machines and then blackjack, where they lose more than $4,000. Eventually, their losses grow to more than 10 times that figure.

The couple spend so much time at the casino that they leave their daughter, RV, to face her teenage problems by herself. The death of Ray's father inspires him to become a full-time gambler. Spending night and day in the casino, he loses more money until eventually the couple is in debt for more than $49,000. Ray and Jewel sell their home and belongings and move in with Ray's widowed mother. Eventually they discover the value of living a less "exciting" life.

RAY AND JEWEL'S PSYCHOLOGICAL TRAITS

Ray and Jewel are a healthy, unremarkable married couple with a daughter from Jewel's previous marriage. Initially, no member of the familiar shows signs of having any psychological problems. That changes slowly after Ray and Jewel visit a casino.

GAMBLING DISORDER

Most people who gamble treat it as a diversion or entertainment. It does not become an addiction. Some people like Ray and Jewel, however, are not able to control their gambling behavior and it disrupts their lives.

Assuming neither Ray nor Jewel experience manic episodes, they would each need to satisfy four of nine criteria to be diagnosed with gambling disorder.

They feel the need to increase the amount of money they bet to experience greater excitement.

"With the gambling you want to jack up the stakes, you know what I mean?"

They are preoccupied with gambling.

"And I'm going over there all the time, and when I'm not there, I'm thinking about it."

Jewel tells Ray how their new interest seems to be taking over her life.

They often feel unhappy, guilty, anxious, or depressed when gambling.

"I felt s**tty about the money we'd lost, but I thought we might win it back, sooner or later. I was trying to understand the attraction—Jewel said it was like drugs, same thing, but I wasn't sure."

They often gamble to "get even," to make up for previous gambling losses.

"Losing meant you had to play more, try harder."

Bob has lost his career as a result of gambling. This criterion would also include losing or nearly losing an important job, an educational opportunity, or a significant relationship.

Bob is forced to close his office and can no longer find work in his chosen field of architecture.

Due to gambling losses, they end up depending on funds provided by others in order to compensate for lack of money.

"We'll get rid of everything and move in with Ray's mother for a while . . . "

In this case, they depend on a relative providing free rent in her home.

Other criteria are feelings of discomfort when cutting back on gambling, repeated failed attempts to cut back on gambling, and lying about time and money spent gambling. Although the couple don't meet these criteria, their behavior certainly qualifies as gambling disorder.

Their gambling started when "Jewell hit a jackpot on a Wild Cherry slot and was two hundred dollars ahead." It ended when they lost their possessions, home, and Ray's career. "Lots of people could afford it. I just wasn't one of them," Ray observed. Remarkably, after moving into Ray's mother's home, the couple learn that their new simplified lifestyle offers much more than their former lifestyle.

Neurocognitive Disorders

Profile #44: Dr. Alice Howland in the Film *Still Alice*; Screenplay by Wash Westmoreland and Richard Glatzer

I find myself learning the art of losing every day, losing my bearing, losing objects, losing sleep, but mostly losing my memories.

PLOT SUMMARY

While giving a lecture, noted Columbia University linguistics professor Dr. Alice Howland begins to show signs of memory loss. The loss is subtle at first, but progresses steadily. Then she begins to lose her intellectual or cognitive functioning as well. Diagnosed with early-onset Alzheimer's disease, she struggles to maintain her memory, her sense of self, and her dignity.

ALICE'S PSYCHOLOGICAL TRAITS

Alice is 50 years old and an ambitious, accomplished professor, teaching at an Ivy League university. She prides herself on her intelligence, independence, and notable accomplishments in the field of linguistics. After noticing memory losses and declining mental abilities, she learns that she has a rare form of dementia, early-onset Alzheimer's disease (AD).

EARLY-ONSET ALZHEIMER'S DISEASE

AD is the most common form of dementia. It is a progressive disorder caused by the degeneration of brain tissue. Symptoms include memory loss, impaired ability to think and reason, impaired language skills, and changes in behavior.

If AD develops before age 65, the patient is diagnosed with early-onset AD. It is a rare form of dementia affecting approximately 5 percent of all AD patients. Most of those affected by this form of the disease are, like Alice Howland, in their 50s, although there have been cases in which people develop the disease in their 30s and 40s. Some people believe that the symptoms of early-onset disease progress faster than symptoms of the late-onset form. There is, however, no convincing evidence that this is the case.

In a minority of cases, early-onset AD is, except for the age of onset, the same as the more common form that strikes after age 65. Most cases of early-onset disease have a clear genetic component involving mutations in one of three genes.

Difficulty recalling the right word, completing sentences, following directions, learning new tasks, following conversations.

Alice: "But I hope to convince you that by observing these baby steps in to the . . . into . . . uh . . . I knew I shouldn't have had that champagne."

While lecturing on a familiar topic, Alice experiences an unusual memory lapse. In most cases, this would not be an unusual event; everyone suffers such brief lapses that increase with age. In light of her developing symptoms, this particular lapse is a harbinger of future problems.

Memory loss

Husband: "Honey, we all have memory lapses. That's a sign of getting older. The other day I couldn't remember the word 'glucose.' "

Alice: "It's not like that. It's not like that. It's like something just drop—drops out under me."

Alice senses that her memory loss is not like the common memory lapses people experience as they age without disease.

Disorientation and misinterpretation of spatial relationships

Alice: "I've started forgetting things, little annoying things like words and names. And I got lost, completely lost running on campus."

While jogging, Alice becomes briefly disorientated and anxious when she cannot recognize the familiar Columbia University campus where she works.

Problem speaking and writing

"I . . . I use this . . . Yellow . . . Yellow thingy to mark it, so I don't have to read the same line over and over and over and over again . . . It took me three days to write this." Alice spends three days writing a short speech and must use a highlighter to read it out loud to prevent her from rereading the same line repeatedly.

Problems thinking and reasoning

Alice's student: "The content was often muddled and delivered with little focus and care . . . I found Linguistic 201 very erratic . . . I had a hard time following Dr. Howland's lectures. Even she seems like she gets lost in them."

Alice was once a popular and skilled lecturer. After her diagnosis, the decline in her cognitive abilities is reflected in the student reviews of her course.

Anxiety

Alice: "It feels like my brain is f**king dying! And everything I've worked for in my entire life is going. It's all, all going."

The film doesn't stress the ***personality and behavioral changes*** that also occur with the disease.

During her diagnosis, her doctor asks "Are you taking any pills, medications, supplements? . . . Have you had any head injuries? Would you consider yourself depressed or under undue stress at the moment? . . . How is your sleeping?" to rule out other possible causes of her symptoms.

With all medical tests negative, he explains his concern: "what worries me are the memory tests that I sent you for. You have sporadic memory impairment totally out of proportion to your age. And there is evidence of decline in your level of mental function."

Before her disease advances to the point where Alice is unable to function, Alice gives a short speech to people with AD and their families. She concludes: "Our strange behavior and fumbled sentences change others' perceptions of us and our perceptions of ourselves. We become ridiculous, incapable, comic. But this is not who we are. This is our disease. And like any disease, it has a cause, it has a progression and it could have a cure."

Profile #45: Henry Reifsneider in the Short Story "The Lost Phoebe" by Theodore Dreiser

---

> In age and with the feeble it is not such a far cry from the subtleties of illusion to actual hallucination, and in due time this transition was made for Henry.

PLOT SUMMARY

Seventy-year-old Henry Reifsneider and his 64-year-old wife Phoebe have lived for 48 years together on a small Indiana farm. The nearest town stopped growing years ago. Its population is falling. The couple's farmhouse, located three miles outside of town, is like its furniture: "old and mildewy and reminiscent of an earlier day."

The apparently dreary life of the Reifsneiders is offset by one thing: "Old Henry and his wife Phoebe were as fond of each other as it is possible for two old people to be who have nothing else in this life to be fond of." Despite Henry's complaining and grumping about Phoebe, and Phoebe's false threats to leave him, they are devoted to each other. Henry's devotion, however, has an unhealthy component. He is so emotionally dependent on his wife that he has no other meaningful relationships with anyone else. And he worries deeply about losing her.

When Phoebe dies, Henry's isolation increases after he rejects offers of help from his neighbors. The couple's five surviving children (three died young) are scattered and distant but still they offer to take the widower father in if he will leave his farm. He refuses.

Henry's grief takes over his life. He neglects his home and ignores its decay. Then he begins to see what he wants to see more than anything: Phoebe. He catches glimpses of her in shadows of the old house and, later, outside in the yard. " 'Phoebe,' he called, thrilling from head to toe and putting out one bony hand, 'have yuh come back?' " The glimpses turn into longer sightings, which he hopes to encourage. "If he only thought sufficiently, if he made it perfectly clear by his feeling that he needed her greatly, she would come back, this kindly wife, and tell him what to do."

In time Henry begins wandering the countryside looking for his mate whom he is convinced has left him temporarily after a spat. During the seven years he searches for her, calling "O-o-o Phoebe! O-o-o Phoebe!," he first visits homes, and then searches the roads and fields and woods of the isolated Indiana farmland for his wife. Everyone in three counties come to know about the pathetic, demented man.

One final vision of Phoebe, young and beautiful this time, brings Henry happiness at last. The farm boys who find Henry's body after he falls chasing his hallucination see "a molded smile of peace and delight upon his lips."

HENRY'S PSYCHOLOGICAL TRAITS

Henry is a self-sufficient farmer and a devoted husband, but he is insecure emotionally. He is overly dependent on his wife and rejects offers of help from what could become a social network of relationships. His isolation, grief, and the extreme sense of loss that he feels after Phoebe dies are linked to the delusion he develops that she is alive. It is also linked to the hallucinations that let him see her again. It is likely that Henry suffers from some form of dementia, although it is not possible to identify the type of dementia based on the information in the story.

DEMENTIA

Farmer Dodge, a neighbor:	"It can't be your wife yuh're talkin' about. She's dead."
Henry:	" 'Dead! Shucks!' retorted the demented Reifsneider."

Although Henry attended his wife's funeral, he is now convinced that she is alive. The author describes Henry as demented but there is not enough information to determine which type of dementia or neurocognitive disorder Henry might have. Dementia is a chronic disorder that causes changes in personality and problems with reasoning and memory. It is caused by brain disease or damage. One possibility is that Henry has Lewy body disease. Its symptoms develop gradually. One of the core diagnostic features is repeated visual hallucinations that are very lifelike and detailed. Not enough information is provided, however, to determine if Henry has other core features of this form of dementia such as parkinsonism and variations in his ability to concentrate.

Delusion

"His mind had gone. In its place was a fixed illusion. He and Phoebe had had a senseless quarrel. He had reproached her for not leaving his pipe where he was accustomed to find it, and she had left. It was an aberrated fulfillment of her old jesting threat that if he did not behave himself she would leave him."

What the author refers to as a "fixed illusion" is a delusion, an idiosyncratic, firmly held belief that his wife is alive. Delusions are symptoms of a mental illness.

Hallucinations

"Of a sudden there came to him now for the first time in many years the full charm of her girlish figure as he had known it in boyhood, the pleasing, sympathetic smile, the brown hair, the blue sash she had once worn about her waist at a picnic, her gay, graceful movements. . . . On she moved before him, a will-o'-the-wisp of the spring, a little flame above her head, and it seemed as though among the small saplings of ash and beech and the thick trunks of hickory and elm that signaled with a young, a lightsome hand."

In the beginning of the story, Henry has *illusions* that he sees his dead wife. He thinks he may see her in "a certain combination of furniture—a chair near a table, with his coat on it, the half-open kitchen door casting a shadow, and the position of a lamp near a paper." He misinterprets these real things as his late wife.

Later, he has full-blown *hallucinations*. Visual hallucinations look exactly like real beings or objects but are not caused by external stimulation of the eyes, as illusions are. Hallucinations can affect other senses besides sight including hearing, taste, smell, and touch. Some people may recognize that they are having hallucinations. Others, like Henry, are convinced they are real.

Personality Disorders

Profile #46: Alex Forrest in the Film *Fatal Attraction*; Screenplay by James Dearden

This is not gonna stop. It keeps going on and on.

PLOT SUMMARY

Dan Gallagher (played by Michael Douglas) is a successful lawyer living in New York with his wife Beth (Anne Archer) and their daughter. One evening when his family is away, he has a brief fling with a stranger named Alex (played by Glenn Close). Dan thinks of their two-day encounter as a casual affair. Alex sees it differently. When Dan tries to end the relationship with Alex, she begins to display unstable behavior. First she pursues him aggressively, despite his insistence that their relationship must end for the sake of his family. Then she begins to stalk him and display obsessive and paranoid behavior. Her behavior escalates until it leads to a frightening and violent conclusion.

ALEX'S PSYCHOLOGICAL TRAITS

Alex is highly insecure and unstable. These traits are not evident when one first meets her but they become apparent when she becomes involved in a relationship or experiences stress. Her character is often cited, not exactly accurately, as a prime example of a person dealing with borderline personality disorder.

Of course, in the manner often seen in Hollywood productions, her symptoms and behaviors lie on the most extreme end of the spectrum of mental disorders. While this film is a skillfully made and successful thriller, it could easily contribute to misconceptions about the true threats posed by mental illness and thus contribute to the stigma that still clings to issues surrounding mental disorders.

The National Alliance on Mental Illness indicates that approximately 1 of every 20 to 25 individuals may struggle with borderline personality disorder.

Very few have symptoms as severe as Alex, although the personal distress caused by this disorder is considerable. While Alex has many features of the borderline personality, they are confounded by her stalking behavior.

A minority of patients with borderline personalities stalk others and few do so with such extreme intensity. In fact, at least four studies that included people who had been charged with a crime found that somewhere between 4 and 15 percent of stalkers have borderline personality disorder. In one sample of patients who were not charged with crimes, 45 percent of the stalkers had the disorder. These preliminary studies provide no data suggesting that Alex's extreme, violent behavior is typical or common among borderline personalities although they do suggest that a minority of stalkers have the disorder.

BORDERLINE PERSONALITY DISORDER WITH STALKING BEHAVIOR

If Alex received a formal diagnosis of borderline personality disorder, we would not be surprised if she had many strained and failed romantic and nonromantic relationships before meeting Dan Gallagher. It is likely that her problems began when she was a young adult. Her self-image would have lacked stability, she would have acted impulsively, and her emotional responses would have been extreme and inappropriate.

Borderline personality disorder has not received as much attention from researchers as have several other serious conditions such as bipolar disorder. However, according to the director of outpatient psychiatry at Rhode Island Hospital and director of the Rhode Island Methods to Improve Diagnostic Assessment and Services project, Dr. Mark Zimmerman, it causes as much, or more, suffering and suicidal thoughts and actions as bipolar disorder. Zimmerman believes that diagnosing and treating patients with borderline personalities is just as important as detecting and treating bipolar patients.

One of the reasons borderline personality is hard to diagnose is that it is often present in people with bipolar disorder. Although the two disorders are not identical, some of their symptoms often overlap. Some mental health care providers suspect that borderline personality disorder is sometimes a risk factor for bipolar disorder.

Viewers can't tell if this applies to Alex. In addition to her childhood and medical history, Alex's diagnosis of borderline personality disorder would depend on her showing five of the following nine behaviors.

She would act desperately to avoid being abandoned by another person. It wouldn't matter if the threat of abandonment was real or imaginary. In either case, she would behave in a troublesome and frantic way to prevent the threat of abandonment she perceived.

Alex to Dan: "What happened? I woke up, you weren't here. I hate that." Also "Well, what am I supposed to do? You won't answer my calls; you change your number. I mean, I'm not gonna be ignored, Dan!" Dan then confides in his friend Jimmy about Alex: "She keeps calling the apartment. Every time Beth [his wife] answers the phone, she hangs up. I'm scared Jimmy, and I don't want to lose my family."

When involved in a relationship, she would tend to view the person as either perfect or deeply flawed. She almost certainly had a history of troubled relationships marred by her irrational, intense feelings.

Dan: "Why are you trying to hurt me?"
Alex: "I'm not trying to hurt you Dan, I love you!"
Dan: "You what?"
Alex: "I love you!"
Dan: "You don't even know me."

She would have a history of engaging in at least two dangerous and reckless behaviors. For example, she might engage in unsafe sex, use street drugs, go on spending or eating binges, associate with dangerous individuals, drive dangerously, or act impulsively in other ways that could lead her to harm herself.

Alex to Dan: "We were attracted to each other at the party, that was obvious! You're on your own for the night, that's also obvious . . . we're two adults."

She might have deliberately harmed herself or have a history of threatening or attempting to take her own life.

Alex to Dan's wife: "And you're playing happy family. Aren't you?" [Here Alex begins to cut her own leg with a large kitchen knife. Also, when Dan first tried to end the affair, Alex cut her wrists.]

Most of the time, Alex would feel as if she were empty inside.

Dan: "You're so sad. You know that, Alex? Lonely and very sad."

She may have serious problems controlling her anger and/or become angry without justification. She might, for example, argue or fight with people far more often than is normal. She might rage or have temper tantrums. It's also possible that she would feel angry most of the time.

Telephone Operator: "I'm sorry, the number's been changed to an unlisted number."

Alex: "Operator, this is a real emergency please. You need to give me that number."
Operator: "I'm sorry. We're not allowed to give out that information."
Alex: "Well f**k you!"
Operator: "My place or yours?" [Alex slams down the phone.]

When especially stressed, Alex might experience temporary but serious episodes during which she feels emotionally and/or physically detached from herself. Or, she might have temporary episodes during which she has paranoid thoughts.

Alex to Dan's wife: "And don't you think I understand what you're doing? You're trying to move him into the country . . . and you're keeping him away from me!"

For the majority of her adult life, Alex's sense of self would be very weak. She would lack a healthy and strong self-image. And she might overreact to certain events or personal interactions. She might feel unhappy, restless, anxious, sad, or irritable, for example, for a few hours up to a few days. If, during these episodes, she feels unwell or unhappy, these feelings might be interrupted by periods dominated by anger, anxiety, or even panic. However, positive feelings of happiness or contentment would rarely interrupt her generally negative feelings.

Alex: [from her tape, which Dan is listening to] "Hello, Dan. Are you surprised? This is what you force me to do. I guess you thought you'd get away with it. Well . . . you can't. 'Cause part of you is growing inside of me, and that's a fact, Dan. You'd better start learning how to deal with it. Just so you know, I feel you. I taste you. I think you. I touch you. Can you understand? Can you? I'm just asking you to acknowledge your responsibilities. I—Is that so bad? I—I don't think so. I don't think it's unreasonable. And you know, another thing—And it's that you thought you could just walk into my life, and turn it upside down, without a thought for anyone but yourself. You know what you are, Dan? You are a c**ks**king son of a bitch. I hate you. I bet you don't even like real girls, do you? Ha! You disappoint me, you f**king faggot!"

Profile #47: Mavis Gary in the Film *Young Adult*; Screenplay by Diablo Cody

I have a lot of problems.

PLOT SUMMARY

Single, divorced, 37-year-old Mavis Gary (played by Charlize Theron) is a ghostwriter living in Minneapolis. She is struggling to write the last book in her series for young adults. Her readers have lost interest and her publisher has canceled the series. This doesn't help Mavis's deeper problem. Mavis has experienced little or no true pleasure in life since she was in high school. Now, in the midst of her writing block, she learns that her high school boyfriend Buddy Slade and his wife Beth just had a baby.

This news inspires Mavis to steal Buddy from his wife. Although her book is unfinished and past its deadline, she drives to rural Minnesota, where Buddy lives and where she went to high school.

Mavis's unhealthy desperation is clear to another high school classmate she meets during her trip, Matt Freehauf (played by Patton Oswald). Mavis doesn't remember Matt until he reminds her that he was the "hate crime" kid in their school. He is the kid who was severely beaten by classmates who mistakenly thought he was gay. Matt has lasting physical injuries and needs a leg brace, but he is psychologically healthy compared to Mavis, despite his resentment at what happened to him. Although still physically attractive, Mavis is clearly as psychologically impaired as Matt is physically impaired. As her drinking buddy, Matt tries to get Mavis see how unrealistic her goals are and how important it is that she faces the reality of becoming an adult.

MAVIS'S PSYCHOLOGICAL TRAITS

Mavis appears to suffer from alcohol abuse syndrome. Also, from time to time, she pulls individual hairs from the back of her scalp. Since her teen years at least, she has suffered from a mild case of trichotillomania, a mental disorder that causes a person to have repeated, irresistible urges to pluck hair from her body. Hair pulling in Mavis's case appears to be focused rather than automatic; she does it intentionally to relieve her psychological distress.

Mavis's general outlook is cynical and bored. She is perpetually dissatisfied and unfulfilled. Mavis seems to be incapable of enjoying her life, yet she is not clinically depressed. Despite her past success as a writer, she has no sense of accomplishment and no close, stable, personal relationships. She doesn't even get pleasure from her pet dog, which she often leaves alone for long periods of time. She gets little or no fulfillment from sleeping with strangers.

Mavis has many of the traits seen in people with borderline personality disorder. In fact, she illustrates the typical dysfunction and pain associated with this condition better than the overly dramatic, violent stalker Alex does in the Hollywood thriller *Fatal Attraction*.

BORDERLINE PERSONALITY DISORDER

People like Mavis who struggle with borderline personality disorder are extremely sensitive to real or perceived threats of abandonment and rejection by others. They consequently have unstable relationships. Their problems are compounded by the difficulty they have controlling their emotions, thoughts, and actions, which can be reckless and impulsive.

Mavis acts desperately to avoid being abandoned. It doesn't matter if the threat of abandonment is real or imaginary. In either case, she behaves in a troublesome and frantic way to prevent the threat of abandonment she perceives.

Mavis: "Here's the deal: Buddy Slade and I are meant to be together. And I'm here to get him back."
Matt: "Buddy Slade. Alright. I'm pretty sure he's married with a kid on the way."
Mavis: "I'm cool with it. I mean I've got baggage too . . . "
Matt: "I would keep all of this to yourself. I would find a therapist. Talk to a professional."

Mavis's impulsivity is revealed when she packs some clothes suddenly and drives to her old hometown after she decides to steal Buddy from his wife. Mavis's behavior hints at, but never crosses, the line into stalking.

When involved in a relationship, she would tend to view the person as either perfect or deeply flawed. She may have a history of troubled relationships marred by her irrational, intense feelings.

Mavis: "Buddy, you're my moon. My stars. You're my whole galaxy."

She believes her former boyfriend still wants to be in a relationship with her. She regards him unrealistically as perfect.

She has a history of engaging in at least two dangerous and reckless behaviors. For example, she might engage in unsafe sex, use street drugs, go on spending or eating binges, associate with dangerous individuals, drive dangerously, or act impulsively in other ways that could lead her to harm herself.

Mavis jeopardizes her career and future by not taking calls from her editor and not finishing the book she was contracted to write. She also abuses alcohol. She has sex with men she sneaks away from in the morning.

Most of the time, Mavis feels as if she is empty inside.

Mavis: "It's really difficult for me to be happy."

Mavis makes a poignant admission to Matt about a problem commonly seen in people with borderline personalities.

She has serious problems controlling her anger and/or becomes angry without justification. She might, for example, argue or fight with people far more often than is normal. She might rage or have temper tantrums. It's also possible that she would feel angry most of the time.

Mavis runs into Beth, her former boyfriend's wife. The collision causes Beth to spill her drink on Mavis.

Mavis: "My God!"
Beth: "I'll get some . . . "
Mavis: "F**k you. F**k you! You f**king bitch! Oh my God . . . you should see your face. It's a joke! Are you just gonna stand there like a big lump? I love your sweater!"

For the majority of her adult life, Mavis's sense of self has been very weak. She lacks a healthy and strong self-image. And she might overreact to certain events or personal interactions. She might feel unhappy, restless, anxious, sad, or irritable, for example, for a few hours up to a few days. If, during these episodes, she feels unwell or unhappy, these feelings might be interrupted by periods dominated by anger, anxiety, or even panic. However, positive feelings of happiness or contentment would rarely interrupt her generally negative feelings.

Mavis crying to Matt: "I'm crazy! And no one loves me. You don't love me."

Mavis's interactions with Buddy and Beth reveal the extent of her troubled psychology. Her actions suggest that emotionally she has failed to grow into a mature functioning adult. Like a character in her young adult novels, she has never matured beyond adolescence. Mavis realizes that her plan to win back her married former boyfriend reflects her desperation and sadness. (In the real world, it is likely that a character with Mavis's disorder would start to despise Buddy.) Mavis manages to find consolation with Matt—for one night—before she returns to Minneapolis alone.

Profile #48: Blanche DuBois in the Play *A Streetcar Named Desire* by Tennessee Williams

I was on the verge of—lunacy, almost! So Mr. Graves—Mr. Graves is the high school superintendent—he suggested I take a leave of absence.

PLOT SUMMARY

Blanche DuBois takes a streetcar named Desire, and then transfers to one called Cemeteries and rides six blocks and gets off at Elysian Fields. That is how she arrives at her sister Stella's apartment in New Orleans.

Blanche, a former English teacher, has nowhere else to go after being forced to leave her hometown of Laurel, Mississippi, following a sexual scandal involving a student and other indiscretions. Her once plantation-owning family's assets have been squandered, but she maintains the pretense of an elite Southern belle. The pretense is not appreciated by Stella's rough husband Stanley Kowalski or his friends. During the clash between Blanche's past and present, and her struggles with her self-image, she finds no allies and receives no help, not even from Stella. Blanche's psychological fragility is completely shattered after Stanley rapes her. Her pretensions become delusions and she is led away to an asylum.

BLANCHE'S PSYCHOLOGICAL TRAITS

Blanche's over-the-top behavior suggests that she has features of histrionic personality disorder.

Tennessee Williams

Tennessee Williams said he began to write because he "found life unsatisfactory" after his parents moved from Mississippi to St. Louis, Missouri. Before he became one of America's most famous playwrights, he studied at three different universities and also spent time working for his father who owned a shoe company.

Williams wrote for years, and worked at a variety of jobs, until he achieved his first success at the age of 33 when his play *The Glass Menagerie* was produced in Chicago. When Tennessee moved to New Orleans, he fell in love with the city and used it as the location of one of his best known plays, *A Streetcar Named Desire*.

During his late 30s and 40s when his works were most popular, Williams had success with plays like *Sweet Bird of Youth*, *Cat on a Hot Tin Roof*, and the Pulitzer Prize–winning *A Streetcar Named Desire*. He also wrote a novel called *The Roman Spring of Mrs. Stone*.

Critics made Williams's 50s difficult. Some objected to the sex and violence in his past and present works. His characters dealt with alcohol abuse, mental illness, pederasty, venereal disease, and lost hope. Some people were upset by the honesty with which he addressed issues in his plays, including

The Night of the Iguana and *The Milk Train Doesn't Stop Here Any More*. Another setback came when he lost his life partner, Frank Marlowe, who died of cancer. After that tragedy, Tennessee became self-destructive and abused alcohol and other drugs. When he was 58 years old, his brother stepped in and had him hospitalized.

Williams continued writing after getting out of the hospital. He produced more plays, poems, short stories, and a novel, *Moise and the World of Reason*. His memoir, published when he was 64 years old, was honest—and like his plays—did not avoid discussing then taboo topics; he wrote about his addictions and his homosexuality. He died, sadly, in a New York City hotel room surrounded by pills and wine bottles in 1983. He will be remembered for his insights into human suffering and for his honest treatment of human weaknesses and failings in his characters and in himself.

HISTRIONIC PERSONALITY DISORDER

Individuals who have a history of excessive emotional, often theatrical, attention-seeking behavior that begins by early adulthood may be diagnosed with histrionic personality disorder if they demonstrate this behavior in different aspects of their lives and they have five or more of the following specific traits or behaviors:

Shows discomfort when not the center of attention in a gathering or situation

Blanche: "I want to be near you, got to be with somebody, I can't be alone! Because, as you must have noticed—I'm—not very well."

Blanche's need for attention makes it necessary for her to be around people. It partially explains her promiscuity after her husband's death. She is not introspective or self-reliant. She needs affirmation from others, but the benefits are always fleeting. She is also aware that recent setbacks in her life—including the death of her husband and other relatives, and her scandal-inspired exile from Laurel—have made her more vulnerable than usual. She implies that she is unwell and it is clear that her psychological health is becoming more fragile.

Interactions often involve provocative or inappropriately sexually seductive behavior.

Blanche: "Young man! Young, young, young man! Has anyone ever told you that you look like a young Prince out of the Arabian Nights?"

While waiting for Mitch, one of Stanley's friends, to arrive for a date, Blanche flirts with and kisses a youth who knocks at the door to collect payment for a newspaper subscription. Her reference to the Arabian Nights is characteristic of her theatrical outlook, manner, and speech.

Expresses shallow and quickly changing emotions

Blanche: "Yes, yes, magic! I try to give that to people. I misrepresent things to them. I don't tell the truth, I tell what ought to be truth. And if that is sinful, then let me be damned for it! Don't turn the light on!"

Misrepresenting things to people because you think that is what they should hear reflects a shallow approach to interpersonal relationships. Turning on the light will illuminate not only Blanche's fading looks, but her superficiality as well.

Consistently draws attention to oneself based on physical appearance

Blanche: "You haven't said a word about my appearance . . . I was fishing for a compliment, Stanley."

One of the reasons Stanley disrespects Blanche so much is her habit of calling attention to herself. Even though Blanche is aware her beauty is fading, her frequent references to herself show how important appearance is to her and how much her self-image is based on it.

Speech content lacks details, facts, and specific knowledge, and instead features general thoughts or feelings.

Blanche: "There are thousands of papers, stretching back over hundreds of years, affecting Belle Reve as, piece by piece, our improvident grandfathers and father and uncles and brothers exchanged the land for their epic fornications, to put it plainly!"

Stanley accuses Blanche of squandering the wealth of her family's estate and selling her family home, thus depriving her sister—Stanley's wife—of her inheritance, which, not coincidentally, is actually *his* inheritance under Louisiana law. Blanche responds by referring to "thousands of papers stretching back over hundreds of years." It's true the property was foreclosed but this nonspecific response seems like an attempt to bury the issue in a murky past. It also blames the financial losses on the "epic fornications" of her male relatives when her own, similar behavior has forced her from her hometown.

Exaggerates emotions, self-dramatizes, and acts theatrically

Blanche: "I don't want realism. I want magic!"

Blanche explains herself to Mitch, a suitor. On another occasion she says: "We are going to be very Bohemian. We are going to pretend that we are sitting in a little artists' café on the Left Bank in Paris!"

Another feature of some people with histrionic personalities is their highly suggestible natures. They are often easily influenced by people around them and their circumstances.

Overestimates the intimacy of relationships

Blanche: "Whoever you are—I have always depended on the kindness of strangers."

Even after she loses touch with reality, Blanche retains significant features of a histrionic personality. After first trying to run away and resist her transfer to an asylum, the doctor speaks kindly to her. That is enough for Blanche to depend on this stranger to provide support she never had and to give her a feeling of worth, something she has always lacked. "Yes," Blanche says, "I had many intimacies with strangers. After the death of Allan [her husband]—intimacies with strangers was all I seemed able to fill my empty heart with."

Profile #49: Dorian Gray in the Novel *The Picture of Dorian Gray* by Oscar Wilde

> The sense of his own beauty came on him like a revelation...
> ... How sad it is! I shall grow old, and horrible, and dreadful. But this picture will remain always young. It will never be older than this particular day of June ... If it were only the other way! If it were I who was to be always young, and the picture that was to grow old! For that—for that—I would give everything! Yes, there is nothing in the whole world I would not give! I would give my soul for that!

PLOT SUMMARY

Young, handsome, and wealthy, Dorian Gray is struck by his own beauty when he sees his image in an oil portrait painted by the artist Basil Hallward. He is devastated by the realization that his own beauty will be lost with age while the beauty in the painting will never fade. Dorian desperately and fervently wishes that the reverse were true. He gets his wish. He retains his youthful beauty unchanged for many years despite living a life that becomes more and more selfish, decadent, and, finally, criminal. At the same time, his portrait becomes more hideous, reflecting each act of self-indulgence and unkindness and each of his sins. In the end, Dorian destroys the portrait, causing his own destruction.

DORIAN'S PSYCHOLOGICAL TRAITS

Dorian Gray has several distinguishing psychological and personality traits. He is emotionally shallow and immature, and has an obsessive preoccupation with his physical attractiveness. His most defining trait is narcissism.

Oscar Wilde

Oscar Wilde was born in 1854 in Dublin, Ireland, to a surgeon/writer father and a political activist/poet mother. At age 24, Wilde graduated from Oxford University with a well-deserved reputation for having a quick wit and a sharp intelligence. After graduating, he wrote and edited articles for magazines. He was a lecturer and essayist, reviewing books, art exhibits, and plays. On two occasions he applied to be an Inspector of Schools in England, but he didn't get the job.

But Wilde is best known for using his considerable literary talents and the attributes he demonstrated at Oxford to succeed as a playwright; *The Importance of Being Earnest* and *Lady Windermere's Fan* are two of his best known plays. He also wrote poetry and one novel: *The Picture of Dorian Gray*, which he published when he was 37 years old. He had two children with his wife, Constance Lloyd.

In 1895, Wilde was accused of homosexuality, a crime in Great Britain at the time. (In fact, homosexuality was illegal in Great Britain until 1967. Ignorance regarding this aspect of human sexuality prevailed across the Atlantic Ocean too: The American Psychiatric Association considered homosexuality to be a "psychiatric disorder" until 1973.)

Wilde was convicted of committing homosexual acts after the last of three, very sensational trials, during which prosecutors included his authorship of *The Picture of Dorian Gray* in the evidence presented against him. The two years he spent in jail following his conviction destroyed Oscar's reputation, ruined his finances, and severely damaged him emotionally. He moved to Paris and died from an ear infection and meningitis in 1900. He was 46 years old.

The Greek mythological character Narcissus, from whom narcissism gets its name, was, like Dorian, renowned for his good looks. (The word "Dorian" historically referred to people from ancient Greece.) Like Dorian, Narcissus became obsessed with himself. In Narcissus's case, it was when he saw his reflection in a pool of water. Dorian saw his image in his portrait. The connection between the two characters is made obvious when Basil Hallward, the artist who painted Dorian's portrait, says to him: "You had leaned over the still pool of some Greek woodland and seen in the water's silent silver the marvel of your own face."

Both characters become obsessed with their beauty to such an extent that it destroys them. Narcissus wastes away looking at his reflection. Dorian lives a dissolute life, which for a time has no impact on his appearance. At the same time, his portrait—locked away in his childhood nursery—becomes uglier with each immoral act Dorian commits. Gazing at his changing portrait "He grew more and more enamored of his own beauty, more and more interested in the corruption of his own soul."

NARCISSISTIC PERSONALITY DISORDER

Dorian has several of the defining features of narcissistic personality disorder listed by the American Psychiatric Association in its *DSM-5*. He would qualify for a diagnosis of this condition if a psychiatrist or clinical psychologist determined he had at least five of the nine characteristic features of the disorder. These features reflect a pattern of grandiosity, the need for admiration, and a lack of empathy that, as in Dorian's case, show up in childhood, or in early adulthood. Key features of the narcissistic personality are listed below, along with quotes that suggest Dorian has very strong narcissistic traits.

Dorian grossly overestimates, and has an inaccurate sense of, his importance.

A person with a narcissistic personality may exaggerate his or her accomplishments, talents, and overall value. She or he may expect other people to recognize her or his superiority despite the lack of real accomplishments that would justify the demands. "There were times when it appeared to Dorian Gray that the whole of history was merely the record of his own life."

He is unrealistically preoccupied with thoughts of great power, success, intelligence, beauty, or achievements.

"A man who is master of himself can end a sorrow as easily as he can invent a pleasure. I don't want to be at the mercy of my emotions. I want to use them, to enjoy them, and to dominate them."

He believes he is extraordinary so he believes he can be appreciated only by successful, high-status individuals.

A person with narcissistic personality disorder may also want to associate exclusively with such people, people who are in the same "special class." "He had dreamed of her as a great artist, had given his love to her because he had thought her great."

He requires admiration far in excess of what most people normally expect.

"He has certainly not been paying me compliments. Perhaps that is the reason that I don't believe anything he has told me." And: "As he strolled home, smoking his cigarette, two young men in evening dress passed him. He heard one of them whisper to the other, 'That is Dorian Gray.' He remembered how pleased he used to be when he was pointed out, or stared at, or talked about."

He feels he is entitled to special treatment.

The person believes that he deserves favorable treatment beyond what others deserve, or that he deserves quick and unquestioning acceptance of his demands or expectations. "This thing that has happened does not affect me as it should. It seems to me to be simply like a wonderful ending to a wonderful play. It has all the terrible beauty of a Greek tragedy, a tragedy in which I took a great part, but by which I have not been wounded."

He uses or exploits others.

He does not hesitate to take advantage of others to get what he wants. "Through vanity he had spared her. In hypocrisy he had worn the mask of goodness. For curiosity's sake he had tried the denial of self."

He lacks empathy.

Dorian cannot or does not "feel" what others are feeling or needing. He does not identify or care about others' feelings unless he can use them to benefit himself. "Cruelty! Had he been cruel? It was the girl's fault, not his."

He envies others and/or believes others envy him.

"I am jealous of everything whose beauty does not die. I am jealous of the portrait you have painted of me. Why should it keep what I must lose?"

He behaves in an arrogant manner or has a superior attitude.

"Then she had disappointed him. She had been shallow and unworthy."

People like Dorian who have marked narcissistic traits frequently also have traits associated with other personality disorders such as borderline and histrionic personality disorders. If narcissism is a feature of several personality disorders, the question arises: "Which diagnosis is most appropriate?" In the future, it is possible that, instead of limiting diagnosis to specific disorders, psychiatrists may instead develop a system that stresses personality traits that result in problems getting along with other people, or functioning day-to-day. Using this approach, people need not receive a diagnosis of having a single personality disorder. Instead, they might receive a profile describing dysfunctional personality traits. In other words, descriptions of difficult personalities or personality problems might be as, or even more, useful than a diagnosis involving a single label referring to a specific disorder.

Profile #50: Claude Frollo in the Novel *The Hunchback of Notre Dame* by Victor Hugo

One fixed idea haunts me and pierces my brain like a red-hot iron.

PLOT SUMMARY

Esmeralda is a 16-year-old orphan girl living in Paris in 1482. She is poor with no social connections. She is, however, strikingly beautiful. Her beauty, unfortunately, attracts a variety of unworthy men. They include the shallow and insincere soldier Captain Phoebus, the unsuccessful playwright Pierre Gringoire, and the unbalanced Archdeacon Claude Frollo who is in charge of Notre Dame Cathedral. Claude's interest in Esmeralda is, sadly, nothing more than a pathological obsession. Only the deaf, hunchbacked, bell-ringer Quasimodo, who was raised by Claude, offers anything resembling true, lasting concern for Esmeralda in the form of his platonic love. Claude Frollo's obsession with the girl leads to a climax that sees both criminals and soldiers storming the sanctuary of Notre Dame Cathedral and the deaths of innocent and guilty parties alike.

CLAUDE'S PSYCHOLOGICAL TRAITS

In his youth, the priest was idealistic and generous. He cherished knowledge and showed kindness to his brother Jehan whom he raised after the death of their parents. He adopted the severely deformed Quasimodo after he was abandoned as a baby at the cathedral. He raised Quasimodo and made him the cathedral's bell-ringer. He tried to teach Quasimodo to read and write but Quasimodo's deafness, caused by deafening clanging of the giant bells he rang, prevented him from learning. Sadly, Claude's brother disappointed him just as intensely. Jehan preferred drinking and gambling to learning. Discouraged by these failures, Claude became bitter and began to study the occult. His infatuation with the beautiful street dancer Esmeralda turns into obsessive lust. He stalks her.

According to forensic psychologist J. Reid Meloy, many people who stalk others experience strong feelings of shame, sadness, and humiliation. Their response is powerful anger driven by their narcissism. Rejected by the target of their desire, they begin to demean, insult, and punish their victims. In the most tragic cases, such as Claude's stalking of Esmeralda, stalking victims can die.

OBSESSIVE LOVE

Claude: "I love you. Nothing can be more true. No fire can be fiercer than that which consumes my heart. Ah! Maiden, night and day—yes, night and day—does this deserve no pity? It is a love, torture, night and day, I tell you."

Claude cannot stop wanting or thinking about Esmeralda without feeling unbearable anxiety. He continues his obsession in an attempt to avoid the terrible anxiety that tortures him when he thinks of not having her. Obsessive love is very different from healthy love.

Psychologically healthy love affairs may begin with a period of infatuation. Partners think about each other often and can't wait to be reunited when separated. This phase of a relationship often lasts for months. Over time the obsessive nature of a healthy, new romance evolves and matures. Infatuation is replaced by contentment, respect, commitment, and appreciation of the love interest. Mature love is not possessive. Partners recognize each other as separate individuals and encourage each other to have interests outside of the relationship. This is made possible by mutual support, respect, and appreciation of a partner's individuality.

The initial feeling of being consumed with desire for someone that started this evolution to a mature relationship is appropriate if the desire is mutual. It can be pathological if it is not.

If Claude Frollo had actually been in a relationship with Esmeralda, then his jealousy and infatuation with her would clearly have been pathological. Delusional jealousy and obsessive behavior such as Claude displays are estimated to occur in less than one-tenth of 1 percent of the population.

Victor Hugo

Victor Hugo put off writing *The Hunchback of Notre Dame* several times as his publisher waited. Finally, in 1831 at the age of 29, in only four months he finished writing the historical novel that brought him fame.

Hugo was the third son of Joseph-Léopold-Sigisbert Hugo, who eventually became a general in Napoleon's army. Victor did not share his father's interest in military life. His interest was in writing. Encouraged by his mother, he began writing when he was a teenager. Later he studied law, but dropped the pursuit of that career to found a literary review and write poetry, plays, and novels. Like many students, he had little money while attending school. His memories of these times are reflected in the plight of the poverty-stricken character Marius in his famous novel *Les Misérables*.

Hugo's mother opposed his relationship with his childhood sweetheart, Adele Foucher. A year after his mother died in 1821, Victor married Adele. They eventually had five children. He also published a well-received book of poetry. And the next year he published his first novel, *Hans of Iceland*. Throughout most of the rest of his life, he was a prolific author enjoying success as a poet, playwright, and novelist.

In his mid-40s, Hugo was elected to the French Assembly and served until he was forced to flee to Belgium following a coup in 1851. He returned in 1870 when the French Republic was reconstituted. The death of his wife in 1868 and two of his sons between 1871 and 1873 affected him deeply. The sadness he felt is reflected in his writing after this time.

Many of Hugo's works reflect his liberal ideals including his concerns for the poor and for political and social justice. The French public appreciated his liberal views. Upon his death in Paris at the age of 83, he received a national funeral. After he was honored by having his body lay in state beneath the Arc de Triomphe, he was laid to rest in the Panthéon, a former church dedicated to the memory of France's greatest heroes.

STALKING BEHAVIOR

Claude: "I will have you. You will not have me for a slave; you shall have me for a master. You shall be mine. I have a den to which I will drag you. You will come, you must come with me, or I will give you up! You must die, my beauty, or be mine—be the priest's, the apostate's, the murderer's! Do you understand? Come now! Kiss me, darling! The tomb or my bed!"

Claude and Esmeralda were strangers when he became obsessed with her. They had no personal relationship. Claude stalks his victim in an attempt to have his fantasies about her become true. Furthermore, he expects Esmeralda to go along with his plans, to play the role of his lover, a role he has assigned to her despite her disdain for him.

Claude can be excluded from the ranks of a second type of stalker, the simple obsessional stalker. These individuals begin stalking people with whom they have had a previously friendly, intimate, or work relationship. Claude has several traits often seen a third type of stalker, the erotomanic stalker. He is single, with above-average intelligence, and has psychiatric problems. Although he wasn't a convicted criminal like some erotomanic stalkers, he became a criminal when he stabbed Captain Phoebus to death after he saw Esmeralda flirting with him. However, he is not an erotomanic stalker because he does not believe that Esmeralda loves him back.

Claude's unhealthy, indeed psychopathological, interest in Esmeralda is distinguished from healthy love by, among other things, the fact that she does not return his interest. When one person refuses to accept that a love interest does not reciprocate his or her feelings, but nevertheless continues to hound the victim and try to force an unwanted relationship, without regard to the other person's desires or concerns, the love has become an unhealthy romantic obsession.

Another indication that Claude is unbalanced is his inability to care about or even to consider the blatant evidence that Esmeralda wants nothing to do with him. Claude, like other people in the grip of a romantic obsession, lacks insight into the cause of his behavior and the torments that both inspires it and results from it.

As a stalker, Claude's behavior goes far beyond simple unrequited love, an experience many, and very likely most, psychologically healthy individuals have experienced, particularly during adolescence or young adulthood.

According to the definition offered by Meloy and Gothard: "Stalking is typically defined as the willful, malicious, and repeated following or harassing of another person that threatens his or her safety." Although this behavior has serious psychological implications, it is not a mental disorder by itself. (In some cases, stalking behavior can be traced to psychosis. For example, some people suffering from major depression, schizophrenia, delusional disorder, or bipolar disorder may develop erotomanic delusions, which cause them to believe they have a relationship with someone who does not know them or does not want to have anything to do with them.)

It is not uncommon to discover a history of domestic violence, antisocial personality disorder, or a criminal record in stalkers. In others, it sometimes can be attributed to one or more personality disorders such as narcissism or borderline personality disorder. (See *Fatal Attraction.*)

When the target of a stalker is a celebrity, the problem is often covered in the media when the stalker makes threats and/or is taken to court after the victim requests a restraining order or order of protection. Madonna, David Letterman, Jodie Foster, and many other well-known personalities have had, and have, stalkers. Of course, like Esmeralda, you don't have to be famous or rich to receive intrusive attention from a stalker. Most victims aren't. Claude saw Esmeralda on the street talking to Phoebus and felt overwhelming desire for her and jealousy of anyone else who might attract her attention. But, it is more common for stalker and victim to have met or have had some kind of intimate or causal relationship prior to the start of the harassment.

Profile #51: Unnamed Despot in the Poem "A Foreign Ruler" by Walter Savage Landor

He says, My reign is peace, so slays/A thousand in the dead of night.

The Poem

He says, My reign is peace, so slays
A thousand in the dead of night.
Are you all happy now? he says,
And those he leaves behind cry quite.
He swears he will have no contention,
And sets all nations by the ears;
He shouts aloud, No intervention!
Invades, and drowns them all in tears.

THE DESPOT'S PSYCHOLOGICAL TRAITS

The statements in the poem reveal the cynical, manipulative, and power-seeking behavior of a despotic ruler. His false proclamations of peaceful intentions contrast with the brutal reality of his actions.

MALIGNANT NARCISSISM

Malignant narcissism differs from narcissistic personality disorder and from the term "narcissism" as many people use it.

Narcissism in common usage refers to excessive vanity, selfishness, and a grandiose view of one's abilities and worth. Many public figures and people with influence in government and industry circles frequently have significant narcissistic traits. Psychologist Gerald M. Post, MD, who has prepared psychological profiles of foreign leaders for the CIA described those leaders as "successful narcissists."

Narcissistic personality disorder is a mental disorder described in the *DSM-5* (see the entry about Dorian Gray).

Malignant narcissism is not mentioned in the *DSM-5*, but is often used to describe dangerous people whose behavior is influenced by a constellation of traits that include narcissism, sadism, aggressiveness, and psychopathy. They are self-centered, lack empathy, and have grandiose self-images.

People with strong malignant narcissistic traits are not good at accepting criticism. Despots like Saddam Hussein, Nikolai Ceausescu, Muammar Qaddafi, Mao Tse-tung, and Joseph Stalin whose behavior and actions were consistent with this type of abnormal personality, tortured and killed many individuals who were brave or naïve enough to criticize them. The same fate awaited anyone who actually posed, or was assumed to pose, a threat to their power.

Some features of malignant narcissism are:

A lack of empathy and compassion, and little or no conscience due to extreme narcissism or self-absorption.

"Are you all happy now? he says,
And those he leaves behind cry quite."

Those left behind are the survivors of the despot's terror and atrocities. He feels nothing for his victims, their relatives, or those he spared who live in fear under his despotic rule.

No hesitation about using violent means to get what he wants.

"Invades, and drowns them all in tears."

Invading a weaker nation to increase his wealth and power is to this foreign ruler simply a logical step to achieve his goals.

Deceitful and manipulative

"He swears he will have no contention" and "He shouts aloud, No intervention!"

This foreign ruler lies to mislead his neighbors to give them a false sense of security before attacking them. Adolf Hitler demonstrated this type of behavior when he signed a nonaggression pact with the Soviet Union. Together, Germany and the Soviet Union invaded Poland in 1939. Two years later, with the nonaggression pact still in place, Hitler invaded the Soviet Union (see *Downfall*).

Cruelty and suspiciousness bordering on paranoia

" . . . slays thousand in the dead of night."

There is no way such a despot can remain in power without being highly suspicious of everyone, even family members and others close to him. He is constantly on the lookout for traitors within his own circle of associates. Saddam Hussein, for instance, declared that he could spot a traitor before his victim knew he was a traitor. As a result of this malignant narcissistic paranoia, Saddam Hussein ordered the murder of many people including advisers who opposed or criticized him. In some cases, he killed with his own hand. To protect himself from real or imagined threats, the foreign ruler of the poem does not hesitate to slaughter as many people as he feels necessary to protect himself or to achieve his goals. Joseph Stalin and Mao Tse-tung each caused the deaths of millions of their own people and they did so without remorse.

Grandiosity is another feature of the malignant narcissist. There is no explicit hint of this feature in the poem but it would be highly unusual if the foreign leader's portrait was not as widely displayed during his reign as were the portraits of Saddam, Stalin, and Mao during theirs.

Profile #52: Captain Ahab in the Novel *Moby Dick* by Herman Melville

> " . . . it was Moby Dick that dismasted me; Moby Dick that brought me to this dead stump I stand on now. Aye, aye," he shouted with a terrific, loud, animal sob, like that of a heart-stricken moose; "Aye, aye! it was that accursed white whale that razed me; made a poor pegging lubber of me forever and a day!"

PLOT SUMMARY

"Call me Ishmael," the narrator of *Moby Dick* famously introduces himself as he seeks to leave the confines of New York City for the freedom of the seas. He heads to New Bedford, Massachusetts, and signs up as a crew member on the Pequod, a whaling vessel. Although he is warned that the Pequod's captain, Ahab, is "strange," Ishmael joins the crew anyway and so embarks on a doomed expedition.

The expedition is doomed because Captain Ahab is more than "strange." He is morbidly obsessed with an elusive white whale named Moby Dick. This almost mythical creature bit off Ahab's leg and has become the focus of his all-consuming obsessive desire for revenge. Killing the white whale has become Ahab's one purpose in life.

After seeking his prey around the globe, Ahab spots Moby Dick near Japan. During the climactic battle between Ahab and the mysterious white—in a sense, blank—creature, the Pequod is destroyed. The whale wins and Ishmael alone survives to tell the tale.

CAPTAIN AHAB'S PSYCHOLOGICAL TRAITS

Ahab's vengeful preoccupation with Moby Dick, the creature that took off his leg, leaves him solitary and brooding. He experiences no pleasure, a condition called anhedonia. He does not entertain opinions that differ from his on the subject of his mission, to kill the white whale. Nevertheless, even Ahab recognizes on a deeper level that his monomaniacal obsession with his nemesis represents more than a simple all-encompassing desire to seek revenge on a "dumb animal." He recognizes that his preoccupation with the white whale extends to "whatever lies behind" the beast. Ahab's struggle is against a force or forces over which he has no control and which he cannot comprehend. Toward the end of the journey, he shows some paranoid features by not trusting his crew, even while they continue to follow his orders.

NARCISSISTIC RAGE

Psychoanalyst Heinz Kohut uses Captain Ahab as an example of a man whose life has been taken over by narcissistic rage. Narcissistic rage, according to Kohut and other psychologists, is a narcissist's response to an insult or injury that threatens the narcissist's grandiose self-image, an image some believe is founded on strong insecurities. The response to a slight provokes an all-consuming desire for revenge and a quest to correct the wrong the narcissist feels he has suffered.

Like others who exhibit narcissistic rage, Ahab is consumed by righting the wrong he has suffered. Ahab clearly sees not only injury but also insult when the whale bites off his leg. He will literally go to any lengths, travel anywhere in the world and even sacrifice others, to satisfy his need for revenge. This compulsion leaves no time or room for other concerns in his life.

This abnormal behavior is very different from more common examples of aggression in at least one profound sense. People who are not in the throes of narcissistic rage perceive the object of their aggression as someone or something who is distinct from themselves. But as Kohut points out, the narcissist who is seeking revenge sees his target "as a flaw in a narcissistically perceived reality." A narcissist's reality is that he is grandly important and truly gifted. Whatever has threatened this picture is a threat to his sense of entitlement, all that is important to him and all that he perceives himself to be. Anyone or anything that damages him seriously threatens everything he believes in. The response to such a serious threat is a narcissistic rage such as that shown by Capt. Ahab in his pursuit of Moby Dick. Kohut sees a strong self-righteous component in Ahab's behavior, as exists in all cases of narcissistic rage.

Ahab has a grandiose self-image.

"Talk not to me of blasphemy, man; I'd strike the sun if it insulted me." This is how the captain answers his crew member Starbuck's suggestion that an obsessive desire for revenge against a dumb creature might be blasphemous (and, perhaps by implication, irrational). And here is Ahab's response to some images on a coin: "look here,—three peaks as proud as Lucifer. The firm tower, that is Ahab; the volcano, that is Ahab; the Courageous, the undaunted, and victorious fowl, that, too, is Ahab; all Are Ahab."

Ahab's response to injury or insult is exaggerated to the point of pathology.

"All evil, to crazy Ahab, were visibly personified, and made practically assailable in Moby-Dick. He piled upon the whale's white hump the sum of all the general rage and hate felt by his whole race from Adam down; and then, as if his chest had been a mortar, he burst his hot heart's shell upon it." Ahab has placed all his pain associated with life itself into a creature that doesn't even know he is alive. The tormented captain has personified this pain—which he sees as his arch enemy—by naming a wild animal and declaring unremitting war on it.

Ahab's desire for revenge takes over his life, absorbing all of his time and energy.

"Aye, aye! and I'll chase him round Good Hope, and round the Horn, and round the Norway Maelstrom, and round perdition's flames before I give him up. And this is what ye have shipped for, men! to chase that white whale on both sides of land, and over all sides of earth, till he spouts black blood and rolls fin out. What say ye, men, will ye splice hands on it, now? I think ye do look brave."

Ahab cannot be easily dissuaded from seeking revenge.

"The path to my fixed purpose is laid with iron rails, whereon my soul is grooved to run. Over unsounded gorges, through the rifled hearts of mountains, under torrents' beds, unerringly I rush! Naught's an obstacle, naught's an angle to the iron way!"

Profile #53: Charlie Brown in the Comic Strip *Peanuts* by Charles Schulz

---

My anxieties have anxieties.

PLOT SUMMARY

Charlie Brown is the main character in Charles Schulz's comic strip *Peanuts*. In one sense, he represents the average person who has good times and bad. His universe consists of his neighborhood and his school populated by at least 15 other characters including his dog Snoopy, pushy, abrasive Lucy, and his good friend Linus. Sometimes Charlie Brown's discussions with these and other characters relate to his level of insecurity, which far exceeds the average. He is lonely and thoughtful, gentle and sweet, innocent and gullible. He very much would like to be more popular but his shyness and insecurity prevent him from acting on his wish. This character remains immensely popular.

CHARLIE BROWN'S PSYCHOLOGICAL TRAITS

Charlie Brown is gentle, introspective, and sometimes seems optimistic—but only sometimes. Charlie Brown also exudes insecurity. He has a poor self-image and obsesses about his shortcomings. He expects rejection by others and hesitates to interact with new people for fear of being rejected. He cannot bring himself to approach the redheaded girl he likes because he is convinced she won't return his affection.

His self-doubt and low self-esteem more than trouble him; they are the source of his discontent and they dominate his life. Therefore, they are a legitimate concern for psychological or psychiatric counseling. He seems to require more help than he gets from his frequent consultations with Lucy, who treats him as he sits in front of a lemonade stand equipped with a crudely written "Psychiatrist" sign.

Of the major personality traits, Charlie Brown rates very high on the neurotic end of the emotional stability spectrum. He also seems to have many of the features of avoidant personality disorder.

AVOIDANT PERSONALITY DISORDER

People with this disorder typically begin to have symptoms as children, which persist through adulthood. Having a history of feeling inadequate, being socially inhibited, and being extremely sensitive to negative opinions may be traced to avoidant personality disorder if four or more of the following behaviors or traits are present:

Refusal to interact with or get involved with people without a guarantee that he will be liked.

Charlie Brown: "I think I'll ask the teacher if I can move my desk next to that little redhead haired girl . . . Then, one day I can reach over and touch her hand . . . And she can look at me like I've lost my mind! Maybe I'll ask the teacher if I can move my desk out into the hallway."

Sitting at his school desk, Charlie Brown considers the prospect of approaching someone he likes but doesn't know. The redheaded girl symbolizes Charlie Brown's desire for affection, acceptance, and an idealized relationship. These desires are not unusual in people with this disorder.

Hesitation at committing or getting close to someone in an intimate way for fear of being made fun of or shamed.

Charlie Brown: "Real love is standing behind a tree so you can see her when she leaves her house. Of course it can sometimes be embarrassing. Like when you discover you've been standing on the wrong side of the tree."

Based on his past history, Charlie Brown isn't stalking the little red-haired girl. This behavior, like his daydream about moving his desk closer to hers, is as close as he can get to approaching her to establish a friendship. His fear keeps him away from her.

Worrying to the point of preoccupation about being rejected or criticized in social gatherings.

Charlie Brown: "Awkward is my specialty."

This might also be his motto.

Acting and feeling inhibited when dealing with new people or social situations due to feelings of inadequacy.

"Yes, ma'am, I'd like to buy a book of poems for this girl in my class . . . Well, she's really out of my class but we are in the same class, but I'm not in her class . . . Actually, she probably doesn't know I even exist . . . Don't cry, ma'am . . . I'll survive."

Charlie Brown's feelings of inadequacy are on display when he approaches a clerk in a bookstore. His lack of confidence is seen in his explanation about his relationship with the girl he wants to buy a present for, and in the pitiful, apologetic tone with which he explains his desire to the clerk.

Seeing himself as unappealing, socially inept, and generally inferior to other people.

Lying in bed at night, Charlie Brown recalls: "Sometimes I lie awake at night, and I ask myself, 'Is this all there is?' Then I hear a voice that says . . . 'What kind of question is that?' " And: "Sometimes I lie awake at night, and I ask, 'Where have I gone wrong?' Then a voice says to me, 'This is going to take more than one night.' "

Charlie Brown believes his list of failings is so long, it would require hours and hours to explore them all. The irony is Charlie Brown has many endearing characteristics and traits; it is his poor self-image alone that makes him ignore his strong points and emphasize his few weak points.

Avoiding jobs or work that require close or frequent contact with the public or other individuals due to fears of being rejected or criticized.

Charlie Brown is too young to work so he can't meet this criterion.

Out of fear of embarrassment, rarely taking chances participating in new activities.

Charlie Brown rarely takes chances on new activities but this might be because his life is essentially confined to school, football, and conversations with his fellow *Peanuts* characters.

Playwright Jules Pfeiffer attributed the longevity of Charlie Brown, Linus, Lucy, and other *Peanuts* characters to the fact that, like real children, they were troubled by insecurities, doubts, and anxiety. In other words, they were like us. This, in addition to the skill of creator Charles Schulz, helps explain why the comic strip was read by an estimated 355 million people in 75 countries and in 21 languages during the course of its 65-year run.

Some of Schulz's own personality traits may have contributed to Charlie Brown's experiences. Schulz was described by his biographer, Rheta Grimsley Johnson, as being frequently lonely and depressed. He also experienced panic attacks and remembered personal slights encountered years earlier. And yet his creation, hapless Charlie Brown, despite his constant failures and disappointments, nevertheless has several indicators of positive psychology. He perseveres in spite of his insecurities. And he never becomes bitter or mean.

NEUROTIC (OR EMOTIONAL INSTABILITY) PERSONALITY TRAITS

Charlie Brown: "I've developed a new philosophy. I only dread one day at a time."

Charlie Brown is a model neurotic, according to psychologist James Kaufman, PhD, an Associate Professor of Psychology at California State University of San Bernardino: "He is prone to depression and anxiety and paralyzing fits of over-analysis. Constantly worrying if he is liked or respected, he has a perpetual, usually dormant crush on the little redheaded girl, taking small joys in her foibles (like biting her pencil) that may make her more attainable. He is noted for his inability to fly a kite."

Profile #54: Adolf Hitler in the Film *Downfall*; Screenplay by Bernd Eichinger. Based on the Books *Der Untergang: Hitler und das Ende des Dritten Reiches*, by Joachim Fest, and *Bis zur Letzten Stunde*, by Traudl Junge and Melissa Müller

---

Adolf Hitler: "Who do you think you are to dare disobey an order I give?"

PLOT SUMMARY

By 1945, Germany's Nazi Führer (played by Bruno Ganz) had led his nation to devastating defeat and destruction. The war he started took as many as 80 million lives including the 6 million Jews he is responsible for killing in the Holocaust. As Hitler retreats into his bunker 55 feet beneath his Berlin headquarters, the Soviet Army pushes toward the city from the east while the Americans, British, and their allies drive toward it from the west.

Hitler alternates between unrealistic plans and hopes for defeating his enemies and raging despair at the realization that the thousand-year Reich he promised the German people is doomed. He shows signs of breaking down physically and mentally as he blames everyone but himself for his defeat, including the Jews and the German people themselves. After marrying his longtime mistress Eva Braun, Hitler escapes capture by taking cyanide and shooting himself in the head. His wife dies beside him after taking cyanide.

HITLER'S PSYCHOLOGICAL TRAITS

Adolf Hitler's reprehensible behavior has been the subject of speculation for more than 70 years. Dozens of books and thousands of articles have attempted to explain the sickening behavior of the man whom many simply dismiss as a "madman."

It is likely that the difficulty of understanding how anyone could behave like Hitler can be traced to the diversity and complex nature of his negative psychological traits, including apparent indications of narcissism, paranoia, lack of empathy, and grandiose delusions.

Many psychiatrists are convinced that Hitler showed signs of multiple mental disorders. For example, psychologists Frederick L. Coolidge and his collaborators asked five Hitler historians to complete a personality inventory using the dictator as the subject. The researchers reported their findings in a 2007 report in the journal *Individual Differences Research* titled "Understanding Madmen: A DMS-IV Assessment of Adolf Hitler." They claim that their results "support the reliability and preliminary validity of informant reports for psychological investigations of historical or contemporary figures."

Agreement about Hitler's personality and behavior among the historians was described as "moderately high." The results indicate that the dictator had features of PTSD, psychotic thinking, and paranoid schizophrenia. Furthermore, there were indications of paranoid, antisocial, narcissistic, and sadistic personality disorders.

The author of a psychological and medical biography of Hitler, psychiatrist and neurologist Dr. Fritz Redlich doesn't agree completely. In his book *Hitler:*

Diagnosis of a Destructive Prophet, Redlich acknowledges that the Nazi leader's unquestioned paranoia might be viewed as a symptom of mental disorder, but he asserts that most of Hitler's personality "functioned more than adequately." He insists that Hitler knew what he was doing and, furthermore, did it willfully, enthusiastically, and with pride despite the fact that Hitler's personality demonstrated features of paranoia, narcissism, depression, anxiety, and hypochondria.

Hitler also seems to satisfy the description of a person with malignant narcissism (see the unnamed despot in the poem "A Foreign Ruler" by Walter Savage Landor). Although it is not a disorder described in the *DSM-5*, many psychologists feel this combination of narcissism, psychopathy, aggression, and sadism is useful when describing some dangerous individuals. Despots like Hitler who have these traits seek and hold on to absolute power and will suppress and murder their countrymen to retain it. They are ruthless and often are convinced they have been specially chosen by fate (see the description of the messiah complex in this entry). Their grandiose self-images can veer close to the delusional. They lack empathy and remorse but are liable to welcome, demand, and reward flattery if they suspect no hidden threat or agenda on behalf of the flatterer. Their survival instincts are often highly developed and they will adjust their behavior to stay in power if faced with strong opposing forces. Tyrants frequently deal with real or imagined threats by torturing and/or executing their countrymen. Other historical persons who fit this picture include Saddam Hussein, Muammar Qaddafi, and Joseph Stalin.

Other syndromes and personality traits—which are not included in the *DSM*—might explain some aspects of Hitler's behavior. One—narcissistic rage—is described in this volume in the entry about Captain Ahab in *Moby Dick*. A second is called the messiah complex. The third is a defense mechanism called projection, which often appeared in Hitler's speeches and conversations.

NARCISSISTIC RAGE

Hitler: "Traitors! I've been betrayed and deceived from the very beginning! What a monstrous betrayal of the German people, but all those traitors will pay. They'll pay with their own blood. They shall drown in their own blood!" And: "Centuries will pass, but from the ruins of our cities and cultural monuments our hatred will be renewed for those who are responsible, the people to whom we owe all this: The international Jewry and its supporters."

When an insult or slight results in an overwhelming desire for revenge in a person with strong narcissistic features, the response is called narcissistic rage. Hitler leveled massive rage against the Jewish population of Europe for a variety of perceived slights directed against non-Jewish Germans. There were also suggestions of such rage when his orders were not carried out.

MESSIAH COMPLEX

Hitler: "I never attended an academy, and yet I have conquered Europe all by myself." And: "In those three decades, all my thoughts, actions and my life were dictated by my love for and loyalty to the German people."

Hitler believed he had been chosen by fate to lead the German people to a thousand-year-long period of European domination. He believed he had been chosen to rid Europe of peoples he considered undesirable, including Jews, Roma people, homosexuals, and communist and other political enemies. He saw himself as the savior of the German people and thus provides a good example of an individual with a messiah complex. Combined with narcissistic and paranoid traits, such rare individuals can cause nearly unimaginable destruction.

PROJECTION

Hitler: "The outstanding features of Polish character were cruelty and lack of moral restraint."

It is both tragic and ironic that Hitler would accuse the people of a country he invaded, conquered, and subjected to ethnic cleansing of being cruel and without moral restraint. It is a perfect example of projection.

Projection is a psychological defense mechanism a person uses to divert attention to, or deny to themselves, negative characteristics or features of their own personality by attributing them to others. The Hitler character in the film *Downfall* is based on accounts by his subordinates who shared the bunker with him. It is an accurate portrayal as they saw him. The historical Hitler demonstrated projection repeatedly in his speeches and discussions as illustrated by Hitler's actual quote above.

Profile #55: Mr. Kurtz in the Novella *Heart of Darkness* by Joseph Conrad

---

> But his soul was mad. Being alone in the wilderness, it had looked within itself, and, by Heavens! I tell you, it had gone mad.

PLOT SUMMARY

As Marlow sits on the deck of a ship anchored in the Thames River in England, waiting for the tide to change, he tells his fellow sailors a troubling tale.

Years ago, he had been hired by a company (called the Company) to pilot a steamship up the Congo River in the Belgian Congo.

After arriving in Africa from Europe, it wasn't long before he saw overworked and worn-out locals discarded and sent off to die. It was one of the first signs that the Company that hired him was exploiting and mistreating the native population as it stole their natural resources and, especially, ivory.

He waited months for the steamship he was hired to captain. During this time, he heard about an exceptional Company employee named Kurtz. Kurtz ran a station outpost deep in the jungle, far up the Congo River. Kurtz had the reputation of being an exceptionally able leader and a moral man. Based on what he heard of Kurtz's reputation, Marlow wanted to meet him.

When Marlow's ship was finally ready, he started up the river on a mission to find Kurtz, who was rumored to be ill. The journey was difficult and hazardous. The ship was attacked and its helmsman killed by a spear. When the ship finally arrived at Kurtz's station, a Russian trader, dressed oddly in multicolored clothes like a harlequin, told Marlow that Kurtz was not the man Marlow expected. Kurtz once had threatened to shoot the Russian if he wouldn't surrender the ivory he had collected. Still, the Russian was in awe of Kurtz, praising his unique insights and one-of-a-kind brilliance.

Kurtz had established himself as a godlike figure among the local peoples. They feared him and worshiped him. His camp was surrounded by heads on spikes. Kurtz had used his subjects to raid neighboring villages to steal their ivory, a prize that obsessed him.

Despite the dangers of dealing with Kurtz, who had life-and-death powers over everyone around him, Marlow managed to persuade Kurtz to board the steamer to return to the outside world. Kurtz, however, was too ill to survive the voyage. Marlow witnessed Kurtz's last moments:

> I saw on that ivory face the expression of somber pride, of ruthless power, of craven terror—of an intense and hopeless despair. Did he live his life again in every detail of desire, temptation, and surrender during that supreme moment of complete knowledge? He cried in a whisper at some image, at some vision—he cried out twice, a cry that was no more than a breath: "The horror! The horror."

KURTZ'S PSYCHOLOGICAL TRAITS

Kurtz, perhaps more than many fictional characters, is easier to understand as a symbol of a rotten-at-the-core imperialistic civilization than he is as a psychologically tormented man. His conversion in the deep jungle from an exceptional moral Company man into an immoral one is understandable from a literary standpoint but less so from a psychological one.

In reality, long-standing positive traits, including strong moral sense, competence, altruism, and a strong work ethic don't turn into negative traits like cruelty, greed, narcissism, and hunger for power without some earlier hints or indications of what lies below the surface. Such a transformation reflects the nature of European civilization and colonialism, as seen by its critics, as it stole the wealth of African colonies and exploited and abused their peoples. A literary explanation for Kurtz's psychological transformation is that his positive traits were nothing more than a veneer. The veneer of civilization fell away as he spent more time in the Congo.

If anyone ever encountered a real Kurtz, his brutal and sadistic actions after he set himself up as a god among the Africans might suggest that his personality change revealed elements he had consciously hidden from his employers and even from his fiancée whom he left in Europe and who, according to Marlow, never really knew him. Such deception in a real person would be a feature of Machiavellianism, willingness to act deceptively and unethically to gain personal advantage. Allowing oneself to be worshipped as a god almost goes beyond narcissism. And unnecessarily cruel behavior is consistent with sadism and/or psychopathy.

THE DARK TRIAD

When someone has a combination of personality traits that include strong features of narcissism, Machiavellianism, and psychopathy, he or she has what many psychologists refer to as the dark triad. When sadism is included in the profile, the term is expanded to "dark tetrad." Kurtz seems to have shown many of these traits when he abandoned his noble attributes after isolating himself from European civilization.

Narcissism

The Russian: "His ascendency was extraordinary. The camps of these people surrounded the place, and the chiefs came every day to see him. They would crawl."

Kurtz went far beyond negotiating with the local people for ivory. He dominated them and encouraged them to treat him like a special being.

Marlow: "And I wasn't arguing with a lunatic either. Believe me or not, his intelligence was perfectly clear—concentrated, it is true, upon himself with horrible intensity, yet clear."

Kurtz's concentration upon himself with "horrible intensity" is consistent with narcissism.

Marlow: "He had been absent for several months—getting himself adored, I suppose."

Kurtz's lust for ivory is accompanied by his lust for power and adoration. People with narcissistic traits need the admiration of others.

Machiavellianism

A defining feature of Machiavellianism is the manipulation of other people in unethical and cynical ways for personal gain.

Kurtz wasn't playing Company office politics when he first arrived at his remote outpost. He played on a bigger playing field than that. He manipulated the local people by making alliances with some, persuading some to follow and then to worship him, and forcing others into submission. But force alone would not have allowed him to dominate the people in his territory; he was one man. He needed other, Machiavellian methods to achieve influence and later domination. And if Kurtz was a real person, his Machiavellian traits would have been used to deceive his fellow Europeans before he set up his station.

Psychopathic Traits

Marlow: "But I want you clearly to understand that there was nothing exactly profitable in these heads being there. They only showed that Mr. Kurtz lacked restraint in the gratification of his various lusts, that there was something wanting in him —some smaller matter which, when the pressing need arose, could not be found under his magnificent eloquence."

Impulsivity ("lack of restraint"), superficial charm ("magnificent eloquence"), and callous behavior are key features of a psychopathic personality. The terrible punishments Kurtz meted out to the natives, which resulted in their heads being displayed on spikes, are consistent with sadistic ("gratification of various lusts") psychopathy. The "something wanting" in Kurtz was a conscience. At least, it was missing until Conrad gave him one on his deathbed. Having suddenly gained or regained a conscience, Kurtz realized just before he died the horror of what he had become. More profoundly, he experienced the horror of discovering that his transformation from civilized to barbaric meant he was, in Marlowe's words, "hollow at the core."

Most people with personality traits like Kurtz's are not as dangerous or as threatening as he is. Kurtz is a literary device, a symbol of an empty, corrupt civilization. People with the dark triad or tetrad of personality traits, however, do exist, and they can make life unpleasant for everyone they interact with, in or outside the Company office.

Profile #56: Felix Krull in the Unfinished Novel *Confessions of Felix Krull, Confidence Man* by Thomas Mann

Krull sees "the world and mankind as great and glorious phenomena, capable of affording such priceless satisfactions that no effort on my part could seem disproportionate to the rewards I might reap."

PLOT SUMMARY

Felix Krull proudly recalls his unconventional life when he writes his memoirs (through his creator, Thomas Mann), at age 40. He is proud of his history as a conman who gains people's trust and deceives them. He is skilled at spotting people's needs and wants, and he is particularly good at playing a role that satisfies these needs, always for his own enjoyment and advantage.

He convinces doctors he is unfit for military service by producing symptoms that disqualify him. He simultaneously convinces them that he is devastated that he cannot serve. He works as a hotel pageboy during the day and pretends to be a hotel guest at night. He is also a thief. In exchange for money, he pretends to be a nobleman and manages to play the part so well he fools all he encounters. Mann's novel is a parody that criticizes the superficiality of appearance and class in society. The character he uses to do this, Felix, is a charming, even likable, amoral "artist" whose performances reveal the superficiality of his world.

FELIX'S PSYCHOLOGICAL TRAITS

As a child Felix liked to pretend—much more so than other children—that he was someone else. His imagination offset the boredom he felt at school. As an adult, Felix is an imposter, a conman, and a petty criminal with a very high opinion of himself. He enjoys deceiving people, sometimes in innocent ways and sometimes less innocently. Like other people who successfully assume different identities to deceive for personal gain, Felix is imaginative and clever. In his memoir, he provides enough information about himself to suggest he satisfies the criteria for a diagnosis of antisocial personality disorder.

NARCISSISTIC FEATURES

Felix: "If someone accuses me of self-complacency, it is a matter of complete indifference to me, for I should have to be a fool or a hypocrite to pretend that I am of common stuff, and it is therefore in obedience to truth that I repeat that I am of the finest clay."

Felix repeatedly indicates that he has a natural superiority over others. This is one reason he uses to justify his conning lifestyle.

ANTISOCIAL PERSONALITY DISORDER

Felix has displayed an ongoing pattern of behavior that violates or disregards the rights of others. The predominant feature of his personality was apparent when he was a child and is even more apparent as an adult. These are the essential features of antisocial personality disorder.

This disorder is not the same as psychopathy, although many people and even many psychiatrists and psychologists equate the two. Psychopathy includes key features not included in the description of antisocial personality disorder: fearlessness, superficial charm, and lack of empathy, conscience, and emotional depth. Seventy-five or 80 percent of men in prison have antisocial personalities but only around 16 percent have psychopathic personalities. (Felix's superficial charm, lack of conscience, and lack of emotional depth suggest he might even have some of the features of psychopathy.)

Felix has never conformed to social norms. He does not respect the law and often violates it.

Felix: "No doubt I shall be accused of common theft. I will not deny the accusation, I will simply retreat and not confront anyone who chooses to take the paltry word into his mouth. But the word—the poor, cheap, worn-out word, which does violence to all the finer meanings of life—is one thing, and quite another the living, primeval, and absolute deed, forever shining with newness and originality."

Felix first stole some pralines when he was a child. Many children experiment with theft but soon stop. As the above quote suggests, Felix never recognized a reason to not take what he wanted when he could get away with it.

Felix is deceitful, uses alias, cons people and uses them for personal profit and pleasure.

Felix: ". . . in each disguise I assumed, I looked better and more natural than in the last."

Felix delights in his impersonations and deceptions. Although he often profits from them, he also truly enjoys the experience of fooling people. He sees himself as an artist. He can sense what people want to see in him and he has developed his innate abilities to give it to them, to present himself as they want him to be.

Felix lacks remorse for his actions.

Felix: "And in carrying out my idea another game I had long practiced was of signal service to me: that of imitating my father's handwriting."

Although he cried at his father's grave after his father took his own life following the failure of his business, Felix never felt remorse for forging his father's signature as a schoolboy nor, later in life, for deceiving people whom he misled to believe he was someone else.

Felix seems to meet more than enough criteria for a diagnosis of antisocial personality disorder. In addition to the three listed above, he also showed signs of conduct disorder as child (see Alex DeLarge in *A Clockwork Orange*), he was at least 18, and his behavior was not due to bipolar disorder or schizophrenia. Other criteria for the disorder are a history of aggressiveness, impulsivity or poor planning ability, disregard for one's own or others' safety, and consistent irresponsibility.

Profile #57: Gordon Gekko in the Film *Wall Street*; Screenplay by Stanley Weiser and Oliver Stone

He had an ethical bypass at birth.

PLOT SUMMARY

Young, ambitious stockbroker Bud Fox (played by Charlie Sheen) is dissatisfied with his routine job trying to sell stocks by making "cold calls" over the phone to prospective customers. He wants to be a Wall Street "player," someone who negotiates big deals and enjoys the big rewards that come with them. After trying for nearly two months, he finally gets an audience with the biggest player on Wall Street, corporate raider Gordon Gekko (played by Michael Douglas). Bud impresses the ruthless Gekko by giving him insider information about an airline for which his father works as a mechanic and union leader.

Impressed, Gekko mentors Bud and so brings him deeper into his world of unethical and illegal practices, the sole point of which is to make money and more money. When Gekko attempts to enact a typically greedy and unethical plan that would make millions for him but would devastate Bud's father (played by Martin Sheen) and his father's coworkers, Bud tries to outmaneuver his mentor before paying the price for his own moral and legal transgressions.

GEKKO'S PSYCHOLOGICAL TRAITS

Gekko is ruthless. He does not physically harm anyone, but he will do nearly anything—no matter how unethical or illegal—to make money. He has no empathy for the people who lose jobs or are harmed by his financial maneuverings. He has no problem breaking the law to make more money. And since he believes he never has enough money, he never stops hustling. His behavior is a good example of what some psychologists have termed "corporate" psychopathy.

It is sometimes referred to as "successful psychopathy" because the person manages to stay out of jail. (Gekko becomes less successful by the movie's end.)

"CORPORATE" PSYCHOPATHY

Psychologists Paul Babiak and Robert Hare refer to predators in the financial and business worlds as "snakes in suits." A preliminary study involving 203 corporate professionals who were screened for psychopathic traits found that nearly 4 percent placed high on the psychopathic spectrum compared to approximately 1 percent of the general population. Gordon Gekko has many of the traits that characterize corporate psychopathy.

Gordon Gekko will deceive, con, or manipulate people if it will benefit him in the long term and will not hesitate to mislead others about his true intentions by creating a facade or "psychopathic fiction" to appear friendly, dependable, or loyal.

Bud: "You f**kin' used me!"
Gekko: "Well, you're walking around blind without a cane, pal. A fool and his money are lucky enough to get together in the first place."
Bud: "But why do you need to wreck this company?"
Gekko: "Because it's wreck-able, alright!"

Gekko uses his assistant Bud to help arrange a deal and lets Bud think it will save his father's airline and the workers' jobs. Gekko instead plans to shut down the company and sell off its assets for a quick profit. For the money, Gekko manipulated Bud and deceived the airline workers.

Gekko lacks empathy and compassion.

Gekko tells an employee how to deal with the competition: "Rip their f**king throats out. Stuff 'em in your garbage compactor." And as a competitor tells him: "Not only would you sell your mother to make a deal; you'd send her COD [collect on delivery]."

He lacks a conscience.

Gekko to Bud: "Astonish me pal. New info. I don't care where or how you get it."

His actions are damaging.

Bud: "If these people lose their jobs, they got nowhere to go. My father has worked there for 24 years. I gave him my word."
Gekko: "It's all about bucks, kid. The rest is conversation."

He does not hesitate to engage in economic crimes to achieve his goals.

Gekko to his protégé: "Spread your buy orders over different accounts: you won't get caught." And, "You stop sending me information. And you start getting me some [illegal insider information]."

Gekko is a very high functioning Wall Street player with corporate or successful psychopathic traits. Psychologists studying corporate psychopathy report that often less impressive people with psychopathic traits are capable of talking their way into positions of some power. Once on the job for a while, their psychopathic behavior often leads to problems in the workplace including low worker morale and poorly executed projects. Evidently, mediocre middle managers with corporate psychopathic traits can't all be Gordon Gekkos.

Gekko does not experience emotions like most people.

Gekko to Bud's girlfriend (and his former lover): "You and I are the same, Darien. We are smart enough not to buy into the oldest myth running: love—a fiction created by people to keep them from jumping out of windows." And, "I got roasted the other night. A friend of mine asked, 'Why are we honoring this man? Are we running out of human beings?' "

Gekko's lack of morality is summed up in the movie's most famous quote: "The point is ladies and gentleman, that greed—for lack of a better word—is good. Greed is right. Greed works. Greed clarifies, cuts through and captures the essence of evolutionary spirit." Gekko, like many wealthy financial executives whose unethical behavior and greed caused the Great Recession of 2008, is convinced that this antisocial attitude with its inherent endorsement of social Darwinism is a legitimate excuse for accumulating wealth at the expense of innocent victims. An ethical person realizes that his or her actions may affect society as a whole. Ethical people act knowing that they are part of a community and have a responsibility toward it. Justifying greed as a virtue is an abdication of that responsibility.

Profile #58: Anton Chigurh in the Novel *No Country for Old Men* by Cormac McCarthy

I thought I'd never seen a person like that and it got me to wonderin if maybe he was some new kind. (Note: McCarthy writes in dialect and leaves out apostrophes and often the final "g" in verbs as indicated in the quote above and in those below.)

PLOT SUMMARY

Tom Bell has served the people of Terrell County in West Texas as their sheriff for decades after returning from World War II. Now, things are changing. South American drug smugglers are moving more drugs and more money across the border. They are also bringing a level of brutality the sheriff has never seen and has trouble understanding.

Vietnam veteran Llewellyn Moss sees proof of this new brutality while he is out hunting antelope. Llewellyn stumbles on the bloody scene of a drug deal that went wrong and he makes the mistake of taking the money he finds there, more than $2 million.

Sheriff Bell tries to help Llewellyn and his wife Carla Jean avoid the retribution sure to come from drug dealers looking for their money, but Llewellyn runs with the cash. Although Llewellyn has excellent survival skills, the Vietnam War vet has never encountered a man like Anton Chigurh, the hit man who now hunts him.

The methodical, efficient, and remorseless killer will not be stopped. His cold-blooded outlook and actions reflect a new level of evil in the country. When the chase is over, Sheriff Bell retires, convinced that this is no country for an old man.

ANTON'S PSYCHOLOGICAL TRAITS

Anton, a man in his 30s, is resourceful, goal-oriented, and driven to succeed. He also sees people as "things." He has the personality traits of an extremely rare individual; he is a classic, violent psychopath. He feels little or no emotion. He lacks empathy. He feels no remorse for his actions, violent or otherwise. His philosophy is that fate rules the universe and that he is fate's arbiter. On several occasions, he flips a coin to determine if a person will live or die by his hand.

PSYCHOPATHY

Psychopathy is a much-misunderstood personality disorder. It is characterized by a collection of different psychological traits that are grouped into three categories, according to the American Society for the Scientific Study of Psychopathy.

The first includes the expression of emotions. Psychologists refer to these as affective features. In persons with high psychopathic traits, important emotional features such as a sense of guilt, feelings of empathy, and the ability to form significant, meaningful emotional attachments to other people are largely missing.

The second defining group of traits concerns interactions with others, specifically narcissism and the ability to charm people in a deceptive and superficial manner.

The third group of traits reflects antisocial and impulsive behaviors. People with psychopathic personalities are, for instance, more likely to be reckless, to manipulate others for their own gain, and to commit other dishonest acts.

Having a psychopathic personality increases the risk that a person will be violent but does guarantee it. There are plenty of people with psychopathy who are not behind bars; researchers estimate that approximately 1 percent of the population has this type of personality. Nevertheless, the characteristic traits of psychopathy lead many of the individuals who belong to this subgroup of humanity to spend time in prison or jail. Psychological testing indicates that between 16 percent and 25 percent of prisoners are psychopathic.

In literature and in film, however, the violent aspect of psychopathy is nearly always stressed and often inaccurately. Other misconceptions about psychopathy include the belief that it is the same thing as serial killing, psychotic behavior, and mental illness. In fact, psychopathy is not the same thing as psychosis or, in legal terms, insanity. People with psychopathy have little or no empathy but they know the difference between right and wrong, they are in touch with reality—they do not hear voices or see things that aren't there—and they are rational. In other words, they are considered legally sane by the justice system. Some psychologists believe people with psychopathy have a true disorder that may someday be treated while others believe it is a personality type.

The American Psychiatric Association includes psychopathy and sociopathy under its category of antisocial personality disorder, but many scientists point out important differences between antisocial personality disorder and psychopathy. For example, antisocial personality disorder is described on the basis of behaviors and does not stress the lack of empathy and other key effective traits seen in psychopathy.

Lack of empathy and inability to form meaningful emotional relationships

"He was not hard to talk to. Called me Sheriff. But I didnt know what to say to him. What do you say to a man that by his own admission has no soul?"; "They say the eyes are the windows to the soul. I dont know what them eyes was the windows to and I guess I'd as soon not know. But there is another view of the world out there and other eyes to see it and that's where this is going."

The sheriff recalls visiting in jail another man with psychopathic traits. This man provides a preview and a warning about something worse to come in the form of Anton Chigurh.

Lack of guilt

"I have no enemies. I dont permit such a thing."

Anton kills without remorse.

Emotional deficits

"You're asking that I make myself vulnerable and that I can never do. I have only one way to live. It doesn't allow for special cases. A coin toss perhaps."

Anton Chigurh cannot feel emotional vulnerability, nor can he feel other emotions like most people.

"Chigurh shot him through the forehead and then stood watching. Watching the capillaries break up in his eyes. The light receding. Watching his own image degrade in that squandered world."

Anton does not respond emotionally to what he has done. He is only capable of viewing it as a phenomenon involving objects where others would see a human tragedy.

Reckless and manipulative behavior

"I got here the same way the coin did."

Although Anton is an efficient hit man, he does show signs of reckless behavior when he flips a coin to see if an innocent store clerk will live or die. The clerk is not a factor in his search for the money. The murder would only bring more attention from the police. Seeing himself as the arbiter of fate determined by a coin toss betrays recklessness and his desire to manipulate others for his own amusement.

Psychopathic, but not psychotic

"Do you have any notion of how goddamned crazy you are?"

Like many people, Anton's next victim has difficulty understanding the nature of psychopathy. By everyday standards, Anton's actions are "crazy," which is slang for psychotic. But the hit man has no delusions and no hallucinations, and he is rational. He knows the difference between right and wrong but does not care. He would have no valid recourse to the insanity defense if he were ever tried. But Anton doesn't need to worry about defending himself in court; at the end of the book, he walks away, injured but free, his job done.

Profile #59: Martin Burney in the Film *Sleeping with the Enemy*; Screenplay by Ronald Bass, Based on the Novel by Nancy Price

---

> I love you Laura. I can't live without you. And I won't let you live without me.

PLOT SUMMARY

Martin Burney (played by Patrick Bergin) is a wealthy investment counselor in Boston. He lives with his wife Laura (played by Julia Roberts) in a large, expensive house on the shore of Cape Cod. In the beginning of their relationship, Martin was loving and tender toward Laura. Now he is intensely, pathologically jealous. Shortly after their honeymoon, he began beating his wife when she displeased him or when he became jealous.

Laura's ordeal lasts "three years, seven months, six days." Then she carefully prepares to escape by secretly learning to swim and faking her death by drowning. She flees to the Midwest and begins to build a new life with a new identity. This life is threatened when Martin discovers her deception and tracks her down. Laura's neighbor and prospective new love interest tries to stop Martin from harming her, but Martin overpowers him. Martin is then surprised to learn he can no longer overpower his wife.

MARTIN'S PSYCHOLOGICAL TRAITS

At work, Martin is confident and competent. At home, he is controlling and abusive in his relationship with his wife. He demonstrates multiple traits common to men who batter and abuse their partners. He displays pathological jealousy, and isolating and controlling behaviors. He forces sex on his wife without regard to her interest or desire, and he insists that she "keep his home" and cater to him. He is obsessive about neatness and order in his home and extends his excessive desire for control of his surroundings to his wife's behavior.

ABUSIVE BEHAVIOR AND PATHOLOGICAL JEALOUSY

Abusive men may be charming and manipulative. They can not only convince a woman to enter into a relationship but also convince outsiders that they behave decently. Psychologists like Matthew Huss of the University of Nebraska suggests that perhaps between 15 percent and 30 percent of people like Martin are psychopathic. Also, many abusers seem to meet the criteria for narcissistic personality disorder, borderline personality disorder, or a combination of these two.

Jealousy

Martin: "When was he in here? Yesterday while I was in town?"
Laura: "Martin, I don't know the doctor."
Martin: "Sure you do. Young. Good looking. Says you've been staring at him out of the window all day."

After talking to a neighbor, a neurologist, who admired his house, Martin assumes the doctor has had sex with Laura. Laura has never seen the man. The doctor never told Martin he saw Laura in the house.

Controlling with rigid traditional views of gender roles

Laura: "Mrs. Clark called from the library. She said they could use me full time now."
Martin: "You already work three mornings a week and I support that because I know you love books. What about our home? Don't you love our home as much?"

Martin pressures Laura to severely limit ties outside of their home unless he accompanies her. He demonstrates his controlling behavior when he "suggests" that Laura wear a certain black dress for an evening out. Laura knows she must do it to avoid her husband's rage.

Violent

After falsely accusing her of being unfaithful, Martin strikes Laura and knocks her down. He asks her "Does it give you that much pleasure to humiliate me?" When she cries in pain, he shouts "Stop it!" and kicks her. "Now you'll sulk won't you?" he says "Yes, you will. You'll pout."

Isolating

Martin: "Need I remind you how I worried?"
Laura: "No. You reminded me enough when I came back."
Martin: "You're not suggesting I enjoyed that?"
Laura: "God no. That would make you a monster."

In order to see her elderly mother, Laura left without Martin's permission. When she returned home, she lied and told him she had attended her mother's funeral. Martin severely beat her for leaving without his permission.

An estimated 1.3 million women in the United States suffer from physical or psychological abuse at the hands of partners or ex-partners. Like Martin, abusers tend to believe that the abuse they inflict is justified. The Florida State University Institute for Family Violence Studies suggests that many abusers have low self-esteem, fear being alone, and lack remorse for their actions.

Profile #60: Hannibal Lecter in the Film *Silence of the Lambs*; Screenplay by Ted Tally, Based on the novel by Thomas Harris

> Oh, he's a monster. Pure psychopath. So rare to capture one alive. From a research point of view, Lecter is our most prized asset.

PLOT SUMMARY

A serial killer called "Buffalo Bill" is eluding the FBI. FBI trainee Clarice Starling (played by Jodie Foster) is selected to approach Dr. Hannibal Lecter (played by Anthony Hopkins) in prison to elicit his advice on catching the killer. Hannibal himself is a murderer, a cannibal, and an extraordinarily intelligent psychiatrist. Clarice's superiors believe her combination of beauty, innocence, and intelligence will appeal to the psychopathic Hannibal Lecter. They are correct. Hannibal is intrigued by the young trainee. He insults, teases, manipulates, and tries to charm her while flaunting his snobbish intelligence. He causes the authorities and Clarice nearly as much trouble as "Buffalo Bill." In the end, one killer is neutralized and one saunters away.

HANNIBAL LECTER'S PSYCHOLOGICAL TRAITS

Hannibal is well-educated, erudite, sophisticated, and charming. He had a successful career as a psychiatrist and traveled in rich social circles. He did not hesitate to kill anyone who he felt deserved death. And then he prepared gourmet meals using his victim's organs as main courses. He is now confined to an institution for the criminally insane after being convicted of murder. Hannibal, however, is not psychotic or legally insane. Rather, he is in touch with reality and knows the difference between right and wrong.

"ELITE PSYCHOPATHY" WITH CANNIBALISM

His superficial charm, manipulative nature, and lack of empathy, remorse, and meaningful personal relationships all are consistent with psychopathy (see Anton Chigurh in *No Country for Old Men*). But Hannibal's version of psychopathy comes with a distinct Hollywood twist.

Criminal psychopaths as vicious, violent, and resourceful as Hannibal are more than rare; they are virtually nonexistent. No forensic psychologist or psychiatrist has ever come face-to-face with such an intelligent, refined professional with Hannibal's off-the-scale psychopathy ratings. The character is intriguing and skillfully portrayed by an excellent actor, but he is essentially a movie supervillain, a mythic evil personality. Every known real psychopathic killer is far less impressive and competent than Hannibal. It is even unlikely that there is a person like Hannibal who has managed not to get caught.

Lack of remorse and lack of emotional response

Psychiatrist: "The doctors managed to reset her jaw more or less. Saved one of her eyes. His pulse never got above 85, even when he ate her tongue."

Hannibal has never shown or felt remorse for his crimes, including this one during which he attacked a nurse who was examining him. His relatively low pulse rate during the assault—he was being monitored when he managed to release his restraints and attack—is consistent with multiple reports that people with psychopathy have lower-than-average resting heart rates. They don't feel emotions the way an estimated 99 percent of the population do, and this may be reflected in their physiology. Another example is the small but detectable difference in their bodies' response to a looming or threatening shock; they don't perspire as much as most people when anticipating the shock.

Cannibalism

Hannibal: "A census taker once tried to test me. I ate his liver with some fava beans and a nice chianti."

Psychologists cannot satisfactorily explain why some people kill in order to eat their victims. In some cases, it can be attributed to psychosis. But nonpsychotic individuals, like Hannibal, also engage in cannibalism. Some psychologists believe past trauma is a factor, but fortunately not everyone who has been traumatized turns to cannibalism. Hannibal was traumatized as a child during World War II and exposed to cannibalism during the trauma. In other cases, it might be a paraphilia, that is, the person may be sexually aroused by the forbidden practice. The thrill of the forbidden may also become addictive for some people susceptible to this behavior. Any of these reasons, except psychosis, might explain Hannibal's dining preferences. Cannibalism is nevertheless *not* a characteristic feature of psychopathy.

Superior intelligence and sophistication

Hannibal: "First principles, Clarice. Simplicity. Read Marcus Aurelius. Of each particular thing ask: what is it in itself? What is its nature? What does he do, this man you seek?"

Clarice eventually persuades Hannibal to help her discover the identity of "Buffalo Bill" after she agrees to share personal details about her past. The doctor has extraordinary, Sherlock Holmes–like skills reading people and deducing facts about their motivations and lives. Here he profiles Clarice during their first meeting: "You know what you look like to me, with your good bag and your cheap shoes? You look like a rube. A well-scrubbed, hustling rube with a little taste. Good nutrition's given you some length of bone, but you're not more than one generation from poor white trash, are you, Agent Starling? And that accent you've tried so desperately to shed: pure West Virginia."

When asked what Hannibal is, Clarice answers: "They don't have a name for what he is." Thirteen years after Hannibal made his appearance on the screen in 1991, forensic psychiatrists Samuel Leistedt and Paul Linkowski of the Erasme Academic Hospital in Brussels, Belgium, proposed a name for what he is: an " 'elite psychopath,' or a psychopath exhibiting exaggerated levels of intelligence, sophisticated manners, and cunning, sometimes up to super-human and super-mediatized levels. Doctor Hannibal Lecter is probably one of the best examples of this type of unrealistic but sensational character."

Profile #61: Livia Soprano in the Television Series *The Sopranos*, Created by David Chase

An almost mystical ability to wreak havoc...

PLOT SUMMARY

New Jersey organized crime figure Tony Soprano arranges for his mother Livia to move to a nursing home when she is unable to care for herself. With no need for the house she lived in, Tony sells it. Livia deeply resents Tony for taking these steps. "Nobody dumped him in the glue factory and sold his house out from underneath him," she complains.

Later, she skillfully manipulates her brother-in-law, Junior, the titular head of Tony's Mafia family, by "letting slip" during a casual conversation that Tony has had several secret meetings with rival Mafia leaders while visiting her nursing home. She knows Junior will view these meetings as a threat to his dominance. She also knows that the information she is leaking will put her son in danger.

LIVIA'S PSYCHOLOGICAL TRAITS

Livia is expert at inducing guilt in other people and portraying herself as a victim of their supposed selfishness and inconsideration. She represents herself as harmless, unappreciated, and victimized. She cannot establish close personal relationships with other people, including members of her own family.

Tony's psychiatrist, Dr. Melfi, tells Tony that his mother very likely has borderline personality disorder. She bases her suspicion on Tony's tales about Livia's behavior during his childhood and on Livia's highly manipulative behavior.

Psychiatrist Glen O. Gabbard, the author of *The Psychology of the Sopranos*, believes that "this diagnosis might actually be charitable because Livia is much closer to being a true psychopath than Tony." For example, Tony remembers her threatening him by holding a fork near his eye when he was a child.

BORDERLINE PERSONALITY DISORDER

People with borderline personalities are typically dissatisfied and unhappy. Their distorted self-image negatively affects their interactions with others. While their relationships are intense, they are also highly unstable. They can be extremely emotional, needy, and impulsive. Symptoms include extreme fear of being abandoned; history of unstable intense relationships; wild mood swings; shifts in self-image, beliefs, and goals; feelings of emptiness and uncalled for expressions of bitterness, sarcasm, or intense anger. Livia Soprano does indeed have some of these traits (compare to Alex in *Fatal Attraction* and Mavis in *Young Adult*).

Livia: "Who says everything has a purpose? The world's a jungle. You want my advice. Anthony, don't expect happiness. You won't get it. People let you down. I won't mention any names. But in the end you die in your own arms . . . It's all a big nothing. What makes you think you're so special?"

Livia shares her outlook on life with her grandson Anthony. We see her bitterness and anger and we also gain insight into her lack of feeling for her grandson. She cares nothing about his development and psychological health. She is exclusively concerned about her own feelings of disappointment in life.

Poor self-image, fear of abandonment, unstable relationships

Livia: "He's talking about his mother, that's what he's doing. Sure, he talks about me and complains. I did this. I did that. I handed over my life to my children on a silver platter. And this is how he repays me."

Livia reacts to the news that her son, Tony, is seeing a psychiatrist. She expresses no concern for Tony, who might be the suffering and in need of help. She is concerned only about herself. Livia's reaction also is consistent with a fear of abandonment; if Tony establishes a relationship with his psychiatrist, he may be less inclined to interact with her.

PSYCHOPATHIC TRAITS

The Society for the Scientific Study of Psychopathy defines "psychopathy" as

> A constellation of traits that comprises affective features, interpersonal features, as well as impulsive and antisocial behaviors. The affective features include lack of guilt, empathy, and deep emotional attachments to others; the interpersonal features include narcissism and superficial charm; and the impulsive and antisocial behaviors include dishonesty, manipulativeness, and reckless risk-taking. Although psychopathy is a risk factor for physical aggression, it is by no means synonymous with it. In contrast to individuals with psychotic disorders, most psychopaths are in touch with reality and seemingly rational. Psychopathic individuals are found at elevated rates in prisons and jails, but can be found in community settings as well.

Psychopathy should not be confused with antisocial personality disorder (see Felix Krull in *Confessions of Felix Krull*), serial killing, psychosis, violence, and a generalized concept of mental illness (compare with Gordon Gekko in *Wall Street*, Anton Chigurh in *No Country for Old Men*, Hannibal Lecter in *Silence of the Lambs*). Livia's psychopathic traits include manipulation, lack of empathy, lack of remorse, lack of true, deep emotional attachments, and antisocial behavior, as demonstrated by her willingness to have her son killed.

Manipulative and antisocial behavior

Junior: "If this is true, Livia, you know what, I, I mean—I'm the boss for Chrissake! If I don't act, blood or no—I have to."

Livia: "Oh God! What, what did I say now? I suppose I should've just kept my mouth shut, like a mute. And then everyone would've been happy."

Livia deliberately drops hints that her son Tony is conspiring against the nominal head of his Mafia family, Uncle Junior. Livia is manipulating Junior into killing her son. The assassination attempt fails. When Livia sees a news report about the attempt, she acts surprised. "How could this happen?" she asks innocently.

Lack of empathy

Livia: "But little babies are animals. They're no different from dogs."

Livia shares her views on rearing children. It reveals her inability to relate to others, even to infants, as fellow human beings. Tony recalls that his mother once threatened to smother her children if her husband, Johnny, relocated the family from New Jersey to Las Vegas.

Lack of deep emotional attachments

Livia: "I suppose now you're not going to kiss me. You're cruel. That's what you are."

Livia cries after an argument with Tony. Frustrated, Tony storms out of the nursing home and trips on the stairs going down. He looks back and sees Livia interrupt her sobbing. She smiles with victory. Then immediately she resumes sobbing. She is faking her distress. Livia feels no emotional attachment to Tony or to any of her other relatives.

The combination of borderline traits with its pattern of unstable relationships, bitter outlook, and severe fears of abandonment combined with the lack of conscience that characterizes psychopathy makes Livia Soprano a memorable and fascinating character illustrating an extreme combination of personality disorders.

Paraphilic Disorders

Profile #62: Jean-Jacques Rousseau in His Memoir *The Confessions of Jean-Jacques Rousseau*

The foolish pleasure I took in displaying it before their eyes cannot be described.

SUMMARY

A political philosopher and novelist, Jean-Jacques Rousseau began writing his memoir with the intention of hiding nothing, no matter how embarrassing or unflattering. He succeeded, and his *Confessions* introduced to the literary world a new way of writing about oneself. Jean-Jacques was less concerned about documenting the historical details and dates of each event in his life than he was about capturing the effect they had on his feelings and their importance to him personally. This emphasis on complete honesty, with his acknowledgment that memory is not perfect, influenced how people wrote and how they evaluated literature for generations after the memoir's publication in 1782, four years after his death.

JEAN-JACQUES'S PSYCHOLOGICAL TRAITS

Jean-Jacques's mother died during childbirth and his father was forced to flee their home in Geneva to avoid jail. Just 16 years old, Jean-Jacques left Geneva and managed to survive on his own until he reached France.

He was convinced that progress associated with modern civilization corrupted people who would otherwise be good. Perhaps without realizing it, he demonstrated this personally by abandoning the five children he had with his wife Thérèse Levasseur. He dropped all of them off at a foundling hospital.

His views attracted much controversy, which he may have welcomed; he appeared to have "something of a persecution-complex," according to Professor Robert Garner and his coauthors of the textbook *Introduction to Politics*.

As a teenager, Jean-Jacques displayed a paraphilic behavior, that is, he received sexual pleasure by engaging in a practice that his culture viewed as abnormal. For a time, Jean-Jacques had exhibitionistic disorder.

EXHIBITIONISTIC DISORDER

People who think about exposing their genitals to unsuspecting strangers in order to achieve sexual satisfaction or pleasure have exhibitionistic interests. If they act on this need, or if their interest in this behavior distresses them, they may have exhibitionistic disorder. This is determined by two criteria.

Repeatedly being sexually aroused over a six-month period by thought, urges, or acts involving exposure of one's genitals to unwilling people, usually strangers

"My agitation became so strong that, being unable to satisfy my desires, I excited them by the most extravagant behavior. I hunted dark alleys and hidden retreats, where I might be able to expose myself to women in the condition in which I should have liked to have been in their company."

Jean-Jacques's urge to expose himself to unsuspecting women is clearly documented in his memoir.

Acting on sexual urges involving exhibitionism or being distressed by the urges

"One day, I took up my position at the bottom of the court where there was a well, from which the girls of the house were in the habit of fetching water . . . This adventure, without having the consequences which I dreaded, nevertheless made me careful for a long time."

The future philosopher repeatedly exposed himself on the streets to unsuspecting women. On one occasion he was chased down by some women in the company of a man armed with a sword. After being cornered, Jean-Jacques claimed that he was from a good family, but had brain damage and had run away from home. The man let him go. It's not clear if Jean-Jacques resolved to be more careful when exposing himself or if he was more careful by limiting or suspending his paraphilic behavior.

There is no age limit for a diagnosis of exhibitionistic disorder. Like many males, Jean-Jacques's urges began in adolescence; he was between the ages of 16 and 19. His actions appear to have gone beyond normal adolescent sexual curiosity but they decreased with age, something that has been observed in other people with the disorder.

Profile #63: Frank Alpine in the Novel *The Assistant* by Bernard Malamud

---

> He remembered with regret and strange sadness how often he had wished for better control over himself, and how little of it he had achieved.

PLOT SUMMARY

Morris Bober and his Brooklyn grocery store are failing. He and his wife Ida struggle to keep their unprofitable store afloat during what should be their retirement years. They depend on the income their daughter Helen earns as a secretary to support their family.

Morris's situation worsens when he is beaten during a robbery. During his recovery, a drifter named Frank Alpine volunteers to work at his store despite Ida's doubts and dislike for the stranger. Morris, however, is much more trusting than Ida and sees good in people where Ida sees threats. As he recovers from his injuries, Morris accepts Frank's offer to work for free as he learns the business. He lets Frank live in the basement, and later in an apartment above the store. He is rewarded by Frank's hard work and cheerful personality, which attracts more customers. He does not know that Frank steals from the cash register and spies on his daughter. Even before he volunteered, Frank was more involved in Morris's life then the trusting grocer could ever have suspected.

Frank wants to be good, but struggles against his very ingrained desires for money and his unhealthy interest in Helen, whom he lusts after but wants to love. Eventually Morris catches Frank stealing and regretfully bans him from the store. Desperate to change, Frank helps Morris in other ways and even saves the old man's life. Despite the harm Frank does to Morris's family, Morris's example of humility and goodness eventually help Frank come closer to becoming the person he struggles to be. In time, he replaces Morris after the old man dies, not long after shoveling snow in front of his grocery store. Frank continues the struggle to make the store profitable and to support Helen, emotionally and financially.

FRANK'S PSYCHOLOGICAL TRAITS

Frank enters the story with many antisocial traits including serious disregard for social norms illustrated by robbery and theft. Later he commits rape. From the first time he sees Helen, he demonstrates voyeuristic behavior. He does not, however, have a psychopathic personality. He has a conscience. He feels empathy. And he feels remorse. He doesn't want to be antisocial and strives to overcome his criminal inclinations.

VOYEURISTIC DISORDER

One defining feature of voyeuristic disorder is experiencing sexual arousal by spying on someone without his or her knowledge when that person is partially clothed, unclothed, or engaged in a sexual activity. It doesn't matter if the person denies experiencing sexual arousal if there is proof that the person has engaged in such behavior. If, however, a person admits to having voyeuristic urges but does not act on them and experiences no psychological stress because of them, then the diagnosis does not apply. This does not describe Frank. He acts on his voyeuristic urges, and they cause him to feel guilt, anxiety, and shame. Frank satisfies the three diagnostic criteria for this disorder:

Frank repeatedly experiences intense sexual arousal by spying on Helen as she undresses or is naked. This behavior must have been going on for at least half a year and could involve actual observation (as it does in Frank's case), urges, or fantasies.

"But then he took to doing things he had promised himself he never would again. He did them with dread of what he would do next. He climbed up the air shaft to spy on Helen in the bathroom. Twice he saw her disrobe . . . He swore to himself that he would never spy on her again, but he did."

If Frank only had fantasies or sexual urges to spy on Helen but was able to resist them, he would still meet this criterion for a diagnosis of voyeuristic disorder because his behavior troubles him considerably. But Frank acts on his sexual urge to observe an unsuspecting person and so clearly meets the second criterion.

"The girl was in his mind a lot. He couldn't help it, imagined seeing her in the things that were hanging on the line—he had always had a good imagination. He pictured her as she came down the stairs in the morning; also saw himself standing in the hall after she came home, watching her skirts go flying as she ran up the stairs." And: "Leaning forward, though not too far, he could see through the uncurtained crossed sash window into the old-fashioned bathroom. He thought she would stand there forever, but at last she unzippered her housecoat, stepping out of it. He felt a throb of pain at her nakedness, an overwhelming desire to love her . . . Her body was young, soft, lovely, the breasts like small birds in flight, her ass like a flower . . . He felt greedy as he gazed, all eyes at a banquet, hungry so long as he must look."

Frank is over the age of 18.

Morris: "You are young yet."
Frank: "Twenty-five," he said bitterly.
Morris: "You look older."
Frank: "I feel old—damn old."

Profile #64: A Man in the Short Story "An Encounter" in *Dubliners* by James Joyce

> In my heart I thought that what he said about boys and sweethearts was reasonable. But I distilled the words in his mouth and I wondered why he shivered once or twice as if he feared something or felt a sudden chill.

PLOT SUMMARY

The young narrator is bored with the routine of school, the routine of playing "cowboys and Indians" with classmates, and the routine of his life in Ireland. Seeking excitement, he convinces two of his friends, Leo and Mahony, to skip school with him and explore the streets of Dublin. Leo doesn't show up at the rendezvous point the next morning, but the narrator and Mahony set off on their adventure.

After wandering for a while they rest in an open field. They are alone until an older man approaches them. The seedy figure walks past them, then slowly turns back toward them, greets them, and begins to talk about innocent things: books he enjoys and childhood experiences. Then he asks them about girlfriends and talks about girls. Evidently excited by his own talk, the disturbing stranger rises and walks to the end of the field. Mahony expresses his dismay and shock when the man exposes himself.

The narrator suggests to his schoolmate that they call each other Smith and Murphy, instead of their real names, for their safety. When the man returns, Mahony gets up to chase a cat but the narrator is unsure about what to do. He stays seated, looking down at the grass.

The man resumes talking and his topics become more and more troubling. It culminates in the declaration that any boy who talks to a girl should be whipped and that he would very much like to do the whipping. Finally, the narrator stands. He yells for "Murphy," and Mahony runs toward him.

THE MAN'S PSYCHOLOGICAL TRAITS

We don't know how often the man in Joyce's story engages in the type of behavior he displays on the day the boys play hooky, but his conversation and behavior indicate he has paraphilic interests and may possibly have paraphilic disorders. People with paraphilia are sexually excited by acts that go against what most people consider healthy and normal. During the brief encounter with the boys, he displays pedophilic interest, interest in sexual sadism, and exhibitionistic behavior. Comorbidity, or having more than one disorder such as paraphilic disorders, is not unusual.

PEDOPHILIC INTERESTS

"He began to speak to us about girls, saying what nice soft hair they had and how soft their hands were and how all girls were not so good as they seem to be if one only knew. There was nothing he liked, he said, so much as looking at a nice young girl, at her nice white hands and her beautiful soft hair. He gave me the impression that he was repeating something which he had learned by heart or that, magnetized by some words of his own mouth, his mind was slowly circling round and round in the same orbit. At times he spoke as if he were simply alluding to some fact that everybody knew, and at times he lowered his voice and spoke mysteriously as if he were telling us something secret which he did not wish others to overhear."

The man's conversation clearly indicates that he has a sexual interest in children. People 16 years or older who are sexually excited by young children—usually under age 13—may be diagnosed with pedophilic disorder (see Humbert Humbert in *Lolita*).

Interestingly, this character fits the stereotypical image some people still have when they imagine people with this disorder: creepy, unkempt, old men hanging around schools, playgrounds, and other public places where prepubescent children are found. But as Thomas G. Plante, PhD, a Santa Clara University professor of psychology, explained in an article in the *Washington Post*: "Pedophiles come in all shapes and sizes and from all walks of life. Some are rich and others poor; some are highly educated while others aren't; some are very socially skilled and delightful conversationalists and some more reticent. So often we hear that people would never in a million years expect so-and-so to harm children, be a pedophile or engage in child pornography because they're charming, clean cut, fun to be around, successful in their careers, have a nice family life, and so forth. We wonder how such a winner could be a pedophile."

Unlike Joyce's stranger, most—8 out of 10—people with pedophilic disorder know the children they victimize. They are frequently relatives.

EXHIBITIONISTIC BEHAVIOR

"After a long while his monologue paused. He stood up slowly, saying that he had to leave us for a minute or so, a few minutes, and, without changing the direction of my gaze, I saw him walking slowly away from us towards the near end of the field. We remained silent when he had gone. After a silence of a few minutes I heard Mahony exclaim:

'I say! Look at what he's doing!'

As I neither answered nor raised my eyes Mahony exclaimed again:

'I say . . . He's a queer old josser!' "

The man apparently became sexually excited during his monologue and exposed himself or performed an obscene act when standing in view of the two boys.

INTEREST IN SEXUAL SADISM

"He described to me how he would whip such a boy as if he were unfolding some elaborate mystery. He would love that, he said, better than anything in this world; in his voice, as he led me monotonously through the mystery, grew almost affectionate and seem to plead with me that I should understand him."

There is much misunderstanding about pedophilia. Although many people use the term "pedophiles" to describe people who victimize teens, this is technically inaccurate. Pedophile victims are aged 13 or younger. Sex crimes against teens are much more common than crimes against preteens, according to Plante. For instance, 9 out of 10 victims of sexual abuse committed by Catholic clergy members were teens, not preteens, Plante reports in the book *Sexual Abuse in the Catholic Church: A Decade of Crisis, 2002–2012.*

Profile #65: Frank Booth in the Film *Blue Velvet*; Screenplay by David Lynch

---

Frank . . . is a very sick and dangerous man.

PLOT SUMMARY

This dark, highly disturbing tale begins when Jeffrey Beaumont, a naïve and innocent college student (played by Kyle MacLachlan), finds a severed human ear in a vacant lot near a nice neighborhood in a clean, peaceful, and apparently wholesome middle-class American town. Jeffrey reports his bizarre find to the police. He becomes impatient with the slow progress the police make with their investigation. Jeffrey and a police detective's daughter (played by Laura Dern) decide to investigate the case of the severed ear on their own. Their investigation leads Jeffrey to discover that there is a reverse side to the middle-class life he has always known, a side that is hidden, twisted, and repulsive.

The center of this evil is a perverse, cruel, sadistic, obscenity-spouting, drug-dealing, blackmailing, and generally depraved man named Frank Booth (played by Dennis Hopper). Frank has kidnapped the husband and child of Dorothy

Vallens, a nightclub singer (played by Isabella Rossellini), and forces her into sexual slavery. As the nightmarish plot unfolds, it is clear that the innocent Jeffrey and the depraved Frank Booth represent two opposing sides of life, each struggling to prevail despite the presence of the other.

FRANK'S PSYCHOLOGICAL TRAITS

Frank is a blackmailing criminal with strong sadistic, psychopathic traits. He lacks empathy and compassion. He is controlling and shows no sign of remorse for any of his actions. By abusing and forcing his unwilling victim to satisfy his sexual urges, he demonstrates several features characteristic of sexual sadism disorder.

SEXUAL SADISM DISORDER

Jeffrey Beaumont asks "Why are there people like Frank?" No one can answer definitively. Sexual sadism is poorly understood. There has been little research on it compared to other disorders, so we don't know much about why or how it develops. As Jeffrey Beaumont observes: "It's a strange world."

Two criteria lead to a diagnosis of this disorder:

Frank has repeatedly been sexually aroused by the suffering of a victim over the course of at least half a year. This criterion can also be satisfied if a person experiences strong sexual arousal by watching or fantasizing about the suffering of a victim. The suffering can be physical or psychological.

Frank satisfies this criterion by kidnapping Dorothy Vallens's family and forcing Dorothy into sexual slavery for his own pleasure. Furthermore, he constantly demeans Dorothy; for example,

Dorothy: "Hello, baby."
Frank: "Shut up! It's Daddy, you s**thead! Where's my bourbon? Can't you f**king remember anything?"

Frank acts on his sexual urges with an unwilling or coerced partner, someone who does not consent with freewill. (This criterion could also be satisfied if a person is distressed because his sexual fantasies or preoccupations involved harming or producing suffering in a victim.)

Frank: "Baby wants to f**k! Get ready to f**k. You f**ker's f**ker. You f**ker. Don't you f**kin' look at me! Baby wants blue velvet . . . Don't f**kin' look at me. Don't f**kin' look at me. Don't you look at me. Daddy's coming. Daddy's coming home. Don't you f**kin' look at me. Daddy's coming home . . . Don't you f**kin' look at me!"

Profile #66: Humbert Humbert in the Novel *Lolita* by Vladimir Nabokov

> I was consumed by a hell-furnace of localized lust for every passing nymphet whom as a law-abiding poltroon I never dared approach.

PLOT SUMMARY

Lolita has become a modern classic, in part, by humanizing a sad character that many would consider a monster. Middle-aged, British expatriate professor of literature Humbert Humbert is obsessed with Lolita, the 12-year-old daughter of his landlady. The account of Humbert's obsession is obviously disturbing, but, owing to the author's skill, it also manages to make readers see the abuser as a pitiful, doomed human being.

Few writers could use an adult protagonist's sexual desire for an underaged girl as a plot for a successful and critically acclaimed novel. This finely crafted, post–World War II road novel begins with an introduction by fictional psychologist John Ray Jr., PhD. Ray explains that he received a manuscript, titled *Lolita, or the Confession of a White Widowed Male*, from a lawyer who represented its author. The author of the manuscript, who referred to himself as Humbert Humbert, died awaiting trial for murder. In his own words, Humbert describes his obsession with 12-year-old Dolores "Lolita" Haze, his former landlady's daughter and, later, his stepdaughter. Ray offers the account as an instructive case study of a psychologically abnormal character.

In learned, articulate, and elegant style, Humbert's account begins with the loss he suffered as a 13-year-old when his first love, 12-year-old Annabel Leigh, dies of typhus only four months after they meet. Humbert never recovers from the loss psychologically.

Humbert supports himself working as an unskilled laborer, is treated for a time in a mental institution, and later marries an age-appropriate woman. The marriage fails. Humbert is forever sexually attracted to girls the age of his first love, girls who appear—in his eyes—to be aware of their attractiveness.

Humbert immigrates to the United States. He teaches for a while and works on a book about French literature, but his mental health declines and he spends several years in different sanitariums. He easily misleads his psychotherapists, and in time manages to get a job teaching at a college in a small New England town. He rents a room in Charlotte Haze's house. Charlotte is a widow and the mother of preteen Dolores, aka Lolita. Charlotte is attracted to Humbert and has no idea that Humbert is infatuated with her daughter. Humbert describes his infatuation in detail in his private diary, which also documents his disdain for Charlotte.

Afraid of losing contact with Lolita, Humbert marries Charlotte. But Charlotte finds his diary and discovers his true feelings about her and her daughter. Charlotte confronts him. She does not believe his denial and runs out of the house straight into the path of a passing automobile. She dies instantly. Lolita, it seems to Humbert, is finally his.

He collects her from summer camp and begins a long road trip with her. After two years, he gets another teaching position in another eastern college. He teaches while Lolita attends a girl's school. As Lolita gets more involved with the school's extracurricular and social activities, Humbert becomes suspicious and jealous.

Humbert's doomed and desperate quest to retain control of Lolita is challenged not only by boys her own age but also by another devious pedophile named Clare Quilty, a playwright who lures her away. Humbert's attempts to bring her back into his life ends years later in tragedy, but not before he realizes how much he has harmed Lolita.

HUMBERT'S PSYCHOLOGICAL TRAITS

Humbert is introverted, intelligent, and bookish. He is snobbish and disdainful of American culture. At first glance, he does not appear different from many other middle-class college professors. He does, however, move through life with an air of general dissatisfaction and sadness, which is most certainly related to

Vladimir Nabokov

As a child in St. Petersburg, Russia, where he was born in 1899, Nabokov enjoyed a privileged life in an aristocratic family. His family was well known and well-off. He attended a good school, learned Russian, French, and English, and read widely.

Nabokov fled Russia in 1917 when the Bolsheviks overthrew the Czar and took over the country. He enrolled at Trinity College, Cambridge, and graduated at age 23, having studied biology, literature, and languages. He lived in Europe for the next 18 years. When Nazi anti-Semitism became an obvious threat, he moved first to Paris and then to the United States.

Nabokov wrote a total of nine novels in Russian, but after he moved to the United States, he wrote in English while teaching at several universities including Harvard and Cornell. He published *Lolita* in 1955 and became widely known. Although he regretted having to give up writing in Russian, he became a famous American author. Besides his best known work, *Lolita*, he wrote *Invitation to a Beheading*, *The Real Life of Sebastian Knight*, *Pnin*, *The Defense*, *The Gift*, *Ada*, *Pale Fire*, and his memoir *Speak, Memory*. In addition to his writing, he had an interest in butterflies, which led him to become a respected lepidopterist. He was also well known for his interest in chess.

Nabokov died in 1977 in Switzerland.

his troubled childhood. It is his sexual interest in very young girls, and his acting on that interest, that makes it clear that he has a paraphilic disorder.

Two conditions may lead to a diagnosis of a paraphilic disorder. First, it may be diagnosed when a person's sexual interests cause him or her personal distress that goes beyond the distress associated with society's general condemnation or disapproval of the interest. Second, it may be diagnosed when one person's sexual behavior or desires harm another person psychologically or physically, or when a person's desire for sexual behaviors involves persons who do not want to participate, or who cannot legally agree to participate, in such behaviors. The eight paraphilic disorders are exhibitionistic, frotteuristic, fetishistic, sexual masochism, sexual sadism disorder, voyeuristic, transvestic, and pedophilic, the disorder associated with Humbert.

PEDOPHILIC DISORDER

Pedophilic disorder is classified as a paraphilia because it involves a dangerous or harmful sexual interest or behavior that is considered unusual and socially unacceptable. In this paraphilia, the sexual interest is directed toward underage children. The diagnosis applies both to individuals who act on their interest and to those who do not act on their interests but are troubled by them. Individuals who admit to being attracted to children but who have never abused them and who are not distressed by their interests are considered to have pedophilic sexual interests rather than pedophilic disorder.

There are several theories that attempt to explain the attraction of an adult to a child under the age of 13.

Scientists have observed differences in brain structure in a number of mental and personality disorders including psychopathy, obsessive-compulsive disorder, impulse control disorders, PTSD, and substance abuse disorders. For example, some studies have reported decreased gray matter in the brains of people with pedophilic and other disorders. Of course, not everyone diagnosed with one of these disorders also has pedophilic tendencies, but in some individuals, pedophilic interest may co-exist—that is, be comorbid with—another psychiatric condition.

Many individuals diagnosed with one of these disorders have detectable abnormalities in their frontal and temporal lobes, and in the connections between their frontal lobes and other parts of the brains. These abnormalities might even be a consequence of another psychiatric disease. If pedophilic disorder is, in fact, related to brain abnormalities, then the brain changes that underlie this condition might be traced in some cases to a typical or improper development of the brain and/or to traumatic experiences occurring early in life.

Unlike Humbert Humbert, many people with this disorder are reported to have low IQs. If the speculations of some therapists are correct, then some cases of pedophilic disorder can be attributed to incomplete psychosexual development. These individuals would have become fixated or stuck at an early stage of development, resulting in a sexual interest in children, an interest they find natural and one that they justify by claiming that their young victims initiate or welcome their advances.

Humbert's behavior meets the three diagnostic criteria for pedophilic disorder:

Humbert has repeated, intense sexually arousing urges, fantasies, or sexual contact with one or more children aged 13 years or younger over a period of at least six months.

"Between the age limits of nine and fourteen there occur maidens who, to certain bewitched travelers, twice or many times older than they, reveal their true nature which is not human, but nymphic (that is, demoniac); and these chosen creatures I propose to designate as 'nymphets.' " Humbert admits to having been attracted to girls under the age of 13 since he himself was a teenager.

Humbert acted on his paraphilic urges. (If he had not acted on them but was significantly distressed by his interest or fantasies, he would still meet this criterion.)

"It had become gradually clear to my conventional Lolita during our singular and bestial cohabitation that even the most miserable of family lives was better than the parody of incest, which, in the long run, was the best I could offer the waif." He sexually abused Lolita for years after he gained custody of her when her mother died.

Humbert meets the criterion that he is at least 16 years old and at least five years older than the child he is sexually interested in. (If, however, Humbert was in late adolescence and had a sexual relationship with a 12- or 13-year-old girl, the diagnosis of pedophilic disorder would not apply to him.)

Humbert was 38 years old and Lolita was 12 years old when he began abusing her.

Other Disorders and Syndromes

Profile #67: Leonard Shelby in the Film *Memento*; Screenplay by Christopher Nolan, Based on the Short Story "Memento Mori" by Jonathan Nolan

I have no short-term memory.

PLOT SUMMARY

When Leonard Shelby (played by Guy Pearce) tried to rescue his wife from a rapist, the rapist slammed Leonard's head into a mirror. Since then, Leonard can no longer remember anything long enough for it to become a permanent memory. Although he can remember everything before his injury, the only way he now can keep track of people and events now is to make notes—some on scraps of paper, some on photographs, and some on his body in the form of tattoos.

Despite this handicap, Leonard works every day, all day, to find the man who attacked his late wife—and kill him. His search brings him into contact with people who exploit his unusual memory problem for their own purposes. In the end, even Leonard deliberately takes advantage of his problem to deceive himself.

LEONARD'S PSYCHOLOGICAL TRAITS

Before his injury, Leonard was a dedicated husband. At work, he was an insurance investigator with average abilities. After his injury, his dominant psychological feature becomes his inability to form new memories.

ANTEROGRADE AMNESIA

Leonard's anterograde amnesia is sometimes called short-term memory loss. It differs from generalized and localized amnesia, which produce memory deficits of past events (see the entry about Jason Bourne). Anterograde amnesia involves an inability to transfer short-term memories into long-term memories.

Short-term memory loss

Leonard: "I know who I am. I know all about myself. I just . . . since my injury I can't make new memories. Everything fades. If we talk for too long, I'll forget how we started. The next time I see you, I'm not gonna remember this conversation."

A person with this rare condition can talk to someone for an hour and not recognize that person if she leaves the room and returns a few minutes later. Leonard demonstrates this when he has a fight with a woman who then goes out to her car and reenters the apartment. Leonard does not remember the fight.

Leonard's injury evidently damaged a part of his brain called the hippocampus. This brain structure plays a key role in transferring new memories into permanent memories. Another cause of anterograde amnesia is Korsakoff's syndrome, which is associated with long-term vitamin B1 deficiency. It can result from years of alcohol abuse. This syndrome has been linked to widespread brain damage.

Motel Clerk: "What's it like?"
Leonard: "It's like waking. It's like you just woke up."

Profile #68: Plyushkin in the Novel *Dead Souls* by Nikolai Gogol

When Chichikov opened the door in question, the spectacle of the untidiness within struck him almost with amazement.

PLOT SUMMARY

Chichikov is a clever con man. He is so clever that he has a scheme to make money by buying "dead souls."

In pre-Revolutionary Russia, "dead souls" referred to serfs who died in a landowner's service. They were a problem for landowners because the landowners had to continue paying taxes on their "dead souls" until the next census was completed. Chichikov offers to buy "dead souls" for cash as part of his con. Few can resist his unusual offer.

Chichikov meets many characters as he travels the dirt roads of the poverty-stricken Russian countryside on his mission. When he visits a landowner named Plyushkin, Chichikov clearly sees evidence of a psychological syndrome familiar to many people. The signs of the syndrome are expressed in the appearance of the man and in the state of the man's house.

PLYUSHKIN'S PSYCHOLOGICAL TRAITS

Plyushkin is a dour, 70-plus-year-old, humorless landowner who lives in squalor. His living conditions strongly suggest he is affected by Diogenes syndrome.

DIOGENES SYNDROME

Diogenes syndrome is a behavioral disorder described by several common alternative names: messy house syndrome, senile breakdown, self-neglect, social withdrawal in the elderly, and senile squalor. It is a symptom, not a mental disorder. It may be seen in some patients with dementia, alcohol abuse syndrome, obsessive-compulsive disorder, and depression.

The syndrome is misnamed after a Greek philosopher who lived in the fourth century BCE, Diogenes of Sinope. Diogenes promoted independent living and fulfillment without the need for material goods. He lived without amenities and even begged for food in order to simplify his lifestyle. This inherently contradictory philosophy seemed to reject outside help (if you forget about Diogenes's begging) and so inaccurately became associated with the syndrome. Diogenes, ironically, did not have enough of the following traits to be diagnosed with Diogenes syndrome.

Extreme neglected physical state

"In short, had Chichikov chanced to encounter him at a church door, he would have bestowed upon him a copper or two (for, to do our hero justice, he had a sympathetic heart and never refrained from presenting a beggar with alms), but in the present case there was standing before him, not a mendicant, but a landowner."

Chichikov is stunned by the poor condition of Plyushkin's appearance, including his filthy clothing and neglected personal hygiene.

Self-imposed social isolation

"It is long since I last received a visitor," he [Plyushkin] went on. "Also, I feel bound to say that I can see little good in their coming."

More than once, Plyushkin announces to Chichikov that he does not welcome social interaction or visitors.

Domestic squalor

"My late wife made the stuff," went on the old man, "but that rascal of a housekeeper went and threw away a lot of it, and never even replaced the stopper. Consequently, bugs and other nasty creatures got into the decanter, but I cleaned it out, and now beg to offer you a glassful."

It is not unusual for a person like Plyushkin to begin to neglect himself after losing a spouse who cared for him. By one estimate, approximately one-third of Diogenes syndrome cases develop after such a loss.

Syllogomania

"It would seem that the floor was never washed, and that the room was used as a receptacle for every conceivable kind of furniture." And: "and everything he came upon—an old sole, a peasant woman's rag, an iron nail, a shard of earthenware—he would haul off to his house and place on the heap which Chichikov had noticed in a corner of the room."

Syllogomania means excessive hoarding. Hoarding disorder is described in the *DSM-5*. It applies to anyone who has serious difficulty discarding excess possessions and extreme stress associated with the thought of discarding them.

Diogenes syndrome, by contrast, includes symptoms in addition to hoarding that potentially can make life especially difficult for senior citizens.

Profile #69: Alice in the Children's Book *Alice in Wonderland* by Lewis Carroll

"The first thing I've got to do," said Alice to herself, as she wandered about in the wood, "is to grow to my right size again."

PLOT SUMMARY

One quiet summer day, Alice sees a white rabbit rush past her and disappear down a rabbit hole. Alice follows the rabbit and enters a world of her imagination called Wonderland. Her adventure underground begins when she glimpses an enticing garden but realizes she can't fit through the door to enter it. She drinks a potion that makes her shrink in size. Realizing she now can't reach the key to the door, Alice eats some cake that makes her grow and grow until her size is grotesque. As her adventure continues, she experiences more changes in size.

In Wonderland, Alice meets the always grinning, disappearing-and-reappearing Cheshire Cat, and Wonderland's unstable ruler, the Queen of Hearts. Alice is frustrated by the Mad Hatter, puzzled by the hallucinogen-loving Caterpillar, meets the self-absorbed Mock Turtle, and interacts with many other remarkable creatures who share her seemingly nonsensical dream adventure.

Lewis Carroll

Shy, introspective Charles Lutwidge Dodgson was a gifted, multitalented lecturer at Oxford University. He was a mathematician, a logician, and a photographer. He also wrote original and creative fantasies ostensibly for children under the pen name Lewis Carroll.

A deacon of the Anglican Church, Carroll stammered and was uncomfortable around adults. Based on his diaries and contemporary accounts of his behavior, he seemed to prefer the company of children over that of adults. More than half of his photographs—taken when photography was a new art form that required considerable technical skill—were of children, especially girls.

Carroll combined his understanding of what interested children with his wit, his specific knowledge of logic, and his considerable general knowledge to write the classic tales of *Alice in Wonderland* and *Through the Looking Glass*. The books were based on stories he told Alice Liddell and her sisters Lorina and Edith, daughters of his Oxford colleague, classics scholar Henry George Liddell.

The unique combination of fantasy, satire, playful use of logic, and clever wordplay continues to make *Alice in Wonderland,* published in 1865, popular with adults as well as children. It is widely quoted; some claim only the Bible and works by Shakespeare are quoted more often. Sixteen years after its publication, Carroll quit his job at Oxford to become a full-time writer. He wrote more children's books, poems, and even puzzle books featuring logic games and problems. He died in 1898 at the age of 66.

Thirty years after Carroll's death, scholars began speculating that his affection for children might not have been innocent. The speculation continues to this day based largely on his close friendships with children and on the hundreds of photos of children he took, including at least 30 of children partially clothed or nude. But, there is no conclusive evidence that Carroll had what would today be called pedophilic disorder. His strong interest in children and the fact that he photographed some children in the nude strongly suggest to some people that he may have had repressed pedophilic interests.

Victorian society, however, was not like modern society. Photographs similar to those Carroll took were not unusual in his day. Although the age of consent was 12, the average Briton during Queen Victoria's reign may have seen young children as innocent examples of purity, not as potential victims of sex abuse. Portraits of nude children were not uncommon back then. There are even examples on birthday cards. On the other hand, the sexual abuse Virginia Woolf suffered as a child in Victorian England made her question the way Victorians really viewed children. Until historians find some evidence regarding Carroll's motivations, the nature of his friendships with, and photographs of, children will remain a matter of speculation and controversy.

ALICE'S PSYCHOLOGICAL TRAITS

Alice's strange experiences in Wonderland frequently cause her to question who she is. Her worries about her basic, core identity, of course, are related to the surreal circumstances surrounding her presence in Wonderland and to the strange and curious characters she meets there.

Her questions about her true self are also inspired by the frequent changes she experiences in the size of her body. These visual disturbances follow her ingestion of unknown substances and could, therefore, be attributed to the effects of psychedelic drugs. It is perhaps more interesting, however, to discuss them in terms of a set of symptoms named after Alice herself.

ALICE IN WONDERLAND SYNDROME

Alice in Wonderland syndrome (AIWS) is a collection of symptoms related to changes in a person's body image. Like Alice, a person with this group of symptoms feels as if her body, or parts of it, grow larger or smaller, or change in shape. Visual hallucinations frequently accompany the syndrome, which can also include distortion of space and time. No one knows what causes it.

It was described in 1955 by John Todd, a British psychiatrist, in the *Canadian Medical Association Journal*. He initially associated it with patients suffering with epilepsy or migraines who reported feelings of altered body size. The symptoms may also occur with fever, lesions in the cerebral cortex, schizophrenia, and infectious diseases like mononucleosis and other viral infections. Two conditions associated with the syndrome have especially close associations with Lewis Carroll's book: use of hallucinogenic drugs and migraine headaches.

As mentioned, Alice experienced her AIWS symptoms after drinking an unknown drink and eating an unknown type of cake. Hallucinogenic drugs in those items might easily explain Alice's experience. The inspiration for Alice's repeated body size changes, however, may not rest entirely with hallucinogens. As Todd pointed out, "Lewis Carroll himself suffered from migraine." This fact, Todd wrote, "arouses the suspicion that Alice trod the paths and byways of a Wonderland well known to her creator."

Alterations in body image

"She went on growing and growing and very soon she had to kneel down on the floor. Still she went on growing, and, as a last resource, she put one arm out of the window and one foot up the chimney."

Patients with AIWS often report feeling as if their heads and hands are larger than normal. They may also lose their sense of time and misjudge the actual size of objects.

" 'I must be growing small again.' She got up and went to the table to measure herself by it and found that she was now about two feet high and was going on shrinking rapidly."

Symptoms of shrinking in size are less common than symptoms of growing larger but are still a feature of the syndrome.

While Lewis Carroll may have used his migraine-induced body image alterations as inspirations for Alice's experiences, he also appears to use Alice's questions about who she is and her changing body as a metaphor for a child's concerns about imminent puberty. This is a time when a child faces losing her familiar child's identity and prepubescent body as she grows into adolescence on the way to adulthood.

Part 2

Positive Psychological Traits

The characters in the next section have personalities with attributes that have been largely ignored by psychologists until relatively recently. If psychology is the study of the mind and human behavior, then to be complete it must recognize both the positive and the negative aspects of its subject.

The importance of this field of psychology is reflected in a 2002 study of more than 3,000 adults in the United States between the ages of 25 and 74. Fewer than 20 percent of them were flourishing—that is, were mentally healthy, with no illnesses, no distress, and enjoying a sense of vitality. About 57 percent were moderately mentally healthy. A little more than 12 percent were languishing—bored, apathetic, disinterested, and listless. Languishing is associated with emotional distress, more missed days of work, and other problems. Fourteen percent of the 3,000 plus subjects had symptoms that matched the criteria for major depressive episode at some point during the year.

People in the languishing group were close to six times more likely to experience a major depressive episode than the people in the flourishing group. They were also twice as likely to experience a major depressive episode as people in the moderately mentally healthy group.

Important goals of positive psychology research are to study positive emotions, character traits, institutions, social relationships, and achievements to identify and promote the benefits they offer to individuals and society.

Many of the 24 positive character traits, which are grouped into the six major catagories of wisdom, courage, humanity, justice, temperance, and transcendence (see Appendix B) are illustrated by the characters in the literature and films discussed in the next section. These traits were selected because they are valued and recognized as desirable by diverse peoples and cultures around the world, according to psychologists Christopher Peterson, PhD, and Martin Seligman, PhD.

Profile #70: Sherlock Holmes in the Novel *A Study in Scarlet* by Sir Arthur Conan Doyle

> "My mind," he said, "rebels at stagnation. Give me problems, give me work, give me the most abstruse cryptogram or the most intricate analysis, and I am in my own proper atmosphere. I can dispense then with artificial stimulants. But I abhor the dull routine of existence. I crave for mental exaltation. That is why I have chosen my own particular profession, or rather created it, for I am the only one in the world."

PLOT SUMMARY

Mr. Stamford, an acquaintance of Dr. John Watson, introduces Watson to Mr. Sherlock Holmes. Watson has recently returned from fighting in Afghanistan and is looking for a place to live, one that he can afford on his meager disability pension. Sherlock is also looking for a new living arrangement. The two agree to share a flat at 221B Baker Street in London.

Watson discovers that his new roommate is unlike anyone he has ever encountered. Sherlock is eccentric but highly intelligent. He has a vast amount of knowledge, but only in subject areas that help him in his work as a consulting detective. He has developed his powers of observation, reasoning, and deduction to such a degree that he can identify both important and trivial facts about anyone he directs his attention toward. He often smokes a pipe when thinking and plays the violin to relax. He currently regrets that he has no new cases to occupy his superior intellect.

It's not long, however, before a Scotland Yard detective requests Sherlock's help in solving a recent murder. Sherlock invites Watson to come along as he inspects the crime scene: a corpse lying on the floor of a house in Brixton; the word "Rache," is written in blood on the wall near the body. While Watson observes, Sherlock uses his deductive reasoning skills to uncover facts crucial for solving the case. After Sherlock solves the case, the newspapers give most of the credit to Scotland Yard detectives. Sherlock shows a fleeting touch of bitterness before shrugging off the unfairness.

With this case, Watson becomes the private detective's chronicler and goes on to narrate his future adventures in 3 additional novels and 56 short stories.

SHERLOCK'S PSYCHOLOGICAL TRAITS

Sherlock Holmes is brilliant, successfully self-employed, solitary, and uninterested in making friends or socializing. He is completely devoted to his career and is liable to experience depressed moods when he has no case to work on. At these times, he sometimes abuses cocaine or opiates.

Sherlock is the author of several monographs on diverse topics related to criminology. He has a vast amount of background knowledge on every topic he can identify that is connected with this field. Sherlock has no interest in learning about or knowing anything in fields of knowledge not directly related to his specialty: solving crimes. He didn't know, for example, that Earth revolved around the Sun until Watson told him. And then he was sorry to hear it because, he said, the useless knowledge just took up valuable room in his brain.

POSITIVE PSYCHOLOGICAL ATTRIBUTE

Wisdom and Knowledge—Judgment

Sherlock's single-minded purpose in life—solving criminal cases—allows him to showcase his remarkable ability to think critically, to avoid jumping to conclusions, to consider all facts, and to change his opinion when the facts dictate.

Sherlock has no mental disorders. His behavior is sometimes unusual and he avoids people who waste his time. Nevertheless, readers and fans have diagnosed the consulting detective with several mental disorders including obsessive-compulsive disorder, bipolar disorder, schizoid personality disorder, and most frequently Asperger's or high-functioning autism spectrum disorder. While Sherlock has some, superficial features, of two of these disorders—as many people do—he does not meet the criteria for any of them.

The first two disorders can be dismissed quickly. Sherlock is not troubled by the anxiety that results from not preforming compulsive acts. Nor does he perform compulsive acts to avoid experiencing anxiety. He shows no sign of troubling obsessive thoughts that interfere with his work. There is little or no evidence to suggest that Sherlock suffers from obsessive-compulsive disorder. People not familiar with mental disorders sometimes confuse meticulous attention to detail—a positive professional trait in Sherlock's line of business—with compulsion and obsession.

Sherlock experiences depressed moods sometimes when he is not working but quickly regains his energy when he has the opportunity to return to work. These moods never strike unless he is unoccupied. They are a response to lack of intellectual stimulation. While working, he is often energized but his enthusiasm is not manic. Occasional depressed moods and enthusiastically pursuing a chosen line of work are not signs of bipolar disorder.

NOT HIGH-FUNCTIONING AUTISM SPECTRUM DISORDER/ASPERGER DISORDER

People with autism spectrum disorder have difficulty interacting and communicating with others. Symptoms can range from a total inability to connect with others to difficulty recognizing and understanding others' feelings. People at the high end of the spectrum have less severe symptoms and are diagnosed with high-functioning autism, which is still sometimes called Asperger's syndrome. They may have trouble recognizing facial expressions and emotions in others. They often have average or above average intelligence and may want to be involved with other people but aren't sure how to do it.

If Sherlock was on the autism spectrum, he would have the following characteristics:

Have poor social skills; difficulty interacting with others

Stamford: "No; he is not a man that it is easy to draw out, though he can be communicative enough when the fancy seizes him."

Sherlock has little interest in small talk or speaking to anyone who cannot advance his knowledge in criminology or help him solve a case. When interested in a topic under discussion, he is perfectly capable of participating in an intelligent conversation. He interviews witnesses and communicates well with the police, clients, and Dr. Watson. When necessary, he can disguise himself physically and adopt different behaviors. Sherlock does not have difficulty interacting with others but, instead, chooses not to interact unless he finds the interaction useful to him personally. He does not meet this criterion for high functioning autism/Asperger's syndrome.

Be unable to appreciate humor and subtle nuances in conversation

"Didn't I tell you so when we started?" cried Sherlock Holmes with a laugh. "That's the result of all our Study in Scarlet: to get them a testimonial!"

Sherlock clearly demonstrates emotion and an ironic sense of humor when he shows Watson a newspaper story that barely credits Sherlock for solving the crime. There are multiple examples of Sherlock laughing and smiling, such as when Watson recalls: " 'You appear to be astonished,' he said, smiling at my expression of surprise." When he fails to show interest in humor or mundane conversations, it is very likely because they don't interest him, not because he is unable to react to them.

Have obsessive interest in specific subjects or topics

Watson: "Yet his zeal for certain studies was remarkable, and within eccentric limits his knowledge was so extraordinarily ample and minute that his observations have fairly astounded me. Surely no man would work so hard or attain such precise information unless he had some definite end in view."

This is the only criterion for high functioning autism/Asperger's syndrome that Sherlock seems to satisfy. But he doesn't satisfy it. His interests in life are solving crimes and gathering any information in any field of knowledge that can improve his ability to do this. But, as Sherlock explains to Watson,

> I consider that a man's brain originally is like a little empty attic, and you have to stock it with such furniture as you choose. A fool takes in all the lumber of every sort that he comes across, so that the knowledge which might be useful to him gets crowded out, or at best is jumbled up with a lot of other things so that he has a difficulty in laying his hands upon it . . . Depend upon it there comes a time when for every addition of knowledge you forget something that you knew before. It is of the highest importance, therefore, not to have useless facts elbowing out the useful ones.

It is obvious that Sherlock's desire to be the best he can be at his chosen profession accounts for his decision to concentrate on learning what will help him in his goal.

A small number of people with autism spectrum disorder are able to live independent lives as adults. This minority tends to have superior language skills and above average intelligence. They also tend to obtain work that matches their specialized interests and abilities. This profile describes Sherlock Holmes but it also describes many other people who are not on the autism spectrum.

NOT SCHIZOID PERSONALITY DISORDER

This disorder is characterized by clear signs that a person is detached from social relationships. These people also show a limited range of emotional expressions when dealing with other people. They are frequently described as "loners" with no close confidants except perhaps close family members. They have little or no interest in sexual activities. They do not care about other people's opinions of them and get pleasure from very few or no activities. Their lives often lack direction; their goals shift and are indistinct.

This disorder is easily confused with mild forms of autism spectrum disorder. Just as it is clear that Sherlock does not meet the criteria for autism spectrum disorder, it is clear he does not meet the criteria for schizoid personality disorder. For example, he has a close confidant in Dr. Watson. He shows that he cares about what other people think of him when he expresses irritation at not being given credit for solving a murder. While it is true Sherlock appears to be celibate with no interest in sex, he is very directed in his work and he has a clear goal. He is the opposite of directionless, a trait that distinguishes from many people with schizoid personality disorder.

If it is necessary to make a diagnosis about this fictional character, the most accurate "diagnosis" would be that he is a rare, eccentric, solitary, and brilliant individual who has chosen to devote himself to his chosen career.

A long retired Sherlock comes to terms with his decision to live a solitary life limited to intellectual interests in Mitch Cullin's novel *A Slight Trick of the Mind* and in its film version. (See Sherlock Holmes in *Mr. Holmes.*)

Profile #71: Santiago in the Novella *The Old Man and the Sea* by Ernest Hemingway

Fight them, he said. I'll fight them until I die.

PLOT SUMMARY

Santiago, "thin and gaunt with deep wrinkles in the back of his neck," is a poor, aging Cuban fisherman who hasn't caught a fish in nearly three months. His friend and fishing partner, a boy named Manolin, has been forced by his parents to leave Santiago to work for more successful fishermen. One night Santiago has a dream inspired by a memory from his younger days when he served on a ship that passed close to the coast of Africa; he dreams of the lions he saw on the beach.

The next morning, the 85th day since he last caught a fish, the old man sails alone far out into the Gulf Stream. He is convinced his luck will change. And it does when he hooks a giant marlin. But, following an epic, exhausting, three-day-long struggle to bring in the magnificent creature, the old man's fortunes reverse. He ties the giant fish to the side of his boat and sails toward home. Then, still far from shore, sharks appear. They circle and attack the dead marlin. The old man tries to fight them off despite his flagging energy. He harpoons and clubs and, finally, has to resort to knifing the predators. But the sharks win. They steadily, bite by bite, devour the old man's greatest catch until no flesh remains. Santiago reaches home at night when everyone is asleep. The marlin's skeleton is still tied to his skiff. Too exhausted to get out of the skiff, he sleeps in it. Manolin finds him in the morning. He brings the old man coffee with milk and sugar, and he brings him his friendship. Manolin tells the old man they will sail again together despite his parents' wishes. That night the old man dreams once again of lions.

SANTIAGO'S PSYCHOLOGICAL TRAITS

Santiago's life illustrates many positive traits that can be seen in quiet, hard-working individuals who never seek to become famous. Santiago began teaching Manolin how to fish when the boy was only five years old. And he tutored him as he grew into a teen and loyal friend. Now they are devoted to each other. Santiago's work ethic is indomitable, as is his persistence even as he faces the trials of aging, setbacks, and disappointments. After a monumental struggle, he fails. But he is not defeated.

A dominant feature of Santiago's personality is his sense of purpose. Behavioral scientist Paul Dolan, PhD, the author of *Happiness by Design*, suggests that happiness is closely tied to experiences or feelings of pleasure *and* purpose.

Based on his conversations with Manolin, it is clear that Santiago takes pride in being a fisherman and that he cherishes the victories he has experienced. Despite the difficulty of the job, despite the long months without success, despite the physical challenges of aging, Santiago gives us the impression that he can find pleasure in his work. His sense of purpose is obvious. Fishing, for the old man, is not part of a meaningless job. It offers the opportunity for personal triumph and success.

Ernest Hemingway

Hemingway is out of fashion with many academic critics now, but in the first half of the 20th century he was considered one of the world's greatest writers. In 1954, at the age of 55, he was awarded the Nobel Prize in literature "for his mastery of the art of narrative, most recently demonstrated in *The Old Man and the Sea*, and for the influence that he has exerted on contemporary style."

Hemingway's writing style is heavily influenced by his days as a newspaper correspondent. It is sparse, simple, and straightforward. This, along with his legendary, macho lifestyle involving hunting, fishing, and boxing, and the super masculine persona he presented to the world, is one reason many English professors dismiss his novels today. His short stories alone, however, establish him as one of America's greatest writers.

Hemingway grew up in Oak Park, Illinois, and began writing early. He volunteered as an ambulance driver in Italy during World War I and was wounded. The romantic attraction he felt for Sister Agnew von Kurovsky, a nurse he met during his recovery, inspired the novel *A Farewell to Arms*. Its publication brought him fame around the age of 30.

Other successful works followed but the writer's creativity seems to have come at a great price. He could be friendly and gracious and then bullying even with his friends. His relationships with women were rocky and he had four marriages. He looked back fondly on the years he shared with his first wife Hadley in Paris, but long regretted leaving her for another woman. Late in life, he would write a nostalgic memoir, *A Moveable Feast*, describing this time.

Hemingway was deeply affected at the age of 29 when his father, who was himself a bully, shot himself in the head. His mother, whom he detested, later gave Hemingway the pistol his father used to kill himself. Hemingway's active lifestyle (some would suggest he was pursuing a "death wish") resulted in many head injuries, which may have contributed to his later health problems.

Psychiatrist Christopher D. Martin, MD, studied Hemingway's life closely and concluded that "significant evidence exists to support the diagnoses of bipolar disorder, alcohol dependence, traumatic brain injury, and probable borderline and narcissistic personality traits. Late in life, Hemingway also developed symptoms of psychosis likely related to his underlying affective illness and superimposed alcoholism and traumatic brain injury."

Many of Hemingway's relatives and descendants apparently suffered from bipolar disorder including his parents and their siblings, his son, and his granddaughter. Altogether, at least five members of the Hemingway clan spread across four generations took their own lives.

By 1960, the great writer was suffering from depression and paranoid delusions. He was depressed at his inability to write or to make love. He died by his own hand from a shotgun blast to the head. The macho writer, who once confided in movie actress Ava Gardner that he spent "a hell of a lot of time killing animals and fish so I won't kill myself," was finally overcome by his psychological burdens.

POSITIVE PSYCHOLOGICAL ATTRIBUTES

Wisdom and Knowledge—Personal Intelligence

"I may not be as strong as I think," the old man said. "But I know many tricks and I have resolution."

Courage—Bravery

"What kind of a hand is that," he said. "Cramp then if you want. Make yourself into a claw. It will do you no good." The old man's hand seizes up during the long battle with the fish but he endures the pain bravely as he does all of the physical and psychological challenges he faces.

Courage—Perseverance, Persistence

Santiago fights the giant marlin alone for three days, demonstrating that once he commits, he does not give up when challenged. Remembering the past, when he was a crew member on boats that caught a different kind of sea creature, he observes: "Most people are heartless about turtles because a turtle's heart will beat for hours after he has been cut up and butchered. But the old man thought, I have such a heart too and my feet and hands are like theirs."

The old man's heart—his will, his resolve, his determination—will not quit.

Courage—Perseverance, Industriousness

"Now is not the time to think of baseball, he thought. Now is the time to think of only one thing. That which I was born for." The old man is a professional and devoted fisherman.

Courage—Zest, Vitality

"Everything about him was old except his eyes and they were the same color as the sea and were cheerful and undefeated." Santiago does not give in to despair, although it would be understandable if he did. Age leaves him weaker than he once was. He has endured failure for months, but he still plans to recover and takes steps to succeed. He acts wholeheartedly.

Humanity—Love

"The old man had taught the boy to fish and the boy loved him." And Santiago "no longer dreamed of storms, nor of women, nor of great occurrences, nor of great fish, nor fights, nor contests of strength, nor of his wife. He only dreamed of places now and of the lions on the beach. They played like young cats in the dusk and he loved them as he loved the boy." Santiago cherishes Manolin and his love is reciprocated. He values their friendship and the way they care for each other.

Temperance—Forgiveness

"They sat on the Terrace and many of the fishermen made fun of the old man and he was not angry." Santiago accepts that a vocal minority of persons are petty, hurtful, and even hateful. He is strong enough to ignore or forgive this common type of behavior.

Temperance—Humility

"He was too simple to wonder when he had attained humility. But he knew he had attained it and he knew it was not disgraceful and it carried no loss of true pride." The old man does not feel superior to others. He knows his strengths and weaknesses. He is strong without feeling the need to broadcast it to others.

Profile #72: Luke Jackson in the Film *Cool Hand Luke*; Screenplay by Donn Pearce and Frank K. Pierson, Based on the Novel by Donn Pearce

---

Yeah, well, sometimes nothin' can be a real cool hand.

PLOT SUMMARY

The last defiant act of Luke (played by Paul Newman) against authority, before he is convicted and sentenced to two years on a Florida prison chain gang, is to drunkenly and methodically use a pipe cutter to "behead" a row of parking meters along a quiet street late at night.

The prison warden, "Captain" (played by Strother Martin), is surprised by Luke. No one has ever come to his prison for "maliciously destroyin' municipal property while under the influence." And he doesn't see many prisoners with war records like Luke's: a sergeant who left the service as a buck private with a Bronze Star, a Silver Star, and a few Purple Hearts.

After a painful beginning in the prison during which he refuses to quit a boxing match he is losing badly, Luke's individuality and bullheaded defiance of authority win the affection of the 50 other prisoners. They begin to feed off his independent attitude and savor his acts of defiance against the prison authorities. They come to live vicariously through him.

After repeatedly escaping and being recaptured, Luke's spirit is broken by the guards' brutal punishment. His "worshipers" now abandon him. But when his spirit returns, he makes one last gesture that will make him live forever in their memories. Dragline (played by George Kennedy), Luke's former tormentor and now greatest disciple, calls Luke a "natural-born world-shaker."

LUKE'S PSYCHOLOGICAL TRAITS

Luke is an aimless army veteran who believes he has wasted much of his life. His nonconformist, independent, individualistic attitude has self-destructive, even masochistic, features. And yet, this antihero loner still manages to inspire those who have been victimized by "The Establishment" or by any authority that unjustly uses power. Luke stubbornly resists while other men acquiesce to authority's demands to make it easy on themselves. In this sense, Luke sacrifices himself for others by resisting "bosses" others will not or cannot resist. Luke's Christ-like role in the lives of the other prisoners is obvious.

POSITIVE PSYCHOLOGICAL ATTRIBUTES

Despite Luke's personal weaknesses, he is an inspiration to others.

Wisdom and Knowledge—Perspective

Boss: "Sorry, Luke. I'm just doing my job. You gotta appreciate that."
Luke: "Nah, calling it your job don't make it right, Boss."

A prison guard—all guards are called "Boss" in the prison—is ordered to lock Luke in "The Box," a windowless punishment cell barely big enough for one man. Luke is being locked in it because his mother recently died and the warden is afraid he might get "rabbit in his blood" and escape to attend the funeral. Luke doesn't accept the guard's excuse that someone ordered him to treat Luke unfairly. The excuse is reminiscent of the excuse Nazi war criminals used to justify their murderous actions during World War II: "Just following orders."

With his rebuff of the guard's excuse, Luke is telling everyone who hears it that they are responsible for their actions and cannot put the responsibility for what they do onto anyone else (see "Teachers" in *Experimenter: The Stanley Milgram Story*). Others may not be strong enough to accept Luke's perspective on this point, but it is nevertheless wise advice.

Courage—Perseverance

Dragline: "Stay down. You're beat."
Luke: "You're gonna have to kill me."

Luke's independent attitude threatens the dominant prisoner in the cellblock, Dragline. Although Dragline is bigger and stronger, Luke agrees to box him. Luke is beaten, knocked down repeatedly, and beaten more when he stumbles to his feet, again and again. The other prisoners scream at him to stay down and even Dragline tells him to stay down. Finally, Dragline walks away rather than kill his opponent. Luke earns everyone's respect by not quitting. In reality, Luke could have been beaten to death. In terms of the story, his refusal to stay down symbolizes his unwillingness to ever surrender. Dragline beats him literally, but Luke wins the battle of wills. And everyone watching realizes it.

Courage—Zest, Vigor, Vitality

Dragline: "Nothin'. A handful of nothin'. You stupid mullet-head, [Luke] beat you with nothin'. Just like today when he kept comin' back at me—with nothin'."
Luke: "Yeah, well, sometimes nothin' can be a real cool hand."

After the fight, Luke wins a poker hand by bluffing. Dragline berates the prisoner Luke bluffed. His respect for Luke increases. Luke's response reveals his wholehearted approach to life. By society's standards, Luke's life has pretty much amounted to "nothin'," but he is making what he can with what he has. Luke's comment leads Dragline to give him the nickname "Cool Hand Luke."

Transcendence—Humor

Prisoner: "It's not your fault. He's just too big. Let him hit you in the nose and get some blood flowing. Maybe the bosses will stop it before he kills you."
Luke: "I don't want to frighten him."

Offered an escape from his brutal beating during the boxing match with Dragline, Luke mocks himself and uses humor to dismiss the suggestion that he quit.

Another example of Luke's use of humor comes after one of his escape attempts. The Captain says he is punishing Luke for "his own good." Luke replies: "I wish you'd stop bein' so good to me, Captain."

Off the screen and off the pages of the novel on which the film is based, Luke would be considered masochistic and antisocial. But in the context of the film and the novel, Luke's persistent defiance of unjust authority, his ability to see humor in events despite the suffering and challenges they pose for him, and his ability to inspire less charismatic, less original, less vibrant people turn the character into a symbol rich with positive traits.

Profile #73: Juror #8 in the Film *12 Angry Men*; Screenplay by Reginald Rose

This is somebody's life. We can't decide in five minutes.

PLOT SUMMARY

After a nearly week-long trial in a hot Manhattan courtroom, 12 male jurors are about to determine the fate of a 19-year-old man accused of stabbing his father to death. The defendant, who has a criminal record, will be executed if the jurors find him guilty. In the first vote, that is what all but one of the jurors want.

The holdout is juror #8 (played by Henry Fonda). His fellow jurors are surprised and annoyed at this setback in their plans to escape early from the un-air-conditioned deliberation room. The 12 male jurors represent a cross-section of New Yorkers who expect a quick verdict and a quick return to their regular routines. Juror #7, for example, is anxious to get the voting over quickly so he can get to a baseball game.

Despite the derision and invective directed at him, juror #8 persists in asking the others to at least discuss the case before condemning a young man to death. Slowly, over the course of 90 minutes, he tactfully and deliberately raises convincing questions about the evidence as he challenges his fellow jurors' reasons for voting guilty. Tempers flare and insults fly in the hot jury room, but juror #8 remains calm, rational, and steady. With each new vote taken, one or a few jurors change their original verdict. In the end, reason replaces emotionality, and the jurors do their duty by incorporating reasonable doubt into their collective decision.

JUROR #8'S PSYCHOLOGICAL TRAITS

Juror #8 is an architect with a calm, thoughtful demeanor. He is quiet, analytical, intelligent, and empathetic. He is self-confident without being arrogant. He is open-minded but not persuaded by peer pressure. Without being bossy, he is persuasive when the facts support his viewpoint. He is more interested in seeking truth, wherever the search leads, than in winning an argument for the sake of winning.

POSITIVE PSYCHOLOGICAL ATTRIBUTES

Justice—Fairness

Juror #8: "I just think we owe him a few words, that's all."

Juror #8's attitude contrasts sharply with juror #7's initial assertion that he honestly thinks "the guy is guilty. Couldn't change my mind if you talked for 100 years." There is little justice in denying a man fair treatment during jury deliberation because you want to get home quickly.

Justice—Leadership

Juror #8: "Now, let's take two pieces of testimony and try to put them together."

Throughout the deliberations, juror #8 patiently listens to the arguments of his fellow jurors and tactfully points out the flaws in their reasoning and, in several cases, the prejudice behind their opinions.

Temperance—Humility

Juror #8: "I don't really know what the truth is. I don't suppose anybody will ever really know. Nine of us now seem to feel that the defendant is innocent, but we're just gambling on probabilities—we may be wrong. We may be trying to let a guilty man go free, I don't know. Nobody really can. But we have a reasonable doubt, and that's something that's very valuable in our system. No jury can declare a man guilty unless it's sure."

Juror #8 acknowledges that the questions he has about the case may never reveal the truth. He does not insist that he is "right," compared to many of his fellow jurors who initially declare that they "know" that the defendant is guilty.

Wisdom and Knowledge—Critical Judgment

Juror #8: "I began to get the feeling that the defense counsel wasn't conducting a thorough enough cross-examination. I mean, he . . . he let too many things go by."

Juror #8's thoughtful approach to analyzing the evidence presented by the prosecution and the defense contrasts sharply with the prejudice and thoughtlessness his fellow jurors bring to the deliberation room. Despite opposition and the unpopularity of his values, he persists and skillfully convinces the others to examine the facts.

Courage—Bravery

Juror #3 referring to #8:	"Somebody's in left field. You think he's not guilty? . . . The man's a dangerous killer. You could see it."
Juror #7:	"So what'd you vote not guilty for?"
Juror #10 to #8 threateningly:	"You're a pretty smart fellow, aren't you?"

Throughout most of the deliberations and especially in the beginning, juror #8 is pressured to conform and agree with the majority. He resists despite how unpopular it makes him.

Juror #8 is not as well-known as Atticus Finch of *To Kill a Mockingbird*, but he exemplifies the positive traits of respect for justice, sense of fairness, leadership skills, humility, critical judgment, and bravery in the face of strong opposition and peer pressure, in a way that matches those shown by Atticus.

Profile #74: Peter Parker/Spider-Man in the Comic Book *Amazing Spider-Man 2*; the Junior Novelization Adapted by Brittany Candau and Nachie Marsham

> She and Peter had been together long enough for her to know he had his issues and crises to handle and she had hers.

PLOT SUMMARY

Peter Parker, as Spider-Man, rushes to his self-assigned job as superhero right before his high school graduation. This time his private life is interrupted by a bad guy named Aleksei Sytsevich. Aleksei is speeding through the New York streets in a stolen truck carrying a cargo of plutonium.

During the chase, Peter takes time to lift an onlooker named Max Dillon out of the path of an oncoming car. Max is thrilled that his hero takes the time to speak kindly to him during the act.

After catching Aleksei and recovering the plutonium—and after taking time to acknowledge his adoring fan Max—Peter turns back to his civilian duties. He rushes to his high school graduation ceremony, arriving late. After the ceremony, he tells his girlfriend, Gwen, that he reluctantly must stop seeing her because he had promised her dying father he would end their relationship. Her father did not want Gwen exposed to the dangers associated with a superhero's life.

Meanwhile, Max suffers a life-changing accident at work. He slips and falls into a tank filled with genetically modified electric eels (an accident presumably not covered by workers' compensation insurance). The eels attack and Max survives—but not as he was. He becomes a living, high-voltage power source, just the kind of supervillain readers expect a superhero to save the world from.

Still coping with his split from Gwen, Peter encounters Max in Times Square. Peter tries to reason with Max but things go badly. Max becomes the evil villain Electro, intent on punishing Peter for his perceived betrayal. Peter has significant trouble doing it, but eventually he succeeds in short-circuiting Max's power before returning to the challenges common to new high school graduates.

PETER'S (SPIDER-MAN) PSYCHOLOGICAL TRAITS

Early in his superhero career, Peter Parker ignored a thief he assumed was a small-time crook. Telling himself he had his own problems, Peter did not bother apprehending the man. Later that evening, Peter's beloved uncle Ben was shot and killed by the criminal Peter dismissed as a petty thief.

Peter dealt with this tragedy in a surprisingly positive way. Instead of becoming cynical, resentful, and bitter, Peter resolved to use his superpowers more efficiently and conscientiously to prevent further tragedies. Just as remarkably, his resolution to fight crime became less of an obsession and more of a positive endeavor, which he approaches with humor, sensitivity, and compassion for the innocent.

Despite the stresses associated with being a teenager approaching adulthood and challenges that come with being a superhero, Peter Parker illustrates multiple positive psychological traits. The teenager retains his perspective, his sense of humor, and a generally optimistic outlook.

POSITIVE PSYCHOLOGICAL ATTRIBUTES

Resilience

"From the disappearance of his parents when he was a little boy to the loss of his uncle Ben right after he got his spider powers, Peter had faced tragedy his entire life. But he had been dealing with it and May [his aunt] was a large part of how and why he'd been able to do so."

By successfully "dealing with it," Peter demonstrates the trait of resilience. A key factor in his ability to recover from the shock resulting from tragedy, adversity, trauma, and other negative events is his relationship with his aunt May and his past relationships with his uncle and other family members who have since passed away.

Having the support of others increases the chances that a person will be able to "bounce back" from a serious setback. Peter has other characteristics that help explain his ability to recover, and even thrive, after suffering a serious loss or traumatic event. He has self-confidence and self-control. He sets goals and makes plans to solve his problems. And he is disciplined enough to execute his plans.

These are traits Peter shares with many others who have experienced highly distressing times. Resilience itself is not rare, but it is not universal either. Fortunately, according to the American Psychological Association, "resilience is not a trait that people either have or do not have. It involves behaviors, thoughts and actions that can be learned and developed in anyone."

Humanity—Love

"He cared for Gwen, deeply."
Peter appreciates and values those closest to him, including May and his girlfriend.

Wisdom and Knowledge—Interest, Openness to Experience

"He pulled off his mask and took in the view: the New York City skyline at sunrise. It was beautiful. And yet, he was excited to leave it behind. Spider-Man put his mask back on and swung over the city. He was ready for the new challenges ahead. It was time for new, amazing adventures."

All forms of fiction, from classic literature to graphic novels or comic books, provide readers with heroes through whom they can have vicarious experiences. The heroes of classic literature, like Odysseus in Homer's *The Odyssey*, are more complex and realistically flawed than heroes like Spider-Man. Nevertheless, psychologists are still able to identify positive traits in a character like Peter Parker. These same traits have been shown to have beneficial effects on both physical and mental health in experimental subjects.

Transcendence—Humor

" 'Can we just cut to the part where you start to cry and give up?' Spidey, hanging casually off the side of the van, asked Aleksei."

Catching up with a criminal, Peter's first words to him might suggest a degree of arrogance, but, given Peter's overwhelming positive personality, they more likely reflect his sense of humor as well as his self-confidence.

Humanity—Compassion, Empathy

" 'Hey! Max! You're one of the good guys. I don't think you want to be here,' Spider-Man said, slowly walking toward him."

Peter's initial approach to a potential threating figure whom he recognizes is to address him with respect. This act is also an example of fairness, not prematurely condemning people.

Justice—Citizenship, Social Responsibility

"Spidey hadn't been planning on getting involved. He had places to go and people to see . . . But, as soon as he heard about the radioactive materials rocketing through the streets of New York, he knew what needed to be done."

Peter displays his sense of social responsibility by voluntarily neutralizing supervillains. As Spider-Man, he also cooperates with the authorities when they let him, an example of teamwork. His ability to be a good team player, unfortunately, is complicated by bad press put out by the *Daily Bugle* newspaper, which portrays him as a menace in a cynical ploy to sell more newspapers.

Positive psychology does not insist that life is or can be always positive. It is based on the supposition that life is full of difficulties, unpleasant challenges, and tragedies that can be counterbalanced by recognizing and developing positive traits.

Profile #75: Bruce Wayne/Batman in *Batman Begins*; Screenplay by Christopher Nolan and David S. Goyer, Based on Characters Created by Bob Kane and Bill Finger

---

Well, a guy who dresses up like a bat clearly has issues.

PLOT SUMMARY

At age eight, Bruce Wayne (played as an adult by Christian Bale) falls into a cave on the sprawling estate of his wealthy parents. He survives the fall but his arrival startles a huge colony of bats nesting deep underground. Bruce is terrified as a giant storm of "hand-winged" animals envelops him as it rushes past. The experience produces a deep fear of bats in Bruce, a phobia called chiroptophobia.

Not long after this traumatic experience, Bruce attends the opera *Mefistofele* with his parents but asks to leave when he sees bats portrayed on stage. Outside the opera house, a robber kills his parents as Bruce watches. His father's dying words to him are: "Don't be afraid." From this time on, his loyal family butler, Alfred Pennyworth (played by Michael Caine), looks after Bruce.

Bruce later travels to Asia, testing himself, hoping his experiences will help him master all his fears. He trains intensively in the fighting techniques of the ninja under the direction of Henri Ducard (played by Liam Neeson). Ducard is part of the League of Shadows, a secret, nihilistic organization.

When Ducard informs Bruce that the shadowy group plans to destroy Gotham City, Bruce leaves Asia and returns to the city. He enlists Alfred and a technology expert employed by his late father's company, Lucius Fox (played by Morgan Freeman), to help him become a crime fighter who dresses like the thing he feared most: a bat. Among his first opponents is the entire League of Shadows.

BRUCE WAYNE'S (BATMAN) PSYCHOLOGICAL TRAITS

The psychology of the orphaned boy, and the young man he becomes, is dominated by fear that goes beyond chiroptophobia. Witnessing the trauma of his parents' murder instilled more fear in him. He is determined to neutralize and compensate for his fears by become more terrifying than they are.

According to Dr. Robin S. Rosenberg, a clinical psychologist, Bruce's successful, self-directed transition from fearful youth to crime-fighting superhero is an example of posttraumatic growth. Dr. Robinson, the author of *What's the Matter with Batman? An Unauthorized Clinical Look under the Mask of the Caped Crusader*, notes that psychologists have observed that some people reevaluate their purpose in life and the meaning of life after suffering traumatic experiences such as the loss of loved ones and personal injury. They begin to work for goals that help others. Bruce's experiences and his desire to rid himself of fear are redirected into social activism. (Actually it is vigilantism, but in the world of superheroes they are the same thing.)

In the make-believe world of comic books into which Bruce was born, he is not mentally ill. He has, as he admits, "issues," but that makes him like nearly everyone else in his make-believe world and in ours.

If a very rich man (or any man) were to dress like a bat and become a vigilante in the real world, it is unlikely he would be as mentally healthy. It would not be surprising if he turned out to be delusional at best and psychotic at worst. But, if he showed the same personality traits and behaviors, the same sense of control as the Batman, he would not meet any of the criteria for mental illness described in the *Diagnostic and Statistical Manual of Mental Disorders, 5th Edition*. Bruce Wayne is in control and fighting against real—or at least, comic book real—threats. He is obsessive but no more so than ambitious workaholics who are still regarded as being healthy. He is aware of his motivation, of what drives him to fight crime. He has a realistic appreciation of his abilities and strengths.

POSITIVE PSYCHOLOGICAL ATTRIBUTES

Posttraumatic Growth

Alfred: "Why bats, Master Wayne?"
Bruce: "Bats frighten me. It's time my enemies shared my dread."

Bruce resolves to deal with his intense fear of bats and of criminals, such as the one who gunned down his parents as he watched, by acknowledging them and converting the anxiety they produce into positive action. He has internalized

Henri Ducard's fortune cookie insights: "To manipulate the fear in others, you must first master your own." And "To conquer fear, you must become fear."

Courage—Honesty

Bruce: "They told me there was nothing out there, nothing to fear. But the night my parents were murdered I caught a glimpse of something. I've looked for it ever since. I went around the world, searched in all the shadows. And there is something out there in the darkness, something terrifying, something that will not stop until it gets revenge. Me."

The desire for revenge is an understandable response to being harmed. While it is a prime motivation for Bruce becoming Batman, he admits it and, as the next quote indicates, uses this motivation not just to satisfy his desire for revenge, but also to help others.

Humanity—Kindness

Alfred: "You're getting lost inside this monster of yours."
Bruce: "I'm using this monster to help other people, just like my father did."

Bruce is intense and committed to his goal of helping others. It is dangerous and difficult work and he is definitely at risk of burnout, as are physicians who work in emergency departments and others with high-stress jobs. But his motivation is a humane one, and he does not become "lost in this monster," at least not during this film.

Most superheroes have been around so long they undergo both physical and psychological changes. Batman first appeared 77 years ago. Different incarnations of Batman display different psychological traits, but in *Batman Begins*, it is clear that he is mentally healthy.

Psychologist Travis Langley, the author of *Batman and Psychology*, agrees. She concludes that Batman "is driven—haunted—but we can no more label that drive a mental illness for him then we can for the revolutionaries who stand up to tyrants or the activists who fight against great odds to make this world a better place."

Profile #76: Hugh Conway in the Novel *Lost Horizon* by James Hilton

> I have often found since then that others who met Conway, even quite formally and for a moment, remembered him afterwards with great vividness.

PLOT SUMMARY

After successfully organizing the evacuation of Europeans from the war-torn Central Asian region of Baskul, diplomat Hugh Conway and three very different companions board what they think is the last flight to safety. Instead, they are hijacked and flown over the Himalayas into Tibet where the plane crashes deep in the mountains, killing the pilot.

The passengers are rescued by a mysterious Chinese man who takes them to a remarkable retreat hidden in "the valley of the blue moon." Protected from the brutal Himalayan winds and snows, Shangri-La offers peace, beauty, and tranquility. The inhabitants live contented lives uncomplicated by materialism, competition, and conflict. The High Lama in the monastery at Shangri-La believes the refuge will help preserve culture sure to be destroyed by impending world war.

Now facing death, the High Lama wants Conway to take over his job. The appeal of the offer conflicts with the responsibility Conway feels toward his companions and his country. The difficult choice he faces and the reactions of the others to the knowledge that they cannot leave "the valley of the blue moon" ultimately lead to tragedy for some and contentment for others. Conway's conflict leads to extreme hardship and, finally, purpose and meaning that he had been missing all of his life.

CONWAY'S PSYCHOLOGICAL TRAITS

Conway was an exceptional student and athlete at Oxford, impressing all who knew him. Brilliant, charming, and multitalented, he excelled at languages, sports, music, theater, and Oriental studies. He was immensely liked and admired. His teachers and fellow students expected him to go far after graduation, perhaps as far as becoming prime minister of Great Britain.

But World War I intervened, and like so many young people who survived that conflict, Conway was forever changed by it (for a more tragic example of a World War I veteran, read the entry about Virginia Woolf's character Septimus Warren Smith in *Mrs. Dalloway*).

Conway's war experiences left him sadder, with less passion but a deeper knowledge and understanding of human behavior and its limitations. He maintained his impressive abilities, talents, and skills but was disinclined to promote himself. He lost his ambition but retained his social intelligence. And although he is now world-weary, he nevertheless retains the leadership traits people saw in him before the war.

POSITIVE PSYCHOLOGICAL ATTRIBUTES

Wisdom and Knowledge—Love of Learning

"A pity you didn't know him [Conway] at Oxford. He was just brilliant—there's no other word." And: "He gave a Speech Day oration in Greek, I recollect, and was outstandingly first-rate in school theatricals."

Conway's record indicates that he enjoys mastering new skills and adding to his store of knowledge.

Justice—Leadership

"There was something rather Elizabethan about him [Conway]—his casual versatility, his good looks, that effervescent combination of mental with physical activities . . . Our civilization doesn't often breed people like that nowadays." And: "And even when he and I met in the middle of China, with his mind a blank and his past a mystery, there was still that queer core of attractiveness in him."

Conway's charisma attracts people to him and plays a big part in them having confidence in him and in his abilities.

Humanity—Kindness, Caring

"We seem to be in a queer fix," he [Conway] said, leaning forward to her ear, "but I'm glad you're taking it calmly. I don't really think anything dreadful is going to happen to us." And, "Conway meanwhile was busying himself with a very practical task. He had collected every scrap of paper that they all had, and was composing messages in various native languages to be dropped to earth at intervals. It was a slender chance, in such sparsely populated country, but worth taking."

After being hijacked, Conway takes steps to help and reassure his fellow captives in a frightening situation.

Courage—Honesty

"He [Conway] preferred the less formal and more picturesque jobs that were on offer, and as these were often not good ones, it had doubtless seemed to others that he was playing his cards rather badly. Actually, he felt he had played them rather well; he had had a varied and moderately enjoyable decade."

Despite his considerable interpersonal skills and intellectual abilities, Conway honestly evaluates his interests and sets his goals accordingly, despite what his colleagues might think of his apparent lack of ambition.

Humanity—Social Intelligence

"I've worked with him [Conway] at the Consulate. I happen to know that he hasn't been in bed for the last four nights. As a matter of fact, we're damned lucky in having him with us in a tight corner like this. Apart from knowing the languages, he's got a sort of way with him in dealing with people. If anyone can get us out of the mess, he'll do it. He's pretty cool about most things."

Conway understands people's motivations, interests, and flaws. He uses this knowledge to help the people he is responsible for.

Hilton's novel was and still is a popular adventure story. Besides its entertainment value, it is best known for introducing the word and the utopian concept of Shangri-La into many languages. Critics never considered *Lost Horizon* a literary work in the same category as the best novels by more famous authors like Ernest Hemingway and F. Scott Fitzgerald, for example. But this was not Hilton's intent. He was a storyteller.

It is not a coincidence that Hilton named the High Lama of Shangri-La Father Perrault. The spiritual leader of the utopian refuge shares his last name with the 17th-century French author Charles Perrault. Charles's writings were inspired by European folktales. His interest in these tales led him to develop a new category of storytelling illustrated by his works, which include *Cinderella*, *Little Red Riding Hood*, and *Sleeping Beauty*; Charles Perrault pioneered the fairytale. James Hilton continued the tradition in his popular novel.

Profile #77: L. B. Jefferies in the Film *Rear Window*; Screenplay by John Michael Hayes, Based on a Short Story by Cornell Woolrich

> I've seen bickering and family quarrels and mysterious trips at night, and knives and saws and ropes, and now since last evening, not a sign of the wife. How do you explain that?

PLOT SUMMARY

It's a hot summer and a broken leg has L. B. Jefferies (played by Jimmy Stewart) stuck in his New York City apartment—without air-conditioning. The photojournalist broke his leg filming a crash during an automobile race. Now he is bored, as bored as a man used to daily adventure can be when he can't leave his small apartment.

He occupies himself by observing his neighbors. He knows them all very well, well enough to notice when something curious happens in the apartment directly across the courtyard from his rear window. He suspects that his neighbor (played by Raymond Burr) has killed his wife and removed her body in pieces in a suitcase. L. B. has a difficult time convincing his aide (played by Thelma Ritter) and fiancée (played by Grace Kelly) that he has uncovered a murder. The police don't believe him either.

L. B. uses persistence and reasoning to gather evidence without leaving his apartment. His perseverance pays off in both positive and threateningly negative ways when his fiancée enters the suspect's apartment to find solid evidence of the crime. Soon, L. B. receives an unexpected visitor to his own apartment.

L. B.'S PSYCHOLOGICAL TRAITS

L. B. is a successful photographer who enjoys the adventure and freedom that come with his job. He resists settling down with his beautiful, sophisticated fiancée whom he thinks might not enjoy the hardships that come with his work.

He makes good use of his powers of observation and deduction. When he suspects a crime, he pursues the case persistently when no one else—not even those close to him—believe in what he is doing.

POSITIVE PSYCHOLOGICAL ATTRIBUTES

Wisdom and Knowledge—Curiosity

L. B.: "Why would a man leave his apartment three times on a rainy night with a suitcase and come back three times?"

Wisdom and Knowledge—Critical Thinking

L. B.: "He killed a dog last night because the dog was scratching around in the garden. You know why? Because he had something buried in that garden that the dog scented."

Courage—Persistence

Detective: "You didn't see the killing or the body. How do you know there was a murder?"

L. B.: "Because everything this fellow's done has been suspicious: trips at night in the rain, knifes, saws, trunks with rope, and now this wife that isn't there anymore."

Detective: "I admit it does have a mysterious sound. But it could be any number of things for the wife disappearing. Murder is the least part."

L. B. persists in gathering evidence despite initial lack of encouragement and even some disapproval from those around him.

Profile #78: Will Kane in the Film *High Noon*; Screenplay by Carl Foreman, Based on the Short Story "The Tin Star" by John W. Cunningham

I think I ought to stay.

PLOT SUMMARY

Five years ago, Marshal Will Kane (played by Gary Cooper) turned the lawless frontier town of Hadleyville, New Mexico, into a safe community by leading his deputies in a campaign to arrest the criminals who were victimizing the settlers. The most dangerous, unstable man he arrested was Frank Miller. Will was responsible for sending Miller to prison, where he was scheduled to be executed. At his trial, Miller swore he would kill Will.

At 10:40 a.m. on the day of Will's wedding and his retirement as marshal, Will learns that Miller has been pardoned and that he is on the noon train heading back to Hadleyville. Three of Miller's gang are already waiting for their boss at the station. Despite the fact that the new marshal will not arrive in town until tomorrow, the townspeople urge Will to leave immediately. Will leaves with his new bride. But 10 minutes later, against the objections of his Quaker wife, Amy (played by Grace Kelly), he heads back into town to face Miller and his men.

The showdown with the bad guys plays out differently for Will this time than it did five years before. Will spends the short amount of time he has before noon trying to recruit men to help him deal with the threat posed by the Miller gang. His single deputy quits. His friends abandon him. His wife says she will leave on the train that drops off Miller if Will insists on fighting. Among all the townspeople, only a 14-year-old boy and a one-eyed intoxicated man offer to help Will. He thanks them but knows he can't risk their safety. Despite his fear, and the abandonment by everyone he thought he knew well, Will stays to face the threat, which he feels it is his job to face.

WILL'S PSYCHOLOGICAL TRAITS

Will is a quiet, introspective man dedicated to upholding the law. He is unpretentious and soft-spoken. He shows lack of insight into the character of his neighbors and "friends" who turn out to be self-righteous and cowardly.

POSITIVE PSYCHOLOGICAL ATTRIBUTES

Courage—Bravery

Former deputy [to Will]: "Scared?"
Will: "I guess so."
Former deputy: "Sure. It stands to reason."

Despite his fear, Will faces the danger that he feels it is his responsibility to face.

Courage—Honesty

Will: "Well, he [Miller] was always wild and kind of crazy. He'll probably make trouble."
Amy, Will's wife: "But that's no concern of yours, not anymore."
Will: "I'm the one who sent him up."
Amy: "That was part of your job. That's finished now. They've got a new marshal."
Will: "Won't be here until tomorrow. Seems to me I've got to stay. Anyway, I'm the same man with or without this [puts badge back on]."

Temperance—Humility

Bartender [to bar patrons]: "I'll give you odds, Will's dead five minutes after Frank gets off the train . . . That's all Frank will need because I . . . "

Will enters bar and hears him. Angry, Will punches the bartender, knocking him down.

Bartender, from the floor: "You carry a badge and a gun, Marshal. You had no call to do that."
Will: "You're right."

Under pressure, Will loses his temper and strikes a cowardly man who is enjoying Will's predicament. In an instant, his basic conviction that he is not special enough to defy the law reasserts itself. He apologizes and offers to help the man up.

Humanity—Kindness

Will: "I kind of hate to do this without your new marshal being here."

Before he learns Miller is returning for revenge to threaten him and possibly the town, Will is uncomfortable leaving the town without a marshal even for a day despite the blessing of the townspeople.

Justice—Leadership

Amy: "Then don't go back, Will."
Will: "I've got to. That's the whole thing."

Justice—Fairness

Mr. Trumbull: "Here's those three killers walking the streets bold as brass. Why didn't you arrest 'em, Marshal? Why didn't you put 'em in jail where they ought to be? Then we'd only have Miller to worry about instead of the four of 'em."
Will: "I haven't anything to arrest them for, Mr. Trumbull. They haven't done anything. There's no law against them sittin' on a bench at the depot."

Justice—Teamwork, Loyalty

Amy: "Don't try to be a hero. You don't have to be a hero, not for me."
Will: "I'm not trying to be a hero. If you think I like this, you're crazy. Look, Amy, this is my town. I've got friends here."

Will returns to town to face the dangers posed by the outlaws because he feels it is his duty and because he feels an obligation to his "friends." People he thought were friends, however, abandon him. He nevertheless decides to meet the obligation he feels he has as the town's sheriff.

After he defeats the Miller Gang—with some unexpected help—the townspeople who abandoned him crowd around him, congratulating him. Will acknowledges only one of them, the young boy who offered to help. He then throws his sheriff's badge at the feet of the others and rides out of town with his wife.

Profile #79: Shane in the Film *Shane*; Screenplay by A. B. Guthrie Jr., Based on the Novel by Jack Schaefer

---

Joey's mother: "You were through with gun fighting."
Shane: "I changed my mind."
Joey's mother: "Are you doing this just for me?"
Shane: "For you Mary. And for Joe [her husband] and little Joe."

PLOT SUMMARY

This classic Western features Shane (played by Alan Ladd), an experienced and skilled gunfighter who is tired of the mercenary and violent life he has led. Wandering the West after the Civil War, he seeks an escape from his past. He befriends a homesteading family consisting of a man, his wife, and their young boy Joey (played by Brandon De Wilde). The boy's admiration for Shane approaches worship. After dispelling the father's initial distrust, Shane moves in and helps the family develop their small plot. It appears he has found some peace and an escape from his past.

This idyllic scenario is threatened by a rich and powerful cattleman who wants to drive the family and their neighboring homesteaders off their lands. Shane initially resists getting involved, even when humiliated and provoked by the cattleman's gunmen. The second time Shane is provoked, he fights back, thus setting the stage for a larger conflict between the two sides. Realizing the threat Shane represents, the cattleman hires Jake Wilson, a professional gunfighter (played by Jack Palance).

Joey's father decides to confront his enemy but Shane and Joey's mother know Joey's father will not be able to win against a professional killer like Wilson. Shane fights the father, knocks him out, and rides into town to fight for the homesteaders. Joey follows him on foot and arrives in time to witness the fight. Shane wins but is seriously wounded. He slumps in his saddle as he rides away for the last time from the violent life he sought to escape. Joey yells his name as he watches his hero ride off.

SHANE'S PSYCHOLOGICAL TRAITS

The former gunfighter is reticent and introspective. At the same time, he gives the impression that he is self-confident, competent, and resourceful. And yet he is subdued, almost as if he has lost someone and is in mourning. His quiet demeanor and humility suggest that he wants to avoid confrontation, and his efforts to help the struggling family until violence cannot be avoided support this impression.

POSITIVE PSYCHOLOGICAL ATTRIBUTES

Shane voluntarily assumes the role of the family's savior and sacrifices himself for them.

Courage—Bravery

Joey's father: "I told Shane to stay away from trouble. He did right."

On a trip to town to buy work clothes and fencing wire, one of the men who wants to drive Joey's father off his land insults Shane in a saloon, throws a drink on him, and tells him to leave. Despite his violent history, Shane refrains from fighting back and leaves.

Justice—Teamwork, Loyalty

One of Shane's first acts is to help Joey's father take out a giant tree stump he had been trying to remove for a long time. Later, after the second time a thug attempts to drive Shane out of the saloon, Shane defends himself and wins. When the thug's accomplices join the fight, Joey's father jumps in to help Shane; they help each other win.

Justice—Leadership

Shane: "You know what he wants you to stay for? Something that means more to you than anything else—your families. Your wives and kids. Like you, Lewis, your girls; Shipstead with his boys. They've got a right to stay here and grow up and be happy. That's up to you people to have nerve enough to not give it up." Shane addresses his adopted family and their neighbors who meet to discuss the threat they face from the cattlemen determined to drive them off their land.

Temperance—Humility

Joey: "Shane, I know you ain't afraid."
Shane: "It's a long story, Joe."
Joey's mother: "I think we know. Shane."

Joey's mother has figured out who and what Shane is: a former gunman trying to redeem himself. When Shane backs down from a fight, Joey reassures him that Joey doesn't think he is a coward. Shane does not brag that he was once a feared gunman and does not feel the need to justify to the boy or to anyone else his aversion to violence.

Humanity—Kindness

Shane: "You were watchin' me down the trail for quite a spell, weren't you?"
Joey: "Yes I was."
Shane: "You know, I . . . I like a man who watches things go on around. It means he'll make his mark someday."

Joey adores Shane and Shane is repeatedly kind to the boy. Shane encourages Joey, teaches him, respects him, and speaks to him like an adult.

Wisdom and Knowledge—Perspective, Self-knowledge

Shane: "I gotta be going on."
Joey: "Why, Shane?"

Shane: "A man has to be what he is, Joey. Can't break the mould. I tried it and it didn't work for me."

Joey: "We want you, Shane."

Shane: "Joey, there's no living with . . . with a killing. There's no going back from one. Right or wrong, it's a brand. A brand sticks. There's no going back. Now you run on home to your mother, and tell her . . . tell her everything's all right. And there aren't any more guns in the valley."

Even though Shane believed he was acting to defend the law-abiding family and community he wanted to join, he nevertheless killed as he had in his past life, something he desperately wanted to avoid. He does not want his actions to brand Joey and his family by association.

Profile #80: Marge Gunderson in the Film *Fargo*; Screenplay by Ethan and Joel Coen

> So that was Mrs. Lundegaard [dead] on the floor in there. And I guess that was your accomplice in the wood chipper. And those three people in Brainerd. And for what? For a little bit of money. There's more to life than a little money, you know. Don't you know that? And here you are . . . And it's a beautiful day . . . I just don't understand it.

PLOT SUMMARY

Jerry Lundegaard (played by William H. Macy) is a car dealer, ineffectual and deeply in debt. He hires two incompetent thugs to kidnap his wife in the hope his rich father-in-law will pay a million-dollar ransom, most of which he will keep after paying the kidnappers a mere $40,000.

He plans for no one to be harmed, but he hires the wrong thugs. Carl Showalter (played by Steve Buscemi) is talkative and hot-tempered. Gaear Grimsrud (played by Peter Stormare) is quiet and psychopathic. After abducting Jerry's wife, Gaear kills a state trooper and then chases down and kills two witnesses on the highway.

Marge Gunderson is woken up early the same morning to work on the case. She is the pregnant police chief of Brainerd, Minnesota, a part of the country where people are known for their friendly demeanors. Unperturbed by the triple homicide, she quickly surmises how the killings occurred. With little help from her far less intelligent deputies, Marge investigates the case, which eventually involves not three, but a total of seven homicides, including Jerry's wife, his father-in-law, a parking lot attendant, and Carl.

When Marge locates the kidnapper's hideout, she interrupts Gaear feeding Carl's body into a wood chipper. She singlehandedly apprehends Gaear, loads him into the back of her police care, and drives him to jail. Glancing at him in the rearview mirror, she asks the unresponsive killer why he would kill for a little money. Despite her highly effective, professional abilities and intelligence, she simply is not capable of understanding how anyone could do that. It is clear that the kindness behind her manners is a real feature of Marge's character.

MARGE'S PSYCHOLOGICAL TRAITS

Although she is a fictional character, Marge's positive psychological traits could easily make viewers wish she were real. (*Fargo* is not based on true events that occurred in Minnesota, despite the written notice at the start of the film claiming it is.) She is soft-spoken, unassuming, very clever, emotionally intelligent, and a partner in a nurturing, loving marriage.

POSITIVE PSYCHOLOGICAL ATTRIBUTES

Wisdom and Knowledge— Critical Thinking

Marge: "So we got a trooper pulls someone over. We got a shooting. These folks drive by. There's a high-speed pursuit, ends here, and then this execution-type deal." Marge rapidly and accurately assesses the events behind a crime scene involving victims separated by a considerable distance. Throughout her investigation, she repeatedly demonstrates her intelligence while never calling attention to it for recognition or praise.

Humanity—Emotional Intelligence

Lou [Deputy]: "The last vehicle that the trooper cited was a tan Ciera at 2:18 am. Under the plate number, he put DLR—I figure they stopped him or shot him before he could finish fillin' out the tag number. So I got the state lookin' for a Ciera with a tag startin' DLR. They don't got no match yet."

Marge: "I'm not sure that I agree with you a hundred percent on your police work there, Lou."

Lou: "Yeah?"

Marge: "Yah. I think that vehicle there probably had dealer plates. DLR?"

Lou: "Oh geez" [looks dully pained].

Marge: "Say Lou. Did ya hear the one about the guy who couldn't afford personalized plates, so he went and changed his name to J3L 2404?"

Lou: "Yeah, that's a good one."

Marge has to correct her slower subordinate but immediately softens the blow by telling him a joke to distract him and reassure him that he is not in trouble.

Humanity—Love

Marge: "You can sleep. It's early yet."
Norm [her husband]: "Gotta go?"
Marge: "Yeah."
Norm: "I'll fix you some eggs."
Marge: "It's okay, hon. I gotta run."
Norm: "You got to eat a breakfast, Marge. I'll fix you some eggs."
Marge: "Hon, you can sleep."
Norm: "You got to eat a breakfast."
Marge: "Ah, Norm. . ."
Norm: "Love you, Margie."
Marge: "Love you, hon."

Throughout the film, Marge and her husband support and show affection for each other. While some viewers might see only the sappiness in these characters' relationships and lives, the Coen brothers manage to make the rural, seemingly unsophisticated characters like Marge and Norm the heroes of their film. They provide a complete, healthy contrast to the behavior of Jerry, Carl, and Gaear.

People with good social connections, including marriages, are more likely to enjoy better health and longer lives than people without strong social networks. Support provided by close friends and family may ease stress and limit its harmful physical and psychological effects.

Profile #81: The Dream in the Poem "Kubla Khan; Or, a Vision in a Dream" by Samuel Taylor Coleridge

In Xanadu did Kubla Khan
A stately pleasure-dome decree:
Where Alph, the sacred river, ran
Through caverns measureless to man
Down to a sunless sea.

THE POEM'S BACKSTORY

Psychologists cannot yet explain the basis of the creativity that—together with sometimes years of hard work—leads to a finished book or film. Some people believe the process may be related to varying degrees to our ability to dream.

Coleridge claimed that his famous poem, "Kubla Khan," appeared to him in 1797 "in a sort of Reverie brought on by two grains of Opium taken to check a dysentery." In his preface to the poem published in 1816, he told his readers, referring to himself in the third person, that

> The author continued for about three hours in a profound sleep, at least of the external senses, during which time he has the most vivid confidence that he could not have composed less than from two to three hundred lines; if that indeed can be called composition in which all the images rose up before him as things, with a parallel production of the correspondent expressions, without any sensation or consciousness of effort. On awaking he appeared to himself to have a distinct recollection of the whole, and taking his pen, ink, and paper, instantly and eagerly wrote down the lines that are here preserved.

Coleridge said he managed to get much of what we now know as the complete poem down on paper before he was interrupted by a visitor knocking at his door. He answered the door and proceeded to discuss business with the visitor (who has never been identified) for about an hour. When he returned to this writing desk, he found he could recall less than a dozen lines or images of the hundreds he wanted to record.

He described the poem to his readers in 1816 as a "psychological curiosity." For years after its publication, many readers accepted the story that the poem was created in a dream and they enjoyed it simply as a reverie about a mysterious, exotic land. More recently, scholars have suggested that the colorful, evocative, sensual imagery reflects the poet's interest in mythology, dreams, the working of the human mind, and his thoughts on the nature of genius.

THE DREAMY ORIGIN OF THE POEM

There is no evidence that Coleridge actually dreamed the complete and polished lines of "Kubla Khan." Nor is there any evidence that he lied about its origin. He certainly may have been inspired by dream imagery. Other writers claim to have developed plots inspired by the content of their dreams. Robert Louis Stevenson's novella "Strange Case of Dr. Jekyll and Mr. Hyde" is said to have sprung from a nightmare he had while suffering from a lung ailment. The horrors of the first two versions of his classic story (see Henry Jekyll in *Strange Case of Dr. Jekyll and Mr. Hyde*) were toned down in the third, published version. And Frankenstein and his monster owe their existence to a vivid early morning vision, according to author Mary Shelley. She recalled that "with shut eyes but acute mental vision—I saw the pale student of unhallowed arts kneeling beside the thing he had put together. I saw the hideous phantasm of a man stretched out, and then, on the workings of some powerful engine, show signs of life."

It is possible that Coleridge exaggerated or even made up his account of the poem coming to him in a dream. By explicitly linking the exotic and mysterious references and allusions in the poem to a story about its dream-vision origin, he made the poem even more romantic than it would have been without the backstory. The poem, after all, is finely crafted and the published version is not identical to an earlier manuscript of the poem. Nevertheless, even if Coleridge exaggerated the role dreaming played in the poem's creation, the poem and its supposed origin raise the interesting topic of the role dreams play in such creative processes and in our lives.

PSYCHOLOGY OF DREAMING

Sigmund Freud believed that dreams were creations full of symbolism, and that they were like poems that provided clues and insights into our subconscious concerns and desires. Since everyone dreams, everyone is, in a sense, a poet, according to Freud. "Dreams," clinical psychologist Ilana Simons wrote in her blog the *Literary Mind*, "are a lot like poetry." Simons, who has PhDs in both literature and psychology, explains that in both dreams and poetry, "we express our internal life in similar ways. We conjure images; we combine incongruent elements to evoke emotion in a more efficient way than wordier descriptions can; and we use unconscious and tangential associations rather than logic to tell a story."

Some researchers, like the Nobel Prize–winning biologist and codiscoverer of the structure of DNA, Francis Crick, dismiss the literary quality of dreams. They believe dreams are meaningless. They explain them as random firing of neurons onto which people project meaning where there is none. The random neuronal activity, according to this theory, is actually the way the brain resets itself, like a hard drive being defragmented.

Other theories attribute less housekeeping and more therapeutic functions to dreams. They suggest that dreams may help us work out problems, serve as rehearsals for dealing with threats, and/or reinforce important memories and allow less important ones to fade. It is likely, however, that dreams will continue to be linked to creativity.

POSITIVE PSYCHOLOGICAL ATTRIBUTES

Wisdom and Knowledge—Creativity and Originality

We still do not understand the human mind and the neurobiological structure and function on which it is based well enough to explain complex phenomena like dreaming or the creation of a good story.

Profile #82: Harry Potter in the Young Adult Novel *Harry Potter and the Sorcerer's Stone* and sequels by J. K. Rowling

> Love as powerful as your mother's for you leaves its own mark . . . To have been loved so deeply, even though the person who loved us is gone, will give us some protection forever.

PLOT SUMMARY

Harry Potter will face many challenges as he grows and reaches his potential as a great and famous wizard. But he encounters his first and perhaps greatest challenge—according to developmental and clinical psychology—before he is 11 years old: he grows up in the Dursley household.

Petunia Dursley is his late mother's sister. When Harry is just one year old, he is left on the doorstep of the home she shares with her husband, Vernon. Harry is an orphan; his parents, Lily and James, were killed by the evil, rogue wizard Voldemort.

Although the Dursleys provide Harry a house to live in, they don't provide a supportive or loving home. The Dursleys never wanted Harry. They are embarrassed by his and his parents' magical backgrounds. They spoil their lumpish, obnoxious son Dudley at Harry's expense. Not only do they not like Harry, but also they abuse him. And the abuse lasts until Harry is able, until summer vacation at least, to escape it by enrolling at Hogwarts, a boarding school for young wizards.

Not only does Harry survive his unhappy childhood, but he distinguishes himself at school, lays the basis for two lifelong friendships, and gains extracurricular experience dealing with black magic challenges that even a young, talented wizard should not have to deal with. By the end of the book, Harry demonstrates that he is a remarkable boy and a talented wizard. Through the pages of six more books in the series, he shows how extraordinarily resilient he is.

HARRY'S PSYCHOLOGICAL TRAITS

Bookish, bespectacled, and skinny, the timid young wizard doesn't look or feel like a hero. He feels alone since he has no close relationships—until he makes friends at school. During his first 10 years, Harry survives emotional neglect and abusive treatment at the hands of his caretakers. Harry successfully struggles to overcome these handicaps and thrive. Despite his accomplishments and the recognition he receives in time, Harry never loses his sense of humility.

J. K. Rowling

Born in in England in 1965, Joanne Rowling was interested in writing from at least the age of six. The gift she eventually developed became apparent when she wrote the first of a series of books about a boy wizard, *Harry Potter and the Philosopher's Stone.* (The word *Sorcerer's* replaced *Philosopher's* in the title of the American edition.) She added the initial "K." (in honor of her grandmother Kathleen) to her name after her first publisher worried that young boys might not relate to a book about a young male wizard written by a woman. Hence, her famous pen name: J. K. Rowling.

Although she wished she had studied English, Rowling majored in French at the University of Exeter. After studying a year in Paris, she graduated and worked at several jobs in London. During a train trip between Manchester and London in 1990, she began thinking about a boy wizard. Although she had nothing to write with on the train—and was too shy to borrow writing materials from anyone—she nevertheless formulated the idea for a series of fantasy books that would become one of the most popular in children's literature.

After moving to Portugal in 1991, Rowling married her first husband, a journalist, and became a mother in 1993. The couple divorced a few years later and Rowling moved to Edinburgh, Scotland, with her child. She continued working on her book despite her struggles as a single parent living on state benefits and suffering from depression.

Rowling later said: "Depression is the most unpleasant thing I have ever experienced. . . . It is that absence of being able to envisage that you will ever be cheerful again. The absence of hope. That very deadened feeling, which is so very different from feeling sad. Sad hurts but it's a healthy feeling. It is a necessary thing to feel. Depression is very different."

Despite her challenges, Rowling managed to finish the book. She found an agent who, after a year and a dozen rejections by large publishing houses, managed to sell the book to a small publisher called Bloomsbury. The Bloomsbury editor agreed to publish the book because his eight-year-old daughter loved the first chapter. To everyone's surprise, the book began to sell well in just a few weeks based on word-of-mouth recommendations. Rowling's money problems disappeared after Scholastic purchased the rights to publish in America and she sold the movie rights to Warner Bros. She completed the seventh, final, and her favorite book in the series, *Harry Potter and the Deathly Hallows*, in 2006. She and her second husband live with their three children in Scotland where she continues to write short stories and novels.

POSITIVE PSYCHOLOGICAL ATTRIBUTES

Resilience

Resilience is the ability to "bounce back" from adversity. It involves adapting to the challenges and injuries, which can be physical or psychological, following stressful or harmful experiences. For a young child like Harry to adapt to a lack of affection and love—not to mention physical abuse—between the ages of 1 and 10 and then to grow into a psychologically healthy adolescent is a remarkable example of resilience.

Albus Dumbledore to the Dursleys: "You have never treated Harry as a son (as I asked). He has known nothing but neglect and often cruelty at your hands. The best that can be said is that he has at least escaped the appalling damage you have inflicted upon the unfortunate boy sitting between you."

The head of Hogwarts and Harry's father figure, Albus Dumbledore, left Harry on the Dursleys' doorstep after Harry's parents were killed. He also left the Dursleys instructions to care for the boy as they would a child of their own. Instead, they subjected Harry to emotional neglect. They not only failed to offer the small boy any indication of love, affection, or even acceptance, but also denied him the memories of his lost parents: Harry "couldn't remember his parents at all. His aunt and uncle never spoke about them, and of course he was forbidden to ask questions. There were no photographs of them in the house."

The Dursleys also force Harry to sleep, and spend long periods of time, in a closet under the stairs. They deny him presents while showering their son Dudley with excessive gifts and attention. They deny him meals and do nothing when Dudley hits Harry. Yet, as Dumbledore points out to the Dursleys, Harry "escaped the appalling damage" they inflicted upon him. In fact, he not only escapes the damage, but also grows into a well-adjusted, secure, and admired figure.

Psychologists Danielle Provenzano and Richard Heyman, authors of "Harry Potter and the Resilience to Adversity" in the book *The Psychology of Harry Potter*, estimate that the odds of a child as maltreated as Harry ending up functioning "in the 'non-pathological' range" are about one in four. They add that "the odds are much lower of being, like Harry, average to above average in all important life domains."

Resilience can be developed. Positive emotions promote and increase resilience. Being able to find something positive in life in the midst of a tragic or negative experience has been shown to decrease mental health problems, such as depression, later. Resilient people handle stress better than less resilient people. They appear to have more confidence in the face of unknown challenges than someone who worries more. Resilient people are less inclined to view things exclusively as negative. Instead they balance both the negative and positive aspects of a challenging situation. This is in contrast to less resilient people who tend to concentrate on the negative aspects of a situation and on negative possibilities.

Harry's remarkable positive response to his early challenges can be attributed, according to Provenzano and Heyman, to four factors. The first is his adaptable temperament. The second is the safe, loving home life he enjoyed during his first year of life before he lost his parents. The third is the academic environment at Hogwarts, which matches his interests and needs. The fourth is the support he gets from Dumbledore and other adults at Hogwarts. All these help to explain how a psychologically abused boy manages to become an exceptional adolescent.

Profile #83: Lisbeth Salander in the Novel *The Girl with the Dragon Tattoo* by Stieg Larsson

You're not a person who encourages friendship.

PLOT SUMMARY

Liberal journalist Mikael Blomkvist has just been tried and convicted of libel and defamation after publishing an article critical of Hans-Erik Wennerström, a powerful financier. Demoralized by the prospect of spending months in prison, he tells the editor of his struggling journal *Millennium* that he will resign.

Mikael doesn't know he is being considered by the head of a large company for a freelance assignment. This development will bring a unique and intriguing female character into his life: Lisbeth Salander. Lisbeth is a brilliant, unconventional, and unorthodox computer specialist and researcher. She works for the private investigation company Mikael's prospective new employer has hired to gather background information on the journalist. Lisbeth is fiercely independent, resourceful, idiosyncratic, multipierced, and tattooed.

Mikael accepts the job because he needs the money and because it will give him an opportunity to gather incriminating information about Wennerström. Impressed by Lisbeth's computer skills when he sees the report she compiles about him, he asks for her help with his new job. Together, they investigate the long-ago disappearance of a young woman related to his new employer. Together, they uncover hideous secrets that go beyond the search for one woman. In a violent climax, Lisbeth saves Mikael's life and they solve the case.

With Lisbeth's help, Mikael then uncovers new evidence that restores his reputation. Lisbeth, uncharacteristically, decides to admit to Mikael that she has feelings for him. Sadly, as she approaches his apartment, she sees him with his lover. She walks away and retreats back into her protective isolation.

LISBETH'S PSYCHOLOGICAL TRAITS

Lisbeth, 27 years old, is highly intelligent, well-organized, resilient, resourceful, and fiercely independent. She is also unconventional. She is not interested in small talk, office politics, or making friends. Her lack of interest in socializing, her petite frame, her unconventional clothing, and her edgy hair style and body markings frequently mislead people; she is more often than not stronger and more competent than those who judge her.

When abused or attacked, she reacts violently in self-defense and sometimes in an excessively punishing way. Given her past history of abuse and the criminal nature of her adversaries, she would likely be declared not guilty by a jury for these offenses. Her computer-hacking crimes may be less well received by a jury, but again, she might have a case; she only hacks into the accounts of bad guys or as part of her job.

MALADAPTIVE ANTISOCIAL PERSONALITY TRAITS

Although subjected to significant abuse throughout her life, Lisbeth has not developed symptoms of posttraumatic stress disorder. Instead, she has developed a strong—if somewhat insular and socially withdrawn—outlook that stresses independence, competence, and resilience. Lisbeth has been violent only when attacked or seriously threatened. She has never acted aggressively without serious provocation.

She has paid a significant psychological price for the abuse she has suffered. But Lisbeth has adapted to its effects by developing strong, effective defenses, defenses that work for her and make her a productive citizen.

The author suggests that Lisbeth has Asperger's syndrome or a high-functioning autism spectrum disorder. Lisbeth's behavior, however, may be explained without referring to this disorder. Her refusal to socialize and form relationships is a psychological defense she developed after suffering years of abuse. It is not the result of something she was born with, which would be the case if she had high functioning autism.

Psychologist Marisa Mauro concludes in her report published in the book *The Psychology of the Girl with the Dragon Tattoo* that "Ms. Salander is not suffering from severe psychological symptoms. Although Ms. Salander appears to have some features consistent with antisocial personality disorder—including aggression, impulsivity, and problems with the law—they do not appear to be at a level severe enough to adversely affect her well-being or the safety of others."

Antagonism

". . . her casebook was filled with such terms as introverted, socially inhibited, lacking in empathy, ego fixated, psychopathic and asocial behavior, difficulty in cooperating, and incapable of assimilating learning."

Lisbeth "would fold her arms and refuse to participate in any psychological tests." Social service authorities requested these tests after they began supervising Lisbeth. Lisbeth came under their authority when "on the threshold of her teenage years, All The Evil happened" to her. (The nature of the abusive evil is explained in two sequels.) Because of her refusal to cooperate with a system she rejects, Lisbeth's social services file contains many guesses, assumptions, and invalid suggestions, for example, "lacking in empathy" and "psychopathic." A thorough overview of her life suggests that she scores low on the personality traits of agreeableness and high on antagonism. She generally lacks affection, trust, and other positive social attitudes, yet she is capable of feeling love for Mikael and she goes out of her way to help decent clients.

Aggressiveness

"She shoved the taser into his left armpit and fired off 750,000 volts. When his legs began to give way, she put her shoulder against him and used all her strength to push him down on the bed."

After being abused as a teen, Lisbeth is raped as an adult by her new social worker. She fights back in a way many would consider excessive. The author might insist that Lisbeth was protecting herself from a system that would not protect her. As a result of her history of being abused, she fights back with everything she has whenever she is attacked. She goes beyond socially acceptable standards when she tattoos the words "I AM A SADISTIC PIG, A PERVERT, AND A RAPIST" on her attacker's abdomen.

POSITIVE PSYCHOLOGICAL ATTRIBUTES

Courage—Bravery

" . . . her only remaining action was to do what she had always done—take matters into her own hands and solve her problems on her own."

Bravery does not have to express itself physically, although Lisbeth does not shy away from physical bravery when necessary. Facing other types of challenges can require bravery. Lisbeth has been facing both kinds of challenges with bravery most of her life.

Wisdom and Knowledge—Judgment, Love of Learning

Lisbeth's boss Armansky "was bewildered and angry with himself for having so obviously misjudged her. He had taken her for stupid, maybe even retarded." But later he realized that she was "the most able investigator he had met in all his years in the business."

Even a security expert with many years of experience like Armansky is fooled by Lisbeth's appearance and behavior. He later recognizes her ability not only to conduct computer-based investigations but also to process and evaluate the secrets she uncovers. Her analytical skills match her exceptional, self-taught computer-hacking skills.

Courage—Honesty (Lisbeth's Way)

"I call them Salander's Principles. One of them is that a bastard is always a bastard, and if I can hurt a bastard by digging up s**t about him, then he deserves it." And, "But the thing is that when I do a PI [private investigation], I also look at what I think about the person. I'm not neutral. If a person seems like a good sort, I might tone down my report."

Lisbeth has a morality, although it can cross ethical lines. Let down and treated terribly by family and social services all her life, she has adopted a moral code that has elements of vigilantism and fairness. It is her way of compensating for a society that victimized her. However wrong, it does not make her mentally ill.

Profile #84: Atticus Finch in the Novel *To Kill a Mockingbird* by Harper Lee

> "They're certainly entitled to think that, and they're entitled to full respect for their opinions," said Atticus, "but before I can live with other folks I've got to live with myself. The one thing that doesn't abide by majority rule is a person's conscience."

PLOT SUMMARY

Six-year-old Scout Finch, her brother Jem, and their friend and neighbor Dill are growing up in the small town of Maycomb, Alabama, during the depression of the 1930s. Over much of the three years described in the novel, their lives are full of outdoor play involving fanciful games and scenarios. They believe there is only one real "threat" in their world, but it is one they created. They scare each other and themselves with conjectures about a mysterious shut-in neighbor named Boo Radley, whom they have never seen.

They are not aware of real danger when it threatens them. It begins when their well-respected, widower father, attorney Atticus Finch, agrees to defend Tom Robinson. Robinson is a black man falsely accused of beating and raping a poor white girl named Mayella Ewell. Atticus knows that Tom's case is hopeless in this racist part of the deep South but he defends him brilliantly. Atticus proves that Tom is innocent by showing in court that Tom was physically incapable of attacking Mayella as she claims he did; one of Tom's arms was so damaged in an accident long ago that he cannot move it.

Although it is clear there is no way Tom could have attacked and raped Mayella, Tom is convicted, as Atticus expected. His children are mystified that the jury could reach such an obviously unfounded verdict. The consequences of Atticus's principled defense of the innocent man eventually put the children's lives in danger. The threat comes from Bob Ewell, Mayella's father, who has been offended by Atticus's statements. Drunk and embarrassed, Bob Ewell promises revenge. The climax of the novel sees an unexpected attack and an even more unexpected rescue by the least likely rescuer the children could imagine. They learn that the ignorance and racism common among so many adults is more dangerous and far more threatening than any of their childhood fears of "threats" like Boo Radley.

ATTICUS'S PSYCHOLOGICAL TRAITS

Few people will ever meet a person with all the character traits Harper Lee bestowed on her beloved character Atticus Finch in *To Kill a Mockingbird*. In fact, his positive psychological profile has made him into an almost mythical literary figure. He demonstrates significantly well-developed features of the majority of the VIA Classification of Character Strengths & Virtues, including wisdom and knowledge, courage, humanity, justice, and temperance.

POSITIVE PSYCHOLOGICAL ATTRIBUTES

Wisdom and Knowledge—Perspective

"When a child asks you something, answer him, for goodness' sake. But don't make a production of it. Children are children, but they can spot an evasion faster than adults, and evasion simply muddles 'em."

Humanity—Emotional Intelligence

"If you can learn a simple trick, Scout, you'll get along a lot better with all kinds of folks. You never really understand a person until you consider things from his point of view, until you climb into his skin and walk around in it." And "Atticus had said it was the polite thing to talk to people about what they were interested in, not about what you were interested in."

Justice—Fairness

"As you grow older, you'll see white men cheat black men every day of your life, but let me tell you something and don't you forget it—whenever a white man does that to a black man, no matter who he is, how rich he is, or how fine a family he comes from, that white man is trash." Atticus believed in justice under the law for all men, black and white, but he was in no way a radical who challenged the unfair practice of segregation in the South in the 1930s. He was not an advocate for integration of blacks into white society where they could benefit from greater opportunity. This becomes very clear when reading about the version of Atticus Finch in Harper Lee's novel *Go Set a Watchman.*

Courage—Bravery

"Courage isn't a man with a gun in his hand. It's knowing you're licked before you begin but you begin anyway and you see it through no matter what. You rarely win, but sometimes you do." And, "Simply because we were licked a hundred years before we started is no reason for us not to try to win."

Courage—Honesty

"Before I can live with other folks I've got to live with myself. The one thing that doesn't abide by majority rule is a person's conscience."

Temperance—Humility

"In a fog, Jem and I watched our father take the gun and walk out into the middle of the street . . . The rifle cracked. Tim Johnson [a rabid dog] leaped, flopped over and crumpled on the sidewalk . . . He didn't know what hit him." Atticus's children are astounded when they discover that their father is an excellent marksman, and had once been the best in Maycomb County. Why, his daughter Scout wonders, didn't he ever tell them? Their neighbor explains to her: "People in their right minds never take pride in their talents."

How realistic is Atticus Finch? Many people appreciate ideal characters, myths, and stories with happy endings. They are encouraged by them. Such tales maintain hope and partially offset the disappointments and uncooperative reality of actual life. They allow many people to vicariously experience adventures and great feats without risking personal harm or failure. Action heroes like Bruce Willis's character in the *Die Hard* series of movies, Hercules, James Bond, romantic love interests in romance novels, and others provide these vicarious benefits to millions of viewers and readers. Atticus Finch of *To Kill a Mockingbird* gives readers a moral hero who is much steadier, braver, and wiser than the average person. Unfortunately, it is easier to encounter a character like the Atticus described in the next entry, *Go Set a Watchman,* than it is to find one like the Atticus depicted in *To Kill a Mockingbird.*

Part 3

Negative Psychological Traits and Features

Profile #85: Atticus Finch in the Novel *Go Set a Watchman* by Harper Lee

> The one human being she had ever fully and wholeheartedly trusted had failed her; the only man she had ever known to whom she could point and say with expert knowledge, "He is a gentleman, in his heart he is a gentleman," had betrayed her, publicly, grossly, and shamelessly.

PLOT SUMMARY

In the mid-1950s, Jean Louise "Scout" Finch, now 26 years old, returns from New York City to her hometown of Maycomb, Alabama. Her father Atticus is in his early 70s and suffering from arthritis. Jean Louise's friend, Hank, happy to see her, proposes marriage to her, as he has done in the past. Jean Louise considers it but decides against accepting his proposal.

Her trip brings back memories of her childhood when she was known throughout Maycomb as the independent tomboy Scout. The new memories she is making on this visit, however, leave her disturbed and disillusioned.

Jean Louise's return to her childhood home and her visit with Atticus, her aunt, her uncle, and Hank leads her to discover the deeply ingrained flaws in the Deep South's social structure. She is appalled to learn that even the people she loves and admires hold racist, intolerant, and indefensible views. Her memories of the dignity, humanity, integrity, and sense of justice she saw in her father and other role models of her youth are shaken when she discovers their deep-seated prejudicial attitudes.

ATTICUS'S PSYCHOLOGICAL TRAITS

Readers are more likely to meet a real-life version of this Atticus than a real-life version of the Atticus in *To Kill a Mockingbird*. The two characters may share the same outward appearance and demeanor, but inside they have a major difference. The Atticus in *Go Set a Watchman* is a racist. Although he is a successful and respected small town lawyer, his prejudiced attitude indicates that he lacks some important critical thinking skills.

Alternatively, a more sophisticated way to view the two Atticus characters is to merge them. The *To Kill a Mockingbird* Atticus is seen through the eyes of a six-year-old girl who loves and admires her father, a hero in her eyes. Her youth and her adoration of Atticus didn't allow her to discover that, although he believed in everyone's right to a fair trial, he didn't necessarily believe in integration and in the essential equality of black and white peoples. Two decades later, a grown-up Scout, now called by her given name Jean Louise, sees the flaws she couldn't see in her childhood. "What," Jean Louise asks, "turned ordinary men into screaming dirt at the top of their voices?"

Harper Lee

The publication of Harper Lee's first novel, *To Kill a Mockingbird*, in 1960 quickly brought her success and what turned out to be unwanted fame. Her extraordinarily popular novel about race relations in the Deep South during the Depression is told through the eyes of a spirited tomboy called Scout. Scout's character was almost certainly inspired by Lee herself. Her father was a lawyer and, again almost certainly, the inspiration for Atticus Finch. Her mother apparently suffered from a mental illness, which may have been bipolar disorder.

After years of writing and struggling, Lee was fortunate enough to make friends with Joy Brown and her Broadway composer husband Michael Martin. The friendship changed Lee's life. In 1956 the Browns became impressed with Lee's writing efforts. They gave her enough money to support herself as she wrote full-time for one year. The gift/investment paid off. One year after the publication of *To Kill a Mockingbird*, the book won the Pulitzer Prize. One year later it was made into a classic film starring Gregory Peck as Atticus Finch.

Lee also served as Truman Capote's research assistant when he was working on a project that eventually became the pioneering true crime classic *In Cold Blood*. The two writers were childhood friends and neighbors in Lee's birthplace, Monroeville, Alabama, where she had been born in 1926.

Capote was the inspiration for Dill, a character in *To Kill a Mockingbird*. Their friendship later cooled after Lee's extraordinary success.

Despite her financial and critical success, Lee largely withdrew from public life for more than 50 years. Some say the attention overwhelmed her. Many of her fans craved another Lee novel. Though hungry for more of Lee's writings, some appreciated the fact that Lee's book represented a stand-alone lifetime achievement that presumably would never be tarnished by lesser efforts.

This changed in 2015 when HarperCollins said it would publish a second novel by Lee called *Go Set a Watchman*. Lee's lawyer Tonja Carter said that she had found the manuscript in a safe deposit box. The manuscript turned out to be a novel written before *To Kill a Mockingbird*. It featured Scout as a 26-year-old adult who returns to her Southern hometown and discovers that the people she grew up with, including her beloved father Atticus Finch, are racists. The manuscript had been rejected for publication. Lee's agent at the time astutely advised her to rewrite the book with a six-year-old Scout as the main character.

The "rediscovery" of the novel was highly controversial. Lee had been represented for decades by her beloved sister and lawyer Alice. Many people suggested that Lee, who by now was in poor health, was manipulated into agreeing to publish the book. After all, they argued, why would she change her mind after more than half a century of refusing to publish anything more, particularly when she was in failing health? In fact, four years before the new novel's publication, Alice wrote a letter in which she said Lee would "sign anything put before her by any one in whom she has confidence." Carter insists that Lee was not manipulated into agreeing to publish what some critics consider to be a rejected, early version of *To Kill a Mockingbird.* Carter's claim is supported by friends who say Lee was mentally competent when she agreed to the publication and by Alabama investigators who determined that no coercion had taken place.

Although less polished than Lee's beloved first novel, *Go Set a Watchman* is interesting for several reasons. It helps readers appreciate Lee's growth as a writer. It provides a strikingly different, and perhaps more believable, picture of the almost saintly Atticus Finch depicted in *To Kill a Mockingbird*. And it provides a more nuanced discussion of race relations in the Deep South in the mid-20th century.

RACISM AND PREJUDICE

Prejudice is the belief that members of a specific a group are inferior solely because they are part of that group. Racism is a subtype of prejudice. It applies when the group in question is an ethnic group. Despite the fact that it has no biological significance, the word "race" is commonly used to refer to ethnic groups such as people with Asian, African, or European ancestry.

Social psychologist Clay Routledge, PhD, compiled a list of five psychological motives that research psychologists believe may underlie the phenomena of prejudice and racism.

Self-esteem

Atticus: "Negroes down here are still in their childhood as a people."

Some people boost their own self-esteem by adopting racist beliefs. They reason that if a person identified with a different group is inferior, then they must be superior. This type of thinking strongly indicates a lack of critical thinking skills since people in any group are not clones; they are individuals. Oversimplifying complex situations indicates flawed thinking.

Positive distinctiveness

Atticus: "You realize that our Negro population is backward, don't you? You will concede that?"

Positive distinctiveness is the group equivalent of individual self-esteem. Atticus belongs to a group he calls "white." It's important for the racist to see his group as superior; it makes him more significant. The sense of his group's superiority is bolstered by believing that other groups are inferior. Social psychologists find that in many cases people have a higher opinion of other persons if they have something in common with them, a common group identity, such as religion or skin color.

Certainty and structure

Atticus: "I'd like for my state to be left alone to keep house without the advice of the NAACP, which knows next to nothing about its business and cares less."

People like Atticus have a psychological trait called "personal need for structure." They are uncomfortable with social change and want their world to remain stable, even if it means denying equal treatment and rights for many people. Change makes them uncomfortable and can create anxiety. Stereotypical and prejudicial attitudes appear to be associated with this trait in many individuals.

Survival

Atticus: "Do you want Negroes by the carload in our schools and churches and theaters? Do you want them in our world?"

Human beings are social primates. During the course of evolution, they developed specific behaviors and traits that increased their group's chances of survival against competing groups. Some evolutionary psychologists suggest that modern group conflict, including racism, is a holdover from our evolutionary past. According to this view, not everyone's attitude has changed enough to enable them to recognize that this outlook is counterproductive in modern society.

Dominance

Atticus: "Jean Louise, have you ever considered that you can't have a set of backward people living among people advanced in one kind of civilization and have a social Arcadia?"

Human beings frequently compete with one another for dominance in the workplace and even in social settings. Evolutionary psychology suggests that this behavior, like the survival motive discussed above, can be traced to our evolutionary past. This innate tendency to establish hierarchies may explain why racists lack, or unconsciously suspend, critical thinking skills to attribute lower status to some individuals over whom they can claim dominance.

Profile #86: Ahmad Ashmawy Mulloy in the Novel *The Terrorist* by John Updike

> In the year past he has grown three inches, to six feet—more unseen materialist forces, working their will upon him. He will not grow any taller, he thinks, in this life or the next.

PLOT SUMMARY

Ahmad was three years old when his Egyptian father abandoned Ahmad's Irish American mother, who now works as a nurse's aide and an amateur artist. She cares for her son and provides for him, but she is distracted and self-centered. The boy feels alone and alienated from his community.

By age 11, Ahmad turns to religion to find acceptance and a sense of community, to ease his feeling of being separate. Now, at age 18 and a senior in high school, he has become radicalized by Shaikh Rashid, the imam at his local mosque. His nearly burnt-out high school guidance counselor, Jack Levy, can offer nothing as appealing to the youth as the radical teachings of the imam.

Ahmad is taught that the United States is imperialistic, materialistic, and hedonistic. His youth, lack of positive role models, sense of isolation, and lack of worldly experience seem to make him vulnerable to extremists who recruit him to sacrifice himself by detonating a truck bomb in the Lincoln Tunnel.

The novel has been criticized for portraying stereotyped characters but it nevertheless offers a fictional starting point for opening a discussion of terrorist psychology. Author John Updike explained: "I'm trying to get the terrorist out of the bugaboo category and into the category of a fellow human being."

AHMAD'S PSYCHOLOGICAL TRAITS

At age 18, Ahmad is thoughtful, somewhat shy, and unsophisticated. He faces the same stresses associated with late adolescence that many of his fellow students face: dealing with bullies, supporting himself after he leaves high school, and struggling with relationships and sex. Unlike most of his fellow students, however, Ahmad becomes radicalized by men who manipulate him into agreeing to die for their cause. The forces and influences that lead young men like Ahmad to join terrorist groups are complex and still incompletely understood.

THE PSYCHOLOGY OF TERRORISM

There is no simple checklist that can predict who will become a terrorist. In fact, the diverse background and motivations of terrorists who have been studied suggest there is no single terrorist psychological profile. Terrorists may be motivated by a combination of factors. These may include politics, revenge, resentment, a sense of purpose, thrill-seeking or escape from a life offering little opportunity, camaraderie or loyalty to a group or "family" of like-minded individuals, and, in some cases, psychopathological disorders such as psychopathy and narcissism.

In some instances, the desire for recognition may help explain why someone would kill unarmed civilians. "Radical ideology promises glory and significance," Arie Kruglanski of the University of Maryland told NBC News in October 2014. "Therefore, people who are more motivated toward glory and significance are more prone to accept those ideologies."

Of course, many people share these traits without joining terrorist groups or committing even a single violent act. Governments and the psychologists they consult are still trying to figure out why some individuals with these traits join terrorist groups or commit individual acts of terrorism while others never become violent.

One possible explanation that could explain why Ahmad became radicalized has its roots in the field of social psychology. This branch of psychology seeks explanations of human behavior by studying how our interactions with other people affect our feelings, self-image, and actions.

Humans are social organisms. Being accepted by others and included in a group is a basic and common human need. We very likely evolved to value such acceptance, according to evolutionary psychologists, because an individual facing the dangers present in the wildness is much less likely to survive than he is as a member of a supporting group or tribe.

Young people like Ahmad often crave such social acceptance, even more than they crave material goods and personal freedom. Psychiatrist Peter A. Olsson and others have suggested a variety of factors that might influence homegrown terrorists, some of which fit Ahmad.

Seeking purpose, acceptance, and recognition

Joryleen: "You should smile more. . . . People will like you more."
Ahmad: "I don't care about that. I don't want to be liked."

Ahmad has no close friends in high school. Although she supports Ahmad, his mother interacts with him infrequently. And he has no close social connections outside home or school. Ahmad does not have a problem leaving behind a society from which he feels estranged. But since joining the mosque, he has found a place where he is accepted and appreciated. Unfortunately, unlike the majority of mosques around the world, this mosque is led by an extremist who guides Ahmad toward violence.

"In-between" or transitional social status

Jack Levy: "Well, perhaps I shouldn't say this, Ahmad, but in view of your grades and SATs, and your way-above average poise and seriousness, I think you're—what's that word?—imam—helped you to waste your high school years. I wish you had stayed on the college track."

Ahmad has been encouraged by his religious mentor to drive a truck after graduating from high school, instead of furthering his education. Like many potential recruits to terrorist organizations, Ahmad is in-between many stages in his psychological development. He is in-between school and work, in-between his childhood home and marriage, and in-between the dependency of being a minor and the independence of being an adult.

Obedience to an authority

Shaikh Rashid: "Dear boy, I have not coerced you, have I?"
Ahmad: "Why, no, master. How could you?"

After agreeing to become a suicide bomber, Ahmad is questioned by the radicalized religious leader who guided him toward agreeing to this terrorist act. Ahmad never questions Shaikh Rashid or Charlie, the two men who recruit him.

Obsessive beliefs

"The boy knows he is being manipulated, yet accedes to the manipulation, since it draws from him a sacred potential."

Psychologists have found that not all domestic terrorists have strong religious beliefs like Ahmad does. Many have only a superficial understanding of religion. Often their alienation from society is enough to get them to join a terrorist group if it provides a sense of belonging and recognition. Some come from poor backgrounds but many are from middle-class homes. They join for glory and the excitement of being part of something more important than the mundane lives they would otherwise lead.

Part 4

Emotional Instability/Neuroticism

Profile #87: Alexander Portnoy in the Novel *Portnoy's Complaint* by Philip Roth

> These people are unbelievable!
> These two are the outstanding producers and packagers of guilt in our time!

PLOT SUMMARY

Alexander Portnoy is in therapy. His therapist, and you the reader, get to hear every personal, private, troubling, and troublesome complaint Portnoy has about his life. His problems are presented as a monologue, a monologue that shows he has been driven to therapy by his feelings of guilt and unhappiness. He blames both of these complaints on the influence of his strict, controlling, and nagging Jewish mother. Much of his anxiety and unhappiness is related to his feelings about sex and masturbation.

PORTNOY'S PSYCHOLOGICAL TRAITS

Thirty-three-year-old Alexander Portnoy works for New York City as an "Assistant Commissioner for Human Opportunities." His job title is ironic because Portnoy is very far from enjoying any human opportunities. Although intelligent, Portnoy is emotionally crippled by feelings of guilt and worry, which he blames on his domineering mother. His unhappiness and his unpleasant interactions with others distress him so much that he consults a psychiatrist named Dr. Spielvogel.

NEUROTICISM OR EMOTIONAL INSTABILITY

Neuroticism is a personality trait that is situated on the opposite end of the spectrum it shares with emotional stability. The term "neurosis" is outdated and hardly ever used in standard medical practice today. People once described as neurotic might today be described as having an anxiety disorder or obsessive behavior.

The term "neuroticism," however, is still frequently used when discussing the "Big Five" personality traits, which, in addition to neuroticism, include openness, conscientiousness, extraversion, and agreeableness. A better label for neuroticism might be emotional instability or negative emotionality.

People who score high on personality tests that measure neuroticism or emotional instability often tend to worry and react emotionally in response to events that other people deal with more easily. They often experience anxiety, anger, irritability, or depressed moods. They tend to think of themselves a great deal and can be highly vulnerable to criticism or challenging situations. Besides Portnoy, the characters Woody Allen has frequently portrayed in his films are often described as neurotic (see Alvy Singer in *Annie Hall*).

Irritability

" . . . what *was* it with these Jewish parents, *what*, that they were able to make us little Jewish boys believe ourselves to be princes on the one hand, unique as unicorns on the one hand, geniuses and brilliant like nobody has ever been brilliant and beautiful before in the history of childhood—saviors and sheer perfection on the one hand, and such bumbling, incompetent, thoughtless, helpless, selfish, evil little s**ts, little *ingrates*, on the other!"

Portnoy frequently expresses irritability toward those he blames for his insecurities and poor self-image. The book attracted controversy for having its main character blame his Jewish mother and Jewish culture for his psychological problems. Some people criticized it as anti-Semitic and self-hating. Most critics reject these concerns. The book is included on multiple "Top 100 novel" lists including the Modern Library list on which it is ranked #52.

Anger

Portnoy: "How can she rise with me on the crest of my genius during those dusky beautiful hours after school, and then at night, because I will not eat some string beans and a baked potato, point a bread knife at my heart? And why doesn't my father stop her?"

Portnoy frequently rants when telling Dr. Spielvogel about things his parents did when raising him.

Sadness

Portnoy: "Doctor, do you understand what I was up against? My wang was all I really had that I could call my own."

Portnoy's sadness at his situation as the son of his overbearing mother started in childhood.

Anxiety

Portnoy: "The guilt, the fears—the terror bred into my bones!"

Portnoy attributes his anxiety and worry—the reasons he is in therapy—to the unending warnings about present and hidden dangers he heard during his childhood. He also blames his mother's warnings that he was always making potentially disastrous, life-altering mistakes even as an adult.

Worry

Portnoy: "I can lie about my name, I can lie about my school, but how am I going to lie about this f**king nose?"

Portnoy's worries extend beyond his concerns about his behavior to his physical body.

Self-consciousness

Portnoy: "Wouldn't it be nice to have a lot of responsibilities and just go around doing them all day and not even realize they were responsibilities?"

Portnoy frequently observes his actions and criticizes himself.

Hostility

Portnoy: "Doctor, these people are incredible! These people are unbelievable!"

Portnoy expresses the frustration and hostility he feels toward his parents to his psychiatrist throughout his monologue. After listening to nearly 290 pages worth of Portnoy's complaints, his therapist ends the book by asking: "So. Now vee may perhaps to begin. Yes?"

Besides the irony of the unexpected statement, it suggests that all of Portnoy's complaining had no therapeutic value.

Profile #88: Alvy Singer in the Film *Annie Hall*; Screenplay by Woody Allen and Marshall Brickman

Alvy, you're incapable of enjoying life, you know that?

PLOT SUMMARY

Alvy Singer looks directly into the camera and says: "There's an old joke: two elderly women are at a Catskill mountain resort, and one of 'em says, 'Boy, the food at this place is really terrible.' The other one says, 'Yeah, I know; and such small portions.' Well, that's essentially how I feel about life—full of loneliness, and misery, and suffering, and unhappiness, and it's all over much too quickly."

Alvy, a stand-up comic and joke writer, proceeds to tell the story of his relationship with aspiring singer Annie Hall as he looks back on the affair and the events in his life that influenced it. By exploring funny and bittersweet anecdotes and memories about his childhood, his past marriages, and the good and bad times with Annie, Alvy tries to understand why the relationship failed. In the end, it becomes clear that although Annie started the relationship as a silly, scatterbrained girl, she grew, during the course of her relationship with Alvy, into a confident woman who finally realized she was as smart as Alvy. Annie outgrows Alvy, but he finally realizes that he has played a part in Annie's growth.

ALVY'S PSYCHOLOGICAL TRAITS

Alvy is a comedy writer who takes himself so seriously that he cannot see humor in himself. He worries and overanalyzes all aspects of his life. (He's been in psychoanalysis for 15 years.) He is self-obsessed, insecure, pessimistic, and highly neurotic.

NEUROTICISM

Woody Allen is famous for portraying characters that are described as neurotic in his films. Alvy Singer is one of the best examples of this. Like Alexander Portnoy in *Portnoy's Complaint* (described in the previous entry), he does not have a personality or mental disorder. Like Portnoy, Alvy has personality traits that are dominated by emotional instability or neuroticism. (See the section "Personality" in the Introduction.) But unlike Portnoy, Alvy has an undercurrent of conscious self-parody.

Anger

Alvy: "What I wouldn't give for a large sock with horse manure in it! Whaddya do when you get stuck in a movie line with a guy like this behind you?"

Guy in line behind Alvy: "Wait a minute, why can't I give my opinion? It's a free country!"

Alvy: "You can give it. Do you have to give it so loud? I mean, aren't you ashamed to pontificate like that?"

While waiting in line to see a movie, Alvy becomes annoyed by the man behind him. He claims to be annoyed by the loudness of the man's voice, but he is just as or even more annoyed by the opinion the man is expressing (about the influence of media on culture). Alvy's constant low level of dissatisfaction with everything is often mixed with subdued anger toward whatever he cannot agree with.

Sadness

Doctor: "Why are you depressed, Alvy?"

. . .

Alvy: "The universe is expanding."

Doctor: "The universe is expanding?"

Alvy: "Well, the universe is everything, and if it's expanding, someday it will break apart and that would be the end of everything!"

Alvy's Mom: "What is that your business?"

Alvy's worry and chronically depressed mood began early, at age nine, when he read about the fate of the universe. He took it personally and has found reasons to be sad ever since. As an adult he feels "that life is divided into the horrible and the miserable."

Worry

Alvy: "I can't enjoy anything unless everybody is. If one guy is starving someplace, that puts a crimp in my evening."

Worry and irritability contribute to Alvy's breakup with Annie. They interfere with his ability to enjoy Annie's company, to enjoy Annie for who she is, not who he wants her to be.

Self-consciousness

Alvy: "Oh my God, she's right. Why did I turn off Allison Portchnik? She was beautiful, she was willing. She was real intelligent. Is it the old Groucho Marx joke? That I—I just don't want to belong to any club that would have someone like me for a member?"

In a past relationship, Alvy interrupted having sex with a woman to discuss the Kennedy assassination. She says "You're using this conspiracy theory as an excuse to avoid sex with me." Alvy sees that she is correct. The reference to the Groucho Marx joke reveals his low opinion of himself and his self-consciousness.

Hostility

Alvy: "You know, I don't think I could take a mellow evening because I—I don't respond well to mellow. You know what I mean? I have a tendency to—if I get too mellow, I—I ripen and then rot, you know."

Alvy is a New York intellectual who complains about New York intellectuals. He looks down upon people who don't share his humorless preoccupation with failure, death, and other sources of worry that other people manage to live with.

Before they settled on the title *Annie Hall*, the screenwriters considered calling the film *Anhedonia*, a psychiatric term used to describe an inability to derive pleasure from experiences that are generally considered by most people to be pleasurable. *Anhedonia*, although less marketable, would nevertheless have been an appropriate title for the film.

Despite his neurotic traits, Alvy does display signs of growth and a small but significant improvement in his outlook by the end of *Annie Hall*. While Alexander Portnoy is just ready to begin therapy at the end of *Portnoy's Complaint*, Alvy has discovered something very important and positive by the end of *Annie Hall*. After running into Annie following their final breakup, Alvy says: "After that it got pretty late, and, we both had to go, but it was great seeing Annie again. I realized what a terrific person she was and how much fun it was just knowing her."

Part 5

Freudian Themes

Profile #89: Norman Bates in the Film *Psycho*; Screenplay by Joseph Stefano, Based on the Novel by Robert Bloch

A boy's best friend is his mother.

PLOT SUMMARY

Marion Crane (played by Janet Leigh) has fled with $40,000 she stole from her boss. She intends to meet up with her boyfriend, but during her flight, she checks into the Bates Motel to rest. The proprietor of the motel, Norman Bates (played by Anthony Perkins), is polite, if a bit twitchy. He says he shares running the motel with his mother and that his hobby is taxidermy.

Unfortunately for Marion, only one of those statements is true. Norman has serious issues concerning his mother and his attraction toward women. Marion gets a brief glimpse of how severe Norman's psychological problems are when she takes her last shower.

NORMAN'S PSYCHOLOGICAL TRAITS

Norman is a mythical character. He suffers from something like dissociative identity disorder—that is, he has an alternate identity as well as his own identity. Most extraordinarily (except for horror films), his single alternate identity is a serial killer. It is based on his mother, whose stuffed body sits in a rocking chair in the basement like a mummified Whistler's Mother. Norman killed her and a man she brought home because he was jealous. Since then, this alternate identity emerges from time to time and kills any woman Norman finds attractive. Norman also has the delusion that his mother is still alive.

Like other characters that do horrible things, Norman is the focus of great misunderstanding. Much of this misunderstanding is epitomized by the title of the film, *Psycho*. "Psycho" is not a technical or medical term; it is a popular term used to describe someone who is psychopathic or psychotic, two very different and unrelated things. It's unfortunate that the words "psychopathic" and "psychotic" sound similar because they refer to unrelated mental states.

"Psychopathic" describes a legally *sane* person who has a personality dominated by traits like superficial charm, lack of remorse, lack of empathy, reckless risk-taking, and other traits that often lead to selfish and victimizing behavior. This does not describe Norman. (See Anton Chigurh in *No Country for Old Men.*)

The word "psychotic" refers to a legally *insane* person who suffers from a serious mental illness that may produce hallucinations, delusions, and bizarre behavior and thoughts. Surprisingly, if you believe in the existence of dissociative identity disorder (and many mental health professionals do not), and that Norman suffers from it, then Norman is not psychotic. Not surprisingly, even doctors can confuse this disorder with psychotic disorders like schizophrenia. And some skeptics dismiss the notion of dissociative identity disorder and claim that such cases are, in fact, often schizophrenia or other disorders with psychotic features.

Norman Bates and Freudian Psychology

The source of the confusion about Norman's true psychopathology might be related to the popularity of Sigmund Freud's psychoanalytic theories in the last century. Clinical psychologist Lisa Cohen, PhD, explains in her book, *The Handy Psychology Answer Book*, how Freudian ideas influenced Alfred Hitchcock in the 1950s when he worked on the movie *Psycho*.

Norman Bates was abnormally attached to his mother. (See Oedipus in *Oedipus the King.*) He was so jealous that when he felt his relationship with her was threatened by another man, he killed her and her love interest. Unable to part with her, Norman stores her body in the basement of the house they shared (and in which he continues to believe he and his mother still share). In his delusional mind, he believes she is still alive. To strengthen his belief, he adopts her identity—at times, he becomes her. Freudian psychologists might say her identity becomes Norman's alternate personality, or alter ego in Freudian terms.

Freud and his ideas have had a significant impact on the arts but very little impact on modern science. This is ironic in one sense because, in addition to being trained as a neurologist, Freud himself hoped that one day his psychoanalytic theories would be firmly based on neurobiology.

Sigmund Freud revolutionized psychiatry in the late 1800s and early 1900s with his theories on the unconscious state, talk therapy, and psychosexual development. Nowadays, many of these theories—like his conclusion that young girls' sexual development is influenced by jealousy over lack of a penis—seem outdated.

Still, his influence over Hitchcock resulted in the creation of a classic movie character in the character of Norman Bates.

FEATURES OF DISSOCIATIVE IDENTITY DISORDER

At least two distinct identity or personality states

Norman, speaking as his mother: "It's sad, when a mother has to speak the words that condemn her own son. But I couldn't allow them to believe that I would commit murder. They'll put him away now, as I should have years ago. He was always bad, and in the end he intended to tell them I killed those girls and that man, as if I could do anything but just sit and stare, like one of his stuffed birds. They know I can't move a finger, and I won't. I'll just sit here and be quiet, just in case they do, suspect me. They're probably watching me. Well, let them. Let them see what kind of a person I am. I'm not even going to swat that fly. I hope they are watching, they'll see. They'll see and they'll know, and they'll say, 'Why, she wouldn't even harm a fly.' "

After being arrested for Marion's murder, Norman sits in a police interrogation room thinking the thoughts of his alternate personality based on his dead mother.

Memory gaps of everyday or important events

Norman: "Mother! Oh God, what . . . blood, blood . . . mother. . . !"

Norman is shocked to discover that his alternate identity has killed Marion. But Norman's diagnosis of dissociative identity disorder would be complicated by his delusion that his mother is still alive. It's also complicated by what Dr. Fred Richmond, the doctor who examined Norman after his arrest, discovered: Norman "began to think and speak for her [his mother], give her half his time, so to speak. At times he could be both personalities, carry on conversations. At other times, the mother half took over completely. Now he was never all Norman, but he was often only mother. And because he was so pathologically jealous of her, he assumed that she was jealous of him. Therefore, if he felt a strong attraction to any other woman, the mother side of him would go wild."

If you believe in dissociative identity disorder, or what used to be called multiple personality disorder, then Norman's case is further complicated by the fact that he has a serious delusion, a feature of psychosis: he is convinced that the mother he killed is still alive. Thus, in the movie *Psycho*, Norman is depicted as a psychotic individual who has dissociative identity disorder, something not found in the *Diagnostic and Statistical Manual of Mental Disorders, 5th Edition* (*DSM-5*). Norman has the delusion that his mother is alive and that he is sometimes his mother.

Norman, of course, sees things differently: “It’s not like my mother is a maniac or a raving thing,” Norman says to Marion. “She just goes a little mad sometimes. We all go a little mad sometimes. Haven’t you?”

Norman, like Hannibal Lecter in *The Silence of the Lambs*, is more of a memorable Hollywood creation than an accurate representation of a person with a recognizable mental disorder. Both work well for what they were intended to be: creepy entertainment.

Profile #90: Henry Jekyll in the Novella *Strange Case of Dr. Jekyll and Mr. Hyde* by Robert Louis Stevenson

> This, as I take it, was because all human beings, as we meet them, are commingled out of good and evil: and Edward Hyde, alone in the ranks of mankind, was pure evil.

PLOT SUMMARY

An English gentleman named Enfield casually strolling through the streets of Victorian London with his lawyer friend Utterson is reminded of an incredible story when the two pass a particular building. Enfield tells his friend he once saw a brutish, ugly man named Mr. Hyde viciously knock down a young girl in the street. He helped catch the man and watched him enter the building to bring back compensation for the girl’s family. The thug emerged and handed them a check signed by a much more respectable gentleman.

Not too long after, Utterson finds that his client and friend, Dr. Henry Jekyll, has written a will leaving all of his possessions to Mr. Hyde. Utterson investigates the connection between these two very different individuals. Dr. Jekyll is a respectable chemist with a good reputation, a gentleman. Mr. Hyde seems low class and deformed in Utterson’s view, but the deformity seems to reflect his evil nature more than a physical handicap. The depraved Mr. Hyde is later even described as a “troglodyte.”

Utterson speaks with mutual friends about the relationship between Mr. Hyde and Dr. Jekyll. When he speaks with Dr. Jekyll directly, he is told not to pursue his informal investigation anymore.

An uneventful year passes and then another client of Utterson’s, Sir Danvers Carew, a member of Parliament, is brutally beaten to death on the street. Utterson immediately suspects Mr. Hyde. Utterson resumes his investigation and in the following months discovers a bizarre secret that confirms the evil nature of Mr. Hyde and raises great suspicion about the morality of Dr. Jekyll. Utterson discovers from a letter written by Dr. Jekyll that is opened after the doctor's death that he was both Dr. Jekyll and Mr. Hyde. He created a chemical concoction that allowed him to separate the good from the evil in himself. As Mr. Hyde, he could walk through the streets of London unburdened by a conscience. At first, Dr. Jekyll enjoyed exploring the feeling of being Mr. Hyde but he later returned to being himself. Eventually, however, he lost control of the process. Mr. Hyde began appearing at unexpected times until, eventually, he took over completely.

HENRY JEKYLL'S PSYCHOLOGICAL TRAITS

On the surface, Dr. Jekyll seems to be a decent man. He is a respected scientist, liked by his friends, and known to be charitable. But in time, he begins experimenting with a technique to separate opposing forces within himself. And it is his darker side that comes to dominate both of the personas he separates.

The literary significance of these events is more important than a diagnosis like dissociative identity disorder (see Eve White in *The Three Faces of Eve*). Alternate identities or personalities in this disorder do not undergo physical transformations and they do not allow one identity to be simultaneously conscious with a second identity, as happens in the case of Dr. Jekyll and Mr. Hyde.

Although it has little influence on modern-day mental health practices, Freudian psychology still plays a significant role in storytelling (see, for example, Norman Bates in *Psycho*).

Robert Louis Stevenson

Robert Louis Stevenson was sickly from the time he was born in Edinburg, Scotland, in 1850, until he died in Samoa at the age of 44. His poor health did not prevent him from becoming a successful author of fiction, travel books, poetry, and essays. Today, he is best remembered as the author of *Treasure Island*, *Kidnapped*, and *Strange Case of Dr. Jekyll and Mr. Hyde*.

Stevenson received a religious education in a conservative household. As a young child he began telling stories and commenting on the religious teachings he received. He broke away from his religious upbringing only after he began studying at the University of Edinburgh when he was 17 years old. There he paid less attention to his classwork than he did to developing his writing skills and enjoying his bohemian lifestyle and personal freedom. His father insisted he earn a degree that would assure he could support himself. Father and son agreed the answer was law. Stevenson kept his word and earned a law degree when he was 25 years old. But he had no interest in practicing law and hardly used the degree.

Despite his health problems, Stevenson succeeded often in finding enjoyment in life. His positive outlook is reflected in the humorous essays he wrote around this time. His writing, however, did not provide a livable income until many years later. At the age of 29, ill and penniless, he traveled to California to be with a married, but separated, woman, named Fanny Vandegrift Osbourne. He was able to marry her the next year. Fortunately, around this time, his father forgave his son for abandoning the law and his religious upbringing, and offered to help support the struggling writer financially.

Suffering from tuberculosis and other health problems, Stevenson traveled frequently, seeking healthy climates after he concluded that England's climate did not suit him. His travels did not interfere with his productivity; instead they seemed to stimulate it. By the age of 37, he had produced some of his best work. When he visited New York City in 1887, he was offered well-paid publishing contracts. He was famous.

The next year Stevenson and his family sailed for the South Pacific on a chartered yacht partly for pleasure and, as always, in search of a weather condition that would improve his health. After visiting Hawaii, Tahiti, and other South Seas islands, he settled in Samoa because the climate seemed to agree with him. During this time, he wrote well-crafted accounts of his travels. He never stopped writing or growing as a writer. Sadly, in 1894 he suffered a cerebral hemorrhage and died.

For a time after his death, Stevenson was regarded only as an author of children's books. For the last 60 years, however, scholars and fans of his writing have appreciated Stevenson as a prolific author in many genres whose works reflect his psychological insights, ethical concerns, journalistic skills, and superior storytelling ability.

FREUD'S STRUCTURAL THEORY OF THE MIND

Sigmund Freud believed that a person's psyche, the sum total of the mental and psychological attributes that determine behavior, consists of three subdivisions: the id, the ego, and the superego. These do not coincide with specific regions in the brain. Instead, they represent the key elements of Freud's hypothetical model of the mental processes that affect motivation and behavior.

Superego

Dr. Jekyll: "I was born in the year 18—to a large fortune, endowed besides with excellent parts, inclined by nature to industry, fond of the respect of the wise and good among my fellow-men, and thus, as might have been supposed, with every guarantee of an honourable and distinguished future."

Freudian psychologists believe that the superego creates ethical and moral standards with an idealistic bent. Dr. Jekyll was influenced by Victorian social standards. His ideal is to be a respected, honorable, and distinguished gentleman. But another part of his psyche, the id, has less noble goals and drives.

Id

Dr. Jekyll: "When I would come back from these excursions, I was often plunged into a kind of wonder at my vicarious depravity. This familiar that I called out of my own soul, and sent forth alone to do his good pleasure, was a being inherently malign and villainous; his every act and thought centred on self; drinking pleasure with bestial avidity from any degree of torture to another; relentless like a man of stone."

With the transformative concoction Dr. Jekyll cooked up in his laboratory, he unleashed his crassest impulses and most basic, animalistic urges. These are the demands of the id in Freud's view—impatient, aggressive demands that have to be controlled in civilized people. That control is the job of the ego.

Ego

Dr. Jekyll: "Between these two, I now felt I had to choose. My two natures had memory in common, but all other faculties were most unequally shared between them. Jekyll (who was composite) now with the most sensitive apprehensions, now with a greedy gusto, projected and shared in the pleasures and adventures of Hyde; but Hyde was indifferent to Jekyll, or but remembered him as the mountain bandit remembers the cavern in which he conceals himself from pursuit."

Freud assigned the ego to be the mediator between the id and superego. A healthy ego also factors in the demands of reality when regulating motivations and drives in a way that allows a person to function successfully according to the values of his or her society. Dr. Jekyll's ego was not healthy or strong enough to reconcile the demands of his id, Mr. Hyde. He allowed Mr. Hyde too much freedom and consequently lost everything.

Stevenson wrote his classic novella in 1886, close to 40 years before Freud introduced his model of mental function. His belief that every person—just like Dr. Jekyll—has two conflicting sides that must be dealt with as two aspects of a single mind might have pleased Freud.

Profile #91: Oedipus in the Play *Oedipus the King* by Sophocles

Without your knowledge you have turned into the enemy of your own relatives, those in the world below and those up here, and the dreadful scourge of that two-edged curse of father and mother will one day drive you from this land in exile.

PLOT SUMMARY

Oedipus, the king of Thebes, is a respected and famous leader. He makes mistakes—like accusing two innocent men, Creon and Tiresias, of treachery—but his actions are not malevolent. He moves quickly to deal with a crisis that threatens his people: a plague. When he learns that the oracle has declared that the plague will not subside until a murderer living in Thebes is identified, Oedipus does not hesitate begin searching for the killer. Ironically, the traits that make him a successful leader—his decisiveness and his desire to acquire knowledge—lead to his downfall. Tormented by his own actions, he blinds himself and asks his successor on the throne to banish him. His request is granted.

OEDIPUS'S PSYCHOLOGICAL TRAITS

Oedipus is dedicated, conscientious, and quick thinking. He is the victim of fate, a tragic figure who unknowingly fulfills the prophecy that will make him "abhorrent to the gods": he has unknowingly killed his father and married his mother.

PSYCHOANALYTIC THEORY AND THE OEDIPUS COMPLEX

Sigmund Freud developed psychoanalytic theory in an attempt to explain the sources of his patients' complaints, problems, and unhappiness. He believed that behavior is influenced by childhood experiences and unconscious thought processes and desires. Children, according to Freud, pass through several psychosexual stages of development.

The idea that childhood experiences and the unconscious play a role in human behavior is now commonly accepted and it has had a significant impact on literature. During the first half of the last century, psychoanalytic theory and the therapeutic approach based on it, psychoanalysis, were very popular but they have since become much less popular. Critics question their heavy emphasis on sex and note that they lack a strong scientific foundation. Proponents maintain that psychotherapy still has benefits for many people.

The Oedipus complex, in Freud's view, is an important stage in the development of a child. He believed children develop a strong sexual desire for the parent of the opposite sex and a strong rivalry with the parent of the same sex. A healthy, supportive family allows children to pass through this phase naturally, Freud hypothesized. If there are problems in the family, the child might not resolve the issues associated with this stage and grow into an adult with neurotic traits.

The analogous complex in girls is named after Electra. This legendary Greek figure is a central character in plays by Sophocles, Euripides, and Aeschylus.

Electra and her brother Orestes together kill their mother Clytemnestra, who murdered their father Agamemnon.

Source of the term "Oedipus complex"

Oedipus: "Loxias [another name for the Greek god Apollo] once said it was my fate that I would marry my own mother and shed my father's blood with my own hands."

Oedipus, without knowing it, fulfilled this prophecy. He killed a man he did not know was his father. And he married a woman he did not know was his mother. He punished himself by gouging out his eyes and banishing himself from the land he once ruled. And he provided Freud with a name for what would be one of Freud's most controversial theories.

Part 6

Psychologists in Films

Profile #92: "Prisoners" and "Guards" in the Film *The Stanford Prison Experiment*; Screenplay by Tim Talbott, Based on the Book *The Lucifer Effect* by Philip Zimbardo

> Okay, is it just me or are these guys [guards] taking this thing a bit too seriously?

PLOT SUMMARY

In 1971, Dr. Philip Zimbardo (played by Billy Crudup), a psychology professor at Stanford University, recruits 24 young volunteers to participate in what he calls an experiment. Based on coin tosses, half of the volunteers are assigned to play the role of "guards" and the other half the role of "prisoners" in a simulated prison setting.

Zimbardo is interested in observing the relationship that develops between the two groups. He seems to be particularly interested in the consequences of one group having power over another.

The treatment of the "prisoners" by the "guards" becomes so abusive that the demonstration has to be stopped after only six days, although it was scheduled to last two weeks. Zimbardo interprets the results as evidence that normal, decent people can readily become cruel and abusive under circumstances like those that exist in prisons.

RESEARCHER'S MOTIVATION

"This experiment will be an extension of my research into the effects prisons have on human behavior," Zimbardo says at the beginning of the study.

Combined with his directions to the guards on how they should behave before and during the demonstration, Zimbardo gives the impression that he expects a particular result. One of his collaborators admits later that "part of me thinks that we already have the results that we were looking for."

RESEARCHER'S BEHAVIOR AND INFLUENCE DURING THE DEMONSTRATION

Poor experimental design

Jim, a faculty colleague: "What's the independent variable in your study?"
Zimbardo: "I'm sorry?"
Jim: "Have you introduced a variable that might influence your outcome? This is an experiment right? Not just a simulation?"
Zimbardo: "Are you challenging me, Jim?"

If the situation or conditions allow, scientific experiments are designed with independent and dependent variables. The independent variable is the only variable in an experiment that the experimenter controls. For example, an independent variable might be the number of cups of coffee subjects are given to drink during an experiment. The dependent variable might be how long they can run or how jittery they become. Age or gender could also be independent variables because they can be controlled when experimental subjects are selected.

Zimbardo's "experiment" amounted to him telling his volunteer guards to put pressure on the volunteer prisoners, to encouraging tough behavior during the demonstration and to monitor them. The Stanford prison experiment ultimately could not be called a scientific experiment; it was a demonstration or a simulation.

Overinterpretation of results

Zimbardo: "The only thing that separates those two [groups], was a coin flip."

Zimbardo and his collaborators assumed that both groups were essentially the same psychologically. When some prison guards began to behave cruelly, Zimbardo concluded that he had shown that good people placed in powerful situations will behave badly. In fact, some of the guards did not participate in abusive behavior. They did not protest, but they were not abusive. Therefore, despite the results of the screening tests he used to assure that the guards were not psychologically different from the prisoners, Zimbardo failed to see or acknowledge that the group of guards consisted of different personality types, only some of whom would engage in abusive behavior. Additionally, people who volunteer for prison experiments might not have personality profiles similar to people who aren't interested in playing "guards" and "prisoners."

Poor experimental procedure

Zimbardo to guards: "Men, it's your job to keep my prison in order, and right now there doesn't seem to be a whole lot of order out there . . . Why am I hearing excuses? Do not forget you have all the authority . . . And you're stronger than they are. They're starting to create bonds with each other. Break 'em up. Okay? Get back in there."

When the prisoners protest their treatment and assert their rights, Zimbardo steps in and essentially takes the role of a supervisory prison guard. He becomes part of the "experiment." Good scientists do not become part of their experiments. They design them, conduct them, and observe, record, and evaluate the results.

Realizing this and other flaws in the exercise, one of Zimbardo's collaborators announces:

"We have become part of this experiment, whether we like it or not, and frankly, I don't even think we can call this an experiment anymore. It's a demonstration, and part of me thinks that we already have the results that we were looking for."

Current psychological research suggests that the toxic situations people find themselves in may not be the most important factor in producing abusive behavior. Instead, power may belong to whatever group develops a shared sense of identity.

The real Dr. Zimbardo, on whom the character played by Billy Crudup is based, discussed his work that inspired the film in an interview included on the film's DVD version: "We all want to believe in the power of free will, that our decisions come from within, in some magical way, that we choose our destiny and we take it. And this [his Stanford prison experiment] said no, no. If you put really good people in a really bad place, the goodness of the people crumbles against the power of the place." It's not clear that the results as depicted in the film support this conclusion.

Profile #93: "Teachers" in the Film *Experimenter: The Stanley Milgram Story*; Screenplay by Michael Almereyda

How do civilized human beings participate in inhumane acts? How was genocide implemented so systematically, so efficiently? And how did the perpetrators of these murders live with themselves?

PLOT SUMMARY

Yale psychologist Stanley Milgram, based on the real psychologist Stanley Milgram, wants to understand how one group of human beings, like the Nazis, could commit horrendous acts that lead to the annihilation of entire populations. He wonders if there is something basic in human nature that might account for such behavior, so he recruits subjects for an unusual psychological experiment. Its purpose is to determine how people respond when directed by an authority figure to act in an unethical manner.

Specifically, a group of volunteers are designated "teachers" and told their role in the experiment is to administer electric shocks to subjects if the subjects answer questions incorrectly. The intensity of the shocks increases with each error. In time, the shocks elicit from the unseen "learners" painful screams, protests, and desperate pleas to be released from the study as the shocks reach dangerous, and even deadly, levels.

In reality, the "learners" who appear to be receiving the shocks are portrayed by an actor. He receives no shocks but responds as if he does. The true subjects of the study are the volunteer "teachers," who think they are helping Milgram and his colleagues in their study by administering the shocks. Whenever a "teacher" expresses doubts about increasing the intensity of the shocks to dangerous levels, he or she is urged by the experimenters—who are seen as authority figures—to continue. The psychologists claim that the vast majority of "teachers" deliver the full range of shocks despite their concerns that they are harmful. Milgram and his colleagues interpret their findings as evidence that "normal" people are capable of unconscionable acts of cruelty when following the orders of someone they consider as an authority.

THE "TEACHERS' " PSYCHOLOGICAL TRAITS

The movie is a fairly accurate depiction of the actual experiments Milgram conducted in the early 1960s, based on his published account. Milgram's results led him to conclude in 1974 that "the extreme willingness of adults to go to almost any lengths on the command of an authority constitutes the chief finding of the study and the fact most urgently demanding explanation."

In this case, we are lucky to have the results of the real-life experiment on which we can base our understanding of the psychological phenomenon featured in this film. Milgram's conclusion, however, is questionable. Like the Stanford prison experiment described in this book, the Milgram experiments are not as easily interpreted as Milgram and his supporters suggested. Of course, many humans throughout history have demonstrated that they were capable of extreme acts of cruelty. The Milgram experiments, however, do not reveal a general, underlying human capacity for committing evil acts when ordered by those in power.

In fact, in his original experiment, 14 of the 40 subjects "broke off the experiment at some point after the victim protested and refused to provide further answers." Nevertheless, 26 of the subjects "obeyed the experimental commands fully, and administered the highest shock on the generator." Any study involving only 40 subjects must be considered a preliminary study. Because the design of the study is now considered grossly unethical, it cannot be repeated in the exact same way because of the harmful stress it produces in the "teachers." And conclusions derived from it apply only to the circumstances under which the study was conducted. Milgram's defenders point out that similar experiments in different countries produced the same result.

Psychologist Jean Perry, the author of *Behind the Shock Machine: The Untold Story of the Notorious Milgram Psychology Experiments*, questioned the validity of Milgram's observations. She claims that when all of Milgram's data from all of his experiments were analyzed, 60 percent of the subjects defied the experimenters—the authority figures—and refused to continue the experiment.

Like the Stanford prison experiment, the Milgram experiments reveal the range of ethical and moral characteristics of humans. Personalities, strengths, and weaknesses vary widely in different individuals. Some are capable of great cruelty without any instigation; others are capable of cruelty in certain environments; and a significant number are strong enough to resist pressure exerted by peers and authorities to commit unethical acts and even to actively resist them.

In the film, Milgram's character asks: "Why do so many, the vast majority, push all the way through to the final switch?" He concludes: "I designed a series of variations, 25 in all, and continued the experiments over the next two semesters . . . In nearly every case, the essential results are the same. They hesitate, sigh, tremble and groan. But they advance to the last switch, 450 volts, 'Danger Severe Shock XXX,' because they're politely told to. The results are terrifying and depressing. They suggest that the kind of character produced in American society can't be counted on to insulate its citizens from brutality and inhumane treatment in response to a malevolent authority."

New research casts serious doubt on such conclusions. Social psychologist Stephen Reicher and his colleagues observe that Milgram's notes clearly show the "teachers" displaying a wide range of responses to their assigned task of delivering shocks. Some were enthusiastic to take part, some were indecisive, and some simply refused.

According to these researchers, a key factor in determining these various responses is whom the "teachers" most identify with. If they identify with the authority figures running the experiment and believe they are aiding science, they are more likely to deliver the full range of shocks. If, however, they identify with the apparently suffering "learner," they are more likely to resist. The design of the experiment and the statements and actions of the experimental psychologists can have a great influence on whom the "teachers" identify with and thereby affect the results.

AGENTIC BEHAVIOR

Milgram's results led him to propose his agency theory. It postulates that there are two types of behavior in social situations. In the autonomous state, people are in control of their actions and take responsibility for them. In the agentic state, people follow orders from an authority figure and pass the responsibility of their actions onto those giving orders.

The "teachers' " agentic behavior

Teacher #1:	"Incorrect. A hundred and 65 volts. Strong shock."
Learner:	"Ah! Let me out of here! I told you, I have a heart condition. I will not be part of this experiment anymore!"
Teacher #1 to psychologist:	"He says he's not gonna go on."
Psychologist:	"Please continue, teacher."
Milgram:	"He went all the way. Most of them do."

A domino effect kicks in once the person assumes the role of "teacher." In fact, 26 out of 40 "teachers" in the experiment depicted in the film went on to deliver the highest shock. Critics, however, claim that when all of Milgram's data from all of his experiments are tabulated, most of them do not go on to deliver the highest shocks.

Teacher #2:	"Something's happening to that man in there. Can you please go check that everything's okay?"
Psychologist:	"Not once we've started. Please continue, teacher."
Teacher #2:	"So you accept all responsibility?"
Psychologist:	"The responsibility is mine, correct. Continue please."

This "teacher" refers responsibility for his actions to an authority.

A "teacher's" autonomous behavior

Learner:	"Let me out of here. I can't stand the pain."
Dutch Teacher:	"The man, he seems to be getting hurt."
Psychologist:	"There is no permanent tissue damage."
Dutch Teacher:	"Yes, but I know what shocks do to you. I am an electrical engineer, and I have had shocks. You get real shook up by them. Especially if you know the next one is coming. I'm sorry."
Psychologist:	"It's absolutely essential that you do continue."
Dutch Teacher:	"Well, I won't, not with the man screaming to get out."
Psychologist:	"You have no other choice."
Dutch Teacher:	"Why don't I have a choice? I came here on my own free will. I thought I could help in a research project. But if I have to hurt somebody, if I was in his place . . . No, I can't continue. I've probably gone too far already. I'm very sorry."

This "teacher" identifies with the "learner" and takes responsibilities for his own actions.

Part 7

Psychological Growth, Development, Maturity, Loss, and Aging

Profile #94: Winnie-the-Pooh in the Children's Books *Winnie-the-Pooh* and *The House at Pooh Corner* by A. A. Milne

Winnie-the-Pooh:	"I think the bees suspect something!"
Christopher Robin:	"What sort of thing?"
Winnie-the-Pooh:	"I don't know. But something tells me that they're suspicious!"

PLOT SUMMARY

Winnie-the-Pooh is Christopher Robin's stuffed "Bear of Very Little Brain." Christopher routinely rescues Pooh from predicaments the bear gets himself into, usually as a consequence of his search for honey or something else to eat. Their adventures take place in the Hundred Acre Wood and are shared with other stuffed creatures, including the anxiety-ridden Piglet and the dysthymic (mildly depressed) Eeyore.

WINNIE-THE-POOH'S PSYCHOLOGICAL TRAITS

Several psychologists have contributed thoughts about Winnie-the-Pooh's psychological traits. Because this character is a stuffed bear that appears in a children's book, these suggestions are mostly tongue in cheek. Pediatrician Sarah Shea and her colleagues, for example, suggested that the popular character might suffer from attention deficit hyperactivity disorder, binge eating disorder, and intellectual disability.

Psychiatrist Leo J. Bastiaens believes that Winnie-the-Pooh's behavior can be explained with a different diagnosis. According to Bastiaens, Pooh "clearly suffers from Prader-Willie syndrome." This serious, rare genetic condition is present at birth and affects multiple parts of the body and the brain. It is characterized by obesity, reduced muscle tone, little or no hormonal production, and reduced mental ability. Patients with this disease constantly seek food because they never feel full. This constant hunger begins around age two and results in many complications associated with obesity.

In a 2013 article in the journal *Childhood Education*, "Pooh's corner: Teaching educational psychology at the intersection of children's literature and technology," educational psychologist Cynthia Bolton-Gary offered her thoughts on yet another interpretation of Pooh's mental state. She notes that the pioneering developmental psychologist Jean Piaget (1896–1980) used Pooh to illustrate his concept of "the preoperational child."

PIAGET'S THEORY OF COGNITIVE DEVELOPMENT

Piaget's describes four stages of a child's cognitive development. The first is the sensorimotor stage when a child, aged two or younger, learns about the world by touching, tasting, smelling, and feeling his surroundings.

The second is the preoperational stage. It covers ages two to seven. Language develops during this stage but logical thinking does not. Like Pooh, the preoperational child has trouble manipulating information. And he is "egocentric" because he cannot yet take another person's point of view. Pooh has several traits of an egotistical toddler. He explores the world by interacting with it, accepting it, and making as much sense of it as he can with his still undeveloped mental abilities.

The third stage, the concrete operational stage, covers ages 7 to 11. Logical thinking develops but abstract topics are still difficult to grasp.

The fourth stage is the formal operational stage, which covers ages 11 or 12 to adulthood. Logic, deductive reasoning and other advanced cognitive skills develop.

Piaget's theory of child development is still guiding psychologists today.

Egocentricity—inability to take another person's point of view

"The only reason for being a bee that I know of is making honey . . . And the only reason for making honey is so I can eat it."

Pooh's attempt at reasoning is limited by his inability to see anything but his own viewpoint. He repeatedly indicates his assumption that bees think just as he does. He cannot yet understand that other creatures view the world differently from the way he views it. And if he loves honey, then he must be the reason it's made.

Difficulty manipulating information

"... and the more he thought like this, the more the party got muddled in his mind, like a dream when nothing goes right."

When Pooh hears that Christopher Robin is throwing a party for him, Pooh is overcome by his thoughts about who will come, what they would know about the party, what if they forgot, and so on.

Inability to think logically

Winnie-the-Pooh: "When you go after honey with a balloon, the great thing is not to let the bees know you're coming. Now, if you have a green balloon, they might think you were only part of the tree, and not notice you, and if you have a blue balloon, they might think you were only part of the sky, and not notice you, and the question is: Which is most likely?"

Christopher Robin: "Wouldn't they notice *you* underneath the balloon?"

Winnie-the-Pooh: "They might or they might not."

Pooh asks for a balloon so he can float up to a bees' nest to get honey. If he believes it is important for the balloon to be camouflaged to prevent detection, it is not logical to assume that his un-camouflaged body hanging under the balloon might not be noticed.

In addition to being delightful entertainment, the episodic adventures of Winnie-the-Pooh are told from a young child's viewpoint and reflect the reasoning limitations of children who have not yet learned to read. The book provides adult readers with an opportunity to see the world as a young child sees it.

Profile #95: The Poet in the Poem "Childhood" by Markus Natten

---

Where did my childhood go?
It went to some forgotten place,
That's hidden in an infant's face,
That's all I know.

POEM SUMMARY

With a combination of puzzlement, regret, and sadness at the loss of his innocence, the poet asks when, and by extension why, he is no longer a child. Each of the poem's four stanzas reflects a different concern or question posed by the nostalgic and now mature speaker. The first stanza identifies the emergence of logic and reasoning abilities. The second reflects his growing sophistication and the loss of his social naïveté. The third recognizes the intellectual originality and independence that comes with maturity. The fourth (see the above quote) concludes that the innocence and essence of his childhood, his feeling of being a child, are out of his reach. His childhood is irretrievably lost, hidden in a place he can only glimpse.

The poet's questions about his lost childhood illustrate the fourth and final stage of Piaget's influential theory of cognitive development.

The first, sensory motor stage describes development in children up to two years of age. Winnie-the-Pooh (see the entry *Winnie-the-Pooh*) illustrates features of the second stage of development, the preoperational stage, which extends from age two to age seven. The third, concrete operational stage, describes mental abilities common to children between the ages of 7 and 11.

FORMAL OPERATIONAL STAGE OF PIAGET'S THEORY

The poet speaking in "Childhood" illustrates the fourth, formal operational stage when advanced cognitive skills like logic and reasoning ability develop, typically between the ages of 11 or 12 and adulthood. More abstract and sophisticated thinking abilities also appear during this stage.

Emergence of rational, abstract, and logical thinking

Was it the day I ceased to be eleven,
Was it the time I realized that Hell and Heaven,
Could not be found in Geography,
And therefore could not be,
Was that the day!

The emergence of rational thinking abilities after the age of 11 allows the poet to critically evaluate others' statements and beliefs. Lack of evidence now raises intellectual doubts about what he hears and is taught.

Emergence of sophisticated thinking

Was it the time I realized that adults were not
all they seemed to be...

The questioning poet wonders if he lost his childhood when he was able to recognize hypocrisy in adults who "talked of love and preached of love,/but did not act so lovingly." Being able to see hidden contradictions in human behavior is an indication of sophisticated social functioning.

Piaget conducted experiments with children of different ages to test their intellectual abilities. He found that children are like discoverers or little scientists as they grow. They pick up new tools and advanced ways of interacting with, and thinking about, their world as they progress.

The poet finds that the final stage of development brings intellectual independence, featuring personal opinions and expressions of individuality. He wonders if this is when he lost his childhood: "Was it when I found my mind was really mine, to use whichever way I choose . . . "

Profile #96: Romeo and Juliet in the Play *Romeo and Juliet* by William Shakespeare

This bud of love, by summer's ripening breath,
May prove a beauteous flower when next we meet.

PLOT SUMMARY

The feud between two leading noble families, the Capulets and the Montagues in Verona, Italy, during the Renaissance has turned violent. The prince who rules the city threatens to execute anyone who commits the next violent act.

Romeo, a 16-year-old Montague, crashes a Capulet ball in one of a series of desperate attempts to win the affection of a young lady named Rosaline. Rosaline, however, has made it clear she is not interested in the young man. Romeo then sees a 13-year-old Capulet named Juliet. He switches his romantic attentions from Rosaline to Juliet very quickly. Juliet is slightly more cautious than Romeo, but it doesn't take long for her to return his affections. The realization that they are from feuding families concerns them but does not dampen their desire for each other. They swear their mutual love and marry with the help of a friar and a Capulet servant.

The feud between the two families continues and again breaks out in violence. When trying to prevent a fight, Romeo ends up killing Juliet's cousin. He is banished from Verona but manages to spend one night with Juliet before he flees the city. When Juliet's parents try to force her to marry a man they have chosen, she refuses. She takes part in an elaborate scheme to fake her own death and escape with Romeo. Not surprisingly, the plan does not go well. Romeo poisons himself when he thinks Juliet is dead. Juliet kills herself with his knife when she realizes Romeo is dead. Too late, the mourning families agree to end their feud.

ROMEO'S AND JULIET'S PSYCHOLOGICAL TRAITS

Sixteen-year-old Romeo is highly emotional. He is infatuated with Rosaline but, with barely a pause, switches his affections to Juliet. He becomes angry and dejected almost as quickly as he falls in love or, perhaps more accurately, as quickly as he redirects his infatuations. He does seem to mature a bit during the play since he remains devoted to Juliet in the face of tremendous opposition from all but a few friends.

Juliet is three years younger than Romeo and less infatuated with the idea of falling in love than he is—until she falls in love with him. She is less emotionally volatile than Romeo and, although naïve at the beginning of their relationship, she too shows determination and strength when facing the same challenges Romeo faces. Her lingering naïveté, however, may contribute to her agreement to fake her own death in an overly elaborate plan to escape with her lover. Their paired suicides, however, indicate that their relationship was based more on obsessional than on mature love.

INFATUATION, OBSESSION, AND MATURE LOVE

Infatuation

Romeo: "Did my heart love till now? Forswear it, sight,/For I ne'er saw true beauty till this night."

Rejected by Rosaline, Romeo quickly turns his attention to a new potential lover: Juliet. He knows nothing about her, not even that she belongs to the Capulets with whom his family is feuding. But he is convinced he loves her based on her beauty alone. This is not lost on someone who will support the couple later, Friar Lawrence: "Holy Saint Francis!/What a change is here!/Is Rosaline, that thou didst love so dear,/So soon forsaken? Young men's love then lies/Not truly in their hearts, but in their eyes."

Juliet enters the relationship with a little more caution: "Well, do not swear. Although I joy in thee,/I have no joy of this contract tonight./It is too rash, too unadvised, too sudden," but she soon becomes as obsessed with Romeo as he is with her. She later demonstrates this when she says: "Do not swear at all./Or, if thou wilt, swear by thy gracious self,/Which is the god of my idolatry,/And I'll believe thee."

Obsessional love and self-destruction

Juliet: "Yea, noise? Then I'll be brief. O happy dagger!/This is thy sheath; There rust, and let me die."

When Juliet discovers Romeo has poisoned himself because he believed she was dead, she grabs Romeo's knife and stabs herself to death. Sadly, even something as morbid as a dual suicide is sometimes still considered "romantic" by some readers. In a psychological sense, such impulsive behavior by both Romeo and Juliet is evidence of psychopathology: an unhealthy, obsessional love. Hormonal changes may account for the intensity of feelings in young lovers but very few experience the extreme infatuation felt by Romeo and Juliet.

At least their obsessive love did not show signs of delusional jealousy, a mental health problem that fortunately affects only around 0.1 percent of the adult population.

Mature love

Romeo and Juliet did not live long enough for their love to mature. Due to their deaths, which can be traced to the obsessional nature of their relationship, all they experienced was the infatuation and desire to spend every minute with each other. Although not as intense or dangerously dramatic as those of the doomed couple, similar feelings are common in new relationships. People who find love often are infatuated and desperate to spend time together. They also tend to idealize their partners. But the nature of positive, healthy relationships typically changes over time. Infatuation fades and feelings of commitment and respect grow. Psychologically secure couples encourage their partners to develop and flourish as individuals while maintaining the bond that provides emotional support.

Shakespeare understood human psychology well. And when writing *Romeo and Juliet*, of course, he was less concerned about the psychological health of his characters than in the feelings his words, as spoken by them, had on his audience. Shakespeare deserves to have the last word here, not for his depiction of tragic love, but for his poetry. When Juliet anticipates spending her first night with Romeo, she graces the English language with her nervous excitement:

> Give me my Romeo, and when he shall die,
> Take him and cut him out in little stars,
> And he will make the face of heaven so fine
> That all the world will be in love with night
> And pay no worship to the garish sun.

Profile #97: Andrew Crocker-Harris in the Film *The Browning Version*; Screenplay by Terence Rattigan, Based on His Play

Taplow: "I don't think the Crock gets a kick out of anything. In fact, I don't think he has any feelings at all. He's just dead, that's all . . . He can't hate people and he can't like people. And what's more, he doesn't like people to like him."

Student: "Well, he doesn't have to worry much about that."

PLOT SUMMARY

It is Andrew Crocker-Harris's (played by Michael Redgrave) last day teaching classics at an English boys' school. He is middle-aged and not quite old enough to retire, but a heart ailment is forcing him to leave the post he has held for 18 years. He is taking a less stressful teaching position at a less prestigious school.

Today, he faces the realization that his personal life and work life have been failures. His students fear him. They call him "The Crock" and, most cruelly, "Himmler," after the Nazi SS chief, because he maintains such discipline in his classes. The school board has denied him a pension. His wife does not hide her affair with the school's chemistry teacher.

Only one student does not hate Andrew. Taplow (played by Brian Smith) feels sorry for him, and even feels some affection. Of all the faculty and students, he is the only one to give Andrew a going-away present, a copy of Robert Browning's English translation of Aeschylus's *Agamemnon*, the classics teacher's favorite play. This is "The Browning Version" of the title.

The teacher is uncharacteristically touched by the gesture and by the kind Greek inscription Taplow writes in the book. He is so affected by it that he has to hide his tears. But just as Agamemnon's wife, Clytemnestra, murdered Agamemnon, Andrew's wife kills the only joy her husband receives this day; she tells him that Taplow had been mocking him earlier. She implies he likes "The Crock" no more than the other students.

The sad exchange is one of several that causes Andrew to face the fact that he is a failure. His struggle to deal with this realization leads to an impressively honest acceptance of his faults, a moving apology, and a demonstration that personal growth is possible even late in life.

ANDREW'S PSYCHOLOGICAL TRAITS

The introverted schoolmaster was an outstanding student of Greek and Latin at Oxford University. But not long after he began teaching, he lost the ability to share his love of, and enthusiasm for, those subjects. He is now humorless, rigid, strict, stern, stiff, and pedantic. His career, like his marriage to his younger wife, stagnated long ago. Andrew faces a major crisis, one addressed in Erik Erikson's eight stages of psychosocial development.

EIGHT STAGES OF PSYCHOSOCIAL DEVELOPMENT

Developmental psychologist and psychoanalyst Erik Erikson introduced the term "identity crisis" to popular culture. The term is related to his well-known theory on the psychosocial development of human beings. It proposes that humans pass through eight distinct life stages, each of which involves a specific psychological challenge or crisis. The manner in which a person deals with the challenges shapes his or her personality.

The first five stages cover infancy through the teenage years. The sixth covers young adulthood.

It is the seventh and eighth stages that apply to Andrew. Stage 7 covers middle-age, a time when people commonly look back on their lives and evaluate themselves. That self-evaluation can result in regeneration or stagnation/self-absorption according to Erikson. The schoolmaster stagnated before he was prematurely cast into Stage 8, which offers an opportunity to develop integrity or to fall into despair.

Due to his serious illness, Andrew finds himself dealing with the same challenges and struggles that are more common in persons 65 years of age or older. Advanced age is often accompanied by physical decline, illness, disappointment about being replaced, and mortality. Erikson suggests that people facing these issues struggle between accepting the reality of their old age and becoming bitter. Acceptance can lead to wisdom. An inability to come to terms with the challenges can lead to despair.

Andrew spent his career stagnating in Stage 7 but deals directly with his Stage 8 crisis brought on by poor health. Accepting his early mistakes and failures allows him to regain a sense of contentment. The self-knowledge he gains during his struggle with this crisis eases his pain and even gives him hope for the future.

Stagnation/inability to relate to youth

Andrew to his replacement: "Of course, from the very beginning, I realized I did not possess the knack of making myself liked. At the beginning at least, I did try very hard to communicate to the boys—those boys sitting down there—some of my own joy in the great literature of the past. Of course, I failed, as you will fail, 999 times out of a thousand. But a single success can atone, more than atone, for all the failures of the world. And sometimes, very, very rarely it is true, but sometimes I had that success. That, of course, was in the early years."

Andrew gave up trying to be a stimulating teacher—that is, a success—early in his career. His imminent departure stimulates a crisis as he tries to evaluate the 18 years he has spent at the school.

Self-evaluation

Andrew: "At all events, it didn't take much to discern on my part to realize that I became an utter failure as a schoolmaster. Still, stupidly enough, I had not realized that I was also feared. 'The Himmler of the lower fifth.' I suppose that will become my epitaph."

Resolution of past and present crises or challenges

Andrew to a gathering of students: "I am sorry because I have failed to give you what you had the right to demand of me as your teacher: sympathy, encouragement

> and humanity. I'm sorry because I have deserved the nickname of 'Himmler.' And because by so doing, I have degraded the noblest calling that a man can follow: the care and molding of the young. I claim no excuses. When I came here I knew what I had to do and I have not done it. I have failed and miserably failed. I can only hope that you and the countless others that have gone before will find it in your hearts to forgive me for having let you down. I shall not find it so easy to forgive myself."

Ignoring his planned, stuffy, Latin-strewn farewell speech, Andrew is honest with his students about himself for the first time. The unpopular teacher has evaluated the cause of his unhappiness and has a choice. He can accept what he has done and experience personal growth even at his age, or he can continue as he was and become bitter. If he is like many people who go through this process, he will settle somewhere in between acceptance and regret. At the end of his improvised statements, he finally receives respect and admiration from his students. They applaud him wildly.

Profile #98: Sherlock Holmes in the Film *Mr. Holmes*; Screenplay by Jeffrey Hatcher, Based on the Novel *A Slight Trick of the Mind* by Mitch Cullin

---

Sherlock: "I have been alone. All my life. But with the compensations of the intellect."
Ann: "And is that enough?"
Sherlock: "It can be. If one is so fortunate as to find a place in the world. And another soul with whom one's loneliness can reside."

PLOT SUMMARY

It's 1947, and Sherlock Holmes (played by Ian McKellen) is retired and living in his seaside house with a house keeper, Mrs. Munro (played by Laura Linney), and her young son Roger (played by Milo Parker). Instead of catching criminals, the former consulting detective now keeps bees. His memory and intellectual abilities are slipping, and he strives to limit the decline with food supplements and note-taking.

There is one case from his past that Sherlock cannot forget. It is, for him, the unsolved investigation that led to his retirement years before. As he tries to come to terms with his past, he desperately wants to solve the mystery before his memory and intellectual abilities fade any more.

The case involved Ann Kelmot (played by Hattie Morahan), a woman who, like Sherlock, was emotionally isolated from other people, including her husband. Sherlock struggles to discover, to remember, and to understand what happened between the woman and himself.

Roger helps Sherlock as he works on his last case, and the retired detective becomes fond of the intelligent boy. After solving the case, Sherlock realizes that the life of the intellect, the life he lived, is not a complete life. This realization leads to positive changes in his life and in the lives of Roger and his mother as Sherlock now works to build bonds between them.

SHERLOCK'S PSYCHOLOGICAL TRAITS

Sherlock is aging and beginning to experience memory loss. He is also trying to come to terms with decisions he made in the past, decisions that isolated him from other people in favor of purely intellectual pursuits.

Sherlock's struggle to recall and understand the mistakes he made in the past, including his decision to avoid forming a close relationship with a compatible and willing partner, readily fits into Erik Erikson's description of the final stage of psychosocial development (see Andrew Crocker-Harris in *The Browning Version*). Sherlock's physical and mental decline and his approaching death spur him to reconcile himself with his past failure. He knows he will die dissatisfied if he can't, a state that Erikson believed results in despair rather than wisdom.

Sherlock successfully negotiates this important final stage of his life and takes an important step toward wisdom. He makes a gesture toward his housekeeper, Mrs. Munro, with whom he has always maintained an emotional distance, that brings him closer to her and her son.

LATER STAGES OF PSYCHOSOCIAL DEVELOPMENT

Like Andrew Crocker-Harris in the previous entry which describes the film and play *The Browning Version* by Terence Rattigan, the elderly version of Sherlock Holmes in *Mr. Holmes* struggles to resolve his doubts about the meaning and value of his life. Sherlock Holmes is clearly in the final, eighth stage of life as described by developmental psychologist Erik Erikson. Erikson believed that people over the age of 65 face a potential crisis when they look back on their lives. If they believe they have been sufficiently successful and can accept their failures, they may acquire wisdom and contentment in their final years. If they remain dissatisfied with their past life, they may end their days depressed and in despair.

Resolution of past and present crises or challenges

Sherlock: "One shouldn't leave this life without a sense of completion."

Sherlock's statement sums up the key issue addressed in Erikson's eighth and final stage of his theory of psychosocial development.

The resolution of Sherlock's final challenging case results in personal and psychological growth for Sherlock when he realizes that a purely intellectual life is ultimately unfulfilling This insight changes Sherlock and provides the sense of resolution, acceptance, and completion that he seeks as he faces death.

Valuing social relationships

Sherlock: "I'm leaving you the house. You and Roger. House, grounds, apiary, everything within and without. And as I shan't change my mind on this point, you will see, I trust, that it will be greatly less complicated for all concerned if the two of you don't go off to somewhere—like Portsmouth."

Sherlock has developed a fondness for Roger but has never been close to Roger's mother, Mrs. Munro. After Sherlock comes to terms with the mistakes he made in the past, he realizes the importance of social ties. He bequeaths his estate to the two people closest to him and hopes they will not move away as they were planning to do to live with Mrs. Munro's sister in Portsmouth, England.

Research indicates that maintaining quality social relationships improves mental and physical health. A review of 148 previously published studies conducted by Brigham Young University professors Julianne Holt-Lunstad and Timothy Smith concluded that being connected to other people or groups of people improves a person's odds of survival by 50 percent.

"When someone is connected to a group and feels responsibility for other people, that sense of purpose and meaning translates to taking better care of themselves and taking fewer risks," Holt-Lunstad said in a statement released by his university.

Profile #99: Amanda Cleary in the Short Story "Winter Light" by MaryLee McNeal

What's it like to be ninety-three? I mean, like, do you feel like the winner? Like you outlasted everybody?

PLOT SUMMARY

Amanda Cleary's husband Jake died 19 years ago. That's when she moved away from the busy ranch she shared with her family and into a small one-bedroom house in the town of River Springs, 40 miles away. She wanted to get away from her daughter Lynn, Lynn's husband, their son Tom, and the hired hands who lived or worked at the ranch. She was tired of the noise and the activity at the ranch. Amanda wanted independence and solitude. She wanted time to read. And she got it.

She did well on her own through her 80s. Now at age 93, she is feeling the burden of the physical and psychological changes that often come with very advanced age. She has some episodes of depression and even has one episode during which she throws a tantrum. After that, she neglects herself and her home until her one friend, Mae, rescues her. Mae puts her in a bath and cleans her house. Amanda recovers, but after this episode, Mae checks in on her more often.

Lynn and Amanda's other children pester their mother to move back to the ranch so they can care for her. Amanda resists. But one Christmas, the pressure is too great. Her grandson Billy comes to get her in a pickup truck and drives her the 40 miles from her house to the ranch. During the trip, he listens to music and communicates with Amanda with a few nods and thumbs-up signs.

At the Christmas gathering, Amanda is irritated. She feels fussed over but nevertheless separate from everyone. Only when she sees one of her great grandsons approach her does she become interested. The boy has not yet mastered walking. Amanda is frail and bent, but she is inspired to pick up the toddler. She marvels at the smoothness of his skin, his baby-like smell, and his joy at seeing a lit candle that he shares by saying "wite, wite."

When Amanda realizes that the boy is excited about the candle's light, she shares his joy and enthusiasm. "Light!" she says. "Light!" The child slides safely down to the floor and hugs Amanda's legs to support himself. Amanda rests her hands on the boy's shoulder to support herself. For the first time in years, she experiences delight and a sense of connection. She promises herself that she will "warm herself with the memory when life got cold. But now she was exhausted, ready for sleep."

AMANDA'S PSYCHOLOGICAL TRAITS

Until she was in her 90s, Amanda demonstrated the independence and satisfaction that many older people achieve. This was in part due to her voluntary social disengagement when she moved into a house away from her children. After more than a decade, however, like many older people, she finds the physical decline associated with aging difficult to accept. This may have contributed to her episodes of depression.

CHALLENGES AND FEATURES OF LATE ADULTHOOD

Disengagement

Amanda has become more selective in her choice of whom she interacts with. She avoids emotionally complicated or troubling interactions and seeks to concentrate on having more emotionally rewarding interactions. This means she spends more time reading and less time with a noisy family. Unlike Amanda, some elderly people choose to maximize interactions with close friends and family and minimize interactions with nonfamily members. One theory about aging, called "disengagement theory," states that decreased interaction between an older person and society is an inevitable and normal feature of aging.

Depression

"Why let her children see up close the waves of depression that rolled over her more and more often?"

Disengagement often reduces the size of a person's social circle to family members and very close friends. Loss of loved ones and friends, however, often leaves older individuals lonely and can contribute to depression, as can failing health. Other stressful factors than can contribute to depression in late life include poverty and caring for a sick spouse.

Amanda's strong desire for independence leads her to hide her depressed moods from her family. Depression is one of the most common mental disorders affecting older people. The World Health Organization reports that between 10 percent and 20 percent of elderly people around the world suffer from depressive disorders. Depression is the main factor behind high suicide rates among the very old, rates that often exceed those of other age groups.

Cognitive impairment

"She asked Lynn two weeks before Christmas, 'How many great-grandkids do I have? People keep asking me. I can't keep track anymore.'

Lynn sighed. 'How come you can always remember characters from some book you've read, and not your own family?'

'People in fiction are more memorable.' Amanda added 'usually' a minute too late, remembering that Lynn thought it strange and disloyal for her to favor any subject over her own children and grandchildren."

Amanda was a competent but not particularly warm mother. "If you ask me," her daughter Grace said, "she's been cranky for at least a decade unless she's off in a corner by herself, reading a book." Amanda is not motivated to maintain close family ties. Her advanced age may also play a role in her inability to "keep track" of the number of her great grandchildren. The efficiency of short-term memory often declines with age while older memories, such as the names of memorable characters in Amanda's favorite books, are unaffected. Amanda and others her age also experience declines in the speed at which they can take in information.

Amanda shows no recent sign of significant mental confusion until she becomes exhausted after her exciting encounter with her great grandson. For a moment, she imagines her grown daughter is a child: "Finally she opened her eyes and looked at her daughter, trying to comprehend how Lynn could have grown old so quickly."

Amanda lived alone in good health, and with a quality of life that suited her, all through her 80s. She loved books and had an exceptional vocabulary. Only after she entered her 90s did she begin to develop physical and psychological problems that threatened her independence.

A specialized field of psychology called geropsychology is devoted to helping older persons like Amanda and their families adapt to age-related challenges and maximize their well-being.

Profile #100: George in the Novella *A Single Man* by Christopher Isherwood

> It is here that he stops short and knows, with a sick newness, almost as though it were for the first time: Jim is dead. Is dead.

PLOT SUMMARY

In early December 1962, George—a middle-aged British expatriate professor in Los Angeles—just tries to get through his day. He rises, dresses, lectures, visits a friend, drinks, flirts with a student, and falls asleep in his own bed. It would be an unremarkable day except for the fact that George lost his closest friend and lover, Jim, the day before. George is stunned by the loss but struggles through the day as if he should not be affected by his devastating loss.

GEORGE'S PSYCHOLOGICAL TRAITS

George, 58 years old, teaches English literature at a college in California. He is liberal, a bit snobbish but mostly unpretentious and well mannered, and withdrawn. His lover died in a car crash the day before. As George forces himself to follow most of his usual routines, he experiences a remarkable number of the components of grief.

BEREAVEMENT

Bereavement is the grief people feel when someone close to them dies. Different people respond differently to such a loss. Psychiatrist Sidney Zisook, MD, PhD, of the University of California at San Diego has identified important components of the grieving process.

The initial or acute stage of grief may provoke feelings of sadness, anger, anxiety, hopelessness, and pain. There may be a period of shock or disbelief and feelings of guilt and time spent second-guessing past actions. Also, a bereaved person may withdraw for a time from social interactions.

In many instances, people grieve and recover on their own with only the support of friends or family. There is little reason for a doctor to treat someone suffering from bereavement or grief unless he or she develops symptoms of major depressive disorder or the grieving lasts longer than six months. Grief lasting longer than six months is called complicated grief and requires psychotherapy and/or medication.

ACUTE GRIEF

Traumatic distress, shock

"And then, at least five minutes after George had put down the phone when the first shock wave hit, when the meaningless news suddenly meant exactly what it said, his blundering gasping run up the hill in the dark, his blind stumbling on the steps, banging at Charley's door, crying blubbering howling on her shoulder, in her lap, all over her; and Charley squeezing him, stroking his hair, telling him the usual stuff one tells."

George responded unemotionally when Jim's uncle called to tell him Jim had died. The shock of the news soon hit him, however, and he sought comfort from his friend and neighbor.

Depressed mood

"Obediently, it washes, shaves, brushes its hair, for it accepts its responsibilities to the others. It is even glad that it has its place among them. It knows what is expected of it. It knows its name. It is called George."

George is grieving but still carrying on his daily routine. Although he is preparing to go to work where he will lecture, he is still in shock. In a sense, he has undergone social withdrawal without removing himself physically from society.

Daily, acute pain of loss

"Jim wasn't a substitute for anything. And there is no substitute for Jim, if you'll forgive my saying so, anywhere."

George was closer to Jim than to anyone else. His loss is not only painful; it is stunning for an introverted loner like George.

Anger

"All are, in the last analysis, responsible for Jim's death; their words, their thoughts, their whole way of life willed it, even though they never knew he existed. But, when George gets in as deep as this, Jim hardly matters any more. Jim is nothing now but an excuse for hating three quarters of the population of America . . . George's jaws work, his teeth grind, as he chews and chews the cud of his hate."

George's pain and anger at losing Jim is redirected at the superficial aspects of American culture that he looks down upon.

Preoccupation with the deceased person

"This bright place [a supermarket] isn't really a sanctuary. For, ambushed among its bottles and cartons and cans, are shockingly vivid memories of meals shopped for, cooked, eaten with Jim. They stab out at George as he passes, pushing his shopping cart. Should we ever feel truly lonely if we never ate alone?"

George's moods alternate between sadness and bitterness, and excitement. For example, immediately after feeling despair while shopping in the supermarket, he remembers an invitation he rejected earlier in the day from his friend Charley. He phones her, tells her his plans have changed, and asks if he can accept her invitation to have drinks. Then he reconsiders: "But he is so utterly perverse that his mood begins to change again before he has even finished unloading his purchases into the car. Do I really want to see her? he asks himself, and then, What in the world made me do that?"

Later Stages of Grief

Positive memories and emotions

"BREAKFAST with Jim used to be one of the best times of their day. It was then, while they were drinking their second and third cups of coffee, that they had their best talks. They talked about everything that came into their heads—including death, of course, and is there survival, and, if so, what exactly is it that survives."

Positive memories and their associated emotions usually begin to appear after the acute stage of grief. They may relieve long periods of sadness.

Acceptance

"No. Jim is in the past, now. He is of no use to George any more. But George remembers him so faithfully."

Christopher Isherwood did not write *A Single Man* to gain attention for issues surrounding homosexuality, a scandalous subject when the book was published over 50 years ago. He succeeded in writing a book about a grieving man who happened to be homosexual. Without being strident, he was able to humanize his protagonist and demonstrate that a normal, ordinary, common person could incidentally be homosexual. Interestingly, the *DSM* continued to describe homosexuality as a mental disorder for a decade after Isherwood's book appeared. In the early 1970s, reference to homosexuality was finally removed from the manual, but its inclusion for so many years highlights the influence social mores can have on the perception of mental disorders and on our ideas of what is "normal" and healthy.

Profile #101: Gilgamesh in the Poem *The Epic of Gilgamesh* by Anonymous Authors and Sin-Leqi-Unninni (attributed)

I will not die like Enkidu, but weeping has entered into my heart. . .

PLOT SUMMARY

Gilgamesh is the tyrannical ruler of the great city of Uruk in Mesopotamia. He preys on the young women of his realm and does not hesitate to exploit and kill the men. His people plead with their gods for relief from their king's oppressive behavior. The gods create a distraction for Gilgamesh in the form of a primitive creature called Enkidu who begins life as a wild animal living among other wild animals. Enkidu is humanized by a priestess/prostitute after she entices him with nearly a week of nonstop sex. The priestess then takes Enkidu—now more human than animal—to the center of civilization, Gilgamesh's own city of Uruk. When Gilgamesh sees the powerfully built Enkidu, he challenges him and the two alpha males fight for dominance.

Gilgamesh wins the long, macho battle and the two become like inseparable brothers. Together they travel far outside of Uruk, sharing their adventures. They defeat the guardian of the Cedar Mountain, Humbaba, and they kill the Bull of Heaven. This last act infuriates the goddess Ishtar, for she had sent the bull to punish Gilgamesh after he refused her sexual advances. Ishtar takes revenge by arranging Enkidu's death.

Gilgamesh is devastated by the loss of his friend and shaken by the prospect of his own death. He embarks on a long journey to find the secret of immortality. He fails, but returns to Uruk more mature and with as good and satisfying an insight as any mortal is liable to discover.

This tale is one of the oldest works of literature. The standard version of the epic has been assembled from a variety of fragments written in Akkadian, an extinct Semitic language once spoken and written in Mesopotamia. The original story, however, is believed to have originated in Sumar, the first civilization. It was presumably written in Sumarian sometime in the 2100s BCE. The story was evidently very popular since the version we know was first written down about 500 years later. And the current version is translated from fragments written 1,000 years after that. There is no single, complete version of the tale, which was translated into Babylonian, Hittite, Sumarian, and Acadian over the span of one and a half millennia.

GILGAMESH'S PSYCHOLOGICAL TRAITS

Some people who are given or who achieve power and/or fame lack the maturity to meet the responsibilities that come with it. A prime example is the king of Uruk. He is selfish, immature, and domineering. He lacks introspection and does not have a single close friend. But Gilgamesh differs from some flawed rulers and politicians because he learns and grows.

The themes in the story of Gilgamesh reflect some of the most important and often anxiety-producing concerns of human beings. How do I live a meaningful life? How do I cope with the loss of loved ones? How do I come to terms with the certainty of my own death? And the epic does it all with larger-than-life characters.

THE FIVE STAGES OF LOSS AND GRIEF

Gilgamesh: "I will not die like Enkidu, But weeping has entered into my heart . . ."

For the first time in his privileged and protected life, Gilgamesh experiences grief when his close (and only) friend dies. Approximately four millennia after the first version of *The Epic of Gilgamesh* appeared, Elisabeth Kübler-Ross compiled a list of five stages of mourning she believed were common in people experiencing either terminal illness or the loss of a loved one. As described in her 1969 book *On Death and Dying*, people may pass through these stages in a different order. Some may not experience all the stages but most people will recognize many of them in retrospect.

Denial

Gilgamesh: "My friend, the swift mule, fleet wild ass of the mountain, panther of the wilderness, after we joined together and went up the mountain, fought the Bull of Heaven and killed it, and overwhelmed Humbaba, who lived in the Cedar Forest, now what is this sleep which has seized you? You have turned dark and do not hear me! But his eyes do not move, he touched his heart, but it beat no longer."

Anger

Not everyone goes through all the stages of loss and grief. Gilgamesh mourns his friend. He shows little signs of overt anger. Instead, he soon turns his attention to finding a way he can avoid suffering the same fate.

Bargaining

Gilgamesh: "I fear death, and now roam the wilderness. I will set out to the region of Utanapishtim, son of Ubartutu, and will go with utmost dispatch!"

As Gilgamesh begins to change and realizes that he too will die, he attempts to bargain for immortality with Utanapishtim, an immortal being from whom he hopes to learn the secret of eternal life.

Depression

Gilgamesh: "Six days and seven nights I mourned over him and would not allow him to be buried until a maggot fell out of his nose."

Acceptance

Gilgamesh: "Enkidu, the companion, whom I loved, is dirt, nothing but clay is Enkidu."

FEAR OF DEATH

Gilgamesh: "Must I die too? Must Gilgamesh be like that? It was then I felt the fear of it in my belly."

It had never occurred to the vain and powerful Gilgamesh that he would die someday. Only after witnessing the death of his close friend did the prospect of his own mortality occur to him. Once arrogant, boastful, and self-centered, Gilgamesh now fears what every human faces.

Terror management theory suggests that the "terror" or anxiety many people feel when they contemplate their deaths exerts a major influence on their behavior. The theory is based on the work of Ernest Becker, the author of *The Denial of Death*. Becker believed that human behavior is basically motivated by a biological need to control the fear and anxiety that comes with the knowledge that death is inevitable. He viewed behavior as a need to deny the terror of death. According to terror management theory, humans develop various religions, worldviews, and philosophies to give their lives meaning and to attain a sense of self-esteem in the face of their inevitable deaths. Thus, the theory attributes much of human accomplishment to the need to come to terms with our mortality.

So soon after Enkidu's death and the realization that he too will die, Gilgamesh isn't ready to consider terror management theory. Gilgamesh's response to his personal crisis is to search for a way to avoid death. He fails, but he does get some good advice along the way.

ACCEPTANCE OF MORTALITY

Fame, status, great accomplishments, wealth—none of these will prevent death. What is a great king like Gilgamesh (or anyone) to do? A barmaid named Siduri offers Gilgamesh advice, which has not been improved upon in over 4,000 years.

"O Mighty King, remember now that only gods stay in eternal watch. Humans come then go, that is the way fate decreed on the Tablets of Destiny. So someday you will depart, but till that distant day Sing, and dance. Eat your fill of warm cooked food and cool jugs of beer. Cherish the children your love gave life. Bathe away life's dirt in warm drawn waters. Pass the time in joy with your chosen wife. On the Tablets of Destiny it is decreed for you to enjoy short pleasures for your short days."

Gilgamesh's acceptance of the fact that he will die someday is a sign of his increasing maturity. This knowledge can inspire a more meaningful, productive, and rewarding life. Gilgamesh's values at the start of his journey—fame, power, and fortune—offered little satisfaction before he met Enkidu and no satisfaction at the end of his journey. Siduri's advice to cherish love, simple pleasures, and companionship, and to remember that life is brief, stresses quality over superficiality. Gilgamesh's most important step toward becoming a mature being is converting the mental energy he expended on dreading death into energy spent appreciating life.

Appendix A: List of Characters and Their Psychological Traits

Character	Work (Author)	Psychological Traits, Features, or Disorder
Part 1: Mental and Personality Disorders		
Neurodevelopmental disorders		
Profile #1: Charlie Gordon	*Flowers for Algernon* (Daniel Keyes)	Moderate intellectual disability
Profile #2: Benjy Compson	*The Sound and the Fury* (William Faulkner)	Profound intellectual disability
Profile #3: Raymond Babbitt	*Rain Man* (Ronald Bass)	Autism spectrum disorder and savant syndrome
Profile #4: Dylan Mint	*When Mr. Dog Bites* (Brian Conaghan)	Tourette's disorder
Psychotic disorders		
Profile #5: Travis Bickle	*Taxi Driver* (Paul Schrader)	Schizotypal personality disorder
Profile #6: Alan Strang	*Equus* (Peter Shaffer)	Delusional disorder—grandiose type
Profile #7: Alonso Quixano	*Don Quixote* (Miguel de Cervantes)	Delusional disorder—grandiose type
Profile #8: Jerry Fletcher	*Conspiracy Theory* (Brian Helgeland)	Delusional disorder—persecutory type
Profile #9: Ophelia	*Hamlet* (William Shakespeare)	Psychosis with marked stressors
Profile #10: Nina Sayers	*Black Swan* (Mark Heyman, Andrés Heinz, and John McLaughlin)	Psychosis, obsessive-compulsive traits, eating disorder, self-harm, and paranoid thinking

Character	Work (Author)	Psychological Traits, Features, or Disorder
Profile #11: The Narrator	"The Tell-Tale Heart" (Edgar Allan Poe)	Psychosis, Anosognosia
Profile #12: Aksenty Ivanovich Poprishchin	"Diary of a Madman" (Nikolai Gogol)	Schizophrenia
Profile #13: John Nash	*A Beautiful Mind* (Akiva Goldsman)	Schizophrenia
Profile #14: The Boy	"Signs and Symbols" (Vladimir Nabokov)	Childhood schizophrenia
Profile #15: Ebenezer Scrooge	*A Christmas Carol* (Charles Dickens)	Brief psychotic disorder without marked stressors
Profile #16: King George III	*The Madness of King George* (Alan Bennett)	Psychotic disorder due to acute porphyria
Bipolar disorder		
Profile #17: Leonard Bankhead	*The Marriage Plot* (Jeffrey Eugenides)	Bipolar I disorder
Depressive disorders		
Profile #18: Esther Greenwood	*The Bell Jar* (Sylvia Plath)	Major depressive disorder
Profile #19: The Narrator	"I Felt a Funeral in My Brain" (Emily Dickinson)	Imagery of depression
Profile #20: Leonard Peacock	*Forgive Me, Leonard Peacock* (Matthew Quick)	Depression, suicidal thoughts, psychiatric emergency
Profile #21: Miss Havisham	*Great Expectations* (Charles Dickens)	Complicated grief

Character	Work (Author)	Psychological Traits, Features, or Disorder
Anxiety disorders		
Profile #22: John "Scottie" Ferguson	*Vertigo* (Samuel A. Taylor et al.)	Specific phobia—acrophobia and vertigo
Profile #23: Dr. Helen Hudson	*Copycat* (Ann Biderman and David Madsen)	Anxiety disorder—agoraphobia
Profile #24: Arthur Dimmesdale	*The Scarlet Letter* (Nathaniel Hawthorne)	Generalized anxiety disorder
Profile #25: Francis Morton	"The End of the Party" (Graham Greene)	Specific situational phobia—fear of the dark
Obsessive-compulsive disorder		
Profile #26: Melvin Udall	*As Good as It Gets* (Mark Andrus and James L. Brooks)	Obsessive-compulsive disorder
Trauma and stress-related disorders		
Profile #27: Dr. Martin Ellingham	*Doc Martin* (Dominic Minghella et al.)	Dismissive style of avoidant attachment
Profile #28: Septimus Warren Smith	*Mrs. Dalloway* (Virginia Woolf)	Posttraumatic stress disorder and an undetermined disorder with psychotic features
Dissociative disorders		
Profile #29: Eve White	*The Three Faces of Eve* (Nunnally Johnson)	Dissociative identity disorder
Profile #30: Jason Bourne	*The Bourne Identity* (Tony Gilroy and William Blake Herron)	Dissociative amnesia
Profile #31: Marcel	*Swann's Way* (Marcel Proust)	Depersonalization/derealization

Character	Work (Author)	Psychological Traits, Features, or Disorder
Somatic symptoms		
Profile #32: Roderick Usher	"The Fall of the House of Usher" (Edgar Allan Poe)	Somatic symptom disorder
Profile #33: Beatrice Trueblood	"Beatrice Trueblood's Story" (Jean Stafford)	Conversion disorder
Eating disorders		
Profile #34: Lia Overbrook	*Wintergirls* (Laurie Halse Anderson)	Anorexia nervosa
Profile #35: Janie Ryman	*Purge* (Sarah Darer Littman)	Bulimia nervosa
Sleep–wake disorder		
Profile #36: Mike Waters	*My Own Private Idaho* (Gus Van Sant)	Narcolepsy
Gender dysphoria		
Profile #37: Roy Applewood	*Normal* (Jane Anderson)	Gender dysphoria in adolescents and adults
Disruptive, impulse control, and conduct disorders		
Profile #38: Bruce Banner/ The Hulk	*The Avengers* (Joss Whedon)	Intermittent explosive disorder
Profile #39: Ronald Bartel	*Backdraft* (Gregory Widen)	Pyromania and possible psychopathic traits
Profile #40: Alex DeLarge	*A Clockwork Orange* (Anthony Burgess)	Conduct disorder
Substance-related and addictive disorders		
Profile #41: Bobby	*Panic in Needle Park* (Joan Didion and John Gregory Dunne)	Opioid use disorder

Character	Work (Author)	Psychological Traits, Features, or Disorder
Profile #42: Geoffrey Firmin	*Under the Volcano* (Malcolm Lowry)	Alcohol use disorder
Profile #43: Ray and Jewel Kaiser	*Bob the Gambler* (Frederick Barthelme)	Gambling disorder
Neurocognitive disorders		
Profile #44: Dr. Alice Howland	*Still Alice* (Wash Westmoreland and Richard Glatzer)	Alzheimer's disease
Profile #45: Henry Reifsneider	"The Lost Phoebe" (Theodore Dreiser)	Dementia
Personality disorders		
Profile #46: Alex Forrest	*Fatal Attraction* (James Dearden)	Borderline personality disorder with stalking behavior
Profile #47: Mavis Gary	*Young Adult* (Diablo Cody)	Borderline personality disorder
Profile #48: Blanche DuBois	*A Streetcar Named Desire* (Tennessee Williams)	Histrionic personality disorder
Profile #49: Dorian Gray	*The Picture of Dorian Gray* (Oscar Wilde)	Narcissistic personality disorder
Profile #50: Claude Frollo	*The Hunchback of Notre Dame* (Victor Hugo)	Obsessive love and stalking behavior
Profile #51: Unnamed Despot	"A Foreign Ruler" (Walter Savage Landor)	Malignant narcissism
Profile #52: Captain Ahab	*Moby Dick* (Herman Melville)	Narcissistic rage
Profile #53: Charlie Brown	*Peanuts* (Charles Schulz)	Avoidant personality disorder
Profile #54: Adolf Hitler	*Downfall* (Bernd Eichinger)	Narcissistic rage, messiah complex, and projection

Character	Work (Author)	Psychological Traits, Features, or Disorder
Profile #55: Mr. Kurtz	*Heart of Darkness* (Joseph Conrad)	Dark triad
Profile #56: Felix Krull	*Confessions of Felix Krull, Confidence Man* (Thomas Mann)	Narcissistic features and antisocial personality disorder
Profile #57: Gordon Gekko	*Wall Street* (Stanley Weiser and Oliver Stone)	"Corporate" psychopathy
Profile #58: Anton Chigurh	*No Country for Old Men* (Cormac McCarthy)	Psychopathy
Profile #59: Martin Burney	*Sleeping with the Enemy* (Ronald Bass)	Abusive behaviors and pathological jealousy
Profile #60: Hannibal Lecter	*Silence of the Lambs* (Ted Tally, based on Thomas Harris's book)	"Elite psychopathy" with cannibalism
Profile #61: Livia Soprano	*The Sopranos* (David Chase)	Borderline personality disorder and psychopathic traits
Paraphilic disorders		
Profile #62: Jean-Jacques Rousseau	*The Confessions of Jean-Jacques Rousseau* (Jean-Jacques Rousseau)	Exhibitionistic disorder
Profile #63: Frank Alpine	*The Assistant* (Bernard Malamud)	Voyeuristic disorder
Profile #64: A Man	"An Encounter" in *Dubliners* (James Joyce)	Pedophilic interests, exhibitionistic behavior, and interest in sexual sadism
Profile #65: Frank Booth	*Blue Velvet* (David Lynch)	Sexual sadism disorder
Profile #66: Humbert Humbert	*Lolita* (Vladimir Nabokov)	Pedophilic disorder

Character	Work (Author)	Psychological Traits, Features, or Disorder
Other disorders and syndromes		
Profile #67: Leonard Shelby	*Memento* (Christopher Nolan)	Anterograde amnesia
Profile #68: Plyushkin	*Dead Souls* (Nikolai Gogol)	Diogenes syndrome
Profile #69: Alice	*Alice in Wonderland* (Lewis Carroll)	Alice in Wonderland syndrome
Part 2: Positive Psychological Traits		
Profile #70: Sherlock Holmes	*A Study in Scarlet* (Sir Arthur Conan Doyle)	Wisdom and knowledge—judgment
Profile #71: Santiago	*The Old Man and the Sea* (Ernest Hemingway)	Numerous, particularly courage—perseverance, persistence
Profile #72: Luke Jackson	*Cool Hand Luke* (Donn Pearce and Frank K. Pierson)	Numerous, particularly courage—zest, vigor, vitality
Profile #73: Juror #8	*12 Angry Men* (Reginald Rose)	Numerous, particularly justice—fairness
Profile #74: Peter Parker/ Spider-Man	*Amazing Spider-Man 2* (Brittany Candau and Nachie Marsham)	Numerous, particularly justice—citizenship, social responsibility
Profile #75: Bruce Wayne/ Batman	*Batman Begins* (Christopher Nolan and David S. Goyer)	Numerous, particularly posttraumatic growth
Profile #76: Hugh Conway	*Lost Horizon* (James Hilton)	Numerous, particularly humanity—social intelligence
Profile #77: L. B. Jefferies	*Rear Window* (John Michael Hayes)	Numerous, particularly wisdom and knowledge—curiosity
Profile #78: Will Kane	*High Noon* (Carl Foreman)	Numerous, particularly courage—bravery

Character	Work (Author)	Psychological Traits, Features, or Disorder
Profile #79: Shane	*Shane* (A. B. Guthrie Jr.)	Numerous, particularly temperance—humility
Profile #80: Marge Gunderson	*Fargo* (Ethan and Joel Coen)	Numerous, particularly wisdom and knowledge—critical thinking
Profile #81: The Dream	"Kubla Khan; Or, a Vision in a Dream" (Samuel Taylor Coleridge)	Psychology of dreaming and wisdom and knowledge—creativity and originality
Profile #82: Harry Potter	*Harry Potter and the Sorcerer's Stone* and sequels (J. K. Rowling)	Resilience
Profile #83: Lisbeth Salander	*The Girl with the Dragon Tattoo* (Stieg Larsson)	Several maladaptive and several positive attributes
Profile #84: Atticus Finch	*To Kill a Mockingbird* (Harper Lee)	Numerous, particularly wisdom and knowledge—perspective
Part 3: Negative Psychological Traits and Features		
Profile #85: Atticus Finch	*Go Set a Watchman* (Harper Lee)	Racism and prejudice
Profile #86: Ahmad Ashmawy Mulloy	*The Terrorist* (John Updike)	Radical beliefs with violent behavior; terrorism
Part 4: Emotional Instability/Neuroticism		
Profile #87: Alexander Portnoy	*Portnoy's Complaint* (Philip Roth)	Neurotism or emotional instability
Profile #88: Alvy Singer	*Annie Hall* (Woody Allen and Marshall Brickman)	Neurotism or emotional instability

Character	Work (Author)	Psychological Traits, Features, or Disorder
	Part 5: Freudian Themes	
Profile #89: Norman Bates	*Psycho* (Joseph Stefano)	The alter ego
Profile #90: Henry Jekyll	*Strange Case of Dr. Jekyll and Mr. Hyde* (Robert Louis Stevenson)	Id/ego struggle
Profile #91: Oedipus	*Oedipus the King* (Sophocles)	Oedipus complex
	Part 6: Psychologists in Films	
Profile #92: "Prisoners" and "Guards"	*The Stanford Prison Experiment* (Tim Talbott)	Abuse of authority
Profile #93: "Teachers"	*Experimenter: The Stanley Milgram Story* (Michael Almereyda)	Agentic behavior
	Part 7: Psychological Growth, Development, Maturity, Loss, and Aging	
Profile #94: Winnie-the-Pooh	*Winnie-the-Pooh* and *The House at Pooh Corner* (A. A. Milne)	Egocentricity, difficulty manipulating information, and inability to think logically
Profile #95: The Poet	"Childhood" (Markus Natten)	Rationality
Profile #96: Romeo and Juliet	*Romeo and Juliet* (William Shakespeare)	Obsessive love
Profile #97: Andrew Crocker-Harris	*The Browning Version* (Terence Rattigan)	Crisis resolution
Profile #98: Sherlock Holmes	*Mr. Holmes* (Jeffrey Hatcher)	Crisis resolution
Profile #99: Amanda Cleary	"Winter Light" (MaryLee McNeal)	Disengagement

Character	Work (Author)	Psychological Traits, Features, or Disorder
Profile #100: George	*A Single Man* (Christopher Isherwood)	Bereavement and acute grief
Profile #101: Gilgamesh	*The Epic of Gilgamesh* (anonymous)	Fear of death

Appendix B: The VIA Classification of Character Strengths

1. Wisdom and knowledge—Cognitive strengths that entail the acquisition and use of knowledge

Creativity (originality, ingenuity): Thinking of novel and productive ways to conceptualize and do things; includes artistic achievement but is not limited to it

Curiosity (interest, novelty-seeking, openness to experience): Taking an interest in ongoing experience for its own sake; finding subjects and topics fascinating; exploring and discovering

Judgment (critical thinking): Thinking things through and examining them from all sides; not jumping to conclusions; being able to change one's mind in light of evidence; weighing all evidence fairly

Love of learning: Mastering new skills, topics, and bodies of knowledge, whether on one's own or formally; obviously related to the strength of curiosity but goes beyond it to describe the tendency to add systematically to what one knows

Perspective (wisdom): Being able to provide wise counsel to others; having ways of looking at the world that make sense to oneself and to other people

2. Courage—Emotional strengths that involve the exercise of will to accomplish goals in the face of opposition, external or internal

Bravery (valor): Not shrinking from threat, challenge, difficulty, or pain; speaking up for what is right even if there is opposition; acting on convictions even if unpopular; includes physical bravery but is not limited to it

Perseverance (persistence, industriousness): Finishing what one starts; persisting in a course of action in spite of obstacles; "getting it out the door"; taking pleasure in completing tasks

Honesty (authenticity, integrity): Speaking the truth but more broadly presenting oneself in a genuine way and acting in a sincere way; being without pretense; taking responsibility for one's feelings and actions

Zest (vitality, enthusiasm, vigor, energy): Approaching life with excitement and energy; not doing things halfway or halfheartedly; living life as an adventure; feeling alive and activated

3. Humanity—Interpersonal strengths that involve tending and befriending others

Love: Valuing close relations with others, in particular those in which sharing and caring are reciprocated; being close to people

Kindness (generosity, nurturance, care, compassion, altruistic love, "niceness"): Doing favors and good deeds for others; helping them; taking care of them

Social intelligence (emotional intelligence, personal intelligence): Being aware of the motives and feelings of other people and oneself; knowing what to do to fit into different social situations; knowing what makes other people tick

4. Justice—Civic strengths that underlie healthy community life

Teamwork (citizenship, social responsibility, loyalty): Working well as a member of a group or team; being loyal to the group; doing one's share

Fairness: Treating all people the same according to notions of fairness and justice; not letting personal feelings bias decisions about others; giving everyone a fair chance

Leadership: Encouraging a group of which one is a member to get things done, and at the same time maintaining good relations within the group; organizing group activities and seeing that they happen

5. Temperance—Strengths that protect against excess

Forgiveness: Forgiving those who have done wrong; accepting the shortcomings of others; giving people a second chance; not being vengeful

Humility: Letting one's accomplishments speak for themselves; not regarding oneself as more special than one is

Prudence: Being careful about one's choices; not taking undue risks; not saying or doing things that might later be regretted

Self-Regulation (self-control): Regulating what one feels and does; being disciplined; controlling one's appetites and emotions

6. Transcendence—Strengths that forge connections to the larger universe and provide meaning

Appreciation of beauty and excellence (awe, wonder, elevation): Noticing and appreciating beauty, excellence, and/or skilled performance in various domains of life, from nature to art to mathematics to science to everyday experience

Gratitude: Being aware of and thankful for the good things that happen; taking time to express thanks

Hope (optimism, future-mindedness, future orientation): Expecting the best in the future and working to achieve it; believing that a good future is something that can be brought about

Humor (playfulness): Liking to laugh and tease; bringing smiles to other people; seeing the light side; making (not necessarily telling) jokes

Spirituality (faith, purpose): Having coherent beliefs about the higher purpose and meaning of the universe; knowing where one fits within the larger scheme; having beliefs about the meaning of life that shape conduct and provide comfort

Derived from Peterson, C., & Seligman, M. E. P. (2004). *Character strengths and virtues: A handbook and classification*. New York and Washington, D.C.: Oxford University Press and American Psychological Association. www.viacharacter.org and the VIA Institute on Character. Used with permission. © 2004–2014 VIA® Institute on Character.

Glossary of Psychological and Literary Terms

Acrophobia—An extreme, abnormal fear of heights that results in symptoms of panic and often a lack of balance when a person finds himself or herself in an elevated position or high place. See also vertigo.

Adjustment disorder—A stress-related disorder that involves the inability to adapt to or "get over" a problem or change encountered in a person's life. Stressors that may precipitate this disorder include problems at home, school, or work, or illness. The stress can be negative like a death in the family, divorce, or eviction, or it can be positive like getting married or moving into a new home or job. Symptoms, which must occur within three months of the stressful challenge or change, can include significant anxiety, depression, and/or suicidal thoughts.

Affect—The observable expression of a mental state, mood, or emotion. Different types of affect include blunted, restricted, flat, constricted, inappropriate, and labile.

Aggression—A hostile behavior that can cause psychological and/or physical harm. The harm may result from emotional, mental, physical, or verbal aggression directed against oneself or another person. Aggression can also be directed against objects. See also impulsive aggression and instrumental aggression.

Alcohol abuse—See alcohol use disorder.

Alcohol dependence—See alcohol use disorder.

Alcoholism—An outdated term for alcohol use disorder.

Alcohol use disorder—A pattern of drinking alcohol that impairs a person's ability to function successfully in his or her daily life and/or causes the person distress. This mental health diagnosis is made when a person's frequent drinking causes significant problems affecting his or her ability to succeed or function at school, work, or home, or results in legal problems or difficulties getting along with other people. For example, if a person regularly uses alcohol and—while under its influence—operates a car or a machine, gets into fights, gets fired from a job, gets thrown out of school, or neglects a child or dependent, alcohol use disorder may be diagnosed.

Alter ego—"Another self." A different side of a person, which has character traits that are not normally associated with that person.

American Psychiatric Association—Now more than 130 years old, the self-described "voice and conscience of modern psychiatry" is the world's largest organization of psychiatrists. It is responsible for writing and publishing the *Diagnostic and Statistical Manual of Mental Disorders.*

Amnesia—Loss of memories due to psychological or neurological stress or damage.

Anger—A strong emotion involving hostility, annoyance, antagonism, displeasure, or belligerence.

Anhedonia—An inability to experience pleasure.

Anorexia nervosa—An eating disorder that causes people to have a distorted image of their body size and appearance, and to starve themselves despite drastic, dangerous weight loss.

Anosognosia—Impaired awareness or lack of insight about an illness.

Antagonist—A character or thing that opposes or challenges a story's protagonist.

Anthropophagous—(1) Eating human flesh; and (2) a cannibal or cannibalism.

Antisocial personality disorder—A long-term pattern of behavior that demonstrates a blatant disregard for the well-being and rights of others and involves obvious instances of acts that threaten or harm people, animals, and/or property.

Anxiety—A normal response to a stressful situation if it is a reaction to a specific situation of limited duration. In some people, however, anxiety can become a state of excess apprehension, worry, and uneasiness that interferes with daily functioning over a long period of time.

Anxiety disorder—One of a group of disorders characterized by excessive levels of stress lasting a long time and negatively affecting quality of life for approximately one in six adults in the United States. Panic disorder, generalized anxiety disorder, posttraumatic stress disorder, obsessive-compulsive disorder, and social phobia or social anxiety disorder are all anxiety disorders.

Autism—See Autism spectrum disorder.

Autism spectrum disorder (ASD)—A neurodevelopmental disorder that negatively affects many aspects of a person's life involving the development of language, communication skills, and interpersonal relationships. People with ASD often prefer rigid and repetitive behaviors. The severity of the handicaps associated with this disorder varies widely. Some individuals live nearly normal lives while others are so affected that they need to be cared for and closely watched in an institutional setting. The phrase "autism spectrum disorder" now encompasses conditions that were previously called autistic disorder, Asperger's syndrome, pervasive developmental disorder, Rett syndrome, and childhood dissent disintegrative disorder.

Autistic savant—A person with autism spectrum disorder who has exceptional abilities in a specialized field such as mathematics, music, memorization, or art. See also savant syndrome.

Avoidant personality disorder—A mental health condition characterized by a lifelong pattern of extreme shyness, feelings of inadequacy, and sensitivity to rejection by others.

Bipolar disorder—A disorder characterized by widely fluctuating mood swings that range from depressive lows to manic highs. Types of bipolar disorder include bipolar I, bipolar II, cyclothymic disorder, and bipolar disorder not otherwise specified. Bipolar disorders were once referred to as manic depression or manic-depressive disorder.

Bipolar I disorder—A form of bipolar disorder that causes people to experience at least one manic episode, or one mixed episode involving rapidly alternating manic and depressive moods. The manic episode may occur before or after major depressive or hypomanic episodes. Formerly called manic depression.

Bipolar II disorder—A form of bipolar disorder that causes people to experience at least one major depressive episode and at least one hypomanic episode, but no manic episodes. Hypomanic episodes are less intense than manic episodes.

Bipolar not otherwise specified—A mood disorder that causes alternating episodes of depression and mania but does not exactly meet the criteria for bipolar I disorder, bipolar II disorder, or cyclothymic disorder.

Blunted affect—Greatly reduced or nearly absent outward expression of emotion. People with schizophrenia may have blunted affect.

Body dysmorphic disorder—A form of anxiety disorder that causes a person to develop a distorted perception of his or her appearance. A person with this disorder has an inaccurate self-image involving an exaggerated or imagined physical flaw or defect in appearance which results in significant stress and excessive worry.

Borderline personality disorder—A form of mental illness characterized by troubled personal relationships, unpredictable mood shifts, and reckless and impulsive behaviors.

Bulimia nervosa—An eating disorder that is characterized by binge eating during which a person, who is usually preoccupied with food and body weight, consumes large amounts of food and then purges to offset the intake of calories. People with purging bulimia may routinely force themselves to vomit or they may use laxatives, enemas, or diuretics following a binge. Nonpurging bulimia involves the use of fasting, extreme dieting, and/or excessive exercise following a binge. It is not unusual for people with this potentially life-threatening illness to use a combination of approaches to eliminate the calories consumed while binging. As with anorexia nervosa, the cause or causes of bulimia nervosa are unclear. It is possible the disorder is a result of a combination of factors related to neurobiology, social influences and expectations, and emotional health.

Character—A literary term referring to a person or, in the case of science fiction and fantasy literature, an entity, through which the reader relates to, or is engaged by, a story's plot. The character's actions and thoughts drive the plot of a story.

Chivalry—A value system associated with knights in the Middle Ages. The system's code of conduct stressed honor, justice, bravery, duty, courtesy, fairness, and defense of the innocent and weak.

Cognition—The mental processes involved in learning, understanding, and gaining and using knowledge. Problem solving, thinking, evaluating, judging, planning, remembering, perceiving, and imagining are examples of cognitive behavior.

Cognitive science—A field of study that draws on multiple scientific disciplines, including psychology, neuroscience, linguistics, and computer science, to investigate critical aspects of mental organization, thinking, and learning.

Comorbidity—The presence in one person of two or more mental disorders or medical conditions at the same time.

Conduct disorder—A persistent pattern of behavioral and emotional problems seen in children and adolescents with strong antisocial tendencies. Youngsters with conduct disorder typically disrespect and disregard social rules and may engage in criminal activities. In some cases, they consistently display a callous attitude toward others, including victims, and lack a sense of empathy.

Conflict—A struggle between a character in a story and an opponent. The opponent can be another character, a natural force, a large group or organization, or even something originating within the protagonist such as an illness, a flaw, or an attitude.

Conversion disorder—A condition in which mental or emotional stress expresses itself as a physical problem in the absence of any actual, physical injury or impairment. For example, after seeing a horrific event, a person may lose his or her sight although that person's eyes and the rest of the visual system suffered no damage. Paralysis, deafness, and numbness are other typical effects of this condition.

Cyclothymic disorder—A type of bipolar disorder in which a person alternates between periods of less-than-major depression and periods of hypomania. While it might seem that cyclothymia is a type of "mild" bipolar disorder, in fact it is a chronic mood disturbance that often first appears before maturity. As many as one-third of those with cyclothymia later develop bipolar I or II disorder.

"Dark tetrad"—A constellation of personality traits that share the key characteristics of callous and manipulative behavior directed at others. The four components of this type of personality are narcissism, Machiavellianism, subclinical psychopathy, and sadism.

"Dark triad"—A constellation of personality traits that share the key characteristics of callous and manipulative behavior directed at others. The three components of this type of personality are narcissism, Machiavellianism, and subclinical psychopathy.

Delusional disorder—A mental health condition lasting at least a month during which a person has one or more delusions but no other psychiatric symptoms. The delusions can be bizarre or nonbizarre. Nonbizarre delusions involve events or situations that could happen but are not happening to the patient. Examples of nonbizarre delusions are being followed, being poisoned, having a disease or illness, or having a relationship with a celebrity. Bizarre delusions are clearly implausible. Examples are being the focus of extraterrestrial alien attention or believing that one's internal organs have been removed and replaced with those of a stranger, despite a lack of scars.

Delusions—Unusual, irrational, or false beliefs that a person maintains are real or true despite convincing evidence to the contrary.

Dementia—A group of symptoms resulting from impaired brain cell function that results in a loss of intellectual abilities. Symptoms may include loss of memory, language skills, navigational skills, complex motor skills, and other cognitive functions. Alzheimer's disease is the most common a type of dementia although there are several others including Lewy body disease and frontotemporal neurocognitive disorder.

Depersonalization—The experience of feeling detached from one's thoughts or bodily sensations. The detachment may extend to one's feelings and actions and may involve a sense of unreality or a sense that a person is an outside observer and not one's familiar self.

Depression—A state of low mood and aversion to activity that can affect a person's thoughts, actions, feelings, and sense of well-being. Depression is different from normal sadness.

Derealization—The experience of feeling detached from nearby people or objects or feeling as if they are unreal. They may seem as if they are lifeless, dreamlike, or viewed in a fog. They may even seem somewhat visually distorted.

Desensitization—A form of behavioral therapy developed in the 1950s to decrease the symptoms of phobias, fears, or other learned anxieties. It is not designed to treat, and it is not effective as a treatment for, major mental disorders like schizophrenia or major depressive disorder. It involves the gradual, repeated exposure to the feared object or situation, and replacement of the resulting negative feelings and emotions with more positive, relaxed ones.

Despair—A loss of hope. The feeling that there is no hope.

Diagnostic and Statistical Manual of Mental Disorders (DSM)—An authoritative handbook prepared by the American Psychiatric Association, which is used by mental health care professionals to classify and diagnose mental disorders. Its descriptions of the symptoms of mental disorders provide a common language for those who treat and insure patients with mental disorders.

Diogenes syndrome—A set of behaviors that may include social withdrawal, self-neglect, refusal of offers of help, domestic squalor, lack of shame, and hoarding. It can be a response to a stressful event or it may be a secondary symptom of a mental disorder. It has also been called senile squalor syndrome.

Disenchantment—Disillusionment and/or disappointment with a previously admired and respected person, organization, movement, or belief.

Disengagement theory—A theory of aging that states that it is common and natural for older people to withdraw or disengage from social networks. It results in decreased interpersonal relationships and interactions between the older individual and others in society.

Dissociation—A somewhat dreamy, disconcerting mental state in which a person feels as if the mind is detached from the emotions or the body. A person may feel a loss of sense of self and/or the world may seem unreal. Events that occur during periods of dissociation may not be remembered well.

Dissociative identity disorder (DID)—A controversial mental health condition in which a person experiences a fragmentation of personality. This results in the creation of 2 or more—the average is 10—separate, distinct identities that alternately control the person's behavior, leaving him or her with no memory of the experience. DID was known as multiple personality disorder until 1994.

DSM—See *Diagnostic and Statistical Manual of Mental Disorders.*

Dysmorphophobia—Body dysmorphic disorder.

Dysphoria—A mood characterized by depression, anxiety, restlessness, and feelings of discomfort, unhappiness, or general dissatisfaction.

Dysthymia—Mild depression.

Eating disorder—One of several psychological disorders that cause people to develop dangerous, abnormal eating habits and fixations about food and body weight. The unhealthy relationship with food, and the resulting emotional and physical problems associated with eating disorders, can be life-threatening. Major eating disorders are anorexia nervosa, bulimia nervosa, and binge eating disorder.

Eccentric—A slightly odd, strange, unusual, or unconventional person, or a descriptive term for the behavior of such a person.

Ego—A part of the human psyche, according to Sigmund Freud, that attempts to reconcile reality with the basic and primitive drives and demands of the id, and the high moral and idealistic standards of the superego. Freud believed that the ego acts as a break or control over our most animalistic instincts and urges that are products of the id. At the same time, the ego tries to accommodate the demands of the superego. Since the id is strongly associated with the unconscious mind, the ego must operate in the unconscious as well as in the conscious mind.

Emotion—A complex, spontaneous mental state or strong feeling that includes an expressive or behavioral response, a physiological response, and a subjective experience. Some emotions are joy, sadness, anger, fear, and disgust.

Emotional stability—The ability of a person to maintain constant character traits, mood, and emotions, under pressure and in trying circumstances.

Empathy—The ability to relate to, share, and understand the feelings of other people in a sympathetic way.

Erotomania—(1) The pathological and obsessive pursuit of an unwilling romantic partner; (2) a person's false belief that a disinterested individual or stranger, often a celebrity or famous personality, is in love with him or her; (3) An excessive desire for, or preoccupation with, sex.

Evolutionary psychology—A theoretical approach to interpreting and explaining human behavior and psychological traits based on the influence of natural selection. It stresses the influence of evolution on the functioning of the mind and brain.

Exhibitionistic disorder—A paraphilic disorder diagnosed when a person (1) acts on strong urges to expose his or her genitals or be observed having sex or (2) feels significant distress related to those urges.

Extroversion—A personality trait characterized by assertiveness, sociability, talkativeness, outgoing behavior, desire for social stimulation, and excitability.

Fetishistic disorder—A paraphilic disorder diagnosed when a person experiences sexual arousal from objects or body parts that are not generally associated with erotic pleasure or interest.

Fiction—A novel, novella, short story, or other form of prose that uses imaginary characters and events to entertain, to present an author's viewpoint, to explore the use of language, to explore and describe human behavior, and/or to otherwise tell a story.

Flat affect—The absence of outward emotional expression.

Folie à deux—A mental disorder or delusion shared by two closely associated persons.

Frotteuristic disorder—A paraphilic disorder diagnosed when a person experiences—over a period six months or more—intense sexual arousal linked to strong urges, fantasies, or behavior centered on rubbing or touching someone who does not consent to the contact.

Gambling disorder—An uncontrollable urge to bet (or risk something of value to gain greater value despite low odds) even when the activity results in devastating financial losses and serious negative consequences that can damage or destroy a person's life. Also called compulsive gambling, it may be a form of impulse control disorder.

Gender dysphoria—A distressed mental state caused by the feeling that a person's biological sex does not match the gender he or she identifies with. For example, a person born with the body of a man may emotionally and psychologically feel like a woman or vice versa. Other people born with the physical attributes of a man or a woman may nevertheless not strongly identify with either sex. It used to be called gender identity disorder.

Geropsychology—A subfield of psychology that seeks to assist older persons and their families adapt to the challenges associated with growing old by researching and applying knowledge related to the psychological, behavioral, and social aspects of aging.

Gray matter—Brain matter consisting of brain cells called neurons. In popular culture, it is often used in reference to the cerebral cortex, the part of the brain that is associated with higher mental functions such as the intellect, problem-solving, and reasoning. Contrast with white matter.

Grief—Very deep sadness or sorrow.

Guilt—A disquieting feeling that accompanies a person's belief that he or she has done something immoral, unethical, illegal, hurtful, or otherwise wrong.

Hallucinations—False perceptions that result in a person seeing, hearing, feeling, or smelling something that does not exist.

Hedonism—(1) The belief that enjoying self-indulgent pleasures is the primary goal in life; and (2) a philosophical outlook or ethical theory that considers the satisfaction of personal desires to be the highest priority in life.

Histrionic personality disorder—A personality disorder that usually becomes apparent during young adulthood. It is characterized by an excessive display of emotions designed to attract attention. There is often a desperate need for approval and it may involve inappropriate seductive or sexual behaviors.

Hyperactivity—A persistent behavioral pattern that includes a short attention span, ease of being distracted, impulsivity, increased physical activity, difficulty "sitting still," and talkativeness.

Hypomania—A mild or less severe form of mania characterized by increased activity and energy, racing thoughts, and an elevated mood that typically includes marked cheerfulness. It can be difficult to distinguish from extreme happiness. Consequently, some people enjoy their hypomanic episodes and feelings, which they see as periods providing great energy, creativity, and accomplishment. However, hypomania can progress into mania and can be an indication of future trouble in someone with bipolar disorder.

Hysteria—An out-of-date term once used by physicians to describe what they thought were cases of repressed or unconscious memories causing physical symptoms. The diagnosis was mostly applied to women. Today, mental health professionals use the better defined terms "conversion disorder" and "somatization disorder," in place of hysteria.

Id—The animalistic part of Freud's concept of the mind. Id means "the it." The id is the source of the drives that need to be controlled if people wish to become or remain civilized.

Identity—A person's sense, conception, and expression of self and individuality.

Immaturity—The state of not being mature, fully grown, or fully developed psychologically, emotionally, and/or physically to the same extent as a healthy adult.

Impulse control—The ability of a person to control his or her desire for an immediate reward or gratification. Good impulse control in children may be related to future success in life as defined by positive social interactions, educational success, and rewarding employment.

Impulsive aggression—Sometimes called "affective aggression," this "hot blooded" form of aggression is a hostile, often unplanned act motivated by strong anger or other emotions. A jealous man, a woman striking an unfaithful spouse, and someone experiencing road rage are examples of individuals displaying impulsive aggression.

Impulsivity—A tendency to act on the spur of the moment or spontaneously without thought or concern about potentially negative consequences. This behavioral trait is often observed in some personality disorders such as psychopathy and bipolar disorder, and in some individuals with substance use disorders involving alcohol or stimulants.

Inappropriate affect—The expression of emotions that are incongruous or inconsistent with what a person is feeling or thinking. Someone who laughs loudly when describing great loneliness is showing inappropriate affect.

Insomnia—Persistent difficulty falling asleep, sleeping through the night or both. The resulting sleep deficit can result in fatigue, lack of energy, depressed mood, poor health, and poor work performance. Its multiple causes include stress, anxiety, depression, increasing age, a variety of medical conditions, medication side effects, diet, and change in daily routine.

Instrumental aggression—Sometimes called "predatory aggression," this "cold-blooded" form of aggression is motivated less by emotions than by an intent to achieve a goal. Instrumental aggression is often planned. A mugger, for instance, who strikes a victim to commit a robbery and a sadistic person who harms another to achieve pleasure are examples of individuals displaying instrumental aggression.

Integrity—Consistently behaving in an ethical manner that stresses honesty, decency, and fairness.

Intellectual developmental disorder—See intellectual disability.

Intellectual disability—A disability that becomes apparent before the age of 18 involving significantly impaired intellectual functioning and difficulty adapting behavior to respond to common, frequently encountered situations. Intellectual disability has replaced the terms "mental retardation," "mental deficiency," and "mental handicap." Also called intellectual developmental disorder.

Intermittent explosive disorder—A psychological disorder characterized by repeated instances of angry verbal or physical outbursts. These episodes involve impulsive, uncontrolled, and highly aggressive behaviors in response to stimuli or situations that do not provoke such behaviors in psychologically healthy individuals. Examples are temper tantrums, road rage, and spousal abuse. Violent episodes may be followed by feelings of embarrassment or regret.

Introversion—A personality trait characterized by a tendency to turn inward, direct interests toward oneself, avoid external stimulation, seek solitary pursuits, and concentrate on internal thoughts, feelings, and moods. Introversion is at the opposite end of a spectrum it shares with extroversion.

Labile affect—The outward expression of rapidly changing emotions that do not coincide with what is going on around a person.

Leadership—The ability to lead or direct a group of people. It often implies the ability to elicit confidence and admiration from followers.

Machiavellianism—A selfish, callous, manipulative philosophy and code of personal behavior named for the 16th-century political adviser Niccolò Machiavelli, the author of *The Prince*. It is not a personality disorder but rather an outlook and behavior. People who are Machiavellian routinely manipulate others in a cynical and unprincipled way to benefit themselves.

Malignant narcissism—A dangerous personality disorder, according to psychiatrist Otto Kernberg, characterized by extreme, grandiose narcissism and self-absorption, lack of empathy, defective conscience, readiness to use aggression to achieve personal goals, and a suspicious, paranoid outlook.

Mania—An abnormal mental state during which a person experiences racing thoughts, little need for sleep, euphoria, poor judgment, talkativeness, and lack of inhibitions.

Maturity—The state of being fully developed psychologically, emotionally, and/or physically to the same extent as a healthy adult.

Megalomania—A psychiatric term used to describe a symptom of mental illness featuring delusions of power, greatness, importance, fame, wealth, genius, omnipotence, or other unrealized attributes. Everyday definition: An unhealthy and abnormal desire for, and an obsession with, obtaining power and dominating people.

Mental disorder—A mental illness that affects a person's ability to function and successfully interact with others by negatively impacting moods, feelings, beliefs, thought processes, or sense of well-being. Also known as psychiatric disorders, mental disorders have been linked to multiple causes including abnormal brain development, genetics, and environmental stresses. They are distinguished from normal or eccentric personality traits by causing suffering, distress, or an inability to behave in a healthy manner.

Messiah complex—A type of delusion characterized by the conviction that a person has unique and special powers. In politics, rulers with this delusion are convinced that they alone can save and rule their subjects and have been chosen by fate or a higher power to do so.

Metaphor—A figure of speech that compares one thing with an unrelated thing and so illustrates a feature common to both. A metaphorical sentence does not use the words "as" or "like." For example, "Alice experienced a roller coaster of emotions."

Mind—The mental processes and sense of self that result from brain activity. The mind can be changed positively or negatively by altering brain structure and function through injury, surgery, medication, illegal drug use, and—preliminary studies suggest—perhaps even by some forms of psychotherapy.

Modernism—An artistic style that strives to break from techniques used in the past and develop new approaches of expression.

Mood—In psychology, a feeling or psychological state. Moods can be happy, sad, excited, pensive, and so on. In literature, a mood is the tone or emotional atmosphere an author creates to produce specific feelings in readers. A writer can establish specific moods with his choice of dialogue, character descriptions, story settings, plots, and themes.

Multiple personality disorder—An outdated term for dissociative identity disorder.

Narcissism—Extreme self-centeredness and selfishness with an unrealistic and overestimated view of one's abilities and talents together with an unusually extreme need for admiration. It is characterized by lack of empathy and extreme levels of vanity, self-absorption, conceit, self-admiration, and self-centeredness.

Narcissistic personality disorder—A mental disorder characterized by extreme self-centeredness and self-interest including lack of empathy, an unrealistically inflated sense of importance, and a strong need to be admired.

Narcissistic rage—An all-consuming obsession to "settle a score," "right a wrong," or respond to an insult, which is sometimes observed in some people with severe narcissistic traits.

Narcolepsy—A chronic sleep disorder that causes a person to fall asleep suddenly. It is characterized by drowsiness during the daytime and difficulty staying awake for long periods.

Negativity bias—The common tendency to devote more time thinking about negative, as opposed to positive, events in one's experience.

Neurodevelopmental disorder—A disorder characterized by disturbances in the development of the central nervous system—that is, the brain or spinal cord. Improper development can result in mental disorders, movement disorders, and/or and intellectual deficits.

Neurosis—A mental state involving impaired functioning due to feelings of anxiety, distress, or other worries without losing touch with reality. The term "neurosis" is no longer used in the *DSM-5*. People formally diagnosed as neurotic are now likely to be diagnosed as having an anxiety disorder. The word "neurosis," however, is still associated with personality theory although a better term would be "emotional instability."

Neurotic—A long-term emotional state or outlook that tends to be negative in character. The feelings of neurotic individuals are often dominated by guilt, fear, anger, envy, anxiety, stress, hypochondria, or other worries to a much greater extent than those of better adjusted, more content individuals.

Novel—A book length form of prose describing the actions of fictional characters that, most often, interact over the course of a connected series of events.

Novella—A form of fictional prose shorter than a novel but longer than the average short story. Hence, it can be described as a long short story or a short novel.

Nyctophobia—Fear of the dark characterized by unrealistic worries about unseen threats.

Obsession—An unrelenting preoccupation with a belief, idea, or feeling that is unreasonable and results in distress, discomfort, lack of fulfillment, or a feeling of unease.

Obsessive-compulsive disorder (OCD)—A mental illness that causes a person to have unreasonable fears and thoughts called obsessions, repetitive behaviors called compulsions, or both. When both are present, the repetitive behaviors are related to the unreasonable fears and thoughts. Patients with OCD are often driven to engage in compulsive behavior to relieve high levels of stress caused by their obsessive thoughts. Some patients recognize the unreasonableness of their thoughts while others don't. In either case, the persistence of obsessive thoughts leads to ritualistic behavior. Classic examples of OCD are fear of germs resulting in compulsive hand washing, and obsessive counting and/or touching objects to ward off or prevent imagined unpleasant consequences.

Oedipal complex—Sigmund Freud's suggestion that during a stage of his psychosexual development, between the ages of three and five years, a boy experiences anger toward his father and desire for his mother. During this phase, according to Freud, boys want to replace their father so they do not have to compete with him for their mother's affections. It is also called the Oedipus complex.

Oedipus complex—See Oedipal complex.

Panic attack—A sudden episode of intense anxiety and fear that can produce severe changes in respiration, heart rate, perspiration, and other physical responses. The unexpected nature and severity of these changes are often misidentified as heart attack or other life-threatening event.

Panic disorder—A condition that causes a person to experience recurrent panic attacks. The severity and unexpected nature of these attacks cause the person to spend a significant amount of time fearing the next attack.

Paranoia—A symptom of mental illness marked by delusions involving plots and persecution, an unrealistic sense of one's importance, or baseless jealousy. Often these are part of a detailed, organized belief system that may be linked to paranoid schizophrenia, paranoid personality disorder, or use of drugs like cocaine and methamphetamine.

Paranoid personality disorder—A mental illness characterized by extreme and pervasive suspicion and distrust of others in the absence of schizophrenia or other psychotic disorders.

Paranoid schizophrenia—The most common type of schizophrenia that causes patients to develop delusions that others are plotting against or controlling them. These delusions are often part of an elaborate, relatively stable belief system. Auditory hallucinations ("hearing voices") are often associated with this mental disorder.

Paraphilia—A condition characterized by recurring sexual interest in, or behavior related to, harmful, extreme sexual practices. Voyeurism, frotteurism, exhibitionism, pedophilia, fetishism, transvestism, sexual sadism, and sexual masochism are paraphilias.

Paraphilic disorder—One of the eight disorders involving sexual interests or practices that (1) distress a person interested in the behavior or fantasy or (2) result in psychological or physical harm to an unwilling person or to someone who cannot provide legal consent. See also paraphilia.

Pedophilic disorder—Sexual attraction by a person 16 years or older for a prepubescent child or children at least 5 years younger. This attraction must involve sexual activity with a child generally aged 13 or younger, or fantasies or urges that result in distress or problems with interpersonal relationships.

Pedophilic sexual interest—Sexual attraction to children generally aged 13 or younger, which is never acted upon to result in actual molestation and does not result in distress or problems with interpersonal relationships.

Personality—A person's individual, characteristic thought, feeling, and behavioral patterns.

Phobia—An irrational fear of something that poses little or no threat. Phobias are distinguished from understandable, normal fears by their extraordinary, and sometimes crippling, intensity, which causes a person to avoid the object of the phobia and to panic in its presence. Symptoms vary depending on the person and the phobia. They often include physical responses such as a pounding heart, dizziness or shakiness, a sense of dread, a panic reaction, a desire to flee, and an inability to dismiss fearful thoughts. Public speaking, social interactions, elevators, flying, snakes, and spiders are just a few of the situations or objects that are the sources of phobias for some people.

Play—A dramatic form of literature written to be performed by actors in a theater, on a stage, or in a broadcast studio. The scripted dialogue written by the playwright is meant to be heard rather than read.

Plot—The sequence or pattern of events related to the main conflict or central idea a story.

Positive outlook—A way of thinking, point of view, or attitude that emphasizes—when appropriate and realistic—affirmative, constructive, encouraging, and reassuring thoughts while deemphasizing inappropriately self-critical and negative ones.

Positive psychology—A relatively new subdiscipline of psychology that studies positive aspects of human behavior and mental health. It balances psychology's traditional emphasis on the study of abnormal psychology and mental disorders. The Positive Psychology Institute describes it as "the scientific study of human flourishing, and an applied approach to optimal functioning. It has also been defined as the study of the strengths and virtues that enable individuals, communities and organizations to thrive."

Posttraumatic stress disorder—A mental health disorder brought about by witnessing or experiencing a highly a traumatic or terrifying event. Patients may not be able to control their thoughts about the event. They may suffer nightmares, severe anxiety, and episodes during which they feel as if they are reliving the event, called flashbacks.

Prejudice—Ill-founded, baseless, preconceived opinions. Targets of prejudiced thinking can include ethnic groups, members of particular socioeconomic classes, nationalities, genders, or other social groups. It shares with racism the practice of judging people negatively based solely on their membership in a particular group.

Projection—A psychological defense in which a person accuses others of having the same flaws or negative feelings that trouble the person making the accusation. The falsely attributed negative attributes are then seen as external threats. For example, a person with a bad temper may accuse an even-tempered person of being angry even though the target of the projection shows no sign of anger and feels no anger.

Protagonist—A central or main character in a novel, novella, short story, play, or film.

Psyche—The psychological and mental aspects of a person considered as a whole. It is generally considered without reference to the role played by the physical components of the brain in determining motivation and behavior. According to Sigmund Freud's psychoanalytic theory, it consists of the id, ego, and superego.

Psychiatry—A medical discipline devoted to the diagnosis, treatment, and study of mental and emotional disorders and abnormal behavior.

Psychoanalysis—A therapeutic method developed by Sigmund Freud and his followers based on psychoanalytic theory. It postulates that uncovering unconscious mental processes will aid in relieving neurotic symptoms. It uses dream analysis as well as free association during which a person undergoing psychoanalysis speaks freely and uncensored.

Psychoanalytic theory—A theory developed by Sigmund Freud and his followers that seeks to explain the forces and influences that affect the development of a person's personality and behavior. It stresses the importance of unconscious psychological influences and the interaction of the id, ego, and superego. Freud viewed these as basic theoretical components of the human mind useful for explaining unconscious and conscious mental processes.

Psychological fiction—A work of fiction that emphasizes the psychological processes and profiles of its characters over external events and actions. An author of psychological fiction is likely to stress what and how a person is thinking, what his or her motivation is, and how it affects behavior and the events that occur in the story.

Psychologist—A person who specializes in the study of psychology. The American Psychological Association limits the title to those who have earned a doctoral degree from an accredited university. The association suggests that people with a master's degree in psychology be referred to as counselors, clinicians, or specialists.

Psychology—A field of study devoted to understanding behavior. Subdisciplines of the field focus on neuroscience, physiology, mental health care, sociology, economics, politics, and other topics relevant to mental activity and mental characteristics.

Psychopathy—A collection of emotional, interpersonal, and behavioral traits including lack of empathy, lack of guilt, inability to form sincere emotional attachments, insincere or superficial charm, narcissism, manipulativeness, impulsiveness, unsafe risk-taking, and dishonesty.

Psychosis—A psychiatric symptom that includes hallucinations and/or delusions. Psychosis reflects or results in a person losing touch with reality. Patients with schizophrenia and mood disorders such as bipolar disorder and major depressive disorder may experience psychotic episodes.

Psychotic—Afflicted with psychosis.

Pyromania—An impulse control disorder characterized by a pattern of behavior involving the deliberate setting of fires for amusement or to achieve satisfaction by relieving psychological tension experienced prior to the arson. This motivation distinguishes a person with pyromania from an arsonist because he or she acts impulsively as opposed to acting in a carefully organized manner.

Racism—(1) Prejudice, hostility, or discrimination against an individual or individuals because they belong to an ethnic group deemed inferior; and (2) a type of prejudice involving the unscientific belief that individual members of a specific ethnic group all share the same behavioral characteristics, abilities, inclinations, and attitudes, and that these account for an imagined superiority or inferiority of one group compared to another. Like prejudice, racism tends to judge people negatively simply because they belong to a particular group.

Resilience—The ability to respond, recover, and adapt successfully in a healthy manner to adverse situations, or to stressful, traumatic, threatening, or tragic events, situations, or experiences.

Responsibility—(1) An assumed or assigned moral obligation or duty that puts a person in charge of completing a task or job correctly, or of assuring the well-being of other people; and (2) to be accountable for an action.

Restricted affect—Somewhat reduced intensity of outwardly expressed emotions. The reduction is less than that observed in people with blunted affect. It is also called constricted affect.

Risk-taking—A type of behavior that can provide perceived, often questionable, benefits accompanied by potentially significant dangers and possibility of harm. Examples of risky behavior are driving fast without proper training or equipment; abuse of alcohol, medications, or street drugs; engaging in unsafe sex; and performing dangerous physical stunts without training or protection. These activities may provide a temporary thrill but the risk they present can result in injury or even death.

Road novel/road movie—A novel or film in which the plot unfolds while the characters are on a journey. The journey may be a quest for romance, experience, or adventure or for escape from danger. The history of the journey narrative extends as far back as *The Epic of Gilgamesh*. Other examples are *Don Quixote* by Miguel de Cervantes, *The Adventures of Huckleberry Finn* by Mark Twain, *On the Road* by Jack Kerouac, and *Lolita* by Vladimir Nabokov.

Savant syndrome—A rare condition sometimes seen in people with neurodevelopmental disorders, including but not exclusive to autism spectrum disorder. This syndrome is characterized by the simultaneous presence of significant intellectual disability and extraordinary skill at performing highly specialized tasks. For example, a person with savant syndrome may not have the intellectual capability that would allow him or her to live independently, but may be able to perform complex mathematical calculations very rapidly. Other individuals with savant syndrome may have extraordinary memories or remarkable musical ability.

Schizophrenia—An often severe, chronic brain disorder that causes people to interpret reality in an abnormal manner. Symptoms may include delusions, hallucinations, disordered thinking, and odd behavior. Schizophrenia causes "split mind," but the disease does not create a "split personality" in patients. The "split" refers to the gap between reality and what the patient believes is real.

Self-deception—A thought process that causes or enables people to distort or deny reality so that they fail to recognize their true motivations, feelings, or abilities. Self-deceiving individuals may believe they are especially important or have extraordinary attributes and they typically fail to recognize personal flaws or limitations.

Self-pity—Excessive concern or preoccupation with the self-indulgent feeling that you have suffered more than you deserve to suffer due to unfairness, hardship, bad luck, or victimization.

Setting—The time, place, and cultural and social background in which the plot of a story unfolds.

Sexual masochistic disorder—A paraphilic disorder diagnosed when a person is sexually excited by urges, fantasies, or behaviors—lasting at least six months—involving the experience of real pain through humiliation, beating, or other acts that cause suffering.

Sexual sadism disorder—A paraphilic disorder diagnosed when a person is sexually excited by urges, fantasies, or behaviors—lasting at least six months—that involve the infliction of real psychological (including humiliation) or physical pain in a victim.

Short story—A form of fictional prose shorter than a novel or a novella, in most cases consisting of 10,000 words or less.

Social conscience—A sense of responsibility and understanding of what is morally correct and what is unjust in society, coupled with concern for the well-being of everyone including the underprivileged, ill, young, and elderly.

Social intelligence—The collection of skills and abilities that enables a person to successfully interact and get along with others. It requires empathy, intelligence, knowledge, understanding, and patience. Individuals with good social intelligence sometimes are said to have "people smarts," which make them sensitive to the body language, emotions, motivations, and interests of others. Such skills make it easier to succeed in social situations.

Social isolation—Limited interaction with other people causing a person to feel a lack of social belonging and a lack of social connectedness. The few social contacts people in a state of social isolation have are superficial, of low-quality, and unfulfilling. An estimated 10 to 43 percent of older adults in community dwellings may be socially isolated. Often ignored, this condition can have serious health consequences and may be associated with an increased risk of death.

Somatization disorder—A mental disorder in which a person complains of having multiple physical symptoms for which there are no discernible medical explanations. Despite the lack of evidence of a physical cause for the complaints, a person with somatization disorder may not be able to function because of his or her symptoms. The symptoms can involve multiple parts of the body including nervous, cardiovascular, reproductive, and gastrointestinal systems.

Stanza—The poetry version of a paragraph. Each division has four or more lines and a uniform structure.

Stereotyping—Attributing one or more traits or characteristics to an individual based on the person's membership in a particular group. A flaw in the thinking that leads to stereotyping is failure to appreciate or recognize that people have individual traits, preferences, interests, skills, and abilities, which are all not shared with everyone who has the same background, skin color, or ethnic heritage.

Stream of Consciousness—A literary narrative technique that reveals a character's flowing thoughts, feelings, and impressions. Psychologist William James first described the phrase around the year 1890. Virginia Woolf, James Joyce, and William Faulkner are well-known for using stream of consciousness in their novels.

Stress—Physical, emotional, and/or mental tension resulting from internal or external sources. Examples of internal challenges are physiological or mental illnesses. Examples of external challenges are threats in the environment or uncomfortable social interactions. Stress from either source can seriously affect physical and mental health as a result of activation of the "fight or flight" response, which involves multiple systems in the body including nervous and endocrine responses.

Stressor—A condition, stimulus, agent, or event that produces stress.

Sublimation—The redirection of an instinctive biological drive into an apparently unrelated activity. For example, the energy and thought that might normally be directed toward satisfying sexual desires might be applied instead to work or to a hobby.

Substance use disorder—A mental health condition diagnosed when a patient repeatedly uses drugs and/or alcohol in a way that results in poor health or an inability to function successfully at work, school, or home. The condition is described as mild, moderate, or severe, depending on the level of impairment. Subcategories of substance use disorder are alcohol, tobacco, opioid, hallucinogen, stimulant, and cannabis use disorders.

Superego—One of the three elements of the human psyche, according to Freudian psychology. Freud believed that the superego dominated the other two elements of the psyche, the id and ego, by controlling basic, primal instincts and consciously accepting reality.

Syllogomania—Compulsive hoarding.

Syndrome—A collection of symptoms that characterize a specific physical illness or mental disorder. Also, a condition associated with a set of defined symptoms that typically occur together.

Terrorism—A deliberate policy of using violence directed at civilian and military individuals and targets to frighten and intimidate a population with the intention of achieving specific political goals, making a statement, and/or punishing actual or perceived slights perpetrated by the government of the victims or targets.

Theme—The main idea, concept, or topic at the center of a work of fiction. It can reflect the writer's opinion on that topic. The theme may be clearly stated or indirectly implied. References to a major theme appear throughout the work. Multiple minor themes may appear in different sections of a work.

Thought disorder—A disordered and incoherent way of speaking, communicating, or thinking frequently observed in psychotic mental illnesses. Dysfunctional thought processes may be reflected in illogical speech patterns that reflect bizarre or delusional thoughts. Sentences may be delivered rapidly and unrelated to each other. The person may jump from one subject to another in quick succession. In other cases, thoughts are left unfinished. Sometimes patients with thought disorder appear to make up silly or meaningless words called neologisms. Thought disorders can be symptoms of psychotic mental illness such as schizophrenia, and schizoaffective disorder, posttraumatic stress disorder, and trauma disorders and may occur with paranoid delusions or hallucinations.

Tics—Uncontrollable, sudden movements, twitches, or sounds that occur repeatedly in people with tic disorders such as Tourette disorder.

Tone—An author's attitude about, or opinion of, the subject of his or her story or the readers of the story. A story's tone is not the same as the attitudes or opinions expressed by the story's narrator or characters.

Tourette disorder—A neurological disorder that causes patients to display characteristics often consisting of repetitive and stereotyped involuntary movements as well as involuntary vocalizations. Symptoms of this disorder begin in childhood. Although its cause or causes are unknown, scientists suspect that both genetics and environmental factors interact to produce the disorder.

Transvestic disorder—A paraphilic disorder diagnosed when a person is distressed by dressing in clothing typically associated with the opposite gender (cross-dressing) and by sexual arousal connected to the behavior.

Vertigo—The sensation of lost balance and dizziness, spinning, or whirling. It can result from looking down from a high place, or from injury or disease affecting the body's vestibular system in the inner ear and brain, which controls the sensation of movement and balance.

Voice—The author's outlook or way of viewing the world as expressed in a body of work. Oscar Wilde's voice could be described as acerbic, mordant, witty, and sharp.

Voyeuristic disorder—A paraphilic disorder diagnosed when a person is sexually excited by urges, fantasies, or behaviors—lasting at least six months—that involve spying on unsuspecting victims while they are undressing, nude, or participating in sexual activity.

White matter—A component of the central nervous system that consists of electrically insulated nerve fibers that communicate between different regions of the brain and spinal cord. The material that insulates nerve fibers is a white substance called myelin. White matter connects different regions of gray matter, which consist of nerve cell bodies.

Sources and Recommended Readings

Nonfiction Books, Articles, and Lectures

Altschuler, Eric Lewin. "One of the Oldest Cases of Schizophrenia in Gogol's *Diary of a Madman*." *British Medical Journal* (2001; Vol. 323, No. 7327, pp. 1475–1477).

American Psychiatric Association. *Diagnostic and Statistical Manual of Mental Disorders, 5th Edition, DSM-5* (2013; American Psychiatric Publishing).

Arcelus, Jon, et al. "Mortality Rates in Patients with Anorexia Nervosa and Other Eating Disorders: Meta-Analysis of 36 Studies." *Archives of General Psychiatry* (2011; Vol. 68, No. 7, pp. 724–731).

Babiak, Paul, and Hare, Robert D. *Snakes in Suits: When Psychopaths Go to Work* (2006; HarperBusiness).

Babiak, Paul, and O'Toole, Mary Ellen. "The Corporate Psychopath." *The FBI Law Enforcement Bulletin* (November 2012; https://leb.fbi.gov/2012/november/the-corporate-psychopath, accessed December 30, 2015).

Barash, David P., and Barash, Nanelle R. *Madame Bovary's Ovaries* (2005; Delacorte Press).

Becker, Ernest. *The Denial of Death* (1997; Free Press).

Bernstein, Elizabeth. "Not an Introvert, Not an Extrovert? You May Be an Ambivert." *Wall Street Journal* (July 27, 2015; http://www.wsj.com/articles/not-an-introvert-not-an-extrovert-you-may-be-an-ambivert-1438013534, accessed October 3, 2015).

Bianca, P., et al. "The Highly Sensitive Brain: An fMRI Study of Sensory Processing Sensitivity and Response to Others' Emotions." *Brain and Behavior* (2014; Vol. 4, No. 4, pp. 580–594).

Bogerts, B. "Delusional Jealousy and Obsessive Love—Causes and Forms." *MMW—Fortschritte der Medizin* (2005; Vol. 147, No. 6, pp. 26–29).

Bolton-Gary, Cynthia. "Pooh's Corner: Teaching Educational Psychology at the Intersection of Children's Literature and Technology." *Childhood Education* (2013; Vol. 89, No. 6, pp. 387–391).

Boxer, Sarah. "Charles M. Schulz, 'Peanuts' Creator, Dies at 77." *New York Times* (February 14, 2000).

Boxer, Sarah. "The Exemplary Narcissism of Snoopy." *The Atlantic* (November 2015; http://www.theatlantic.com/magazine/archive/2015/11/the-exemplary-narcissism-of-snoopy/407827/, accessed January 2, 2016).

Brozan, Nadine. "The Real 'Eve' Sues to Film the Rest of Her Story. *New York Times* (February 7, 1989; http://www.nytimes.com/1989/02/07/movies/the-real-eve-sues-to-film-the-rest-of-her-story.html, accessed January 18, 2016).

Bryfonski, Dedria (ed.). *Depression in Sylvia Plath's The Bell Jar* (2012; Greenhaven Press).

Cipriani, Gabriele, et al. "Diogenes Syndrome in Patients Suffering from Dementia." *Dialogs and Clinical Neuroscience* (2012; Vol. 14, No. 4, pp. 455–460).

Clemens, John, K., and Wolff, Melora. *Movies to Manage By: Lessons in Leadership from Great Films* (1999; Contemporary Books).

Cox, Timothy M., et al. "King George III and Porphyria: An Elemental Hypothesis and Investigation." *The Lancet* (2005; Vol. 366, No. 9482, pp. 332–335).

DeFalco, Tom. *Hulk: The Incredible Guide* (2003; DK Publishing).

Diamond, Stephen A. "UFO's, Close Encounters, and the Cry for Meaning. What Is the Psychospiritual Significance of the UFO Phenomenon?" *Psychology Today* (October 17, 2010; https://www.psychologytoday.com/blog/evil-deeds/201010/ufos-close-encounters-and-the-cry-meaning, accessed June 4, 2014).

Dolan, Paul. *Happiness by Design* (2014; Hudson Street Press).

Donley, Carol, and Buckley, Sheryl (eds.). *What's Normal? Narratives of Mental & Emotional Disorders* (2000; Kent State University Press).

Dryden-Edwards, Roxanne. "The Difference between Healthy and Obsessive Love." *MedicineNet.com* (http://www.medicinenet.com/confusing_love_with_obsession/views.htm, accessed August 11, 2014).

Foreman, Amanda. "Dreams That Created Literary Masterpieces." *Wall Street Journal* (January 12, 2016; http://www.wsj.com/article_email/dreams-that-created-literary-masterpieces-1452699729-lMyQjAxMTA2MjE3NjAxODY0Wj, accessed January 14, 2015).

Forsman, Anna K., Nordmyr, Johanna, and Wahlbeck, Kristian. "Psychosocial Interventions for the Promotion of Mental Health and the Prevention of Depression among Older Adults." *Health Promotion International* (2011; Vol. 26, Issue suppl. 1, pp. i85–i107).

Fredrickson, Barbara L. "The Value of Positive Emotions: The Emerging Science of Positive Psychology Is Coming to Understand Why It's Good to Feel Good." *American Scientist* (2003, July–August).

Fried, Eiko I., et al. "What Are 'Good' Depression Symptoms? Comparing the Centrality of DSM and Non-DSM Symptoms of Depression in a Network Analysis." *Journal of Affective Disorders* (2016; Vol. 189, pp. 314–320).

Friedman, Richard A. "Discussions about Public Figures: Clinician, Commentator, or Educator?" *Physicians Practice, Your Practice Your Way* (March 11, 2014; http://www.physicianspractice.com/career/discussions-about-public-figures-clinician-commentator-or-educator/page/0/1).

Friedman, Richard A. "How a Telescopic Lens Muddles Psychiatric Insights." *New York Times* (May 24, 2011; http://www.nytimes.com/2011/05/24/health/views/24mind.html).

Fruscione, Joseph. "Hemingway, Faulkner and the Clash of Reputations." *New England Review* (2012; Vol. 33, No. 1, pp. 62–79).

Gabbard, Glen. *The Psychology of the Sopranos: Love, Death, Desire and Betrayal in America's Favorite Gangster Family* (2002; Basic Books).

Garner, Robert, et al. *Introduction to Politics*, 2nd edition (2012; Oxford University Press).

Giammarco, Erica. "Edgar Allan Poe: A Psychological Profile." *Personality and Individual Differences* (2013; Vol. 54, No. 1, pp. 3–6).

Goode, Erica. "Insane or Just Evil? A Psychiatrist Takes a New Look at Hitler." *New York Times* (November 17, 1998).

Haque, Omar Sultan, et al. "Why Are Young Westerners Drawn to Terrorist Organizations Like ISIS?" *Psychiatric Times* (September 10, 2015; http://www.psychiatrictimes.com/trauma-and-violence/why-are-young-westerners-drawn-terrorist-organizations-isis/page/0/2?GUID=A63B218E-11D5-4618-901E-84FB3777F209&rememberme=1&ts=15092015, accessed October 3, 2015).

Holt-Lunstad, Julianne, Smith, Timothy B., and Layton, J. Bradley. "Social Relationships and Mortality Risk: A Meta-Analytic Review." *PLOS Medicine* (2010; doi: 10.1371/journal.pmed.1000316).

Hurley, Dan. "The Return of Electroshock Therapy." *Atlantic* (December 2015; http://www.theatlantic.com/magazine/archive/2015/12/the-return-of-electroshock-therapy/413179/).

Huss, M. T. and Langhinrichsen-Rohlinga, J. "Identification of the Psychopathic Batterer: The Clinical, Legal, and Policy Implications." *Aggression and Violent Behavior* (2000; Vol. 5, No. 4, pp. 403–422).

Johnson, D. R. "Transportation into a Story Increases Empathy, Prosocial Behavior, and Perceptual Bias toward Fearful Expressions." *Personality and Individual Differences* (2012; Vol. 52, No. 2, pp. 150–155).

Kamphuis, J. H. and Emmelkamp, P. M. G. "Stalking—A Contemporary Challenge for Forensic and Clinical Psychiatry." *British Journal of Psychiatry* (2000; Vol. 176, No. 3, pp. 206–209).

Kaufman, Carolyn. *The Writer's Guide to Psychology: How to Write Accurately about Psychological Disorders, Clinical Treatment and Human Behavior* (2010; Quill Driver Books).

Kaufman, G., and Libby, L. "Changing Beliefs and Behavior through Experience-Taking." *Journal of Personality and Social Psychology* (2012; Vol. 103, No. 1, pp. 1–19).

Kaufman, James C. "The Charlie Brown Theory of Personality." *PsychologyToday.com* (https://www.psychologytoday.com/blog/and-all-jazz/201003/the-charlie-brown-theory-personality).

Keyes, C. L. "The Mental Health Continuum: From Languishing to Flourishing in Life." *Journal of Health and Social Behavior* (2002; Vol. 43, No. 2, pp. 207–222).

Kleinman, Paul. *Psych101: A Crash Course in the Science of the Mind* (2012; Adams Media).

Kohut, Heinz. "Thoughts on Narcissism and Narcissistic Rage." *The Psychoanalytic Study of the Child* (1972; Vol. 27, pp. 360–400).

Lahey B. B. "Public Health Significance of Neuroticism." *American Psychologist* (2009; Vol. 64, No. 4, pp. 241–256).

Leistedt, S. J., et al. "Psychopathy and the Cinema: Fact or Fiction?" *Journal of Forensic Science* (2014; Vol. 59, No. 1, pp. 167–174).

Lucas, H. D., et al. "Why Some Faces Won't Be Remembered: Brain Potentials Illuminate Successful versus Unsuccessful Encoding for Same-Race and Other-Race Faces." *Frontiers in Human Neuroscience* (2011; Vol. 5, No. 20; published online March 8, 2011; doi: 10.3389/fnhum.2011.00020, accessed September 22, 2015).

Martin, C. D. "Ernest Hemingway: A Psychological Autopsy of a Suicide." *Psychiatry* (2006; Vol. 69, No. 4, pp. 351–361).

Meloy, J. R., and Gothard, S. "Demographic and Clinical Comparison of Obsessional Followers and Offenders with Mental Disorders." *American Journal of Psychiatry* (1995; Vol. 152, No. 2, pp. 258–263).

Milgram, S. "Behavioral Study of Obedience." *Journal of Abnormal and Social Psychology* (1963; Vol. 67, No. 4, pp. 371–378).

Miller, Richard B., et al. "Marital Quality and Health over 20 Years: A Growth Curve Analysis." *Journal of Marriage and Family* (2013; Vol. 75, No. 3, pp. 667–680).

Mulholland, Neil (ed.). *The Psychology of Harry Potter: An Unauthorized Examination of the Boy Who Lived* (2007; Smart Pop, an imprint of Benbella Books).

Nathan, Debbie. *Sybil Exposed: The Extraordinary Story behind the Famous Multiple Personality Case* (2012; Free Press).

Niemiec, Ryan, M., and Wedding, Danny. *Positive Psychology at the Movies 2: Using Films to Character Build*, 2nd edition (2014; Hogrefe Publishing).

Nocera, Joe. "The Watchman Fraud." *New York Times* (July 24, 2015; p. A2).

Olson, J., et al. "Baseline Physiologic and Psychosocial Characteristics of Transgender Youth Seeking Care for Gender Dysphoria." *Journal of Adolescent Health* (2015; published online, doi:10.1016/j.jadohealth.2015.04.027).

Olsson, Peter A. "Homegrown Terrorists, Rebels in Search of a Cause." *Middle East Quarterly* (2013; Vol. 20. No. 3, pp. 3–10).

Paulhus, D. L. and Williams, K. M. "The Dark Triad of Personality: Narcissism, Machiavellianism, and Psychopathy." *Journal of Research in Personality* (2002; Vol. 36, No. 6, pp. 556–563).

Pérez-Álvarez, Marino. "The Psychology of Don Quixote." *Psychology in Spain* (2006; Vol. 10, No. 1, pp. 17–27).

Phillips, T., and Eisikovits, N. "For Some Muslim Youth, Islamic State's Allure Is a Meaningful Alternative to Western Values." *Global Post* (April 24, 2015; http://www.globalpost.com/article/6527455/2015/04/24/muslim-youth-allure-isis-meaningful-alternative-western-values, accessed September 15, 2015).

Pickren, Wade E. *The Psychology Book: From Shamanism to Cutting-Edge Neuroscience, 250 Milestones in the History of Psychology* (2014; Sterling).

Pinto, Carmen. "Don Quixote." *British Medical Journal* (2007; Vol. 335, No. 7627, p. 997).

Plante, Thomas G. "We're Shocked by Every Nice Guy Caught with Child Porn. But We Shouldn't Be." *Washington Post* (July 8, 2015; http://www.washingtonpost.com/posteverything/wp/2015/07/08/were-shocked-by-every-nice-guy-caught-with-child-porn-but-we-shouldnt-be/?wpisrc=nl_headlines&wpmm=1).

Podrug, Dinko. "Through Hamlet to Narrative Medicine and Neuroscience: Literature as a Basic Science of Psychiatry." *Psychiatric Times* (2005; Vol. XXII, No. 7; http://www.psychiatrictimes.com/articles/through-hamlet-narrative-medicine-and-neuroscience-literature-basic-science-psychiatry accessed May 14, 2016).

Post, Jerrold M. "Current Concepts of the Narcissistic Personality: Implications for Political Psychology." *Political Psychology* (1993; Vol. 14, No. 1, pp. 99–121).

Reicher, Stephen D., et al. "Working toward the Experimenter: Reconceptualizing Obedience within the Milgram Paradigm as Identification-Based Followership." *Perspectives on Psychological Science* (2012; Vol. 7, No. 4, pp. 315–324).

Robinson, David J. *Reel Psychiatry: Movie Portrayals of Psychiatric Conditions* (2003; Rapid Psychler Press).

Rosenberg, Robin S., and O'Neill, Shannon (eds.). *The Psychology of the Girl with the Dragon Tattoo: Understanding Lisbeth Salander and Stieg Larsson's Millennium Trilogy* (2011; Smart Pop, an imprint of Benbella Books).

Rosenberg, Robin S. (ed.). *The Psychology of Superheroes* (2008; Benbella Books).

Rucker, A. *The Sopranos: A Family History* (2001; New American Library).

Sansone, Randy A., and Sansone Lori A. "Fatal Attraction Syndrome: Stalking Behavior and Borderline Personality." *Psychiatry (Edgmont)* (2010; Vol. 7, No. 5, pp. 42–46).

Schreiber, Flora Rheta. *Sybil* (2009; Grand Central Publishing).

Selby, Edward A., et al. "Nonsuicidal Self-Injury Disorder: The Path to Diagnostic Validity and Final Obstacles." *Clinical Psychology Review* (2015; Vol. 38, No. 79, pp. 79–91).

Shea, S. E., et al. "Pathology in the Hundred Acre Wood: A Neurodevelopmental Perspective on A. A. Milne." *Canadian Medical Association Journal* (2000; Vol. 163, No. 12, pp. 1557–1559).

Sheldon, K., and King, L. "Why Positive Psychology Is Necessary." *American Psychologist* (2001; Vol. 56, No. 3, pp. 216–217).

Shutt, Tikmothy B. "Gilgamesh" in *The Modern Scholar: Odyssey of the West I, Hebrews and Greeks.* (2011; Recorded Books).

Simons, I. "What Do Dreams Do for Us?" *The Literary Mind* (November 11, 2009; https://www.psychologytoday.com/blog/the-literary-mind/200911/what-do-dreams-do-us, accessed January 2, 2016).

Singh, A., and Misra, N. "Loneliness, Depression and Sociability in Old Age." *Industrial Psychiatry Journal* (2009; Vol. 18, No. 1, pp. 51–55).

Skalski, Jon E., and Hardy, Sam A. "Disintegration, New Consciousness, and Discontinuous Transformation: A Qualitative Investigation of Quantum Change." *The Humanistic Psychologist* (2013; Vol. 41, No. 2, pp. 159–177).

Spinney, Laura. "Is Evil a Disease? ISIS and the Neuroscience of Brutality." *New Scientist* (November 11, 2015; https://www.newscientist.com/article/mg22830471-000-syndrome-e-can-neuroscience-explain-the-executioners-of-isis/, accessed November 20, 2015).

Stone, Alan A., and Stone, Sue Smart (eds.). *The Abnormal Personality through Literature* (1966; Prentice Hall).

Tesar, G. "Psychiatric Emergencies." Cleveland Clinic: Center for Continuing Education (2010; http://www.clevelandclinicmeded.com/medicalpubs/diseasemanagement/psychiatry-psychology/psychiatric-emergencies/, accessed November 3, 2015).

Tischler, Victoria (ed.). *Mental Health, Psychiatry and the Arts: A Teaching Handbook* (2010; Radcliffe Publishing).

Todd, J. "The Syndrome of Alice in Wonderland." *Canadian Medical Association Journal* (1955; Vol. 73, No. 9, pp. 701–704).

Treffert, Darold A. "The Savant Syndrome: An Extraordinary Condition. A Synopsis: Past, Present, Future." *Philosophical Transactions of the Royal Society B: Biological Sciences* (2009; Vol. 364, No. 1522, pp. 1351–1357).

Tugade, M. M., and Fredrickson, B. L. "Resilient Individuals Use Positive Emotions to Bounce Back from Negative Emotional Experiences." *Journal of Personality and Social Psychology* (2004; Vol. 86, No. 2, pp. 320–333).

Tye, Larry. *Superman: The High-Flying History of America's Most Enduring Hero* (2012. Random House).

Viziolia, Luca, Rousseleta, Guillaume A., and Caldaraa, Roberto. "Neural Repetition Suppression to Identity Is Abolished by Other Race Faces." *Proceedings of the National Academy of Sciences* (2010; Vol. 107, No. 46, pp. 20081–20086).

Wagner-Martin, Linda. *Sylvia Plath: A Biography* (1987; St. Martin's Griffin).

Walters, K., et al. "Panic Disorder and the Risk of New Onset Coronary Heart Disease, Acute Myocardial Infarction, and Cardiac Mortality: Cohort Study Using the General Practice Research Database." *European Heart Journal* (2008; Vol. 29, No. 24, pp. 2981–2988).

Weinstein, Arnold. *Morning, Noon and Night: Finding Meaning of Life's Stages through Books* (2011; Random House).

Weissenstein, Anne, et al. "Alice in Wonderland Syndrome: A Rare Neurological Manifestation with Microscopy in a 6-Year-Old Child." *Journal of Pediatric Neuroscience* (2014; Vol. 9, No. 3, pp. 303–304).

Welton, Randon, and Kay, Jerald. "The Neurobiology of Psychotherapy." *Psychiatric Times* (October 22, 2015; http://www.psychiatrictimes.com/neuropsychiatry/neurobiology-psychotherapy/page/0/1?GUID=A63B218E-11D5-4618-901E-84FB3777F209&rememberme=1&ts=27102015/, accessed November 2, 2015).

Willingham, Daniel T. "Critical Thinking: Why Is It So Hard to Teach?" *American Educator* (Summer 2007, pp. 8–19).

Winter, Angela. "The Science of Happiness: Barbara Fredrickson on Cultivating Positive Emotions." *The Sun* (May 2009; No. 401; http://thesunmagazine.org/issues/401/the_science_of_happiness).

Young, Skip Dine. *Psychology at the Movies* (2012; Wiley-Blackwell).

Zetterqvist, Maria. "The DSM-5 Diagnosis of Nonsuicidal Self-Injury Disorder: A Review of the Empirical Literature." *Child and Adolescent Psychiatry and Mental Health* (2015; Vol. 9, No. 31, published online September 28, 2015; doi: 10.1186/s13034-015-0062-7, accessed November 11, 2015).

Web Sites

Psychmovies.com (https://sites.google.com/site/psychologyinfilm/Home) A Web site created by Brooke J. Cannon, PhD, Director of Clinical Training, at Marywood University is a rich resource for anyone interested in the accurate and inaccurate depiction of psychological principles in film.

The VIA Institute on Character/What Is Character? (https://www.viacharacter.org/www/). Information about positive psychological character strengths, courses, and tests.

Index

About the Author

DEAN A. HAYCOCK is a science and medical writer living in New York. He earned a PhD in neurobiology from Brown University and a fellowship from the National Institute of Mental Health to study at the Rockefeller University. The results of his research, conducted in academia and in the pharmaceutical industry, have been published in *Brain Research*, the *Journal of Neurochemistry*, the *Journal of Biological Chemistry*, the *Journal of Medicinal Chemistry*, and the *Journal of Pharmacology and Experimental Therapeutics*, among others.

His books include *Murderous Minds: Exploring the Criminal Psychopathic Brain: Neurological Imaging and the Manifestation of Evil* (Pegasus Books), *The Everything Health Guide to Adult Bipolar Disorder*, 2nd and 3rd editions (Adams Media), *The Everything Health Guide to Schizophrenia* (Adams Media), and *When Eye Surgery Goes Wrong: Expert Advice on How to Deal with Complications of LASIK and Other Corrective Eye Surgery* (with Ismail A. Shalaby, MD, PhD; Sunrise River Press).

His reporting and feature articles have appeared in many newspapers and magazines including *WebMD*, *Drug Discovery and Development*, *BioWorld Today*, *BioWorld International*, the *Lancet Neurology*, the *Minneapolis Star-Tribune*, *Current Biology*, and the *Annals of Internal Medicine*. In addition, he has contributed articles on a variety of topics to *The Gale Encyclopedia of Science* and *The Gale Encyclopedia of Mental Health*. www.DeanAHaycock.com; @Dean_A_Haycock